How to Use the Companion CD

About the CD

The CD-ROM, which will install in Windows 95 and NT 4, contains code for the examples developed in the book and third-party software to help you in your development of Visual Basic projects.

Installing the Software

Third-party software is in the Software folder on the CD-ROM. You may install most of these software packages simply by double-clicking on a setup executable within their respective folders and following the on-screen instructions. VideoSoft's software is distributed in ZIP format. If you don't already have a ZIP extraction package, you may use the trial version of WinZip found on this CD.

Installing the Code

You will find the code in the Code folder, broken down by chapter. Each chapter's code is in a ZIP file. If you don't already have a ZIP extraction package, you may use the trial version of WinZip found on this CD.

Important Note

This CD-ROM uses long and mixed-case filenames that require the use of a protected mode CD-ROM driver.

DATABASE ACCESS
WITH VISUAL BASIC

DATABASE ACCESS WITH
VISUAL BASIC

Jeffrey P. McManus

SAMS
PUBLISHING

201 West 103rd Street
Indianapolis, IN 46290

Publisher	Joe Wikert
Acquisitions Editor	Renee Wilmeth
Development Editor	Angela Allen
Copy Editor	Andy Saff
Technical Editor	Debra Schnedler
Book Designer	Laura Lamar/MAXX, San Francisco
Cover Designer	Megan Gandt
Production Team	Marcia Deboy, Michael Dietsch, Cynthia Fields, and Maureen West

Composed in Minion and Helvetica by Sams Publishing.

Library of Congress Catalog No.: 98-84227
ISBN: 1-56276-567-1

00 99 98   6 5 4 3 2 1

Interpretation of the printing code: the rightmost double-digit number is the year of the book's printing; the rightmost single-digit number, the number of the book's printing. For example, a printing code of 98-1 shows that the first printing of the book occurred in 1998.

All terms mentioned in this book that are known to be trademarks or service marks have been appropriately capitalized. Sams cannot attest to the accuracy of this information. Use of a term in this book should not be regarded as affecting the validity of any trademark or service mark.

Screen reproductions in this book were created using Collage Plus from Inner Media, Inc., Hollis, NH and Capture from Mainstay, Camarillo, CA.

For my buddy Reni Roberts,
the queen of cheese.

CONTENTS AT A GLANCE

TABLE OF CONTENTS

Thanks to the outstanding editorial team who put in a completely unreasonable amount of effort making this book happen—particularly Angela Allen for being the most capable and conscientious editor on the whole damn planet, Renee Wilmeth for deftly picking up the ball and running with it, and Debra Schnedler for outstanding technical input and excellent nitpicking in general.

Introduction

It's probably safe to say that the majority of Visual Basic developers will use VB to access databases sooner or later. So why aren't there more books on databases and Visual Basic? Because database access is the equivalent of plumbing. Like plumbing, there are dozens of segments you must put together before the whole thing works, and when it doesn't work, the part that's causing the problem isn't immediately obvious. Put bluntly, it's a decidedly unsexy topic.

This book puts the plumbing in order. It won't help you hike up your pants when you reach under the sink, but it will give you exposure to nearly all aspects of database access you're likely to encounter in Visual Basic today. Through it all, the objective is to give you the information you need in a concise manner, using examples and step-by-step procedures rather than brief, acronym-laden blurbs.

One common misconception about VB is that it's only good for building database front-ends. But as this book shows, Visual Basic 5.0 is not your father's VB. If you're one of the thousands of developers migrating to VB 5.0 from version 3.0, you'll notice an even bigger difference. In fact, the majority of material covered in this book — ActiveX components, Remote Data Objects, ActiveX Data Objects, and SQL Server 6.5 — weren't available in version 3.0. It's clear that Visual Basic has come of age as a software development system, and the success of VB 5.0 bears that out.

If you use this book and find it helpful, I'd be interested to hear from you. If you find an element of this book less than helpful, I'd like to know that, too. And if you've used the book to create something cool and just want to crow about it, feel free to drop me a line as well. My email address is jeffreyp@sirius.com, and the Web page for this book is at **http://www.redblazer.com/vbdb/**. This Web site will also contain updates to and corrections for this book.

This book was written in the Summer, Fall and Winter of 1997-98 in San Francisco, California, Pittsburgh, Pennsylvania, Brooklyn, New York, Stamford and Mystic, Connecticut, Chaska, Minnesota, Princeton, New Jersey, Jacksonville, Florida, Berlin, Germany, Halifax, Canada, and Boulder, Colorado.

Database Basics

What is a database?

What is a table?

What are fields?

What are data types?

How do tables interact?

What's the best way to map out the structure of my database?

How do I create a database?

What's the most efficient way to set up a multitable database?

How do I create a simple Visual Basic interface that enables users to view, edit, and add data to a database?

A database lies at the core of many business software applications. Databases are prevalent in the world of business because they permit centralized access to information in a way that's consistent, efficient, and relatively easy to set up and maintain. This chapter covers the basics involved in setting up and maintaining a database for a business, including what a database is, why databases are useful, and how you can use databases to create business solutions.

If you've used Visual Basic before or done any database programming, you might find this chapter to be rather basic; however, it will bring you up to speed on some jargon terms that can vary from one database system to another.

Although database concepts tend to be the same from one database system to another, things tend to have their own names from one vendor implementation to the next. What's referred to as one thing in one vendor's system is called something completely different in another. For example, Oracle programmers refer to queries stored in the database as *views*; Visual Basic and Access programmers refer to them as *queries*.

If you're upgrading to Visual Basic 5.0 from a previous version of Visual Basic—particularly if you're coming from Visual Basic 3.0—you need to know several new things about database programming using Visual Basic. Visual Basic 5.0 includes the latest version of the Jet database engine (which Visual Basic shares with Microsoft Access 97). This version of Jet includes several new additions to the database engine, which are introduced in this chapter and referred to throughout the rest of this book.

WHAT IS A DATABASE?

A *database* is a repository of information. There are several different types; this book is primarily concerned with *relational databases*, the most commonly used type of database in the world today. A relational database

▶ Stores data in tables, which comprise rows and columns.

▶ Enables you to retrieve, or *query*, subsets of data from tables.

▶ Enables you to connect tables together for the purpose of retrieving related data stored in different tables.

What Is a Database Engine?

The basic functions of a database are provided by a *database engine,* a software system that manages how data is stored and retrieved.

The database engine covered in this book is called Microsoft Jet. Jet isn't a commercial product; rather, it is a subsystem that several Microsoft products use. Microsoft introduced this engine in Visual Basic 3.0 and Microsoft Access 1.0; Microsoft has revised the engine and expanded its capabilities regularly since its introduction. The version of Jet covered in this book is Jet 3.5, which ships with Microsoft Visual Basic 5.0 and Microsoft Access 97.

Note: There are many other database engines besides Jet, but because Visual Basic supports Jet natively, this book focuses much of its attention on that engine. Additionally, Jet can support other database engines as if they were Microsoft Access-style databases, so much of the discussion about Jet databases pertains to other database engines. Chapter 5, "Client/Server," discusses a completely different database engine: that of Microsoft SQL Server 6.5.

Business Case 1.1: Introducing Jones Novelties Incorporated Many computer books consist of long laundry lists of software features with hastily scribbled explanations of how they work. If you're lucky, the discussion of software includes some kind of discussion that relates the software to the real world.

However, the mission of this book is to present the software in terms of business solutions. Accordingly, each chapter contains several business cases, in which a fictional company pursues the elusive goal of office automation in the face of real-world business problems.

The business cases in this book follow the merry exploits of Jones Novelties Incorporated, a small business just breaking into the retail souvenir, novelty, and party-tricks business.

The company's CEO, Brad Jones, recognizes that for the business to succeed, it must automate large parts of the company's transactions. Jones must implement customer contacts, inventory, and billing systems in a way that is both tailored to the business and flexible enough to endure change over time.

Brad recognizes that the company will rise or fall on the basis of its access to information, so he decides to use a relational database system to manage the company's information. The design and functionality of that database is the focus of the rest of this chapter.

Tables and Fields

Database comprise tables, which in turn comprise records, which in turn comprise fields. You can use Visual Basic code to refer to and manipulate databases, tables, records, and fields.

A *table* is a way of storing data that organizes information within a database. Tables have a predefined structure; they contain data that fits into this structure.

Tables organize information in rows and columns. Within a table, a row of data is called a *record*, whereas columns of data are referred to as *fields*.

A record represents a particular element of data, such as a person's entry in an address book or a single banking transaction.

A field, meanwhile, represents a subdivision of data in a record. A record that represents an entry in an address book might consist of fields for first and last name, address, city, state, zip code, and telephone number.

Designing Your Database To create a database, you must first determine what information it will keep track of. You then design the database, creating tables composed of fields that define the types of data you'll store. After you create this database structure, the database can then store data in its records. You can't add data to a database that has no table or field definitions, because the database has nowhere to store the data. So the design of the database is crucial, particularly because it can be difficult to change the design of a database once you've implemented it.

This book represents tables in a standard format, with the table's name at the top of the diagram and the list of field names beneath, as follows:

tblMyTable

ID

FirstName

LastName

...

The ellipsis (...) in the last field indicates that this table has one or more fields that the book is omitting for the sake of brevity.

If you're new to the world of database programming, but you have used other computer applications before, you might be surprised that a database application makes you go through so much trouble before you can even start entering data. A word processing application, for example, just enables you to type; how the file is saved is the bailiwick of the application. The reason that you must design databases ahead of time is efficiency. If a computer application knows exactly how much and what kinds of data to store, it can perform certain optimizations on them. As you'll learn after you create your first 100,000 record multiuser database, speed is of paramount importance in the database world. Anything you can do to make the process of adding and retrieving information from the database is worthwhile.

In addition to efficiency, another guiding principle behind database table design is to put fields related to the same category of data in the same table. All the customer records go in a Customer table, the orders that those customers place should go in an Orders table, and so forth.

Just because these sets of data go into different tables doesn't mean you can't use them together; quite the contrary. When the data you need is spread across two or more tables in a relational database, you can access that data by using a *relationship*. This book discusses relationships later; for now, you need to focus on the table design.

Business Case 1.2: Designing Tables and Relationships Brad Jones has determined that Jones Novelties requires a way to store information on customers. He's pretty sure that most of his business will be repeat business, so he wants to be able to recontact customers to send them catalogs twice a year.

So Brad scribbles a basic database schema on a cocktail napkin. "Here's what the business needs to keep track of," he says:

▶ The customer's name

▶ The address, city, state, zip code, and phone number

▶ The region of the country (Northwest, Southwest, Midwest, Northeast, South, or Southeast)

▶ The date of the customer's last purchase

Brad figures that he should easily fit all this information in a single table and keep the database nice and simple.

Brad's intrepid team of database developers tell him that might be possible, but that he would end up with a database that is inefficient, disorganized, and extremely inflexible.

The information that Brad wants to include doesn't all directly map to database fields. For example, because the region is a function of a person's state of residence, it doesn't make sense to have a State field and a Region field in the same table. Doing so would mean that a data-entry person would have to enter similar information on a customer twice. Instead, it would make much more sense for the database to store a State field in the Customer table and store information pertaining to regions in a Region table. If the Region table always knows which states map to which regions, the data-entry people don't have to enter a region for each customer. Instead, they will just enter the state, and the Customer table can work with the Region table to determine the customer's region.

Similarly, splitting up the Name field into FirstName and LastName fields will make it easier to sort on those fields once data has been entered into them. This aspect of the design might seem trivial once you consider it, but it's surprising how many database designs don't take this kind of thing into consideration—and it's awfully hard to recover from this design flaw once it makes its way into your database.

So Brad and his intrepid team determine that Jones Novelties' customers should be stored in a table, called tblCustomer, that contains the following fields:

tblCustomer

ID

FirstName

LastName

continues

continued

Company

Address

City

State

Zip

Phone

Fax

Email

Data pertaining to the customer's region of the country should be stored in a table called tblRegion. This table has the following fields:

tblRegion

State

RegionName

There is relationship between the two tables through the State field. Note that this field exists in both tables. The relationship between the Region table and the Customer table is a *one-to-many relationship*; for each record in tblRegion there can be none, one or many matching records in tblCustomer. (The sections on relationships later in this chapter discuss in more detail how to take advantage of such a relationship when retrieving records.)

Notice how the designer of the database named the tables and fields in her preliminary table designs. First, she named each table with the prefix *tbl*. This enables her to distinguish, at a glance, that this is a table rather than another type of database object that can store records. Next, notice that each field name consists of full words (instead of abbreviations) and doesn't contain spaces or other special characters such as underscores.

Although the Microsoft Access database engine enables you to name database objects with spaces, underscores, and other nonalphanumeric characters, it's a good idea to eschew their use, because using them makes it difficult to remember the exact spelling of the field name later. (You won't have to remember whether the field is named FirstName or FIRST_NAME, for example.) Although this guideline seems like a trivial distinction now, when you start writing Data Access Object (DAO) code against a database consisting of 50 tables and 300 fields, you'll appreciate having named things consistently the first time.

One last thing is missing from Brad's wish list: the answer to the question, "When did this customer last purchase something from us?" The database developer decides that this information can be determined from date values in the table that stores data pertaining to customers' orders. This table has the following layout:

tblOrder

ID

CustomerID

OrderDate

ItemID

Amount

In this table, the ID field uniquely identifies each order. The CustomerID field, on the other hand, connects an order with a customer. In order to attach an order to a customer, the customer's ID is copied into the Order table's CustomerID field. That way, it's easy to look up all the orders for a particular customer (as we'll demonstrate later).

What Is a Recordset?

Now that you have the ability to create tables, you'll need a way to manipulate them. Manipulating tables involves entering and retrieving data from tables, as well as inspecting and modifying the structure of tables. To manipulate the structure of a table, you use a *tabledef* (introduced in Chapter 3). To manipulate the data in a table, you use a recordset.

A *recordset* is a data construct provided by the Jet database engine. It is conceptually similar to a table, but includes some important distinctive properties of its own.

When you work with recordsets in the Jet database engine, each recordset is represented as an object, conceptually similar to the user-interface objects (such as command buttons and text boxes) that you might have worked with in Visual Basic in the past. Just like other types of Visual Basic objects, recordset objects have their own properties and methods.

Jet 3.5 features five types of recordsets. In the Data control, you set the type of recordset in the Data control's RecordsetType property. When creating recordsets in code, you set the type of recordset when you create it.

Table 1.1 outlines some advantages and disadvantages of using the various types of recordsets in Jet 3.5.

Table 1.1: Advantages and Disadvantages of Recordset Types in Jet 3.5

Recordset Type	Advantages	Disadvantages
Table	Editable. Can locate and return records quickly because tables are indexable.	Can't represent the results of a multitable query.
Dynaset	Updatable. Efficient because it represents a set of references to the data in the underlying query (rather than the actual data). Can return records from more than one table through the use of a join, even when those tables are linked from multiple databases. Such recordsets are, in many cases, updatable.	Because a Table can utilize an index, searches on a Dynaset aren't always as fast as searches on a Table.
Snapshot	Can be faster than Tables and Dynasets, particularly for smaller recordsets. Can return records from more than one table through the use of a join. Such recordsets are, in many cases, updatable.	Not updatable under Microsoft Jet; possibly updatable under Open Database Connectivity (ODBC) (see Chapter 5). Unlike Dynasets, which return a set of references to the records in a table, a Snapshot returns a copy of

Recordset Type	Advantages	Disadvantages
		the data, which can make large Snapshots slower than Dynasets.
Forward-Only	Faster than, but similar to, a Snapshot. Can return records from more than one table through the use of a join.	Same as those of a snapshot; you can move forward only.
Dynamic	Updatable. Can return records from more than one table through the use of a join. Particularly well suited to multiuser databases because they can update themselves when other users change records contained by them.	Not as efficient as a Dynaset.

If you used data access under previous versions of Visual Basic and Microsoft Access, particularly the 16-bit versions of Visual Basic or Access, you might find recordsets easier to deal with under Jet 3.5. One reason for this is that you don't have to worry as much about what kind of recordset you're dealing with; the database engine enables you to create a generic recordset object instead of having to specify what kind of recordset object you want.

For more information Although the topic of recordsets has relevance to database access programming with the Data control, it comes into play much more when you're working with DAO in code. For more on DAO, see Chapter 3, "Data Access Objects."

Data Types

If you've programmed in virtually any language before, you're probably accustomed to the use of data types. Visual Basic is a *weakly typed* language, which (for the purposes of this discussion) means that you aren't usually required to declare the data types of the variables you work with, as you would have to do in a *strongly typed* language. If you choose not to type your variables explicitly, they simply default to the Variant data type, which is an easy (although inefficient) method to use.

Here's an example of weakly typed Visual Basic code that does not declare variable types, allowing the data types to revert to their default:

```
Private Function MySquareLoop()

For x = 1 To 10000
   TheValue = TheValue + (x ^ 2)
Next x

MySquareLoop = TheValue

End Function
```

Visual Basic gives you the option of strongly typing the variables in your code. Here's a revised version of the MySquareLoop function that declares all its variable types:

```
Option Explicit

Private Function NewSquareLoop() As Single

Dim x As Integer, TheValue As Single

For x = 1 To 10000
   TheValue = TheValue + (x ^ 2)
Next x

NewSquareLoop = TheValue

End Function
```

There's not much difference between the first and second versions of this function, except that NewSquareLoop runs about 50 percent faster than MySquareLoop. And that's the whole point of declaring your variable types: strongly typed data executes much more quickly, particularly in situations where you have to perform repetitive actions on data.

The same is true for databases. When you design your tables, one of the steps in setting up the fields is to declare the type of each field, which enables the database engine to save and retrieve data much more efficiently. The only difference between data typing in conventional Visual Basic programming and data typing in database programming is that you must strongly type the database fields you create.

Visual Basic's native database format provides 21 different types of data; other types of databases define other data types. Table 1.2 lists the data types available to you in a Visual Basic database application.

Table 1.2: Data Types Available in Visual Basic Databases

Data Type	Description
Binary	A binary data type used to store data such as graphics and digitized sound files.
Boolean	A two-byte true-or-false value.
Byte	A single-byte integer value from 0 to 255.
Currency	A numeric field that has special properties to store monetary values accurately.
Date/Time	An eight-byte value representing a date or time from January 1, 100 to December 31, 9999.
Double	An eight-byte, double-precision numeric data type.
GUID	A number called a globally unique identifier. You can use this number to identify a record uniquely; this number is typically used in replication.
Integer	A two-byte whole number from –32,768 to 32,767.
Long	A four-byte whole number from –2,147,483,648 to 2,147,483,647. You can set this field to be an automatically incrementing field.
Long Binary (OLE Object)	A large-value field that can store binary data structures such as images or files. OLE Objects embedded in your database can be up to 1 gigabyte.
Memo	A large-value field that can store up to 65,535 characters. You do not need to declare the length of this field in advance.

Table 1.2: Data Types Available in Visual Basic Databases (Continued)

Data Type	Description
Single	A four-byte, single-precision numeric data type.
Text	A fixed-length data type, which requires that you declare the size of the field when you declare its data type. Text fields can be from 1 to 255 characters long.
VarBinary	A piece of variable binary data (used with ODBCDirect).

There is not a one-to-one correspondence between Visual Basic data types and database field data types; for example, you cannot set a database field to a user-defined type or a Visual Basic-style Object variable. Also, if you use Microsoft Access to create databases for use with your VB applications, note that some data types that are usable in your VB application, but don't appear in the Microsoft Access' table designer. This is because Visual Basic supports programming databases other than those created in Microsoft Access. ODBCDirect databases, for example, can handle several additional data types. For more information on ODBCDirect, see Chapter 5.

Creating a Database Schema

Although creating a list of tables and fields is a good way to nail down the structure of the database, you will also want a way to look at the tables and fields in a graphical format. Then you not only can see which tables and fields are available to you, but also how they relate to each other. To do this, you create a schema.

A *schema* is a road map to your database. The schema diagrams all the tables, fields, and relationships in your database. It's important to include a database schema as a part of your software design process because it gives you a quick way to see what's going on in your database.

Schemas are important long after the database design process is complete. You'll need the schema to perform multitable queries on the data. A good graphical schema answers such questions as, "Which tables do I need to join together to list all the orders greater than $50.00 that came in from customers in Minnesota in the last 24 hours?"

> **For more information** For more on how to create queries based on more than one table, see Chapter 2, "Queries."

There is no one official way to create a database schema, although there are many tools you can use to create them. The drawing tool Visio is flexible, fast, and easy to use, and integrates well with other Windows applications, particularly Microsoft Office.

> ***For more information*** The section of this chapter that covers Visio is intended to show how to use a drawing program to document a database. But you can use Visio as a development tool as well. With Visio Professional 5.0, which came out as this book went to press, you can design databases graphically. The product has the ability to take your graphical design and actually create the database for you. Visio Professional 5.0 can also document existing databases, essentially reverse-engineering them and generating a graphical schema—even if you didn't use Visio to design the database.
>
> You can learn more about the Visio family of drawing tools at the Visio Web site, located at **http://www.visio.com**.

You're not limited to using Visio when you're creating a graphical database schema. You can use whatever drawing tool feels comfortable; Microsoft Windows Paint is a viable option, as are Microsoft Word's drawing features.

Business Case 1.3: Using Visio to Create a Schema Now that you have your table and field design in place, it's time to create a graphical representation of the database tables, fields, and relationships. This is not the same as creating the tables themselves; for right now, you're just drawing a diagram of how the tables will relate to each other when they exist. To do so, follow these steps:

1 Start Visio (or your favorite drawing package). The New dialog box appears.

2 Select Basic Template, then click OK. The basic Visio drawing window appears, as shown in Figure 1.1.

3 In the drawing template, click the Rectangle shape and drag it into the drawing area. A rectangle shape appears, as shown in Figure 1.2.

4 Click-drag on the rectangle's handles so it is 1.5 inches wide and 1.25 inches tall.

5 In the Visio toolbar, click the Text tool. A caret appears in your rectangle, enabling you to type text, as shown in Figure 1.3.

6 Type the name of the table into the rectangle.

7 From the template, drag another rectangle into the drawing area.

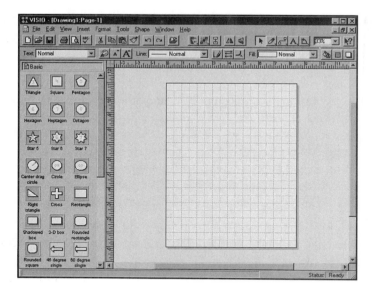

Figure 1.1: The basic Visio drawing window. The drawing template appears on the left, and your drawing area is on the right. You create drawings by dragging items from the template onto your drawing.

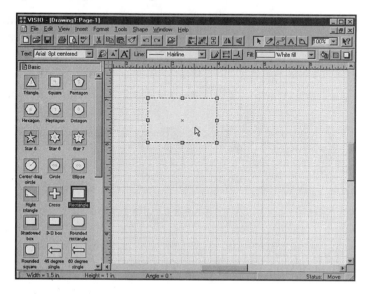

Figure 1.2: You create a rectangle in the drawing area by click-dragging.

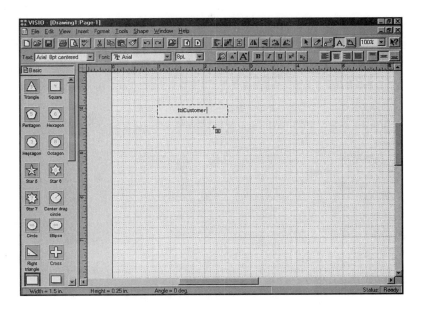

Figure 1.3: Using the Text tool on a shape enables you to type text into the shape.

8 Type the name of the fields for this table into the rectangle. Because you still have the Text Tool selected, you should be able to begin typing immediately.

9 When you're done typing field names, resize the rectangle's handles so it is large enough to display all the fields clearly. When you're done, the graphic should look like Figure 1.4.

Now that you've created your first table drawing, you can draw additional tables to display the relationships between them. The easiest way to do this is simply to copy the table graphic you already have. To do so, follow these steps:

1 Choose Edit, Select All. Then choose Edit, Duplicate.

2 A duplicate tblCustomer appears. Using the mouse, click-drag the duplicate out of the way so it doesn't overlap the original tblCustomer.

3 Click the duplicate field's name rectangle. Using the Text tool, change the field's name to tblOrder.

4 Click tblOrder's field rectangle. Using the Text tool, change the field's list of fields so it matches your design.

5 Click-drag the bottom handle of the field rectangle to make it shorter. The drawing should look like Figure 1.5.

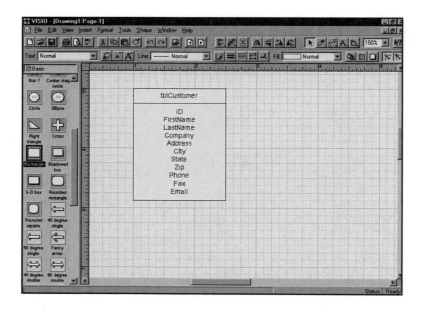

Figure 1.4: A completed table design using Visio rectangles.

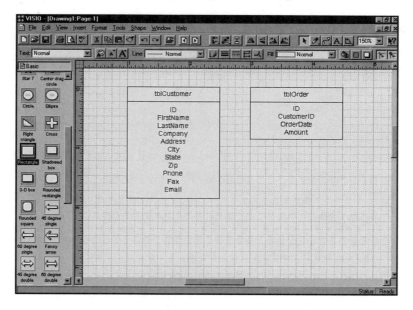

Figure 1.5: A Visio database schema with two tables.

Now that your schema displays both tables in your design, you need to display the relationships between them. The relationship indicates that for a record that exists in one table, there can be one or many related records in another table. Each table in a relationship must share a field in common with the other tables it's related to. A real-world analog for this process is, for example, when you put a green dot on all the file folders that are supposed to be filed in the green file drawer. By storing a matching piece of information on both the file folder and the file drawer, you ensure that nothing gets misplaced. The same applies to records in a database relationship.

We'll discuss more about relationships later in this chapter; for now, create the relationship in your schema by following these steps:

1 In the Visio toolbar, click the Line tool.

2 Click-drag from the ID field in the tblCustomer table to the CustomerID field in the Order table. If you click-drag more than once, you can create a line that bends in several places.

Your schema should now look like Figure 1.6.

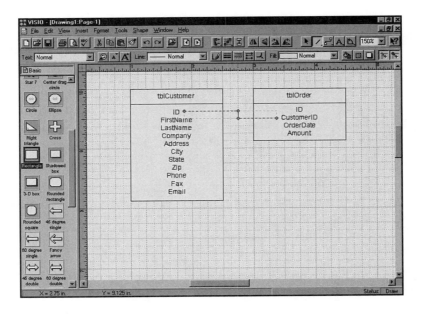

Figure 1.6: The schema now displays a relationship between the two tables.

Note: This is a very simple method of creating a database schema; there are more involved methodologies that might suit your purposes better. In fact, the professional edition of Visio has a number of specialized templates for entity relationship diagrams, which are a more detailed kind of schema diagramming system than the one used in this book.

Often, creating a graphical database schema will reveal flaws in your design. For example, the database design that you have so far enables the business to store information on customers and orders. But orders consist of *items* taken from the company's inventory and sold to the customer. If an order consists of more than one item, there's no way to store it in the database; you would have to create separate orders for each item.

The solution to this problem is to create a new table for line items associated with an order. The design of this new table looks like the following:

tblOrderLineItem

ID

OrderID

ItemID

Quantity

Cost

There is a one-to-many relationship, then, between the tblOrder table and the tblOrderLineItem table. The database schema now looks like Figure 1.7.

Displayed in Microsoft Access, the data entered into this one-to-many relationship looks like that shown in Figure 1.8.

For more information Don't confuse the process of developing a database schema with a software design methodology. Most successful software development organizations have a design methodology in place that dictates such things as what business problems the software is supposed to solve, how the software application will look, and how it will be built. You should consider all these issues before you design the database.

If you're looking for more information on the design process, particularly as it relates to the world of Visual Basic programming, check out Deborah Kurata's *Doing Objects in Visual Basic 5.0* (Ziff-Davis Press, 1997). In addition to serving as a great introduction to the object-oriented programming techniques discussed in Chapter 6, "Classes," of this book, Kurata's book will give you some great ideas about developing software in Visual Basic in general.

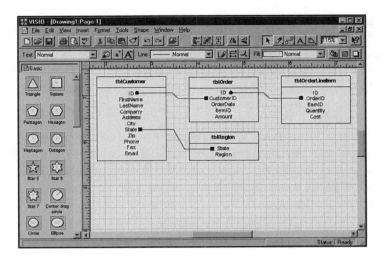

Figure 1.7: The evolved database schema, including relationships among three tables in the database.

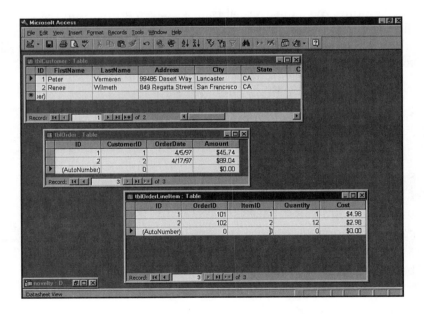

Figure 1.8: Data entered in a one-to-many relationship. Note that for every ID in the Orders table, there are one (or many) corresponding OrderID fields in the OrderLineItem table.

Creating a Database Using Visual Basic

After creating your schema and refining your design, it's time to create the actual database. To create a database using Visual Basic, you use a utility called Visual Data Manager. This utility, which comes with the Professional and Enterprise Editions of Visual Basic 5.0, enables you to create databases that are compatible with Microsoft Access 97 and Microsoft Access 2.0.

> **Note:** Because Visual Basic and Microsoft Access 97 share the same database engine, you can use either Visual Basic or Access to create a database; the resulting database files created with the two systems are identical. Therefore, if you're more comfortable working with Access, you can feel free to use it to create databases. For information on how to create databases using Microsoft Access, see the section, "Creating a Database Using Microsoft Access."

To launch the Visual Data Manager, follow these steps:

1 In Visual Basic, choose Add-Ins, Visual Data Manager.

2 The first time you launch Visual Data Manager, if Microsoft Access is already installed on your computer, a message box appears asking you whether you want to add SYSTEM.MD? (Microsoft Access Security File) to the Visual Data Manager's .INI file. For now, choose No.

The Visual Data Manager window appears.

To create a database using Visual Data Manager, do the following:

1 Choose File, New. From the submenu, choose Microsoft Access, Version 7.0 MDB. A file dialog box appears.

2 Select the folder in which you want to save the new database, then type its name. (For the purposes of subsequent demonstrations in this book, you might want to call the database **NOVELTY.MDB**.)

3 Click the Save button. The new database is created, and the Visual Data Manager displays several windows that enable you to work with the database, as shown in Figure 1.9.

Using the Database Window   Visual Data Manager's Database window stores all the components of the database. In this window, you can view properties of the database, inspect the tables and other elements of the database, and add new components of the database.

Figure 1.9: Visual Database Manager has just given birth to a brand new database.

To view the properties of the database you just created, click the plus sign to the left of the Properties item in the outline. The outline then expands, as shown in Figure 1.10.

Figure 1.10: Visual Data Manager's expanded outline, showing default database properties.

Creating a Table   One idiosyncratic fact about the Visual Data Manager is that it doesn't give you an obvious way to create a new table in the database you've created. This is because the elements that appear in Visual Data Manager's Database window are sensitive to right-clicks. But once you get used to right-clicking, creating a new table is easy. For example, to create a new table, follow these steps:

1 In Visual Data Manager's Database window, right-click Properties. The window's context menu appears.

2 Select New Table. The Table Structure dialog box appears, as shown in Figure 1.11.

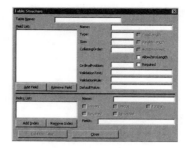

Figure 1.11: Visual Data Manager's Table Structure dialog box, which enables you to create a structure of a new table.

In the Table Structure dialog box, you can create the structure of a table, specifying fields, data types, and indices. For this example, you'll create the structure of a table to store customers. To do so, follow these steps:

1 In the Table Name box, type **tblCustomer**.

2 Click the Add Field button. The Add Field dialog box appears as shown in Figure 1.12.

Figure 1.12: The Add Field dialog box enables you to add a field to a table created with Visual Data Manager's Table Structure dialog box.

3 In the Name text box, type **FirstName**. This will be the name of the field you're creating in the customer table.

4 In the Size text box, type **25**. This specifies that first names can be up to, but not more than 25 characters long, but also means that the database will store names much more efficiently.

5 Choose Fixed Field to indicate that this is not a variable-length field, then click OK. (Note that it's difficult to make a change to a field once you've created it, so make sure you've got everything set correctly.) The field is added to the database structure. The text boxes in the Add Field dialog box are cleared.

6 You can now continue to add additional fields to your table structure. Using the Add Field dialog box, add fields to tblCustomer so you wind up with these fields:

Name	Data Type	Size	Fixed
FirstName	Text	35	Yes
ID	Long, AutoIncrField = True		
LastName	Text	45	Yes
Company	Text	100	Yes
Address	Text	100	Yes
City	Text	100	Yes
State	Text	2	Yes
Zip	Text	9	Yes
Phone	Text	25	Yes
Fax	Text	25	Yes
Email	Text	255	Yes

(You can't specify a size or a fixed value for the ID field because these attributes only apply to Text fields.)

7 You should check the AutoIncrField box when creating the ID field to ensure that every customer you create will have a unique identification number, but because the database engine updates the number in the field automatically, your database application won't have to generate the unique number.

8 When you're done entering fields, click the Close button. The Table Structure dialog box should look like Figure 1.13.

Designating Indexes and the Primary Key Now that you've created the basic table, one thing remains: You must designate indexes. An index is an attribute you can assign to a field that makes it easier for the database engine to retrieve data based on information stored in that field. For example, if you have a database that tracks employees, you will probably look up employees by last name, department, and their individual ID numbers. So it makes sense to create indexes on each of these fields, to make the process of retrieving records based on these fields faster.

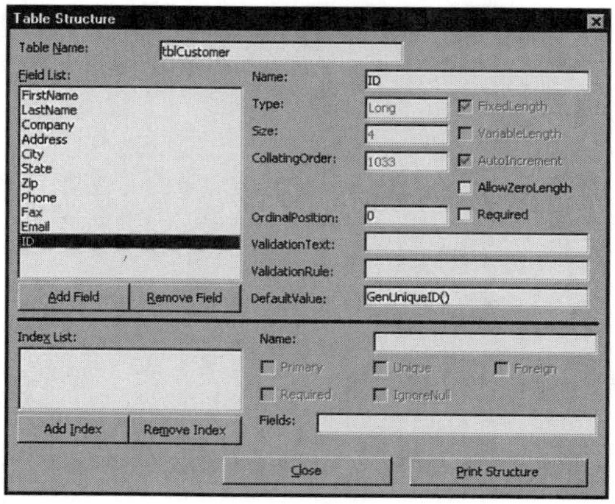

Figure 1.13: The table structure of tblCustomer in the Table Structure dialog box.

Once you've realized the benefits of indexes in database design, you might ask yourself the question: If indexes make lookups faster, why not place an index on every field in every table? The answer is that there's a diminishing return with indexes. Indexes make your database physically larger, so if you have too many indexes, they will consume a ton of memory and disk space, making your computer run more slowly. And this obviously nullifies the benefit of having an index in the first place. There's no hard and fast rule for how many indexes each table should have, but in general, you should created indexes based on the fields that you envision will be used in queries most often. (For more information on how to use the information in a field as a query criterion to retrieve sets of records, see Chapter 2.)

A *primary key* is a special type of index. A field that is designated as a table's primary key serves to uniquely identify the record. So, unlike other types of indexes, no two records in the same table may have the same value in its primary key field. Additionally, if you designate a field in a table as that table's primary key, you can create relationships between that table and other tables in your database.

Every table you create should at least have a primary key, and it should also be indexed on those fields you expect will be queried the most. In the case of the tblCustomer table, as with many database tables, the primary key will be the ID field. The secondary indexes will be the LastName and FirstName fields.

To create indexes and primary keys, follow these steps:

1 In the Table Structure dialog box, click the Add Index button. The Add Index dialog box appears, as shown in Figure 1.14. First, you'll create a primary key for the table.

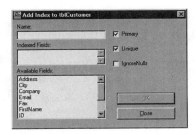

Figure 1.14: The Add Index dialog box, where you add an index to a field in the table you're creating.

2 In the Name text box, type **PrimaryKey**.

3 Double-click the ID field in the list of available fields. ID is added to the list of indexed fields. The check boxes Primary and Unique should already be checked by default.

4 Click OK. The text boxes clear and the primary key is added to the table design. Note that indexes have names just like fields do (although if you're accustomed to using Microsoft Access, you may not know this, since Access hides index names from you in its user interface). It's useful to have access to the name of a field for certain programming purposes; we'll revisit this topic in Chapter 3.

Now you can create two more indexes, for the FirstName and LastName fields. To do so, follow these steps:

1 Type the index name **FirstNameIndex** in the Name text box.

2 Double-click the FirstName field in the list of available fields. FirstName is added to the list of indexed fields.

3 *Uncheck* the check boxes for Primary and Unique, then click OK.

Caution: If you leave the Unique check box selected, you cannot add two people with the same first name to the database.

4 Repeat the process for the LastName field, creating an index called **LastNameIndex**.

5 Click the Close button. You return to the Table Structure dialog box, which now looks like Figure 1.15.

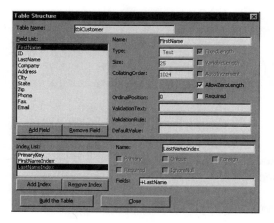

Figure 1.15: The Table Structure dialog box, after all the fields and indexes have been designated.

6 To create the table, click the Build the Table button. The table is created and added to the Visual Data Manager Database window, as shown in Figure 1.16.

Figure 1.16: The Database window after adding a table. You can click the plus sign to expose subitems in the outline.

Changing Existing Field Properties   The Visual Data Manager makes it rather difficult to change most of the important properties of a table—unlike Microsoft Access, which enables you to change almost any part of a table's structure at any time. Generally, when you want to change the properties of a field using the Visual Data Manager, you must delete the field and re-create it.

Suppose that you want to change the length of the LastName field. To do so, follow these steps:

1 In Visual Data Manager's Database window, right-click tblCustomer.

2 From the context menu, choose Design. The Table Structure dialog box appears.

To remove the LastName field, you must first remove its index. To do so, follow these steps:

1 Click the LastNameIndex in the list of indexes.

2 Click the Remove Index button.

3 When the message box appears asking you if you want to remove the index, click on Yes. The index is removed.

Now you can remove the field. To do so, follow these steps:

1 Click the LastName field in the list of fields.

2 Click the Remove Field button. When the message box appears asking you if you want to remove the field, click on Yes. The field is removed from the table.

Now, finally, you can make the change to the field by adding it to the table again, this time with a field length of 50. Don't forget to also add the field's index back to the table after you re-create it.

Tip: If you think the process of modifying an existing field seems more complicated than it needs to be, you're right. In Microsoft Access, making changes to already-existing fields is far easier. For this reason, the astute Visual Basic database programmer keeps a copy of Access lying around, just in case.

Creating an Interface Using Visual Data Manager   One advantage that Visual Data Manager has over Microsoft Access is its capability to create Visual Basic *forms* based on the data structures you create. If you've never used Visual Basic before, a form is the basis of the user interface of your application—just about everything in the way of a user-interface is based in some way on the Visual Basic form, and on the user-interface controls that are placed on a form.

Note: Using the VDM's form-building capabilities are adequate to get started, in time you'll likely want to build your own interfaces with VB's powerful visual design facilities and third-party add-in tools. Chapters 10 through 14 of this book cover building a more customized data access user interface in more depth.

Suppose you're happy with the design of your tblCustomer table and you want to add a Visual Basic form to your project based on the table design. To do so, follow these steps:

1 From the Visual Data Manager menu, choose Utility, Data Form Designer. The Data Form Designer dialog box appears.

2 In the Form Name text box, type **Customer**.

3 In the RecordSource combo box, choose tblCustomer. The Data Form Designer fills in the Available Fields list with the fields found in tblCustomer, as shown in Figure 1.17.

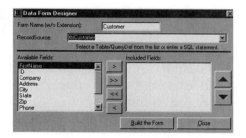

Figure 1.17: The Data Form Designer after displaying a list of the fields available in your table.

4 Click the right-arrow button until all the available fields *except for ID* are added to the form. (There's no point in adding the ID field to a data-entry form because the user cannot edit the ID field.)

5 Click the fields and the up- and down-arrow buttons so that you have arranged the fields in a way that makes sense, as shown in Figure 1.18.

6 Click the Build the Form button. The form is created in Visual Basic.

7 Click Close.

Figure 1.18: The Data Form Designer after all the fields have been added.

Next you'll want to exit the Visual Data Manager to see what your form looks like. But you might want to return later to add new elements to your database, or to make changes to what you've already done. To tell the Visual Data Manager that you want it to reopen your database the next time you return to it, follow these steps:

1 Choose Utility, Preferences. From the submenu, choose Open Last DataBase on Startup.

2 Exit the Visual Data Manager by choosing File, Exit. You are returned to Visual Basic; you should see a new form, called frmCustomer, as shown in Figure 1.19.

To work with this new form, you'll need to make it your project's startup form. To do so, follow these steps:

1 From Visual Basic's Project menu, select Project1 Properties. The Properties dialog box appears as shown in Figure 1.20.

2 In the Startup Object combo box, select frmCustomer, then click OK.

3 From Visual Basic's Run menu, select Start. The application runs, displaying the data-entry interface in frmCustomer.

You can now enter data into the interface that Visual Basic has provided for you. To do so, follow these steps:

1 Click the Add button. You'll notice that the application gives you absolutely no visual feedback that anything has changed. However, rest assured that you are, in fact, now editing a new record.

2 Enter data in each text box in the form.

3 When you're done, click Update. The record is saved; the only visual feedback you get is that the data control displays "Record 1," as shown in Figure 1.21.

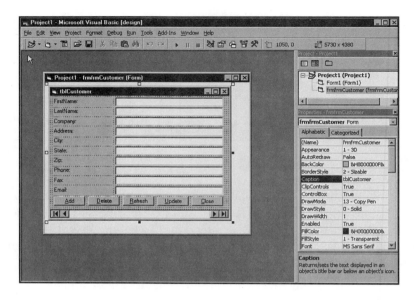

Figure 1.19: The new form created by the Data Form Designer has an interface for all the fields you selected, arranged in the order you selected them. It also includes code that enables you to add and delete records.

Figure 1.20: In the Visual Basic Project Properties window, you can choose which form to display when your application first starts up.

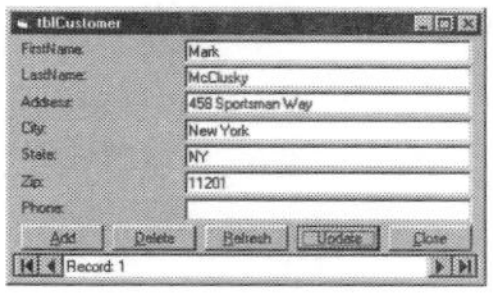

Figure 1.21: The data-entry interface after you enter the first record.

The basic data-entry interface created by the Data Form Designer gives you a sense of the code you must write to make a robust application using the Data control. Even though the Data control is supposed to be a "no-code" solution, if you need to extend its functionality (to perform such actions as lookups and deletion of records) the code can be non-intuitive to a beginner.

Creating a Database Using Microsoft Access

Microsoft Access has a much more sophisticated and easier-to-use interface for creating database objects. To demonstrate this, you'll use Access to create another table for your database. This table will track information pertaining to your business' inventory.

> **Note:** This section assumes you're using Microsoft Access 97. If you have another version of Access, the instructions are basically the same; however, the database you create with Visual Basic's Visual Data Manager might not be compatible with the version of Access you're using.

To add a new Inventory table to your database using Microsoft Access, follow these steps:

1 Start Microsoft Access 97. Access' file dialog box appears.

2 Select More Files, then locate the database NOVELTY.MDB that you created with the Visual Data Manager. (If you didn't use the Visual Data Manager to create the file in the previous section, you'll need to create a new database instead.) The Microsoft Access Database window appears, as shown in Figure 1.22.

Figure 1.22: The Microsoft Access Database window.

3 To create a new table, click the New button. The New Table dialog box appears. Select Design View and click OK. The Access table design window appears, as shown in Figure 1.23.

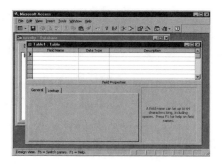

Figure 1.23: Microsoft Access' table design window.

4 In the first row of the Field Name column, type the first field name, **ID**.

5 Press Tab to move to the next column.

6 Change the data type to **Autonumber**. This creates a long integer field that automatically populates itself with a unique number each time you create a new record.

7 To make this field the primary key of this table, choose Edit, Primary Key, or click the Primary Key button from the Access toolbar, as shown in Figure 1.24.

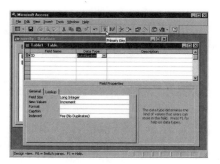

Figure 1.24: You can set a field's primary key in Access with a single click on a toolbar button.

8 Create the remaining fields in the table:

FieldData	Type
Product	Text
CatalogNumber	Text
WholesalePrice	Currency
RetailPrice	Currency
SupplierID	Number (Long Integer)
Description	Text (100 characters)

9 Close the table. Microsoft Access asks whether you want to save it. Save it with the name **tblInventory**.

Changing a Database Using Access   Microsoft Access makes it easy to change an existing database structure. For example, suppose you realize after creating the tblInventory table that your Description field needs to be larger than 100 characters. If you simply change its data type, Access takes care of converting any existing data to that new data type. To do so, follow these steps:

1 In Access' Database window, select tblInventory and click the Design button. The tblInventory table appears in Design view.

2 Change the Description field's data type to **Memo**.

3 Save the table by choosing File, Save. This command automatically converts the field to the new type.

Note: A Memo field can store much more text than a conventional text field. The disadvantage is that a Memo field can't be indexed, so it's inefficient to search on a Memo field.

Relationships

A *relationship* is a way of formally defining how two tables relate to each other. When you define a relationship, you tell the database engine which two fields in two related tables are joined.

The two fields involved in a relationship are the primary key, introduced earlier in this chapter, and the *foreign key*. The foreign key is the key in the related table that stores a copy of the primary key of the main table.

For example, suppose you have two tables, Departments and Employees. There is a one-to-many relationship between a department and a group of employees. Every department has its own ID, as does each employee. In order to denote which department an employee works in, however, you must make a copy of the department's ID in each employee's record. So, in order to identify each employee as a member of a department, the Employees table must have a field—possibly called DepartmentID — to store the ID of the department to which that employee belongs. The DepartmentID field in the Employees table is referred to as the foreign key of the Employees table, because it stores a copy of the primary key of the Departments table.

A relationship, then, tells the database engine which two tables are involved in the relationships and which foreign key is related to which primary key. The Access/Jet engine doesn't require that you explicitly declare relationships, but it's advantageous for you to do so, because it simplifies the task of retrieving data based on records joined across two or more tables (discussed in more detail in Chapter 2).

In addition to matching related records in separate tables, you also define a relationship to take advantage of *referential integrity*, a property of a database engine that keeps data in a multitable database consistent. When referential integrity exists in a database, the database engine prevents you from removing a record when there are other records related to it in the database.

After you define a relationship in your database, the definition of the relationship is stored until you remove it.

> **Note:** You can't create a database relationship using the Visual Data Manager; however, you can create a relationship using either Microsoft Access or DAO.
>
> To create a database relationship using Microsoft Access, see "Creating a Database Using Microsoft Access," later in this chapter. For more information on how to create relationships using DAO, see Chapter 3.

Using Referential Integrity to Maintain Consistency   When tables are linked through relationships, the data in each table must remain consistent with that in the linked tables. Referential integrity manages this task by keeping track of the relationships among tables and prohibiting certain types of operations on records.

For example, suppose that you have one table called tblCustomer and another table called tblOrder. The two tables are related through a common ID field, as shown in Figure 1.25.

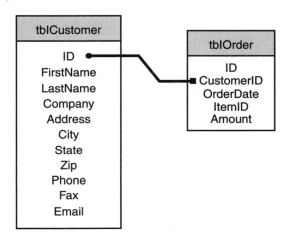

Figure 1.25: The tblCustomer and tblOrder tables are related through the CustomerID field. Referential integrity prohibits the deletion of a customer that has related data in the tblOrder table.

The premise here is that you create customers that are stored in the tblCustomer table, then create orders that are stored in the tblOrder table. But what happens if you run a process that deletes a customer who has outstanding orders stored in the order table? Or what if you create an order that doesn't have a valid CustomerID attached to it? An order without a CustomerID can't be shipped, because the shipping address is a function of the record in tblCustomer. When data in a database suffers from this kind of problem, it is said to be in an *inconsistent state*.

Because it's so important that your database not become inconsistent, the Jet database engine provides a way for you to define formal relationships among tables. When you formally define a relationship between two tables, the database engine monitors the relationship and prohibits any operation that would violate referential integrity.

Creating a Relationship Using Microsoft Access   Microsoft Access enables you to define the relationships among tables. When you define a relationship, the database engine enforces referential integrity among the related tables.

Now that you have a database with two related tables, you can demonstrate how to set up a relationship between the tblCustomer and tblOrder tables. To do so, follow these steps:

1 Create a new table in the database called tblOrder. This table will be related to tblCustomer and should have the following fields and data types:

Field	Data Type
ID	LongInteger, AutoIncrement
CustomerID	LongInteger
OrderDate	Date/Time
Amount	Currency

2 In Microsoft Access, choose Tools, Relationships. The Show Table dialog box appears.

3 Double-click tblCustomer, double-click tblOrder, then click Close.

4 Click-drag between the ID field in the tblCustomer table and the CustomerID field in the tblOrder table. The Relationships dialog box appears, as shown in Figure 1.26.

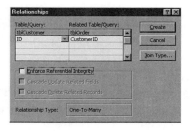

Figure 1.26: Microsoft Access' Relationship dialog box.

5 Click the check box "Enforce Referential Integrity." The Cascade Update and Cascade Delete check boxes become available.

6 Select the "Cascade Update Related Fields" and "Cascade Delete Related Records check boxes."

7 Click Create. Access creates the relationship, as shown in Figure 1.27.

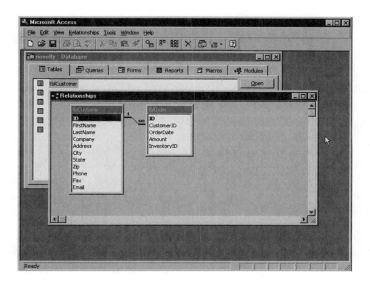

Figure 1.27: A successfully created relationship in Access. This relationship is designed to look like a graphical schema (discussed earlier in this chapter).

To test how the relationship works, follow these steps:

1 Close and save the Relationship window.

2 Open the tblOrder table and attempt to enter a record for a customer who you know isn't in the tblCustomer table.

The database engine generates an error. as shown in Figure 1.28.

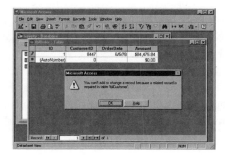

Figure 1.28: Entering a related record with referential integrity causes an error.

Because this error is generated at the database-engine level, the same kind of error is generated whether the referential integrity problem took place in Access or in a Visual Basic application that is based on this database.

Cascading Updates and Cascading Deletes　Cascading updates and cascading deletes are useful features of the Jet database engine. They cause the following things to happen in your database:

▶ With *cascading updates*, when you change a value in a table's primary key, the related data in the foreign keys related to that table change to reflect the change in the primary key. Therefore, if you change the ID of Halle's Hockey Mart in the tblCustomer table from 48 to 72, the CustomerID field of all the orders generated by Halle's Hockey Mart in the tblOrder table automatically change from 48 to 72 as well.

▶ With *cascading deletes*, when you delete a record in a table, all the records related to that record in related tables are automatically deleted as well. Therefore, if you delete the record for Halle's Hockey Mart in the tblCustomer table, all the orders in the tblOrder table for Halle's Hockey Mart are automatically deleted.

> **Note:** You want to be cautious when setting up relationships that perform cascading updates and cascading deletes in your data designs. If you aren't careful, you could wind up deleting (or updating) more data than you expected.

Cascading updates and cascading deletes work only if you've established a relationship between two tables. If you always create tables with Autonumber primary keys, you'll probably find cascading deletes more useful than cascading updates, because you can't change the value of an Autonumber field (so there's no "update" to "cascade").

Creating a Database Using More Exotic Techniques

You can create a database structure entirely in code. You would want to do this in situations where your application needs to create or update data structures. Additionally, you may want to give users of your applications the ability to create their own data structures within the context of your existing data design.

There are two ways of creating databases and database objects in Visual Basic: using Data Definition Language (DDL) queries, and using DAO.

For more information For more on queries using Data Definition Language, see Chapter 2, "Queries." For more on DAO, see Chapter 3, "Data Access Objects."

Normalization

Normalization is a concept that is related to relationships. Basically, the principle of normalization dictates that your database tables will eliminate inconsistencies and minimize inefficiency.

Databases are described as being *inconsistent* when their data elements are entered inconsistently, or when data in one table doesn't match data entered in another table. For example, if half of your staff thinks that Arkansas is in the Midwest and the other half thinks it's in the South, and if both factions of your staff handle their data entry accordingly, your database reports on how things are doing in the Midwest will be meaningless.

An *inefficient* database doesn't enable you to isolate the exact data you want. A database that stores all its data in one table might force you to slog through a slew of customer names, addresses, and contact history just to retrieve one person's current phone number. A fully normalized database, on the other hand, stores each piece of information in the database in its own table, and further identifies each piece of information uniquely by its own primary key. Normalized databases enable you to reference any piece of information in any table given that information's primary key.

You decide how to normalize a database when you design and initially set up a database. Usually, everything about your database application—from table design to query design, from the user interface to the behavior of reports— stems from the manner in which you've normalized your database.

> **Note:** As a database developer, sometimes you'll come across databases that haven't been normalized for one reason or another. The lack of normalization might be intentional, or might be a result of inexperience or carelessness on the part of the original database designer. At any rate, if you choose to normalize an existing database, you should do so early in your development effort (because everything else you do in database development depends on the table structure of the database). Additionally, you will find *action queries* (discussed in Chapter 2) to be useful tools in getting a deficiently designed database in order. Action queries enable you to move fields from one table to another as well as add, update, and delete records from tables based on criteria you specify.

As an example of the normalization choices you make at the database design phase, consider the request made by Brad Jones in Business Case 1.2, "Designing Tables and Relationships." Brad's business needs a way to store the customer's state of residence, as well as the region of the country in which the customer lives. The novice database designer might decide to create one field for state of residence and another field for region of the country, like this:

tblCustomer

ID

FirstName

LastName

Address

Company

City

State

Zip

Phone

Fax

Email

Region

This structure might initially seem rational, but consider what would happen when someone tries to enter data into an application based on this table. The data-entry interface for tblCustomer would look like Figure 1.29.

Figure 1.29: The user interface for the non-normalized version of tblCustomer.

If you were entering data into this form, you'd have to get the normal customer information—name, address, and so forth—but then, after you'd already entered the customer's state, you'd have to do some thinking to determine the customer's region. Is Arkansas in the Midwest or the South? What about a resident of the U.S. Virgin Islands? You don't want to put these kinds of decisions in the hands of your data-entry people, no matter how capable they might be, because if you rely on the record-by-record decisions human beings, your data will ultimately be inconsistent. And defeating inconsistency is one of the primary reasons for normalization.

Instead of forcing your data-entry people to make a decision each time that they type in a new customer, you want to instead store information pertaining to regions in a separate table. You might call this table tblRegion, which would have the following design:

tblRegion

State

Region

The data in a table with this design would look like this:

State	Region
AK	North
AL	South
AR	South
AZ	West
...	...

In this refined version of the database design, when you need to retrieve information about a region, you perform a two-table query with a join between the tblCustomer and tblRegion tables, with one supplying the customer's state and the other providing the region information based on that state. Joins match records in separate tables that have fields in common. See Chapter 2 for more information on how to do this.

Storing information pertaining to regions in a single table of its own has many advantages:

▶ If you decide to carve out a new region composed of an existing region, it is simple to alter a few records in the tblRegion table to reflect the change. Then you need to change only those few records in the tblRegion table, not the thousands of records that might exist in the tblCustomer table.

▶ Similarly, if you started doing business in regions other than the 50 states, it is easy to add a new region to accommodate changes in how your business is structured. Again, you need to add only a single record for each new area to the tblRegion table, and that record then becomes available immediately throughout your system.

▶ If you need to use the concept of regions again somewhere else in your database (to denote that a sales office located in a particular state served a particular region, for example), you could reuse the tblRegions table without modification.

In general, then, you should always plan on creating distinct tables for distinct categories of information. Devoting time to database design before you begin actually creating the design will give you an idea as to which database tables you'll need and how they relate to each other. As a part of this process, you should create a schema, as discussed in the section "Creating a Database Schema," earlier in this chapter.

One-to-One Relationships   Say your human resources database contains tables for Employees and Jobs. The relationship between employees and jobs is referred to as a *one-to-one relationship*, because for every employee in the database there is at most one job. One-to-one relationships are the easiest kind of relationships to understand and implement, because in such relationships, a table (such as the Jobs table) usually takes the place of a field in another table; the fields involved are easy to identify. However, a one-to-one relationship is not the most common relationship you find in most mature database applications. This is for two reasons:

▶ You can almost always express a one-to-one relationship without using two tables. You might do this to improve performance, although you lose the flexibility of storing related data in a separate table. In the previous example, instead of having a separate Employees and Jobs table, you could instead have all of the fields related to jobs stored in the Employees table.

▶ Expressing a one-to-one relationship is nearly as easy as (and far more flexible than) expressing a one-to-many relationship, for reasons we'll go into in the next section.

One-to-Many Relationships   More common than a one-to-one relationship is a *one-to-many relationship*, in which each record in a table can have none, one, or many records in a related table.

For example, suppose that you decide to assign each customer to a specific salesperson. To do this, you'd need a table for salespeople with the following fields:

ID

FirstName

LastName

Department

Because each salesperson is responsible for many customers, you would say that a one-to-many relationship exists between salespeople and customers.

To implement this relationship in your database design, you must copy the primary key of the "one" side of the relationship to the table that stores the "many" side of the relationship. Figure 1.30 shows the tables that implements this design.

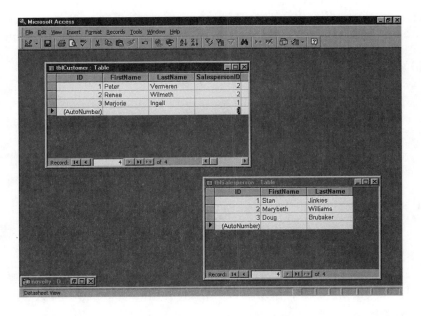

Figure 1.30: The design of a one-to-many relationship includes the primary key of the "one" side duplicated in the related table on the "many" side.

For more information In a user-interface design, you'll commonly implement the process of copying the primary key of one table to the foreign key of a related table with a list box or combo box. For more information on how to implement this in your interface, see Chapter 10, "User-Interface Controls."

Many-to-Many Relationships A many-to-many relationship takes the one-to-many relationship a step further. The classic example of a many-to-many relationship is the relationship between students and classes. Each student can have multiple classes, and each class has multiple students. (Of course, it's also possible for a class to have one or no students, and it's possible for a student to have one or no classes.)

To set up a many-to-many relationship, you must have three tables: the two tables that store the actual data, and a third table, called a *juncture table*, that stores the relationship between the two data tables. The juncture table usually consists of nothing more than two foreign keys—one from each related table.

For example, modify the example in the previous section so the database can store multiple salespeople per customer. Each salesperson can have multiple customers, and each customer can have multiple salespeople. These tables would look like Figure 1.31.

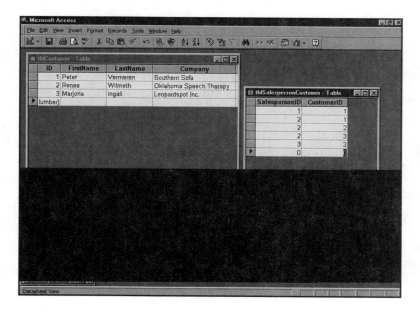

Figure 1.31: Tables involved in a many-to-many relationship. In this design, tblSalespersonCustomer is the juncture table.

A user interface developed in Microsoft Access typically implements many-to-many relationships by using a *subform*. To a VB developer, an Access subform is like a form within a form; the main form displays the "one" side of a one-to-many relationship, while the subform displays the records on the "many" side. The advantage of a subform is that it doesn't require code to keep the relationship between the two tables consistent; you simply set properties to denote the primary and foreign keys.

Unfortuantely, unlike Microsoft Access, VB doesn't provide subforms. In Visual Basic, you often implement many-to-many relationships by using two or more Data controls, one for each recordset involved in the relationship. Unlike Microsoft Access, however, a Visual Basic application typically requires you to write some code to implement a user interface based on a many-to-many relationship. For more information on how this works, see Chapter 10, "User-Interface Controls."

Using the Visual Basic Data Control

The Data control manages the connection between a Visual Basic form and a database. It also provides basic functionality enabling your application to navigate through a recordset and add and update records.

> **Note:** The Data control is available in every edition of Visual Basic 5.0 except the Control Creation Edition. In the Learning Edition of Visual Basic, the capabilities of the Data control are limited; for example, you can't use the Recordset object of a Data control to create other Recordset objects.
>
> Because of the limitations of the Data control in the Learning Edition, this book assumes that you are using the full version of the Data control found in the Professional and Enterprise Editions of Visual Basic 5.0. For more information on the differences between the Data control in the various editions of Visual Basic 5.0, see the *Visual Basic Guide to Data Access Objects*, part of the Visual Basic documentation (which is also available in Visual Basic Books Online).

Data controls are the simplest way of gaining access to databases in Visual Basic, whether the files are in Visual Basic's native format (shared with that of Microsoft Access), in an external format such as that of dBASE, or in a client/server database environment.

Figure 1.32 is a high-level diagram that demonstrates the way the Data control connects your application to a database.

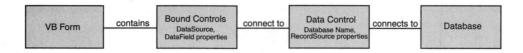

Figure 1.32: The components involved in connecting a Visual Basic application to a database through the Data control.

Note: Although the Data control provides by far the easiest way to connect your application to a database, it's by no means the only way. After becoming more familiar with how database access works in Visual Basic, you might consider using DAO, which is a way of manipulating a database using Visual Basic code. For more information on this, see Chapter 3.

Connecting to a Database and Working with Records

Creating an application that uses the Data control is very simple—in fact, if all you're interested in doing is browsing the database, you don't even have to write a single line of code. It's a two-step process—setting the Data control's DatabaseName and RecordSource properties. To do so, follow these steps:

1 Start a new Visual Basic project.

2 In the Visual Basic toolbox, double-click the Data control. Figure 1.33 shows the Data control's toolbox icon. A Data control appears on the form.

Figure 1.33: The Visual Basic Data control as it appears in the Visual Basic toolbox.

3 In the Properties window, locate the control's Database property.

4 Set the DatabaseName property to the name of a Microsoft Access .MDB database file.

 Note: If earlier in this chapter you didn't create a database to which to connect, you have a few options here. You can either connect to the version of NOVELTY.MDB database included on this book's companion CD-ROM, or you can connect to the BIBLIO.MDB database that comes with Visual Basic. If you use the database that's on the CD-ROM, though, you'll want to copy it to your hard drive first. Otherwise, you cannot create and update records in the database.

5 Now choose the Data control's RecordSource property. In the property's drop-down, you should see a list of tables in the database you assigned previously. Select a table from the list.

The connection to the database takes place when the application runs. However, the connection isn't noticable, because there's no way to display the data. To display data retrieved from a Data control, you must create bound controls connected to the Data control. To do so, follow these steps:

1 Create two text boxes on the form.

2 Set the text boxes' DataSource properties to Data1, the name of the Data control.

3 Select the first text box and set its DataField property to a field in the database. Again, as with the RecordSource property of the database, a bound control's DataField property displays a drop-down list that displays the list of what's available in the database.

4 Set the second text box's DataField property to the name of another field in the database.

5 Run the application. If you used the BIBLIO.MDB database that comes with Visual Basic, you should see something like Figure 1.34.

Using the Data Control to Connect to a Database   After you deposit the Data control on a form, the user can navigate from one record to the next by clicking the control's buttons. The Data control displays four buttons.

Note that the Data control does not by default enable the user to add or delete records. If you want the user to do anything with the Data control besides browse and update records, you'll have to write code. Fortunately, the code that you write to work with the Data control is straightforward and similar to code you've probably written to perform other tasks in Visual Basic.

Figure 1.34: An application displaying two fields from a database with a Data control. You can use the Data control's buttons to navigate through the recordset.

For more information Several third-party ActiveX controls are designed to replace and extend the capabilities of the standard Visual Basic Data control. For examples of third-party Data controls, see Chapter 11, "Using the DBGrid and Apex True DBGrid Controls."

Updating Records Using a Data Control   You need not write any code to perform a database update using the Data control. When a user changes a record displayed by the Data control, that record is updated as soon as the user moves to a new record (if the recordset displayed by the Data control is already updatable). If you're familiar with the way that Microsoft Access updates records, you should expect this behavior.

There are also ways to manipulate a recordset in code. The easiest way to do this is to change the values of user-interface controls that are bound to the Data control; you can also manipulate the Data control's Recordset object to update its records.

Creating a Basic User Interface

Earlier in this chapter, you learned how to use a Visual Basic wizard to create a basic user interface using the Data control. In this section, you create a user interface of your own, also using the Data control, but manually setting up the properties that govern the connection to the database. This process enables you to customize the application and add additional functionality to it.

To connect a database-aware control to a Data control, follow these steps:

1 Make sure your form contains a Data control whose DatabaseName and RecordSource properties have been set to a valid data source.

2 Set the database-aware control's DataSource property to the name of the Data control. (When you use the Visual Basic Properties window to do this, the DataSource property displays the names of all the Data controls on the current form.)

3 If the database-aware control has a DataField property, set it to the name of the field you want the control to represent. Again, you'll notice that if everything is set up properly, a list of available fields drops down in the DataField property when you click it in the Visual Basic Properties window.

Note: Most data-aware controls have DataField properties, but not all do. The DBGrid control (included with Visual Basic 4.0 and 5.0), for example, doesn't have a DataField property, because the control can display all the fields in a data source.

Data-Aware Controls   A *data-aware* control is any control that has a DataSource property. The DataSource property refers to a Data control because this property connects the user-interface control to the Data control (which in turn connects, or "binds" the user interface to the database). The user-interface control is therefore said to be *"bound"* to the database through the Data control.

Several data-aware controls come with Visual Basic 5.0; the following list introduces these controls. Chapter 10, "User-Interface Controls," provides more information on how to use these and other data-aware controls.

- ▶ *Check box.* This control displays a true/false condition. It is typically bound to a Boolean, or yes/no, field in a database.

- ▶ *ComboBox.* This is the standard Visual Basic drop-down combo box. You usually don't use this control for data access purposes; use the more robust DBCombo control instead.

- ▶ *DBCombo.* This data-aware control sports a drop-down list that is similar to the standard Visual Basic combo box control, but can populate its list of choices from a database table.

- ▶ *DBGrid.* This grid can display database data in rows and columns. The commercial version of this control is the Apex True DB Grid control, which Chapter 12 covers.

- ▶ *DBList.* This list box control is similar to the standard Visual Basic list box control, but can populate its list of choices from a database table.

- ▶ *Image.* This image display control is similar to the PictureBox control, but lacks some of its features.

▶ *Label.* This control enables you to display text from a database field, but prevents the user from editing it.

▶ *ListBox.* This is the standard Visual Basic list box. You don't usually use this control for data access purposes; use the more robust DBList control instead.

▶ *MaskedEdit.* This control is similar to a text box, but provides some intrinsic validation functionality as well as a default display that gives users a cue as to what to enter in the text box.

▶ *MSFlexGrid.* New to VB5, the MSFlexGrid control gives you the ability to display database data in a grid format. You can also use the control to pivot data, grouping it and arranging it in ways that let you see trends in your data. The commercial version of this control is the VideoSoft VSFLEX control. Chapter 12 covers the MSFlexGrid and VSFLEX controls in depth.

▶ *OLE.* The OLE container control displays documents created by other OLE-compliant applications.

▶ *PictureBox.* This control displays a graphical image. In previous versions of Visual Basic, the control could display graphics only in Visual Basic's .BMP format; in Visual Basic 5.0, however, the control can also display images in .GIF and .JPG format.

▶ *TextBox.* This ubiquitous control enables the user to enter data in a straightforward way.

Third-Party Data-Aware Controls   In addition to the data-aware controls that come with Visual Basic, there is a third-party market for such controls. Usually, when a control is data-aware, a third-party control vendor promotes the control as "data-aware" or "bound," indicating it can be bound to a Data control.

> ***For More Information*** If you're looking for a fascinating overview of third-party controls that you can use with Visual Basic, check out the *Visual Basic Component Sourcebook for Developers* (Ziff-Davis Press, 1997). The book contains information on over 600 controls, including over 100 database-aware controls.
>
> Both of these books are written by the author of this book, so if you like this book, you won't have to reaccustom yourself to another author's writing style. There are Web pages for both of these books at **http://www.redblazer.com/books**.

Manipulating Records with the Data Control

In addition to enabling you to navigate through the recordset, the Data control also enables you to perform actions on data; many of these actions don't require you to write much code. You can use code with the Data control to navigate through records one by one, delete records, and create new records.

Most of the code you write when working with the Data control is centered around the concept of the Recordset object. A Recordset object becomes available after you've set the Data control's DatabaseName and RecordSource properties. To access a property or method of a Data control's Recordset object, you reference the Data control, then reference the Recordset object, then reference the property or method of the Recordset object in which you're interested.

For example, to move to the first record of the recordset stored by the Data control named datCustomer, you'd write the following code:

```
datCustomer.Recordset.MoveFirst
```

If you haven't written an extensive amount of code involving objects in Visual Basic, this code might seem a bit hard to understand. Why don't you just say **datCustomer.MoveFirst** instead? The answer lies in the fact that the Data control isn't the same as the data; instead, the Data control contains the data, in the form of a Recordset object. The properties of the Data control itself pertain to its appearance and behavior, while the Recordset object has its own set of properties and methods pertaining to the actual data.

Creating New Records Using the Data Control
To create a new record using the Data control, you have two options:

▶ Set the Data control's EOFAction property to **2 - AddNew**. This solution has the appeal of not requiring you to write any code.

▶ Use the AddNew and Update methods of the Data control's Recordset object. This approach is more complicated, but gives you greater control over what happens when the user wants to create a new record. It is also appropriate in situations where you have hidden the Data control from the user.

To enable the Data control to create new records without writing code, do the following:

1 In your Data control project, set the Data control's EOFAction property to **2 - AddNew**.

2 Run your project.

3 Click the Data control's Move Last button. Instead of moving to the last record in the recordset, the Data control creates a new record. You can tell that the record is new because all the bound controls on the form are blank.

4 Enter data in the bound controls.

5 Using the Data control's leftmost navigation button, move to the previous record. The new record is saved in the database.

To use the AddNew and Update methods to create a new record, do the following:

1 Add buttons or other controls to your interface to represent the AddNew and Update methods.

2 In the AddNew button's Click event, enter the code:

```
datCustomer.Recordset.AddNew
```

3 In the Update button's Click event, enter the code:

```
datCustomer.Recordset.Update
```

4 When a user is entering data, she has the option of clicking on the Update record to commit the new record to the database. She can also simply move off the record in order to save it, as is the case with updated records.

It is important to understand that when a user creates new records in a data-entry interface that uses the Data control, many operations are not valid because there is no current record.

For example, if your application enables a user to create a new record by setting the Data control's EOFAction property to AddNew, then enables the user to perform the Delete method on the current record, that application will generate run-time error 3021, "No current record." (This, by the way, is one of the most commonly encountered errors in the world of Visual Basic database access.)

This error occurs because there's no record to delete. To avoid this situation, you have several options. If you've worked with Visual Basic before, the obvious option might be simply to trap the error and disallow the Delete method. But there's an even better way to avoid the problem: Disable the Delete button to prevent the user from clicking it in the first place. A perfect way to do so is to use the Data control's Reposition event.

Using the Reposition Event to Update the User Interface   You can use the
Reposition event of the Data control to initiate changes in the application as the
user moves from one record to the next. The Reposition event is triggered after
a new record becomes current.

You typically use the Reposition event to do the following:

▶ Run a query of records related to a main record—what Microsoft Access
refers to as a "main/subform" interface

▶ Calculate a value derived from one or more values in the record—for
example, a total amount based on a subtotal multiplied by a sales tax constant

▶ Manage user-interface issues that respond to the state of the Data control's
recordset, performing tasks such as hiding or disabling certain features in
the absence of a valid record

Deleting Records Using the Data Control   To delete records in an application
using the Data control, you use the Delete method of the Data control's
Recordset object, as follows:

```
datCustomer.Recordset.Delete
```

There is an important caveat related to using the Delete method of a
Recordset object with the Data control. When you delete a record, no current
record appears to take its place; your recordset is essentially nowheres. So, to
resolve this problem, you must move to another record in the recordset (typically by using recordset methods such as MoveNext or MoveLast).

Note: As discussed in the previous sections on creating new records and
using the Reposition event, you must make sure that there is a current record
in the Data control's recordset when you execute a Delete method, or your
application will raise error 3021, "No current record." To avoid this error, you
should set up your user interface so that users can't delete records that
aren't there. One good way to do that is to inspect the EOF and BOF properties of the recordset before proceeding with the Delete method; if either BOF
or EOF are true, then the Delete method will fail.

Ensuring That Data Is Valid Using the Validate Event   In database programming, *validation* ensures that data entered into the system conforms to rules

defined by the design of your application. These rules are called *validation rules.* One way to implement validation when you're programming with the Visual Basic Data control is to write code in the control's Validate event.

The Validate event takes place whenever the data in a record changes, but before the data is committed to the database. In a typical scenario involving the Data control, the user triggers the Validate event by attempting to move to a new record after changing or creating a new record.

Business Case 1.4: Client-Side Validation   While developing a data-entry interface for the Inventory application, Jones Novelties' database developer realizes that it might be problematic if an item in the product inventory is entered without a catalog number attached to it. Because customers might phone in orders identifying products by their catalog number, and order-takers cannot retrieve an inventory item by its catalog number, they cannot fulfill the order.

The developer brings her concerns to her boss, Brad Jones. Brad agrees that it would be a problem if data-entry operators were to create new inventory items without also including their catalog numbers. However, Brad also envisions situations where it might not be appropriate to assign catalog numbers to products 100 percent of the time. For example, a new product that is not yet for sale might need to be entered in the system without a catalog number.

So, instead of creating a server-side validation rule, the database developer decides to validate data entry in the Validate event of the Data control. This enables her to write another application in the future that can create inventory items without catalog numbers.

In the Inventory example application, the code to perform this type of validation looks like this:

```
Private Sub Data1_Validate(Action As Integer, Save As Integer)

If txtCatalogNumber.Text = "" Then
    MsgBox "Sorry, friend. You must enter a catalog number.", _
    vbExclamation + vbOKOnly, _
    "Validation Error"
    Action = vbDataActionCancel
End If


End Sub
```

When this code exists in the Data control's Validate event and the user deletes a catalog number. The result looks like Figure 1.35.

Figure 1.35: The validation rule is triggered, displaying a message box and rejecting the edit. Because the Data control generates a Validate event, you can include any code in the event you want—not just message boxes.

To see how the application came to trigger a Validate event, you can inspect the value of the Action argument, which the system passes to the Validate event. Table 1.3 lists the possible values for the Action argument.

Table 1.3: Values of the Validate Event's Action Argument

Constant	Meaning
vbDataActionCancel	Whatever caused the Validate event to be triggered is undone
vbDataActionMoveFirst	The MoveFirst method was executed
vbDataActionMovePrevious	The MovePrevious method was executed
vbDataActionMoveNext	The MoveNext method was executed
vbDataActionMoveLast	The MoveLast method was executed
vbDataActionAddNew	The AddNew method was executed
vbDataActionUpdate	The Update method was executed
vbDataActionDelete	The Delete method was executed
vbDataActionFind	The Find method was executed
vbDataActionBookmark	The Bookmark property was set
vbDataActionClose	The Close method was executed
vbDataActionUnload	The form on which the Data control resides is being unloaded

In addition to the Action argument, the Validate event also has a Save argument. The Save argument is set to True if data in bound controls attached to the Data control change, or False if no data has changed. (This suggests that the Validate event is triggered when the user is simply browsing through records—which, in fact, is the case.)

You can use the Save argument in situations where your validation code takes a long time to execute—for example, if a validation code had to perform a database query on the basis of data entered by a user, you might tailor that query to execute only if the data in the bound controls had actually changed. Such code would look like this:

```
Private Sub Data1_Validate(Action As Integer, Save As Integer)
If Save = True Then
    ' Incredibly time-consuming validation
    ' rules get executed here.
Else
    ' Do nothing; we assume that the data is OK
    ' because it's in there to begin with.
End If

End Sub
```

Validation at the Database Engine Level   In addition to doing ad-hoc validation at the time your data is entered, remember that you can also do validation at the database engine level. Such validation is usually more reliable, because the validation is applied no matter what process changes the data. You do not have to remember to implement the validation rule in every application that accesses a particular table. But validation at the database engine level is less flexible, because it's nearly impossible to override. Additionally, you can perform validation at the database engine only at the field level; you can't have database engine validation rules that, for example, are based on a comparison between two fields.

Database engine validation is a function of database design. You create database engine validation rules in the table design view of Microsoft Access.

For example, suppose that you want to make sure that a piece of inventory is *never* entered into the Inventory table without a catalog number. To do this, you' set up a database engine level validation rule, as follows:

1 In Microsoft Access, open the table definition in design view.

2 Click the CatalogNumber field to select it.

3 In the Allow Zero Length setting in the window's bottom pane, select No. The table definition window looks like Figure 1.36.

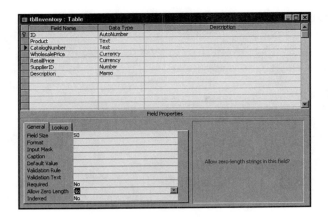

Figure 1.36: Setting validation rules at the database engine level. This ensures that the contents of the CatalogNumber field are never empty, no matter what process performs the data entry.

You can create more sophisticated validation rules at the database engine level as well. For example, suppose that every item in your inventory has a catalog number that must begin with a letter from A through M. In this case, "F123" is a valid catalog number, but "Z3875" is not. To implement this as a database engine validation rule, do the following:

1 In the table definition window for the Catalog Number field in the Inventory table, go to the Validation Rule property.

2 In the Validation Rule property, enter the following expression:

```
Like "[A-M]*"
```

The Like keyword indicates that you want a validation rule that permits any data that is like the expression that follows it. The expression that follows the Like keyword is a pattern; data that matches the pattern is valid, whereas data that doesn't match the pattern causes a validation error.

For more information Like statements are most commonly used as criteria in queries. For more information on how Like expressions work, see Chapter 2, "Queries."

So, in the case of this expression, [A-M] means "any letter of the alphabet between A and M, inclusive," whereas the asterisk means "anything else." So with this rule, "A34584" fits the validation rule, but "W34" does not, nor does "9039."

Data access operations are compared against database-engine validation rules first, before they are compared against any local validation that might exist in your application's Validate event. In your Visual Basic application, if you attempt to enter data that violates a database engine validation rule, the user gets a message box, as shown in Figure 1.37 (generated by the database engine).

Figure 1.37: A generic database engine validation message. Note that this message is a little cryptic; it might not be appropriate for inexperienced users.

Making Validation Clearer with Validation Text   Because an inexperienced data-entry user might have trouble understanding the syntax of a validation rule violation message generated by the database engine, you can specify a more friendly message to display when the user enters a bad value. You do this in the Validation Text property of the table definition window.

For example, to provide a more user-friendly message when the user violates the CatalogNumber's validation rule, do the following:

1 In Access, open the table definition for the tblInventory table.

2 In the CatalogNumber field's Validation Text property, type the following: **"Look, dude. You gotta type a catalog number whose first character is a letter between A and M."**

3 Save and close the table definition and return to your Visual Basic application.

4 Launch the Visual Basic application and try to change a value in the Catalog Number field to an invalid value. A message box appears, as shown in Figure 1.38.

Figure 1.38: Validation text that is set in Access' table definition window appears in your Visual Basic application.

Other Important Properties of the Data Control

The Data control has several additional properties that govern its behavior. You can set most of these properties at design time, so you don't have to write any code to take advantage of them.

The BOFAction Property   The BOFAction property determines what happens when the user moves the Data control's recordset to the beginning-of-file (BOF). The user might do so by clicking the leftmost button on the Data control, or by changing the current record in code.

If you set the BOFAction property to **0 - Move First**, then the Data control moves to the first record when the user clicks the leftmost navigation button.

> **Note:** BOF is actually a property of the Data control's Recordset object. For more information on Recordset objects, see Chapter 3.

The Connect Property   The Connect property determines the type of database to which the Data control is connected. By default, this property is set to Microsoft Access, but you can change the setting if you are interested in connecting to a non-Access data type. Such data types are referred to as *external data types*.

> **Note:** Don't confuse external data types with client/server databases such as Microsoft SQL Server and Oracle; those are supported through the Remote Data control. You can access several databases not directly supported by Jet by using ODBC. For more information on both the Remote Data control and ODBC, see Chapter 5.

Jet 3.5 supports the following types of desktop databases:

▶ dBASE III, IV, and 5.0

▶ Excel versions 3.0, 4.0, 5.0, and 8.0

▶ FoxPro versions 2.0, 2.5, 2.6, and 3.0

▶ Lotus spreadsheets in WK1, WK3, and WK4 formats

▶ Paradox versions 3.x, 4.x, and 5.x

▶ Delimited ASCII text files

One of the easiest ways to test how this works is to connect to an Excel spreadsheet. You can do this whether or not Excel is installed on your computer; simply use the file EXCEL-DB.XLS found on this book's companion CD-ROM. To do so, following these steps:

1 Set up a Visual Basic form with a Data control.

2 Set the Data control's Connect property to the following:

```
Excel 5.0;
```

3 Set the Data control's DatabaseName property to the name of the Excel spreadsheet. The spreadsheet is in the CHAPTER01 folder in the Code folder of this book's companion CD-ROM. You will probably want to copy this file to your hard drive; otherwise, the file is read-only.

4 Set the Data control's RecordSource property to **Sheet1$**. You can now create bound controls on your Visual Basic form as you normally would.

The Excel spreadsheet that stores the data looks like Figure 1.39.

Bear in mind that Jet doesn't support several features on external databases. In particular, such databases do not support several DAO procedures that create databases, fields, and query definitions.

The EOFAction Property The EOFAction property determines what the Data control does when the user moves to the end of the recordset. If you set the property to **2 - Add New**, the control creates a new record when the user moves one record past the last one in the current recordset. (In other words, the setting causes the interface to work like a Microsoft Access form.) But bear in mind that this setting is not the default of a Visual Basic Data control; you must change the property at design time to ensure that the control behaves this way.

To create a new record when the Data control's EOFAction property is set to AddNew, you click the MoveLast button, then click the MoveNext button.

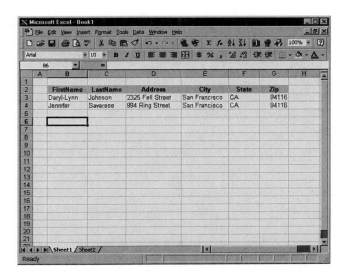

Figure 1.39: The Excel spreadsheet as a Data-control-compatible data source. Note that in Excel, field names are entered as the first row of the data.

The Exclusive Property By setting the Exclusive property of a Data control to True, you ensure that other users can't access the database when your application is running. The advantage of setting the Exclusive property to True is that performance improves, because the Jet database engine doesn't have to worry about such problems as record locking and multiuser contention that can occur if more than one application can access the same record.

The Options Property The Options property of a Data control actually affects the control's Recordset object. You can use the Options property to deny other users the ability to read from or write to the database; there are also options that govern whether your application can make changes to or add data to the recordset.

Chapter 3 discusses the Options property of a Recordset object more fully.

SUMMARY

This chapter covered the basics of databases in general, as well as the easiest ways of connecting your Visual Basic applications to Microsoft Access databases. It's important to remember that although Visual Basic and Microsoft Access share a database engine, Access-style databases aren't your only option in Visual Basic. Chapter 5 describes how to set up and use Microsoft SQL Server; it also talks about ODBC, a Windows technology that enables you to get to databases of all kinds from a Visual Basic application.

QUESTIONS AND ANSWERS

Q: **Given the fact that the Visual Data Manager isn't as powerful or easy to use as Access, is there any reason why I should use it?**

A: Yes—if you don't have Microsoft Access, for one thing. Also, some developers like to have a working familiarity with the Visual Data Manager in case they're stuck in a situation where they don't have access to Access. But in general, it's easier to design tables and queries using Access, so it's a good idea to use Access if you have it.

Q: **The Data control seems easy to use, but it also seems limited in what it can do and a little cumbersome. Are there other ways of doing database stuff in Visual Basic?**

A: Absolutely. Microsoft provided the Data control as a way to provide a no-code solution to the problem of database access in Visual Basic. And the Data control remains the only way to exploit the wealth of database-aware ActiveX controls. But the limitations of the Data control, combined with its inefficiency, lead many developers to disdain its use. In all likelihood, your production database applications will use both Data controls and DAO (discussed in Chapter 3).

There's also a client/server version of the Data control, the Remote Data control (discussed in Chapter 5).

Q: **Is there a way to use data-aware controls without using a Data control?**

A: Yes, although if you do not use a Data control, you'll have to write code to manage the database connection manually. This is not impossible to do, but it can be tricky. You'll use DAO code (covered in Chapter 3) to handle retrieving and updating records in this scenario. (You can also use this kind of code to enable non-data-aware controls, such as the Visual Basic TreeView control, to display data from a database.)

Q: **A Data control exposes a Recordset object. Does that mean I can use that recordset for other purposes?**

A: As long as you remember to use your newfound powers only for good and never for evil, yes. The Recordset object exposed by the Data control is the same as, for example, the Recordset object returned by the OpenRecordset method of a Database object. And you can assign a recordset you generate in code to the Recordset object of a Data control. See Chapter 3 for more on how this works.

Q: **Is it possible to have a primary key composed of more than one field?**

A: Yes. Although not often done, in the database world, this is known as a concatenated key. You might use such a key if you know that all the people in your database are going to have unique first and last names. You choose to make the FirstName and LastName fields the concatenated primary key so that users can never enter the same name twice in the database.

Queries

WHAT IS A QUERY?

HOW CAN I USE STRUCTURED QUERY
LANGUAGE (SQL) TO RETRIEVE DATA?

HOW CAN I USE QUERIES THAT HAVE BEEN
STORED IN MY DATABASE?

HOW CAN I DYNAMICALLY GENERATE QUERIES
AT RUNTIME?

HOW CAN I USE QUERIES TO RETRIEVE RELATED
DATA FROM MORE THAN ONE DATABASE?

HOW CAN I CREATE QUERIES THAT GROUP AND
SUMMARIZE RELATED RECORDS?

HOW CAN I WRITE QUERIES THAT CHANGE
DATA IN MY DATABASE?

Chapter 2

The discussion of database and table structure in Chapter 1, "Database Basics," demonstrated how to create a database using Visual Basic and Microsoft Access. This chapter is concerned with manipulating data in tables, as well as creating and changing the structure of tables by using Structured Query Language (SQL).

SQL queries give you the ability to retrieve records from a database table, match related data in multiple tables, and manipulate the structure of databases. They pertain to the applications you saw demonstrated in Chapter 1 in the sense that certain types of SQL queries can serve as the RecordSource property of a Data control. And they serve as the basis of manipulating databases with Visual Basic code and Data Access Objects, the subject of Chapter 3, "Data Access Objects."

SQL is a standard way of manipulating databases. Generally, it's used for creating queries that extract data from databases, although a large subset of SQL commands perform other functions on databases, such as creating tables and fields.

Generally, SQL commands are broken down into two categories:

▶ **Data Definition Language commands**, which enable you to use SQL queries to create components of the database, such as tables, fields, and indexes

▶ **Data Manipulation Language commands**, designed to retrieve records from databases

While this chapter discusses how to use both types of SQL commands, it's generally more appropriate (and easier) to use Data Access Objects instead of SQL to create databases in Visual Basic applications. Using DAO to create database structures is covered in Chapter 3.

WHAT IS A QUERY?

A query is any set of database commands that retrieves records. Using queries, you can pull data from one or more fields from one or more tables. You can also subject the data you retrieve to one or more constraints, known as criteria, that serve to limit the amount of data you retrieve.

Queries in Visual Basic are, at one level or another, based on a language called *Structured Query Language*, or *SQL*. SQL is a fairly standard language for retrieving and otherwise manipulating databases; it's easy to learn and is implemented across many different databases, so you don't have to learn a totally new query language if you, for example, migrate your Jet database application to Sybase or Oracle.

At least that's the theory. In practice, as with so many other "industry standards," every database vendor has its own way of implementing a standard, and Microsoft is certainly no exception. Though Jet's implementation of SQL isn't radically different than other vendors' implementations, you should be aware as you learn the language that other dialects of SQL exist.

WHERE SQL IS USEFUL

It's intuitive that you'd need to have a way to retrieve records from a database in order to write a database application in Visual Basic. It's not always intuitive where you actually stick the queries you need to retrieve records, however.

The rule of thumb in Visual Basic Jet programming is that any place where you'd use a reference to a table, you can instead use a SQL statement or a reference to a stored query (which is, in turn, based on a SQL statement). The most obvious place to put a SQL statement, based on the limited data access techniques discussed in this book so far, would be the RecordSource property of a Data control.

So instead of setting the RecordSource property to the name of a table (such as tblCustomer), you can set it to the name of a stored query (such as qryCustomerSorted, for example) or a SQL statement (such as `SELECT * FROM tblCustomer ORDER BY State`).

Other contexts in which the use of SQL statements are used include

▶ The *source* argument of the OpenRecordset method of a Database object. You use this method most commonly when you are querying records in code.

▶ The *source* argument of the Execute method of a Database or QueryDef object. You use the Execute method when you are running an action query.

▶ The SQL property of a QueryDef object. You generally use this method when you are defining a query that is to be stored in the database.

All these techniques are discussed in more detail in Chapter 3, "Data Access Objects."

Testing Queries with the DBGrid Control

The DBGrid control is a useful tool for trying out the concepts described in this chapter. In fact, it's not hard to build a simple VB application using the Data control (introduced in Chapter 1) to experiment with different SQL statements in a database. Use the steps here to build this tester application that you can use to test SQL statements as you work through this chapter.

> **Note:** As an alternative to using a DBGrid application, you may want to consider simply using the Visual Data Manager or Microsoft Access to experiment with SQL. For my money, using Access to develop queries is the best option, if you have it. But if you don't have Access, using the Visual Data Manager or a DBGrid application you build yourself works perfectly fine, particularly if all you're interested in doing is testing the SQL code that's discussed in this chapter.

To build a SQL tester application using the DBGrid control, follow these steps.

1 In Visual Basic, create a new EXE project.

2 Select the menu command Project Components. Add the component labeled Microsoft Data Bound Grid Control, then click OK.

3 The DBGrid control is added to the Visual Basic toolbox. Double-click the DBGrid control to add an instance of the DBGrid control to your project.

4 Add a standard text box, a standard command button, and a Data control to the form. Arrange the controls so they look like Figure 2.1.

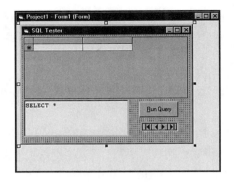

Figure 2.1: The interface of the SQL Tester Application.

5 Assign the following properties to the text box control:

Property	Value
Multiline	True
Text	SELECT *
Font	Courier New, 10 point

Assign the following properties to the Data control:

Property	Value
DatabaseName	The location of the file novelty.mdb from the chapter02 folder on the CD-ROM that accompanies this book. You'll want to copy this file to a location on your hard drive; otherwise, it will be read-only
RecordSource	tblCustomer
Visible	False

6 Assign the following properties to the DBGrid control:

Property	Value
DataSource	Data1
Align	1-vbAlignTop

7 Assign the following properties to the command button:

Property	Value
Caption	&Run Query

8 Finally, add the code shown in Listing 2.1 to the Click event of the command button:

Listing 2.1: Code to Reassign the RecordSource Property of a Data Control

```
Private Sub Command1_Click()

    Data1.RecordSource = Text1.Text
    Data1.Refresh

End Sub
```

The Data control's Refresh method is the way you tell the control to requery the database; it should execute each time you change the RecordSource property of a Data control at run time.

Note: Normally, you'd add some sort of error-handling to an application that lets the user change the RecordSource property of a Data control at run time. But leave that out for now because this is a learning tool rather than a production application.

To test the SQL Tester application, do the following.

1 Run the application.

2 The data grid is populated with the complete contents of the tblCustomer table.

3 In the text box, type the SQL statement shown in Listing 2.2.

Listing 2. 2: A Basic Select Query That Sorts by Two Fields

```
SELECT FirstName, LastName
FROM tblCustomer
ORDER BY LastName, FirstName
```

4 Click the Run Query button. The recordset is requeried according to the SQL statement you entered, as illustrated in Figure 2.2.

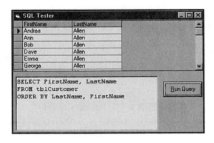

Figure 2.2: Output of the SQL Tester Application after you enter a SQL statement.

Note: It does not matter whether you include line breaks in a SQL statement because SQL is oblivious to line breaks. Including line breaks makes your SQL statements easier to read, however.

The cool thing about the SQL Tester application is that it will enable you to run any valid SQL SELECT statement against any table in the database with a minimum of fuss. For example, try the SQL statement given in Listing 2.3.

Listing 2. 3: A Select Query That Populates a Column with the Results of a Calculation

```
SELECT Product,
[RetailPrice] * 1.1 AS [NewPrice]
FROM tblInventory
```

The SQL Tester will display all the items in the inventory with a 10 percent price increase, as illustrated in Figure 2.3.

You can use the SQL Tester application to experiment with the SQL code introduced in this chapter.

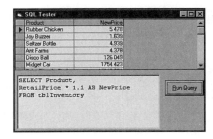

Figure 2.3: The SQL Tester Application displaying the results of a SQL query containing a calculation.

RETRIEVING RECORDS USING THE SELECT CLAUSE

The SELECT clause is at the core of every query that retrieves data. It tells the database engine what fields to return.

A common form of the SELECT clause is

```
SELECT *
```

This clause means "return all the fields you find in the specified record source." This form of the command is handy because you don't need to know the names of fields to retrieve them from a table. Retrieving all the columns in a table can be inefficient, however, particularly in a situation in which you only need two columns and your query retrieves two dozen.

So, in addition to telling the database engine to return all the fields in the record source, you also have the ability to specify exactly which fields you want to retrieve. This limiting effect can improve the efficiency of a query, particularly in large tables with many fields, because you're only retrieving the fields you need.

A SELECT clause that only retrieves the contents of the first and last names stored in a table looks like this:

```
SELECT [FirstName], [LastName]
```

Note that in Microsoft Jet SQL, you conventionally enclose field names in square brackets because field names in Microsoft Jet (unlike many other database engines) can contain embedded spaces and other undesirable characters.

Though I avoid using embedded spaces and the like in the field names I create, I still use square brackets around field names because it makes my SQL statements clearer. In the preceding SQL example, however,

```
SELECT FirstName, LastName
```

would have been perfectly legal as well.

Note also that a SELECT clause is not complete without a FROM clause (so the SELECT clause examples shown in this section can't stand on their own). For more examples of the SELECT clause, see examples for the FROM clause in the next section.

DESIGNATING A RECORD SOURCE USING THE FROM CLAUSE

The FROM clause denotes the record source from which your query is to retrieve records; this record source can be either a table or another stored query. You also have the ability to retrieve records from more than one table; see "Joining Related Tables in a Query" later in this chapter for more information on how that works.

The FROM clauses work with SELECT clauses. For example, to retrieve all the records in the tblCustomer table, you use the SQL statement in Listing 2.4.

Code Listing 2.4: A Basic Select Query

```
SELECT *
FROM tblCustomer
```

This query retrieves all the records and all the fields in the tblCustomer table (in no particular order). The SQL statement produces the following result set.

ID	FirstName	LastName	Address	City	State	Zip	Phone
3	Peter	Vermeren	99485 Desert Way	Lancaster	CA	93534	310 555 9485
4	Eric	Townsend	666 Blue Court	Sunnyvale	CA	94086	415 555 9449
5	Kim	Bassett	8458 Skippy Drive	Seattle	WA	98060	206 555 4993
...	...	...	...	...	...	...	...

To retrieve only the customers' first and last names, you use the SQL statement in Listing 2.5.

Listing 2.5: A Select Query That Limits the Number of Columns It Retrieves

```
SELECT FirstName, LastName
FROM tblCustomer
```

This command produces the following result set.

FirstName	LastName
Peter	Vermeren
Eric	Townsend
Kim	Bassett
...	...

For reasons of efficiency, it's always best to use this technique to limit the number of fields in a SELECT clause to only those fields you know your application will need.

Note that records returned by a SELECT FROM are returned in no particular order. Unless you specify a sorting order (using the ORDER BY clause discussed later in this chapter), the order in which records is returned is always undefined.

SPECIFYING CRITERIA USING THE WHERE CLAUSE

A WHERE clause tells the database engine to limit the records it retrieves according to one or more criteria you supply. A *criterion* is an expression that evaluates to a true or false condition; many of the same expressions of equivalence to which you're accustomed in Visual Basic (such as `>0` and `='Smith'`) exist in SQL as well.

For example, let's say you want to return a list of only those customers who live in California. You might write a SQL query as shown in Listing 2.6.

Listing 2.6: A Basic Select Query with a WHERE Condition, Limiting the Records Retrieved

```
SELECT FirstName, LastName, State
FROM tblCustomer
WHERE State = 'CA'
```

This query produces the following result set.

FirstName	LastName	State
FirstName	LastName	State
Peter	Vermeren	CA
Eric	Townsend	CA
Steve	Hanson	CA
...	...	...

Note again that this result set is returned in no particular order unless you supply an ORDER BY clause; this clause is discussed later in this chapter.

Note also that the delimiter for a text string in a WHERE clause is a single quotation mark. This marker is convenient, as you'll see later, because the delimiter for a string in Visual Basic is a double quotation mark, and SQL statements must sometimes be embedded in VB code.

You can create more sophisticated WHERE clauses by linking two or more criteria together with AND and OR logic. For example, let's say you want to retrieve all the customers who live in Lancaster, California (as opposed to those customers who live in cities called Lancaster in other states). To do this, you need to denote two criteria linked with an AND operator, as you can see in Listing 2.7.

Listing 2.7: A Basic Select Query with a Pair of WHERE Conditions Linked with AND

```
SELECT FirstName, LastName, City, State
FROM tblCustomer
WHERE City= 'Lancaster' AND State='CA'
```

The result set produced by this query looks like this.

FirstName	LastName	City	State
Peter	Vermeren	Lancaster	CA
Steve	Hanson	Lancaster	CA
...	...	...	...

If you are interested in seeing information on people who live in cities called Lancaster in states other than Vermont, you use an OR clause to link the two criteria, as in the code in Listing 2.8.

Listing 2.8: A Basic Select Query with Multiple WHERE Conditions Linked with AND and OR

```
SELECT FirstName, LastName, City, State
FROM tblCustomer
WHERE City= 'Lancaster' AND (State='CA' OR State='PA')
```

The result set of this query might look like the following.

FirstName	LastName	City	State
Peter	Vermeren	Lancaster	CA
Janet	Burns	Lancaster	PA
Steve	Hanson	Lancaster	CA
...	...	...	...

So you can see that you can pretty much go insane linking WHERE criteria together with AND and OR conditions (subject, of course, to Microsoft Jet's limit of 40 criteria linked with AND and OR in a WHERE clause).

Note: One key to successful client-server development is to develop tactics for ensuring that client applications don't retrieve too many records at once. One of your most basic weapons in your client-server arsenal is the WHERE clause. For more on client-server development, see Chapter 5, "Client/Server."

Operators in WHERE Clauses

You can use the operators listed in Table 2.1 when constructing a WHERE clause.

Table 2.1: Operators for Use in WHERE Clauses

Operator	Function
<	Less than
<=	Less than or equal to
>	Greater than
>=	Greater than or equal to

continues

Table 2.1: Operators for Use in WHERE Clauses (Continued)

Operator	Function
=	Equal to
<>	Not equal to
BETWEEN	Within a range of values
LIKE	Matching a pattern
IN	Contained in a list of values

The operators of equality and inequality work exactly the same in SQL as they do in Visual Basic.

The BETWEEN Operator   The BETWEEN operator returns all the records values that are between the limits you specify. For example, to return all the orders placed between June 1 and June 5, you would write the SQL statement shown in Listing 2.9.

Listing 2.9: A Basic Select Query with a BETWEEN Clause

```
SELECT *
FROM tblOrder
WHERE [OrderDate] BETWEEN #6/1/97# and #6/5/97#
```

This query produces the following result set.

ID	CustomerID	OrderDate	Amount
1	5	6/5/97	$45.97
2	101	6/1/97	$995.48
10	105	6/1/97	$25.43
...	...	...	...

Note that date values in Microsoft Jet SQL are delimited with pound signs (#). Note also that the boundaries of a BETWEEN operator are inclusive, meaning that if you ask for all the orders that were placed between June 1 and June 5, the result set will include records that were placed *on* June 1 and June 5 as well.

The LIKE Operator and Wildcard Characters   The LIKE operator matches records to a pattern you specify. This pattern is often a "wildcard" character, such as the * or ? characters with which you may be familiar from working with the MS-DOS or Windows file systems.

The asterisk (*) character indicates a partial match. For example, to retrieve all the records in the tblCustomer table whose last names begin with the letter B, you'd use a query like the one in Listing 2.10.

Listing 2.10: A Basic Select Query That Matches a Pattern Based on a LIKE Expression

```
SELECT ID, FirstName, LastName, Address, City, State
FROM tblCustomer
WHERE [LastName] LIKE 'B*'
```

This query produces the following result set.

ID	FirstName	LastName	Address	City	State
5	Kim	Bassett	8458 Skippy Drive	Seattle	WA
8	Janet	Burns	99485 Desert Way	Lancaster	VT
23	Dave	Burns			
...	...	...	...	...	...

You can also create wildcard characters using the question mark character. The question mark takes the place of a single character in a pattern. For example, to locate all of the customers with five-digit zip codes beginning with the number 9, you use the SQL code in Listing 2.11.

Listing 2.11: A Basic Select Query That Uses Question Mark Wildcards in Its LIKE Clause

```
SELECT ID, FirstName, LastName, Address, Zip
FROM tblCustomer
WHERE [Zip] LIKE '9????'
```

This query produces the following result set.

ID	FirstName	LastName	Address	Zip
4	Peter	Vermeren	99485 Desert Way	99485
5	Eric	Townsend	666 Blue Court	94483
6	Kim	Bassett	8458 Skippy Drive	98060
...	...	...	...	...

You can also use a LIKE operator that returns a range of alphabetic or numeric values. For example, to return a list of customers whose last names begin with the letters A through C, you use the SQL statement given in Listing 2.12.

Listing 2.12: A Basic Select Query That Returns a Range of Values with a LIKE Operator

```
SELECT *
FROM tblCustomer
WHERE [LastName] LIKE '[A-C]*'
```

This query returns the following result set.

ID	FirstName	LastName	Address	City	State	Zip	Phone
5	Kim	Bassett	8458 Skippy Drive	Seattle	WA	88475	206 558 4993
8	Janet	Burns	99485 Desert Way	Lancaster	PA		
9	Steve	Allen					
14	Steve	Armstrong					
19	Steve	Chung	666 Blue Court				
...	...	...	...	...	...	...	...

Note: The wildcard characters in Microsoft Jet SQL are different than the wildcards in ANSI SQL. In Jet SQL, you use an asterisk to match any number of characters, and you use a question mark to match any single character. In ANSI SQL, you use an underscore to match any number of characters, and you use a percent sign to match any single character.

The IN Operator You use the IN operator to retrieve records that match a list of values. For example, to retrieve all the customers in either Wyoming or Vermont, use the SQL statement shown in Listing 2.13.

Listing 2.13: A Basic Select Query That Matches Items in a List Using an IN Clause

```
SELECT *
FROM tblCustomer
WHERE [State] IN ('VT', 'WY')
```

This query produces the following result set.

ID	FirstName	LastName	Address	City	State	Zip	Phone
34	Dave	Gonzales	473 Placid Gulch	Lichen	VT		
41	Mary	Rogers	666 Blue Court	Stevens Gorge	WY		
114	Jennifer	Burns	8849 Asphalt Way	Smoking Crater	WY		

Caution: The Visual Basic Guide to Data Access Objects describes the function of the IN operator incorrectly. As the manual suggests, you can use an IN clause as part of a SELECT statement to "specify records in a database"—specifically, to specify a data source in an external database. But in the role of an equality operator, IN is not used to specify records in a database; instead, you use the IN operator to match a value against a value in a list.

SORTING RESULTS USING ORDER BY

The ORDER BY clause tells the database engine to sort the records it retrieves. You can sort on any field, or on multiple fields, and you can sort in ascending or descending order.

To specify a sort order, you include the ORDER BY clause at the end of a normal SELECT query, followed by the field or fields by which you wish to sort. For example, to return a list of customer orders listed from smallest to largest, you use the SQL statement shown in Listing 2.14.

Listing 2.14: A Basic Select Query That Sorts on a Single Field

```
SELECT *
FROM tblOrder
ORDER BY [Amount]
```

This query produces the following result set.

ID	CustomerID	OrderDate	Amount
5	104	6/10/97	$2.34
50	104	6/7/97	$2.34
15	105	6/1/97	$25.43
...	...	...	...

Sorting in Descending Order

To sort in descending order, use the DESC keyword after the field by which you're sorting. For example, to retrieve records from the tblOrder table according to who placed the most recent order, you'd use the SQL statement given in Listing 2.15.

Listing 2.15: A Basic Select Query That Sorts on a Single Field in Descending Order

```
SELECT [ID], [CustomerID], [OrderDate]
FROM tblOrder
ORDER BY [OrderDate] DESC
```

This produces the following result set, displaying the most recent orders first.

ID	CustomerID	OrderDate
22	119	7/4/97
37	119	7/1/97
18	102	6/30/97
...	...	...

To sort on multiple fields, you list the fields one after the other immediately following the ORDER BY clause. For example, to sort the tblCustomer table by last name then by first name, the SQL would be as shown in Listing 2.16.

Listing 2.16: A Basic Select Query That Sorts on Two Fields

```
SELECT FirstName, LastName
FROM tblCustomer
ORDER BY LastName, FirstName
```

The result set of this query follows.

FirstName	LastName
Andrea	Allen
Ann	Allen
Bob	Allen
Dave	Allen
Emma	Allen
...	...	...	...

DISPLAYING THE TOP OR BOTTOM OF A RANGE USING TOP

You use the TOP keyword to display only the top or bottom few records in a large recordset. You use the TOP keyword with a sort statement to limit the number of records to a set number of records or a percentage of records in the result set.

For example, let's say you want to view the largest orders in your tblOrder table. Normally, to query the top orders in your orders table, you'd write a SQL statement as in Listing 2.17.

Listing 2.17: A Basic Select Query That Sorts in Descending Order on a Single Field

```
SELECT *
FROM tblOrder
ORDER BY Amount DESC
```

Note that the DESC keyword causes the result set to be sorted in descending (biggest to smallest) order. This SQL produces a result set that looks like this:

ID	CustomerID	OrderDate	Amount
2	101	6/1/97	$995.48
57	167	6/8/97	$889.35
12	126	6/30/97	$889.35
42	176	6/30/97	$872.84
...	...	...	...

This is fine, except that in a database that stores every order you've ever fulfilled, you might have to pass thousands of records back to the client when all you're really interested in are the top three outstanding orders. So instead of Listing 2.17, try the SQL statement in Listing 2.18.

Listing 2.18: A Query That Returns the Top Three Items, Sorted in Descending Order by Amount

```
SELECT TOP 3 *
FROM tblOrder
ORDER BY Amount DESC
```

This query provides the following result set, composed of only three records.

ID	CustomerID	OrderDate	Amount
2	101	6/1/97	$995.48
57	167	6/8/97	$889.35
12	126	6/30/97	$889.35

Note that it is not guaranteed that three records will be returned in a TOP 3 query; it's possible that none, one, or two records will be returned if your table has only that many records. If two or more records are tied for last place in your result list, it's possible that four or more records will be returned.

To create a BOTTOM N query, you simply sort in ascending (smallest to biggest) order, as shown in Listing 2.19.

Listing 2.19: A Select Query That Returns the Top Three Items in the tblOrder Table

```
SELECT TOP 3 *
FROM tblOrder
ORDER BY OrderDate
```

Sorting data in ascending order is implicit in SQL; there's no need to use the ASC keyword (to denote ascending sort order) unless you really want to.

This query produces the following result.

ID	CustomerID	OrderDate	Amount
58	101	6/10/96	$94.38
56	119	6/27/96	$766.84
57	102	6/30/96	$83.85

You can see how this type of query might be a problem if you didn't pay attention to what you are doing, because the TOP N query returns the BOTTOM N results from the table unless you remember to sort the field in question in descending order.

Creating Top Percentage Queries

You can write queries that return a percentage of records in a table. For example, if you have a table with 1000 records, and you wish to return the top 1 percent of records, 10 records will usually be displayed. (It's possible that more than 10 records will be displayed in a top percentage query if more than one record stores the same value; this is also the case with a top N query.)

To return the top records in a result set according to their percentage of the total records in your table, you use the TOP N PERCENT clause. For example, to return the top ten percent of outstanding orders in the tblOrder table, you use the SQL in Listing 2.20.

Listing 2.20: A Select Query That Returns the Top Ten Percent of Orders

```
SELECT TOP 10 PERCENT *
FROM tblOrder
ORDER BY [Amount] DESC
```

This query produces the following result set.

ID	CustomerID	OrderDate	Amount
2	101	6/1/97	$995.48
57	167	6/8/97	$889.35
12	126	6/30/97	$889.35
42	176	6/30/97	$889.35
37	119	7/1/97	$869.82
32	119	6/27/97	$769.93

JOINING RELATED TABLES IN A QUERY

You use a *join* to retrieve related information from more than one table.

To create a join in a query, you must designate the primary and foreign keys of the tables involved in the join. For example, consider two related tables with the following designs.

tblCustomer

ID

FirstName

LastName

Company

Address

City

State

Zip

Phone

Fax

Email

tblOrder

ID

CustomerID

OrderDate

Amount

Though the tblOrder table stores information about orders and the tblCustomer table stores information about customers, it's nevertheless likely that you'll want to retrieve a record set that looks like the following.

FirstName	LastName	OrderDate	Amount
Katie	Woodruff	5/6/97	$57.96
Jill	Davidson	6/1/97	$12.92
Gavin	Edwards	5/19/97	$164.04
Gavin	Edwards	6/4/97	$84.08
...	...	...	...

Retrieving a result set like this is easy to do with a join, even though the data is stored in separate tables. As long as you inform the database engine that the primary key in the tblCustomer table (ID) is related to the foreign key (CustomerID) in the tblOrder table, the correct data will be returned.

Note: You'll notice that in this joined recordset, the same customer is displayed more than once, even though his name was only entered in the database once. This is yet another beautiful thing about relational databases; you only have to enter information on the "one" side of a one-to-many relationship once.

Expressing a Join in SQL

In Microsoft Jet SQL, you can set up a join as an expression of equivalence between two fields, as in the following example.

```
SELECT FirstName, LastName, OrderDate, Amount
FROM tblCustomer, tblOrder
WHERE tblCustomer.ID = tblOrder.CustomerID
```

This SQL returns information on all the customers who have related orders in the tblOrder table. It returns four columns of data—the FirstName and LastName fields from the tblCustomer table, as well as the OrderDate and Amount fields from the tblOrder table.

Note that in a query that includes a join, when the same field appears in two tables, you must use full syntax (such as "tblOrder.ID" rather than simply "ID") to denote which table you're talking about.

You can also designate a join between two tables by using the INNER JOIN clause (the syntax is different, but the data returned is the same). For example, the join between the two tables described in the previous example might also be expressed with the SQL shown in Listing 2.21.

Listing 2.21: A Query Based on a Join Between the tblOrder and tblCustomer Tables

```
SELECT FirstName, LastName, OrderDate, Amount
FROM tblCustomer
INNER JOIN tblOrder ON tblCustomer.ID = tblOrder.CustomerID;
```

While the INNER JOIN syntax is unique to Microsoft Jet, it provides an important bonus—when you use INNER JOIN instead of a WHERE clause to join tables in a query, the result set produced by the query can be updatable. For this reason, queries you create using visual query tools (particularly Microsoft Access) will use the INNER JOIN clause to join two tables in a query.

Note that again, the full *tablename.fieldname* syntax is used in the last clause of the joined query. This syntax is required because two ID fields are involved in this query: the ID field belonging to the tblCustomer table and the ID field belonging to the tblOrder table. You can use this full syntax whenever you want in your queries, however.

Listing 2.22: Another Way of Expressing the Same Query, This Time Using Full Syntax

```
SELECT tblCustomer.FirstName, tblCustomer.LastName, tblOrder.OrderDate,
tblOrder.Amount
FROM tblCustomer
INNER JOIN tblOrder ON tblCustomer.ID = tblOrder.CustomerID
```

Caution: I mentioned at the beginning of this chapter that Microsoft Jet SQL is different than some other dialects of SQL. Joins are one area in which this is the case (the INNER JOIN syntax is unique to Jet). If you ever use a database engine other than Jet, be sure to carefully inspect the documentation for that other engine lest you make incorrect assumptions about how that engine implements joins in SQL.

Because creating joins can represent the most complicated part of relational database queries—particularly, when more than two tables are involved—you might find it useful to have some help when creating them. Fortunately, you have two powerful weapons available in your query-constructing arsenal: the Visual Data Manager and Microsoft Access. Techniques for building queries using these tools are discussed later in this chapter.

Using Outer Joins to Return More Data

A join returns records from two tables in which a value in one table's primary key matches a value in a related table's foreign key. But suppose you want to return all the records on one side of a join whether or not there are related records. In this case, you must use an *outer join*.

For example, a query that lists customers and orders—including customers who do not have any orders outstanding—looks like Listing 2.23.

Listing 2.23: A Left Join That Lists Customers Regardless of Whether They Have Orders

```
SELECT FirstName, LastName, OrderDate, Amount
FROM tblCustomer
LEFT JOIN tblOrder ON tblCustomer.ID = tblOrder.CustomerID;
```

Note the *tablename.fieldname* syntax used in the LEFT JOIN clause. This longer name is used to avoid ambiguity because the ID field exists in both the tblCustomer and tblOrder tables. The fact that it's a LEFT JOIN means that the table on the left side of the expression tblCustomer.ID = tblOrder.CustomerID is the one that will display all of its data.

This query returns the following result set.

FirstName	LastName	OrderDate	Amount
Peter	Vermeren		
Eric	Townsend		
Kim	Bassett	6/5/97	$45.97
Steve	Smith		
Steve	Jones		
Janet	Burns		
...	...	...	...

This result set is composed of all the customers in the database whether or not they have outstanding orders. For those customers without orders, *null* values appear in the OrderDate and Amount fields. A null value is a special value indicating the absence of data; in Visual Basic, Null is a keyword that represents a value that is different than zero or the empty string (which are also used to represent empty values in VB). For example, an arithmetic expression that contains a null value anywhere in the expression always evaluates to null.

A right join is the same as a left join, except that it returns all the records from the second table in the join (the right-side table), whether or not there are any matching records in the first table (the left-side table). Other than that, the same data can be returned whether you're using a left join or a right join.

As an example, let's say you want to develop a query to determine the regions of the country in which you have no customers. You're also interested in seeing the names of existing customers. You accomplish this with a right join between the tblCustomer and tblRegion tables, displaying all the states and regions, whether or not they have any customers associated with them. The SQL to perform this query looks like Listing 2.24.

Listing 2.24: A Right Join That Lists All the Regions Whether or Not They Have Customers

```
SELECT FirstName, LastName, tblRegion.State, Region
FROM tblCustomer
RIGHT JOIN tblRegion ON tblCustomer.State = tblRegion.State
```

Note again that the *tablename.fieldname* syntax is used to avoid ambiguity in situations in which a given field exists in both tables involved in the join (in this case, the State field).

This query returns the following result set.

FirstName	LastName	State	Region
		AL	South
		AK	Northwest
		AZ	Southwest
Peter	Vermeren	CA	West
Eric	Townsend	CA	West
...	...	...	...

The rows that contain nulls in the FirstName and LastName fields indicate a region without any customers. For the regions that contain customers, all the customers are listed.

Displaying Zeros Instead of Nulls in a Joined Query

It is very common—particularly when you're creating a query that will be used as the basis of a report—to want to create a query based on a join that displays zeros instead of nulls. To accomplish this, you replace the reference to the field with a calculation.

In this case, the calculation involves the IIf function. IIf takes three arguments: an expression, a value to return if the expression is true, and a value to return if the expression is false.

For example, to return a string that flags whether an order is more than or less than $50, you would write the following IIf expression:

```
IIf([Amount] > 50, ?Big order?, ?Small order?)
```

So, to use IIf to replace nulls with zeroes, you use the IsNull function to inspect the value of the field. If IsNull returns false, then the field already has something in it, so you return whatever's in the field. But if it returns true, that means the field is null, so you return a zero instead. You can see in Listing 2.25 an example of SQL code that accomplishes this.

Listing 2.25: A Query Based on a Join That Returns Zeros Instead of Nulls

```
SELECT FirstName, LastName, OrderDate,
       IIf(IsNull(Amount),0,Amount) AS TotalAmount
FROM tblCustomer
LEFT JOIN tblOrder ON tblCustomer.ID = tblOrder.CustomerID
```

This query returns the following result set.

FirstName	LastName	OrderDate	TotalAmount
Peter	Vermeren		$0.00
Eric	Townsend		$0.00
Kim	Bassett	6/5/97	$45.97
Steve	Smith		$0.00
Steve	Jones		$0.00
Janet	Burns		$0.00
...	...	...	...

Note: Queries with columns based on calculations generally return results significantly more slowly than queries based on fields.

ALIASING FIELD NAMES USING AS

As you saw in the preceding example, you have the ability to *alias*, or rename, a field in a query. You might do this for two reasons:

▶ The underlying table has field names that are unwieldy, and you want to make the field names in the result set easier to deal with

▶ The query you're creating produces some sort of calculated or summation column that requires a name

Whatever your reason for wanting to alias a field name, it's easy to do using the AS clause in SQL. For example, let's say you are doing a complex series of calculations on the Amount field in the tblOrder table. You want to refer to that column as the SubTotal field to remind yourself that you're working with a subtotal rather than an extended total. To do this, you write the SQL code in Listing 2.26.

Listing 2.26: Renaming a Field in a Query Using the AS Clause

```
SELECT [CustomerID], [OrderDate], [Amount] AS [SubTotal]
FROM tblOrder
```

This query produces the following result set.

CustomerID	OrderDate	SubTotal
5	6/5/97	$45.97
101	6/1/97	$995.48
102	6/8/97	$647.65
...	...	...

Note that the field that was formerly called Amount is referred to in this result set as SubTotal; as far as this result set is concerned, the Amount field doesn't exist, although the Amount field still exists in the underlying recordset.

Although using the AS clause can be helpful in situations in which you're trying to simplify field names, aliasing fields is done much more often when you're performing calculations on fields. For example, let's say you need to write a query that calculates sales tax on subtotals in the tblOrder table. Such a query might look like Listing 2.27.

Listing 2.27: A Query with Multiple Calculations: Each Calculated Field Is Named Using the AS Clause

```
SELECT ID, OrderDate, Amount,
CCur(Amount * 0.0825) AS SalesTax,
CCur(Amount * 1.0825) AS Total
FROM tblOrder
```

(The CCur function converts the product of the sales tax calculation to a currency data type; the sales tax calculation assumes a sales tax of 8.25 percent.)

The result set of this query follows.

ID	OrderDate	Amount	SalesTax	Total
1	6/5/97	$45.97	$3.79	$49.76
2	6/1/97	$995.48	$82.13	$1,077.61
3	6/8/97	$647.65	$53.43	$701.08
...	...	...	...	...

Note that the SalesTax and Total fields aren't stored in the database; they're calculated on the fly. Because they aren't stored in fields in the database structure, you *must* name them using the AS clause or you won't have any way of referring to them (and the database engine will generate a syntax error when you try to run the query).

QUERIES THAT GROUP AND SUMMARIZE DATA

Frequently, you'll need to create queries that answer questions like "how many orders came in yesterday?" In this scenario, you don't care exactly *who* ordered material, you only want to know how many orders came in. You can do this using group queries and aggregate functions.

Group queries summarize data according to one or more fields in common. For example, if you're interested in seeing the total number of orders that came in yesterday, you'd group by the OrderDate field (and supply a criterion limiting the data returned to yesterday only). Such a query would look like Listing 2.28.

Listing 2.28: A Query That Groups and Performs an Aggregate Count Function on a Field

```
SELECT OrderDate, Count(CustomerID) AS TotalOrders
FROM tblOrder
GROUP BY OrderDate
HAVING OrderDate=#6/30/97#
```

(The HAVING clause is equivalent to the WHERE clause for grouped queries.)

The result set produced by this query follows.

OrderDate	TotalOrders
6/30/97	10

Note the use of the AS clause; this is done to give the column containing the result of the aggregate function a name, because it's calculated rather than stored in the database.

You could use a simpler version of this query to return a report of sales activity on a day-by-day basis. Such a query would simply eschew the HAVING criterion, as in Listing 2.29.

Listing 2.29: A Query That Groups and Sorts, This Time Without a Limiting Criterion

```
SELECT OrderDate, Count(CustomerID) AS TotalOrders
FROM tblOrder
GROUP BY OrderDate
```

Note that to refer to the field that results from the aggregate grouping, you need to name the new column. You do this by using the AS clause.

This query produces the following result set.

OrderDate	TotalOrders
6/10/96	1
6/27/96	1
6/30/96	1
6/1/97	1
6/2/97	1
...	...

Note that this result set does not generate records for dates on which no orders were taken.

The SUM Function

You're not limited to simply counting records in aggregate functions. Using the SUM function, you can generate totals for all the records returned in numeric fields.

For example, to create a query that generates a day-by-day total of your company's sales, you would write the SQL code in Listing 2.30.

Listing 2.30: A Query That Performs an Aggregate Sum Function on the Amount Field

```
SELECT OrderDate, Sum(Amount) AS TotalOrderAmount
FROM tblOrder
GROUP BY OrderDate
```

This query produces the following result set.

OrderDate	TotalOrderAmount
6/10/96	$94.38
6/27/96	$766.84
6/30/96	$83.85
6/1/97	$1,224.35
6/2/97	$269.04
...	...

Summary of Aggregate Functions

Table 2.2 lists all the aggregate functions available to you in Microsoft Jet SQL.

Table 2.2: Jet SQL's Aggregate Functions

Function	Result
AVG	The average of all values in the column
COUNT	The count of the number of records returned
FIRST	The first value in the field
LAST	The last value in the field
MAX	The maximum (or largest) value in a column
MIN	The minimum (or smallest) value in a column
STDEV	The standard deviation
SUM	The total of all values in the field
VAR	The variance

The syntax of these aggregate functions are essentially the same as the syntax for COUNT, which I discussed in the previous section. For example, to calculate the average order in the tblOrders table on a day-by-day basis, you'd use the SQL query in Listing 2.31.

Listing 2.31: A Query That Performs an Aggregate Avg Function on the Amount Field

```
SELECT OrderDate, Avg(Amount) AS AverageOrderAmount
FROM tblOrder
GROUP BY OrderDate
```

This query produces the following result set.

OrderDate	AverageOrderAmount
6/10/96	$94.38
6/27/96	$766.84
6/30/96	$83.85
6/1/97	$122.44
6/2/97	$269.04
...	...

You must group on at least one field for an aggregate function to work.

Creating Action Queries

An *action query* is a query that has the ability to alter records. Action queries do not return result sets; instead, they make permanent changes to data.

You generally use action queries when you need to make changes to large amounts of data based on a criterion. For example, if you need to initiate a 10 percent across-the-board price increase in your products, you'd use an update query (a type of action query) to change the prices of all the items in your inventory.

Update Queries

An update query has the capability to alter a group of records all at once. An update query comprises three parts:

▶ The UPDATE clause, which specifies which table to update

▶ The SET clause, which specifies which data to change

▶ Optionally, the WHERE criteria, which limits the number of records affected by the update query

For example, to increase the price of all the items in your inventory, you'd use the update query shown in Listing 2.32.

Listing 2.32: An Update Query That Increases All the Values in the RetailPrice Field by 10 Percent

```
UPDATE tblInventory
SET [RetailPrice] = [RetailPrice] * 1.1
```

The contents of the relevant fields in the tblInventory before you run the update query follow.

ID	Product	CatalogNumber	WholesalePrice	RetailPrice
1	Rubber Chicken	AC5	$1.92	$4.98
2	Joy Buzzer	BB1	$0.73	$1.49
3	Seltzer Bottle	AZ401	$2.07	$4.49
...	...	...	...	...

The contents after you run the update query follow.

ID	Product	CatalogNumber	WholesalePrice	RetailPrice
1	Rubber Chicken	AC5	$1.92	$5.48
2	Joy Buzzer	BB1	$0.73	$1.64
3	Seltzer Bottle	AZ401	$2.07	$4.94
...	...	...	...	...

To limit the number of records affected by the update query, you simply append a WHERE clause to the SQL query. For example, to apply the price increase only to big-ticket items more than $100, you'd alter the SQL as Listing 2.33 shows.

Listing 2.33: An Update Query That Increases the Values More Than $100 in the RetailPrice Field by 10 Percent

```
UPDATE tblInventory
SET [RetailPrice] = [RetailPrice] * 1.1
WHERE [RetailPrice] > 100
```

This query increases the retail price of items more than $100 by 10 percent.

Delete Queries

A delete query has the capability to delete a group of records all at once.

For example, to delete all the orders that were placed before (but not on) last Halloween, you'd use the SQL statement shown in Listing 2.34.

Listing 2.34: A Delete Query That Deletes All the Records in the tblOrder Table Created Before October 31, 1996

```
DELETE *
FROM tblOrder
WHERE [OrderDate] < #10/31/96#
```

Append Queries

You use an append query for two purposes:

▶ Adding a single record to a table

▶ Copying one or more records from one table to another

To create an append query, use the SQL INSERT clause. The exact syntax of the query depends on whether you're inserting a single record or copying multiple records.

For example, a single-record append query that adds a new order to the tblOrder table might look like Listing 2.35.

Listing 2.35: An Append Query That Inserts a Single Record into the tblOrder Table

```
INSERT INTO tblOrder ([CustomerID], [OrderDate], [Amount])
VALUES (119, #6/16/97#, 145.94)
```

Executing this query creates a new order for Customer 119 in the amount of $145.94 in the tblOrder table.

> **Note:** In this append query, you don't append anything for the tblOrder table's ID field because it is an Autonumber field; to attempt to do so would generate an error. You can only generate that field's contents automatically.

To create the kind of append query that copies records from one table to another, you use an INSERT clause with a SELECT clause. For example, let's say that instead of deleting old orders, you archive them by periodically copying them to an archive table called tblOrderArchive, which has the same structure as the tblOrder table. (For this to work, you'll first need to create tblOrderArchive, making sure it has the same structure as tblOrder.)

The SQL statement to copy old records from the tblOrder table to the tblOrderArchive table might look like Listing 2.36.

Listing 2.36: An Append Query That Copies Multiple Records from One Table to Another

```
INSERT INTO tblOrderArchive
SELECT * FROM tblOrder
WHERE [OrderDate] < #6/10/97#
```

Executing this statement will copy all the records with order dates before June 10, 1997, into the tblOrderArchive table.

Make-table Queries

A make-table query is similar to an append query, except that it can create a new table and copy records to it in one fell swoop.

To create a make-table query, you use the SELECT INTO clause. For example, in Listing 2.36 you copied records from the tblOrder table to a tblOrderArchive table. This presupposes that the tblOrderArchive actually exists, however. Instead, to copy the same records into a new table with the same structure as the original, you use the SQL action query given in Listing 2.37.

Listing 2.37: A Make-table Query That Copies All the Records from the tblOrder Table into a New Table

```
SELECT * INTO tblOrderArchive
FROM tblOrder
```

Note: Executing this query copies all the records from tblOrder into a new table called tblOrderArchive. If tblOrderArchive already exists when the query is run, it is deleted and replaced by the database engine with the contents of the copied records.

You can apply limiting criteria (by using a WHERE clause) in the same way you apply criteria to an append query, as illustrated in the previous section on append queries. Doing so enables you to copy a subset of records from the original table into the new table you create with a make-table query.

UNION QUERIES

A *union query* merges the contents of two tables that have similar field structures. It's useful in situations in which you need to display potentially unrelated records from multiple record sources in a single result set.

For example, in the previous examples involving make-table queries and append queries, I described a mechanism in the application that stores old orders in a table of their own, called tblOrderArchive. Because of the way your archiving system is set up, the records are physically located in two separate tables. But it's likely that at some point you'd want to view the current records and the archived records in a single, unified result set. A union query lets you do this.

Let's say you now need to view the old records in tblOrderArchive in the same result set as the new records in tblOrder. The union query you'd write to accomplish this shown in Listing 2.38.

Listing 2.38: A Union Query That Displays the Contents of the tblOrder and tblOrderArchive Tables

```
SELECT *
FROM tblOrder
UNION
SELECT *
FROM tblOrderArchive
```

The result set of this query combines old and new orders in a single result set, as follows.

ID	CustomerID	OrderDate	Amount
1	5	6/5/97	$45.97
2	101	6/1/97	$995.48
3	102	6/8/97	$647.65
...	...	...	...

By default, union queries do not return duplicate records (this would be useful if your record-archiving system did not delete records after it copied them to the archive table). You can cause a union query to intentionally display duplicate records by adding the ALL keyword, however, as in Listing 2.39.

Listing 2.39: A Union Query That Displays the Contents of the tblOrder and tblOrderArchive Tables Without Suppressing Duplicate Records

```
SELECT *
FROM tblOrder
UNION ALL
SELECT *
FROM tblOrderArchive
```

CROSSTAB QUERIES

A *crosstab query* is a way of grouping data in two dimensions at once. It is a great a way to see summaries of data in a very compact result set. Crosstab queries are commonly used in database reporting and charting.

Crosstab queries are similar to queries that perform grouping and aggregation. With a conventional grouping query, you group on a single field and perform an aggregate function on another field. An example of this might be a query that shows day-to-day sales figures for a week-long period, as in the following result set.

OrderDate	TotalSales
6/1/97	$1,224.35
6/2/97	$269.04
6/3/97	$83.85
6/4/97	$267.68
6/5/97	$45.97
6/6/97	$178.90
6/7/97	$2.34

But this is a one-dimensional result set; it only displays sales. What if you wanted to see how much each customer purchased on each day? With a crosstab query, you can do this because crosstabs can group on two distinct fields.

To create a crosstab query that shows how much each customer spends per day, you use the SQL statement given in Listing 2.40.

Listing 2.40: A Crosstab Query That Shows Customer Sales Broken down by Day and by Customer

```
TRANSFORM Sum(Amount) AS TotalSales
SELECT CustomerID
FROM tblOrder
WHERE ((OrderDate) Between #6/1/97# And #6/7/97#)
GROUP BY CustomerID
ORDER BY CustomerID, OrderDate
PIVOT OrderDate
```

This statement produces the following result set.

CustomerID	6/1/97	6/2/97	6/3/97	6/4/97	6/5/97	6/6/97	6/7/97
5	$45.97						
101	$995.48	$94.38					
102	$83.85	$83.85					
104	$2.34						
105	$228.87	$89.45	$178.90				
125	$269.04						

Note: Crosstab queries are not part of ANSI SQL. This means that you should not develop crosstab queries in a Microsoft Jet SQL and expect them to function when you migrate your application to a client-server database.

Even if you understand crosstab queries pretty well, it makes sense to use Microsoft Access to create them if you can, because even the simplest crosstabs can be quite complicated to write.

SUBQUERIES

A *subquery* is a query whose result serves as a criterion for another query. Subqueries take the place of normal WHERE expressions. Because the result generated by the subquery takes the place of an expression, the subquery can only return a single value.

The only syntactical difference between a subquery and any other type of expression placed in a WHERE clause is that the subquery must be enclosed in parentheses.

For example, let's say you want to create a query that shows your biggest orders. You define a big customer as a customer that places a larger-than-average order. Because you can determine the value of a larger-than-average order (by performing an aggregate function on the Amount field in the tblOrder table), you can use this value as a subquery in the larger query. The SQL to do this is shown in Listing 2.41.

Listing 2.41: A Subquery That Provides a WHERE Condition to the Main Query

```
SELECT OrderDate, CustomerID, Amount
FROM tblOrder
WHERE Amount > (SELECT AVG(Amount) FROM tblOrder)
```

In this case, the query and the subquery happen to be querying the same table, but this doesn't have to be the case. Subqueries can query any table in the database as long as they return a single value.

The SQL statement in Listing 2.41 returns the following result set.

OrderDate	CustomerID	Amount
6/1/97	101	$995.48
6/8/97	102	$647.65
6/27/97	119	$766.84
6/30/97	167	$889.35
...	...	...

COMMON ERRORS GENERATED BY QUERIES

It's very common to run into errors when creating SQL statements in Visual Basic. This has a lot to do with the fact that SQL is a language-within-a-language, and Visual Basic can't catch errors in your SQL as you type them the way it can catch Visual Basic errors.

As a result, SQL errors don't usually pop up until runtime, and the error messages provided by VB aren't always so helpful. Two of the most common errors encountered when using SQL queries within Visual Basic follow:

▶ "Too few parameters. Expected *n*" (error 3061). This message indicates that one of the fields in the SELECT or WHERE clauses of your SQL statement doesn't exist or is spelled wrong, or you failed to supply one of the parameters in a parameterized query.

▶ "The Microsoft Jet database engine cannot find the input table or query <name>. Make sure it exists and that its name is spelled correctly" (error 3078). This message indicates that misspelled or nonexistent table or query in your SQL SELECT clause.

To see how easy it is to trigger one of these errors (assuming you haven't inadvertently triggered one already), you can use the SQL Tester application described at the beginning of this chapter. The code for this application is in the Chapter 2 folder of the CD-ROM that accompanies this book; to build the SQL Tester application yourself, follow these steps.

1 Start the SQL Tester application.

2 Type in a semi-bogus SQL statement, such as

```
SELECT *
FROM tblKustomurs
ORDER BY [LastName], [FirstName]
```

3 Click the Run Query button. The misspelled table is not found, and the error message illustrated in Figure 2.4 is displayed.

Figure 2.4: The Error Message generated when you don't spell a table name correctly.

This is a relatively straightforward error message, but the error message that is generated when you don't spell a field name correctly is less straightforward. If you use the SQL query

```
SELECT *
FROM tblCustomer
ORDER BY [ListName], [FistName]
```

you get error 3061, "Too few parameters. Expected 2." This message is unexpected because you didn't use any parameters in your query; everything's hard-coded. A glance at the code shows that the problem is obviously the fact that you misspelled the names of two fields (although this problem might be less obvious if the query involved five tables and thirty fields—Visual Basic doesn't tell you which field names are misspelled, just how many were misspelled). But what is this "parameter" thing anyway?

The answer: a parameter is a useful feature of SQL that gives you the ability to supply a parameter (usually the value of a WHERE clause) at the time the query is run. So, rather than having to write a query that is hard-wired always to return the records for a particular date, like this

```
SELECT *
FROM tblOrder
WHERE OrderDate < #6/5/97#
```

you can instead write a query with a parameter, like this:

```
SELECT *
FROM tblOrder
WHERE OrderDate < [TheDateYouWant]
```

Note: The problem with the "Too few parameters" error message, then, is that Jet assumes that any misspelled field names are, in fact, parameters, so it gives you the error message pertaining to parameters even though you may have no idea what parameterized queries are.

In your code, you supply a value for the [TheDateYouWant] parameter before running the query. (In most cases the value for the parameter will be set by something the user does in your application's interface.) In Visual Basic, you use a QueryDef object in Data Access Objects to do this. For more information on Data Access Object programming, see Chapter 3, "Data Access Objects."

USING QUERIES STORED IN THE DATABASE

So far you've seen how to create queries on the fly, composed and executed at runtime by your Visual Basic application. In real Visual Basic database access applications, it's likely that your application will have dozens or even hundreds of SQL queries. To make it easier to maintain and reuse the queries you create, the database engine gives you the ability to permanently store a query definition in the database. This section describes how to create such queries.

> **Note:** In the parlance of Data Access Object programming, queries stored in a database are also referred to as QueryDefs. In the world of client/server programming, queries stored in the database are sometimes referred to as views. In this book, I'll generally refer to such queries as stored queries to make my discussion of them consistent and less jargon-ish.

Database programmers frequently ask why one would go about storing SQL statements in a compiled executable rather than storing them in a database. The answer isn't always clear-cut, but, in general, it's easier and more efficient to embed your queries in the database. There are also some valid situations in which you'd want to compose your query in Visual Basic code at runtime, however. Table 2.3 highlights the advantages and disadvantages of the two techniques.

Table 2.3: Advantages of Stored Queries Versus Queries in Executables

Stored Query	Query in Executable
Executes quickly because it is compiled ahead of time by the database engine	Executes more slowly because it must be interpreted at the time it is run
Requires a change to the database to install	Requires a recompilation and redistribution of that executable
Moderate degree of flexibility (mainly through the use of parameterized queries)	High degree of flexibility (can include parameterized queries as well as concatenated SQL statements generated from any Visual Basic process, including variables, If...Then statements, and other queries)
Easier to maintain because it is stored in the database	Harder to maintain because it is embedded in code

Business Case 2.1: Stored Queries Versus Queries Generated On the Fly
Queries that you store in the database let you modify the way your application works without breaking existing code. For example, let's say you have a payroll application based on a tblEmployee table. If the application generates its queries

on the fly in Visual Basic code, it would interact with the database as illustrated in Figure 2.5.

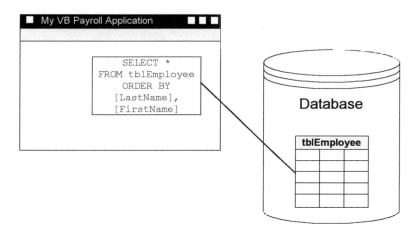

Figure 2.5: An application that generates its own database queries on the fly.

This application might be functional, but it would have the following problems:

▶ It would be extremely difficult to change because the SQL code would be scattered hither and thither throughout your code

▶ The queries scattered throughout your code might be inconsistent; for example, one query might recognize a particular status field in the database while others might ignore it

▶ It would run less efficiently because queries stored in Visual Basic EXEs aren't compiled by the Jet database engine

A better technique is to store the query in the database, as illustrated in Figure 2.6.

In addition to reducing complexity in your VB application by moving the SQL code out of your app and into the database, this design also inoculates your design from change; if a component of the database design changes, you don't have to change your VB code (which would force you to recompile and redistribute your application).

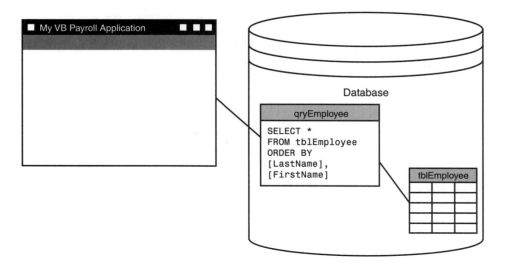

Figure 2.6: The same database application, this time with the query stored in the database.

For an example of how this inoculates your design from change, let's say you alter your database design to accommodate a Hide field in the tblEmployee table. Employees who are hidden are currently inactive—perhaps they don't work for the company anymore, or they haven't been hired yet. You don't want to delete them, because you need to retain information about them indefinitely, but you need to hide them so your system doesn't keep issuing them paychecks. The database design that describes this change is illustrated in Figure 2.7.

As long as you don't change field names or remove a column from the result set of the query, you can use the same query again and again in your application. Your application's code remains unchanged, while your database has the ability to adapt to whatever changing business conditions happen to come along.

Creating Stored Queries Using Visual Data Manager

You have the ability to create queries stored in a Jet database using the Visual Data Manager utility included with Visual Basic. To do this, follow these steps.

1 In Visual Basic, select the menu command Add Ins, Visual Data Manager.

2 The Visual Data Manager appears. In the Visual Data Manager's File, Open menu, open the database `novelty.mdb`.

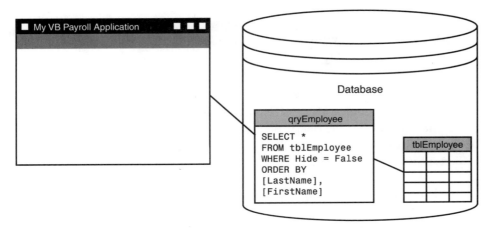

Figure 2.7: The database design after a change has been made. Note that no change in the VB application was necessary.

3 In the Visual Data Manager's toolbar, select the Use DBGrid Control On New Form button, as illustrated in Figure 2.8.

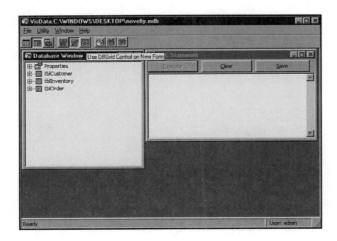

Figure 2.8: Visual Data Manager's Toolbar that displays query results in a grid format.

4 In the Visual Data Manager's SQL Statement window, type the SQL statement shown in Listing 2.42.

Listing 2.42: A Basic Select Query

```
SELECT FirstName, LastName
FROM tblCustomer
ORDER BY LastName, FirstName
```

> **Note:** Pressing Enter when you're entering a SQL statement indicates that you want to execute the query. So if you want instead insert a line break in the SQL Statement window of the Visual Data Manager add-in, press Shift+Enter.

5 When you're done typing the SQL statement, click Execute.

6 The message box "Is this a SQLPassThrough Query?" appears. Because SQL pass-through queries are only relevant in client-server development, click No.

The query executes, as illustrated in Figure 2.9.

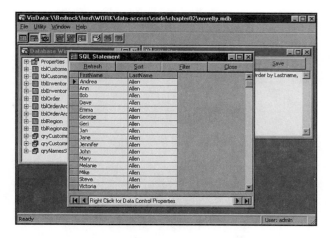

Figure 2.9: The product of a query in the Visual Data Manager displayed in a grid.

7 Now that you know the query works properly, close the query window.

8 In the SQL statement window, click the Save button.

9 In the "Enter QueryDef name" dialog, type `qryNamesSorted`, then click OK.

10 The message box "Is this a SQLPassThrough QueryDef?" appears. Because this is not a client/server database, click the No button.

The query is stored in the database. It also appears in the Database window, as illustrated in Figure 2.10.

Figure 2.10: Visual Data Manager's Database Window after you've saved a query in the database.

You can rerun the query at any time by double-clicking the query definition in Visual Data Manager's Database window. Now that you've saved it in the database, you can refer to `qryNamesSorted` just as you would refer to any table in the database.

Tip: You've probably noticed in this book tables are named with the tbl prefix and stored queries are named with the qry prefix. Now you know why—the fact that the database engine treats tables and queries almost interchangeably means that it can become difficult for developers to know what they're dealing with.

Using the Visual Data Manager Query Builder

You can use the Visual Data Manager's Query Builder to create an SQL statement that serves as the basis of a query. Using the Query Builder can be easier than writing the SQL yourself because the Query Builder presents lists of choices. To create a query using the Query Builder, follow these steps.

1 From Visual Data Manager's Utility menu, select Query Builder.

2 From the list of tables, click tblCustomer.

3 The Fields to Show list is populated with a list of fields in tblCustomer. From that list, select `tblCustomer.FirstName`, `tblCustomer.LastName`, and `tblCustomer.Zip`.

The Query Builder looks like Figure 2.11.

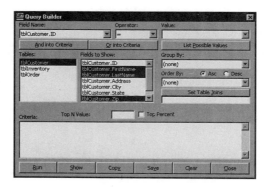

Figure 2.11: The Query Builder dialog box containing choices for a simple query.

Next, you'll specify a criterion for this query to limit the number of records it will return.

1 From the Field Name combo box, select `tblCustomer.Zip`.

2 In the Operator combo, make sure the equal sign is selected.

3 Click the List Possible Values beneath the Value combo box. A list of possible values that can match the field you chose is added to the combo box. Select the value **99485**.

4 Click the And into Criteria button to add the criterion you just constructed to the query definition.

The query looks like Figure 2.12.

5 Run the query by clicking the Run button. The "Is this a SQLPassThru Query?" message box appears. Click on no.

6 The query runs. Only those records whose ZIP codes equal 99485 are displayed in the grid.

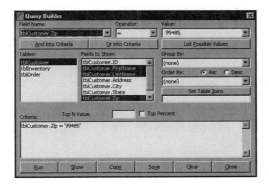

Figure 2.12: Query builder containing a query that has a criterion associated with it.

At this point, you can save the query in the database if you wish. To save the query you've defined, click the Save button, then enter the name `qryCustomersInZipCode99485`.

You can see that by using Visual Data Manager's Query Builder, you can save a significant amount of time developing queries—particularly complicated queries. There's an even easier way to build queries for Jet databases, however: by using Microsoft Access.

Creating Joins in Visual Data Manager

You can create a query based on a join in Visual Data Manager. To do this, follow these steps.

1 If the Query Builder dialog is visible, click on the Clear button to clear out the previous query. If it's not visible, select Query Builder from the Visual Data Manager's Utility window. The Query Builder dialog appears.

2 In the list of tables, click tblCustomer and tblOrder.

3 Click on the Set Table Joins button.

4 The Join Tables dialog appears. Click tblCustomer and tblOrder. The list of fields in both tables appears in the dialog's list boxes, as illustrated in Figure 2.13.

5 In the first column, select the primary key of the tblCustomer table, ID. In the second column, select the foreign key in the tblOrder table, CustomerID.

6 Click the Add Join to Query button, then click Close.

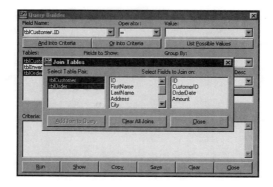

Figure 2.13: The arduous process of creating a Join in the Visual Data Manager.

7 In the Fields to Show list, click `tblCustomer.FirstName`, `tblCustomer.LastName`, `tblOrder.OrderDate`, and `tblOrder.Amount`.

8 Click the Run button. The "Is this a SQLPassThrough query?" message box appears; answer No.

9 The query is run and the result is displayed, as illustrated in Figure 2.14.

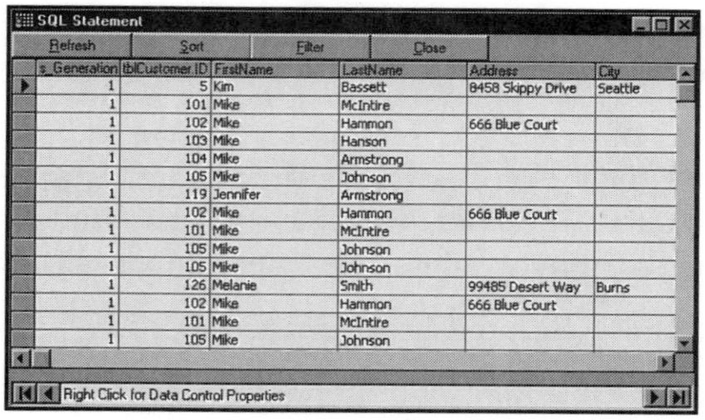

Figure 2.14: The product of a query joining two tables in the Visual Data Manager.

At this point, if you wish to save the query, you can do so by clicking the Save button in the Query Builder. When you're done with the Query Builder, close it by clicking on its Close button.

Creating Stored Queries Using Microsoft Access

Microsoft Access has a much slicker interface for creating queries than that of the Visual Data Manager.

To create a query using Microsoft Access, follow these steps.

1 Launch Access and open the database. The Database window appears.

2 Click once on the table on which you wish to base your query. In this example, I'll use tblCustomer.

3 From the Insert menu, select Query.

4 The New Query dialog appears. Choose Design View.

The query design window appears, as illustrated in Figure 2.15.

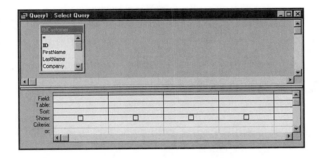

Figure 2.15: Microsoft Access Graphical Query Design Window.

5 For this query, you want to display the customer's first and last name, address, city, and state. To do this, click-drag those fields from the list of fields to the grid at the bottom of the query design window. The query looks like Figure 2.16.

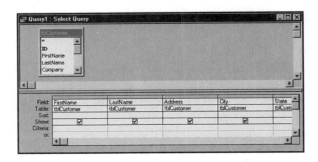

Figure 2.16: Access Query Design Window with fields dragged from the table.

6 To sort the query output, click the Sort row underneath the FirstName and LastName fields. Select Ascending for both fields.

7 Click on the LastName field to select it. Then click-drag the field so it appears in the leftmost column in the query design grid. Doing this will ensure that it is sorted first, before the FirstName field.

8 Run the query by selecting the menu command Query, Run. The result set appears.

9 Go back to design view by selecting the menu command View, Design View.

Now you'll specify a criterion to limit the number of records returned by the query.

1 Type the word Smith in the Criteria row under the LastName field.

2 Run the query. Only records for customers named Smith are returned.

You can save the query you're working on at any time. To save a query you're working on in Access, follow these steps.

1 From the File menu, select Save.

2 The Save As dialog appears. In the dialog, type `qryCustomerSmith`.

3 Click OK. The query definition is saved in the database.

Creating Joins in Microsoft Access
It's extremely easy to create a query based on joined multiple tables in Microsoft Access. To do this, follow these steps.

1 If you need to, open qryCustomerSmith, the query you created in the previous example. Make sure you open this query in design view.

2 From the Query menu, select Show Table. The Show Table dialog appears.

3 Double-click tblOrder, then click the Close button.

4 The table tblOrder appears in the query. If you defined a relationship between tblCustomer and tblOrder in your database in the example in Chapter 1, you should be able to see the relationship expressed graphically, as illustrated in Figure 2.17.

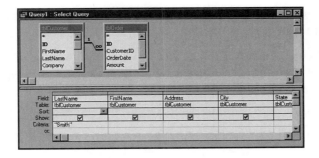

Figure 2.17: Microsoft Access Query Design Window containing two joined tables.

> **Note:** Access is smart enough to know that a predefined relationship exists between two tables when you build a query based on those tables. This capability saves you some steps because you don't have to create the joins in each query you build; it also keeps you from having to remember which fields to connect in the tables.

5 If Access does not create a join between the two tables, you can draw one manually by click-dragging from the ID field in tblCustomer to the CustomerID field in tblOrder.

6 Click-drag the fields OrderDate and Amount from tblOrder into the query design grid. Run the query. You should be able to see the data from both fields, as illustrated in Figure 2.18.

FirstName	LastName	Address	City	State	OrderDate	Amount
Melanie	Smith	99485 Desert W	Burns	KS	6/30/97	$889.35
George	Smith	8458 Skippy Dri	Hayward	CA	6/30/97	$83.85
George	Smith	8458 Skippy Dri	Hayward	CA	6/30/97	$83.85

Figure 2.18: Output of the multitable query created in Microsoft Access.

You can view the SQL behind a query you develop in Access at any time. To do this, follow these steps.

1 From Microsoft Access View menu, select SQL View. The query output window changes in an SQL view window, as illustrated in Figure 2.19.

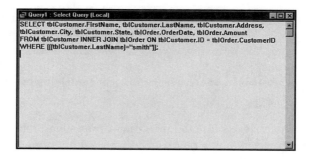

Figure 2.19: Microsoft Access gives the ability to view the SQL behind a Query Design.

You can edit this SQL directly, if you wish. In most cases, you can switch back and forth between Access' graphical query designer, recordsheet view, and SQL View. This capability gives you the ability to take advantage of the power of SQL as well as Microsoft Access' ease of use.

Creating Other Types of Queries in Access

By default, Access assumes you're going to create a SELECT query, but you can easily change the type of query you're writing. Using Access' Query menu, you can create these types of queries:

▶ Crosstab queries

▶ Make-table queries

▶ Update queries

▶ Append queries

▶ Delete queries

▶ SQL-specific queries, which include Union queries, Pass-through queries, and Data Definition queries

There is no graphical user interface for creating SQL-specific queries in Microsoft Access or the Visual Data Manager; you must type in the code for these queries manually. For more information on Data Definition Queries, see "Using Data Definition Language" later in this chapter.

Creating Stored Queries at Runtime

You have the ability to create queries in code at runtime. You'd do this in situations in which some component of the query depends on some other processing performed by your application.

For example, say you are writing a Visual Basic application that acts as a report generator for a particular database. This application must have the ability to output data from any table in the database, constrained by any one of a number of criteria, and sorted any way the user wishes. To avoid hard-wiring any of this information, you use a dynamically-generated query.

To create queries dynamically at runtime, you use the Data Access Objects—specifically, the OpenRecordset method of the Database object and the QueryDef object. For more on dynamically generated queries using Data Access Objects, see Chapter 3, "Data Access Objects."

Using Data Definition Language

Data Definition Language commands are SQL statements that enable you to create, manipulate, and destroy elements of the database structure. Using DDL, you can create and destroy tables and alter the definition of tables.

Data Definition Language commands are perhaps the most seldom-used statements in Microsoft Jet SQL, mainly because there are so many good tools (such as Microsoft Access and the Visual Data Manager) that help you perform chores, such as creating tables, fields, and indexes. It's also more Visual-Basic-like to perform these kinds of tasks using Data Access Objects (discussed in Chapter 3). If you're coming from a client-server environment, however, you might be more comfortable with using DDL to create the structure of your database. Bear in mind, though, that Microsoft Jet doesn't support the use of DDL commands on non-Jet databases.

Like action queries, Data Definition Language commands do not return result sets (which is why they're referred to as "commands" rather than "queries").

There is no support for DDL commands in the user interface of either Microsoft Access or the Visual Data Manager. To execute a DDL command, you must type the SQL directly. In the Visual Data Manager, you type the SQL into the SQL Statement window; in Access, you type the SQL into the SQL view of a query definition window.

Creating Database Elements Using CREATE

You create new database elements using the CREATE clause. To create a table, you use the CREATE TABLE command, followed by the fields and data types you wish to add to the table, delimited by commas and enclosed in parentheses.

For example, to create a new table, you can use the SQL statement in Listing 2.43.

Listing 2.43: A Query that Creates the tblRegion Table

```
CREATE TABLE tblRegion
([State] TEXT (2),
[Region] TEXT (50))
```

The data type TEXT (2) tells the database engine to create a text field that can store a maximum of two characters; TEXT (50) creates a field 50 characters long.

This query creates a table with the following schema.

tblRegion

State

Region

Table 2.4 shows a list of the data types of fields you can denote using Microsoft Jet DDL and the CREATE clause.

Table 2.4: Data Types of Fields Available in Jet

Data Type	SQL	Comments
AutoNumber (Long Integer)	COUNTER	This is the most commonly used autonumber field
Autonumber (Replication ID)	GUID	Generally used only for replication (for more on how replication works, see Chapter 8, "Multiuser Issues")
Currency	CURRENCY	

Data Type	SQL	Comments
Date/Time	DATETIME	
Hyperlink	LONGTEXT	Stored the same as a Memo field
Memo	LONGTEXT	
Number (Byte)	BYTE	
Number (Double)	DOUBLE	
Number (Integer)	INTEGER	
Number (Long Integer)	LONG	The most commonly used integer field
Number (Single)	SINGLE	
OLE Object	LONGBINARY	
Text	TEXT	You must supply the length of the field; example: TEXT (50)
Yes/No	BOOLEAN	

Adding Constraints to Tables

You can also add *constraints* at the same time you create a table. A constraint is similar to an index, but it's used to designate a unique key, a primary key, or a foreign key.

You create a constraint by using the SQL CONSTRAINT clause. The CONSTRAINT clause takes two parameters: the name of the index and the name of the field or fields you're interested in indexing. You can declare the index to be UNIQUE or PRIMARY, in which case the index designates that the field can only accept unique values or that a field or fields serves the table's primary key.

Note: The concept of indexes having names might seem a little strange to you if you're accustomed to Microsoft Access; this is because Access buries the names of indexes in its user interface.

For example, as an enhancement to the tblRegion table created in the previous example, you might add a unique index to the State field because it is used in joins and should therefore be indexed. The SQL to create this table with a CONSTRAINT clause looks like Listing 2.44.

Listing 2.44: A SQL Command That Creates a Table with a Constraint That Forces the State Field to Be Unique

```
CREATE TABLE tblRegion
([State] TEXT (2),
[Region] TEXT (50),
CONSTRAINT StateIndex UNIQUE ([State]))
```

This query creates the table with a unique index called StateIndex on the State field.

Though this example will serve to index the State field, it might make more sense to make the State field the table's primary key. Doing so will index the field, ensure that no values are duplicated in the State field, and ensure that no null values appear in the State field. The SQL to create the tblRegion table with the State field as its primary key is in Listing 2.45.

Listing 2.45: A SQL Command That Creates a Table with a Primary Key

```
CREATE TABLE tblRegion
([State] TEXT (2),
[Region] TEXT (50),
CONSTRAINT StatePrimary PRIMARY KEY ([State]))
```

To designate a field as a foreign key, you use the FOREIGN KEY constraint.

For example, let's say that in your database design, there is a one-to-many relationship between the State field in the tblRegion table and a corresponding State field in the tblCustomer table. Given this fact, the code that you'd use to create a tblCustomer table in code might look like Listing 2.46.

Listing 2.46: SQL Code That Creates a Table with a Relationship, Including a Primary and Foreign Key

```
CREATE TABLE tblCustomer
([ID] COUNTER,
[FirstName] TEXT (20),
[LastName] TEXT (30),
[Address] TEXT (100),
[City] TEXT (75),
[State] TEXT (2),
CONSTRAINT IDPrimary PRIMARY KEY ([ID]),
CONSTRAINT StateForeign FOREIGN KEY ([State])
REFERENCES tblRegion ([State]))
```

Note that designating a foreign key in a CREATE TABLE command doesn't create an index on that foreign key; it only serves to create a relationship between the two tables.

Creating Indexes with CREATE INDEX

In addition to creating indexes at the time you create your table (using the CONSTRAINT clause), you can also create indexes after you've created the table (using the CREATE INDEX clause). This is useful when you want to create an index on a table that already exists (as opposed to the CONSTRAINT clause, which only lets you create indexes on tables at the time you create the table).

To create an index on an existing table, you use the SQL in Listing 2.47.

Listing 2.47: A SQL Command That Creates an Index on the tblCustomer Table

```
CREATE INDEX StateIndex
ON tblCustomer ([State])
```

To create a unique index, you use the UNIQUE keyword, as in Listing 2.48.

Listing 2.48: A SQL Command That Creates a Unique Index on the State Field in the tblRegion Table

```
CREATE UNIQUE INDEX StateIndex
ON tblRegion ([State])
```

To create an index that does not permit null values, you use the DISALLOW NULL clause, as in Listing 2.49.

Listing 2.49: A SQL Command That Creates a Unique Index on the State Field That Does Not Allow Nulls

```
CREATE UNIQUE INDEX StateIndex
ON tblRegion ([State])
WITH DISALLOW NULL
```

To create a primary key on an existing table, you use the SQL in Listing 2.50.

Listing 2.50: A SQL Command That Designates the State Field as the Primary Key in the tblRegion Table

```
CREATE UNIQUE INDEX StatePrimary
ON tblRegion ([State])
WITH PRIMARY
```

Deleting Tables and Indexes Using DROP

You can delete database elements using the DROP clause. For example, to delete a table, you use the SQL statement shown in Listing 2.51.

Listing 2.51: A SQL Command That Deletes a Table

```
DROP TABLE tblRegion
```

You can also drop an index in a table using the DROP clause, as in Listing 2.52.

Listing 2.52: A SQL Command That Removes an Index on a Field in the tblRegion Table

```
DROP INDEX PrimaryKey ON tblRegion
```

Note that to delete a primary key, you must know the primary key's name.

You have the ability to drop individual fields within tables. To do that, you use a DROP clause within an ALTER TABLE clause, as discussed in the next section.

> **Note:** In the client-server world, you also have the ability to drop a database using DDL commands. This doesn't make sense in the Microsoft Jet world; in Jet, to "drop a database," you simply delete the .MDB file from disk.

Modifying A Table's Definition Using ALTER

You can alter the definition of a field in a table by using the ALTER clause. For example, to add a CustomerType field to the tblCustomer table, you use the SQL statement given in Listing 2.53.

Listing 2.53: A SQL Command That Adds the CustomerType Column to the tblCustomer Table

```
ALTER TABLE tblCustomer
ADD COLUMN CustomerType LONG
```

To remove a field from a database, you use the DROP COLUMN clause along with an ALTER TABLE clause, as in Listing 2.54.

Listing 2.54: A SQL Command That Removes the CustomerType Column from the tblCustomer Table

```
ALTER TABLE tblCustomer
DROP COLUMN CustomerType
```

You also have the ability to add constraints to a table by using the ALTER TABLE clause. For example, to create a relationship between the tblCustomer and tblOrder tables using ALTER TABLE, you use the SQL given in Listing 2.55.

Listing 2.55: A SQL Command That Designates the CustomerID as the Foreign Key in the tblOrder Table

```
ALTER TABLE tblOrder
ADD CONSTRAINT OrderForeignKey
FOREIGN KEY ([CustomerID])
REFERENCES tblCustomer ([ID])
```

Again, remember that adding a constraint doesn't create a conventional index on a field; it just makes a field unique, designates a field as a primary key, or creates a relationship between two tables .

SUMMARY

This chapter covered the query technologies available to you in a Visual Basic database access application. Queries that return records as well as queries that create and change database structures were covered.

Much of what's covered in this chapter doesn't stand on its own—it will make much more sense when you start programming with Data Access Objects, which are introduced in Chapter 3. In fact, this chapter was structured to make it easy for you to flip back and forth between this chapter and Chapter 3 as you start creating serious applications based on SQL and Data Access Objects.

QUESTIONS AND ANSWERS

Q: **Given the fact that you can either generate queries dynamically at run-time or use queries that are stored in the database, which technique should you use?**

A: It depends on your application, but it's generally better to embed queries in the database, if you can. Doing so reduces complexity in your application, causes queries to execute more efficiently, and opens the possibility of multiple procedures in your application sharing the same query resources. In a multiuser application, storing queries in the database also means that when you need to alter a query, that alteration doesn't necessarily break the client applications that depend on it. You don't have to redistribute new versions of a compiled executable to all your users just because one of your queries now returns five fields instead of four.

Q: Why would one use straight SQL—as opposed to a visual query-building tool such as Visual Data Manager or Microsoft Access—to build database tables or stored queries?

A: Having the ability to create database components in code is useful if you are writing an application that creates database elements at run time. In this case, your application has no access to the design-time tools provided by the Visual Data Manager or Microsoft Access. Having a handle on the underlying SQL is also very helpful when you move into Data Access Object programming, because many DAO commands take SQL statements as arguments.

It's also useful to write your database using straight SQL code if you need to document everything that went into creating the database. This way, if you need to replicate the design of all or part of the database at some point in the future, you don't have to go digging through Microsoft Access' GUI to figure out what you did to create the database.

Q: This chapter refers to Data Access Objects a lot. I already understand SQL pretty well—why would I want to use DAO when I already know SQL?

A: If SQL is what you know, and you can get by using SQL alone, then by all means do so. The fact that the Visual Basic documentation focuses so much on DAO at the expense of straight SQL is one of the reasons why this chapter covers SQL so thoroughly.

That said, it's important to understand that in Visual Basic, DAO gives you a far more robust and flexible way to get access to data than straight SQL does. And many Visual Basic developers find DAO much easier to deal with than SQL, because DAO expresses many common database operations in terms of VB's object/property/method/event paradigm. You still need to know at least a little SQL to be a successful database developer in Visual Basic, but the choice of how much SQL to use will depend on what you want to do and what you feel comfortable with.

Data Access Objects

What are the advantages of using object-oriented programming to access data stored in a database?

How can I use object-oriented programming techniques to access data in a database?

How can I access data in recordsets using a navigational, rather than procedural, model?

How can I create database structures using object-oriented techniques?

When is it appropriate to use the object-oriented model as opposed to other techniques?

Chapter 3

Y ou can manipulate databases in Visual Basic code using Data Access Objects (DAO). Using DAO, you can run queries, update values in database tables, and create the structure of databases, including tables, stored queries, and relationships among tables.

If you're accustomed to using the features of SQL to perform these tasks in your applications, DAO will represent something of a paradigm shift. But after you ascend the learning curve, you'll find that DAO's programming interface is extremely robust and easy to use. With Microsoft Jet databases, DAO also gives you access to features not available with SQL by itself.

Although it may seem as if there is some overlap between DAO and SQL (described in Chapter 2, "Queries"), you'll actually find that as you become more experienced with using databases in Visual Basic, you use SQL and DAO together. The OpenRecordset method of the Database object, for example, can take a SQL statement as its parameter. If you're familiar with SQL already, this familiarity enables you to leverage your existing knowledge and transfer it into the world of object-oriented programming.

USING THE DAO 3.5 OBJECT MODEL

The DAO object model is complex, with hundreds of elements. Dozens of types of collections own dozens more objects, each of which in turn has properties, methods, and subordinate objects of its own. The model can be a lot to grasp.

Figure 3.1 is a simplified version of the DAO object hierarchy.

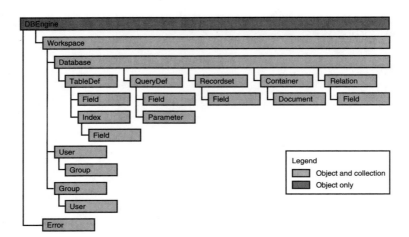

Figure 3.1: The DAO hierarchy, showing relationships among database objects.

One way to digest the complexity of DAO's object model is to start with the Database object and consider its collections. *Collections* are related sets of objects; the Database object has the collections of objects shown in Figure 3.2.

Through the collections owned by the Database object, you can manipulate data and the structure of a database, create new database objects, and inspect the structure and data contained in a database.

Within DAO programming, there is a core set of commonly used techniques used in nearly every program. These include the following:

▶ Running a select query

▶ Iterating through one of the database's collections, or iterating through the recordset in a recordset

▶ Running an action query (including update, delete, and append queries)

▶ Altering the structure of a component of the database

▶ Inspecting errors generated by database access

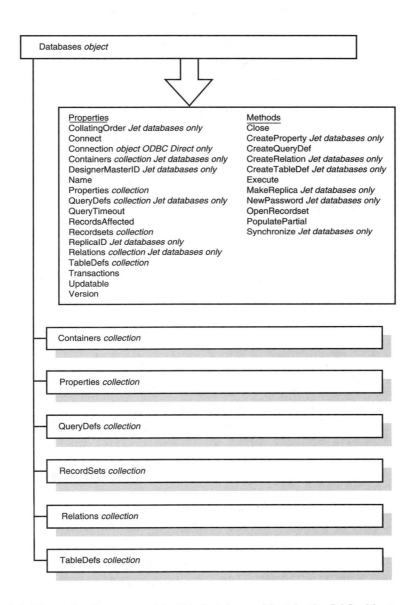

Figure 3.2: The collections owned by the Database object in the DAO object hierarchy.

This chapter serves as a cookbook for these commonly used code constructs, providing typical code examples that work with any database.

To gain access to these features, however, you need a handle on how to reference them. If you're an experienced Visual Basic 4 or Visual Basic 5 programmer and you have experience coding against a complicated object model containing collections and objects that own other objects, you can skip the next section on programming with objects. But if you're relatively inexperienced with Visual Basic, you'll want to peruse the next few sections carefully, because they're crucial to successful programming against the DAO object model.

Programming with Objects

One of the reasons that object-oriented programming is easier than procedural programming is that it describes computer-based abstractions in real-world terms. For example, a procedural program that handles invoices might call one procedure to open the database, another to read invoice data, another to save invoice data, and another procedure to print.

An object-oriented program might perform the same task by creating an Invoice object with properties of Invoice Date, Customer ID, and Due Date. The object also has methods that pertain to actions that an Invoice object is expected to do—a Print method, a Save method, and so forth.

If you're not familiar with object-oriented programming, it might just seem like a competing philosophy, a different way of looking at procedural programming. But the more you use objects, the more you realize that they're easier to code against—at least once you understand what objects are available to you and how they relate to one another. Because objects present themselves consistently, after you learn how to program a particular set of objects, you begin to have a handle on how to use all the objects related to that object. Such is the case with DAO.

Another advantage to using DAO to get to your database is that DAO serves as a *layer of abstraction* on topof your specific database implementation. Therefore, when you're doing database programming in Visual Basic, you don't write code that talks to the database directly; instead, you write code that talks to DAO, which in turn translates your code into something the database engine understands. This means that you can, in many cases, write one set of code that works with any database. You can think of DAO's object model, then, as an something that stands between your program and the specific database implementation, standardizing your access to the database and giving you a consistent, Visual Basic-style set of objects to work with.

All objects have the following:

▶ *Properties.* The data pertaining to the object. Properties can be conventional variables, but they can also be objects or collections—for example, the Name property of a recordset.

▶ *Methods.* The actions the object can perform. These are similar to subroutines or functions.

▶ *Events.* Messages the object can send to the application that uses the object. If you've programmed in Visual Basic at all, you should be accustomed to assigning code to event procedures; Data Access Objects have their own event model that you can write code against.

The process of manipulating a database in code using DAO, then, entails your determining which object is appropriate to use, then excuting its methods and setting and retrieving its properties.

There isn't much difference between manipulating the properties and methods of a Data Access Object and programming the properties and methods of a conventional user interface control, such as a text box. With DAO, however, you must instantiate objects you use (because DAO objects aren't visual, you can't just draw them on a form as you'd draw a list box or a command button).

Additionally, unlike user interface objects, Data Access Objects belong to a hierarchy called an *object model.* This hierarchy dictates that objects own other objects. To gain access to a table, for example, you must understand that a database object owns the table object; the process of creating a table object dictates that you first create a database object.

Using Object Variables   In Visual Basic, you begin using objects by creating an *object variable.* An object variable stores a reference to an object.

In Visual Basic, you must always *declare* an object variable (even if you're not using Option Explicit, the Visual Basic statement that forces you to declare all variables). This is because objects are often complicated constructs that require more memory than other types of variables; the process of dimensioning a variable in Visual Basic tells the computer to set aside memory for the variable.

You declare an object variable using the Dim statement, as shown in Listing 3.1.

Listing 3.1: Creating a Database Object Variable Using the Dim Statement

```
Dim db As Database
```

When you assign a value to an object variable, you must use the Set statement. This is in contrast to conventional Visual Basic assignment statements (such as x = 538) that simply require a variable, an operator, and a value. Listing 3.2 shows an example of an object variable declaration and assignment.

Listing 3.2: Dimensioning and Assigning the Value of an Object Variable Using the Set Statement

```
Dim db As Database
Set db = OpenDatabase("novelty.mdb")
```

This code example uses OpenDatabase to create a Database object. The Set statement assigns this object to the object variable db. At this point, you can program against the object variable db, executing its methods and setting and retrieving its properties.

There's more information about the properties and methods of the Database object later in this chapter.

Working with Collections in Code   One of the most daunting things for new programmers to overcome when learning DAO programming is DAO's object model. Learning this model seems to be particularly tricky for programmers who are accustomed to a more procedural programming model, such as that provided by SQL.

Think of a collection as a type of object that stores a set of references to other objects. You can think of a book's table of contents as a collection because it stores a set of references to chapters and their page numbers. A phone directory is also a collection because it stores a set of references to people and businesses. The advantage of having such a set of references is that you can *iterate* through them quickly and consistently. Iterating through a collection entails acting on all of its members one after another; scanning a table of contents, checking off items on a to-do list, and flipping through a phone directory are examples of iterating through a collection.

Although collections you create can contain references to many types of objects, collections typically store references to one type of object; this is the case for all the DAO collections.

Table 3.1 summarizes all the collections available in DAO 3.5 programming, and what they represent.

Table 3.1: DAO Collections

Collection	Represents	Interface
Workspaces	Represents the open connections to the database engine; normally you'll have only one workspace active at a time	Count property; Append, Delete, and Refresh methods
Databases	All the databases open in a particular Workspace; normally you'll have only one database open at a time	Count property; Refresh method
TableDefs	All the table definitions available in a database	Count property; Append, Delete, and Refresh methods
QueryDefs	All the query definitions available in a database	Count property; Append, Delete, and Refresh methods
Recordsets	All the recordsets open in the context of a single database	Count property; Refresh method
Parameters	The parameters available in a particular QueryDef	Count property; Refresh method
Relations	The relationships defined in a particular database (Jet databases only)	Count property; Append, Delete, and Refresh methods
Connections	The connections to the database owned by a Workspace object; this is the ODBCDirect equivalent of the Database object (ODBCDirect data sources only)	Count property; Refresh method

continues

Table 3. 1: DAO Collections (Continued)

Collection	Represents	Interface
Indexes	The index that belongs to a particular TableDef	Count property; Append, Delete, and Refresh methods
Fields	The fields that exist in a data construct (such as a TableDef or Recordset)	Count property; Append, Delete, and Refresh methods
Groups	The security groups owned by the database; for information on groups, see Chapter 8, "Multiuser Issues"(Jet data-bases only)	Count property; Append, Delete, and Refresh methods
Users	The list of users identified by the security features of the database; for information on users, see Chapter 8 (Jet data-bases only)	Count property; Append, Delete, and Refresh methods
Errors	The errors generated by a particular DAO operation; it's important to note that in DAO, this is a collection rather than a single object, as it is in Visual Basic	Count property; Refresh method
Containers	A group of predefined document objects stored in the database (Jet databases only)	Count property; Refresh method

Collection	Represents	Interface
Documents	Databases, tables, and Relations are examples of Document objects (Jet databases only)	Count property; Refresh method
Properties	The properties of a DAO object; all DAO objects (except for Error and Connection) have a properties collection; properties can either be user-defined or built-in	Count property; Append, Delete, and Refresh methods

If you're experienced with object-oriented programming in Visual Basic, you might have created your own collection classes. One important difference between collections provided by DAO and collections you create yourself is that DAO classes (along with most other collectionsprovided by Visual Basic) are *zero-based*. Therefore, the first element in a DAO collection is numbered zero. The ordinal number of an item in a collection is called its *index*.

You can retrieve an element from a collection by using its index. For example, to display the value of the first field in the current record in a recordset object, use the following code:

```
MsgBox MyRecordset.Fields(0).Value
```

You aren't required to access values in fields by their index number in DAO; this example just shows how you might go about it. Normally, when you know the name of a field, you access it by its name, as in the following code:

```
MsgBox MyRecordset.Fields("LastName").Value
```

The unique textual identifier that designates an element of a collection is called its *key*. To refer to an element of a collection, you can use either its index or its key. (For this reason, keys must always be strings; if they weren't, then Visual Basic wouldn't know that you were trying to access the item whose key is 12 or the 12th item in a collection.)

Accessing a member of a collection by index and by key is a technique that is common to programming all collection objects, whether such objects are created by you or provided for you by Visual Basic. For a complete discussion of accessing values in fields, see the sections on the Recordset and Field objects later in this chapter.

For more information To understand more about how collections can be useful, including how to create your own collection classes, check out Deborah Kurata's *Doing Objects in Visual Basic 5.0* (Ziff-Davis Press, 1997). This book gives you much more detail on how collections work and you can create collections to manipulate data in your Visual Basic applications.

Using Default Collections and Default Properties to Simplify Code   Objects can have *default collections*. These collections make it easier to code against a complicated object model, because you don't have to make references to the most commonly used collections; instead of explicitly referring to a default collection, you can instead use an exclamation point (!) to refer to it.

For example, consider the previous code example, designed to retrieve a value from the LastName field of a recordset:

```
MsgBox MyRecordset.Fields("LastName").Value
```

The code works because you have a Recordset object that has a Fields collection. That Fields collection has a member called LastName, which has some value (which would be a textual value; the name Smith, for example).

But it so happens that the Fields collection is a Recordset object's default collection. So as a shorthand technique for determining the value of the LastName field, you could instead write the following code:

```
MsgBox MyRecordset!LastName.Value
```

You can make this code even less complicated by taking advantage of the fact that a Field object's Value property is its *default property*. You don't have to make reference to a default property of an object at all. So, instead of using the techniques demonstrated in the previous two examples, you could write the following code:

```
MsgBox MyRecordset!LastName
```

All three ways of referring to a value of a field return the same result.

Some argue that taking advantage of default collections and default properties is bad—the rationale is that code readability comes from making as few implicit assumptions as possible. You don't want to do anything invisible or rely on defaults, because when you go back months later to debug your code you won't be able to remember what those defaults are. Consequently, you'll have a hard time figuring out what's going on in your code.

This argument might hold water in general, but in DAO programming, it makes sense to take advantage of default collections and properties when you can. This is because it's extremely common to retrieve the Fields collection from a recordset and somewhat uncommon to retrieve anything else.

In this chapter, the code examples generally spell out references to default collections where it makes the conceptual explanations easier to follow. But later in the book, as you move into more complicated code, the examples use more defaults to make the code less complicated overall.

USING DAO TO WORK WITH DATA

Data Access Objects are most commonly used to manipulate data in an existing database. Running queries, updating records, and performing database mainte-nance are DAO's bread and butter.

Although DAO's object model is vast, you can start creating solutions using DAO even if you understand only a few properties and methods of the most important objects in DAO: the DatabaseRecordset, and Field objects, and the like-named collections that contain them. The next sections describe how to get started programming these objects.

Connecting to a Database Using the Database Object

The Database object is where your application normally begins most of its data-base access. To use a Database object, you begin by dimensioning a database object variable:

```
Dim db As Database
```

If your application is designed to work with a single database, then it makes sense for you to dimension the Database variable at the module level of your application's main form.

However, if many forms in your application need access to the same data-base, it might make sense for you to create a class to manage the connection to the database, instantiate an object from that class when the application starts, and terminate the object when the application ends. For more on this, see Chapter 6, "Classes."

It's best to avoid opening and closing a connection to a database many times in your application, though. A performance overhead is associated with opening a database; you can see this for yourself when you begin running code that opens a database.

You assign the Database object variable to a database using the OpenDatabase method, as described in the next section.

Using the OpenDatabase Method to Create a Database Object   You create a Database object by using the OpenDatabase method. OpenDatabase is a method that returns a Database object (therefore, before you use OpenDatabase, you must declare an object variable of type Database to store in the return value of the method). This technique is shown in Listing 3.3.

Listing 3.3: Creating a Database Object Using the DAO OpenDatabase Method

```
Dim db As Database
Set db = OpenDatabase(App.Path & "\novelty.mdb")

MsgBox "The database " & db.Name & " is now open."
```

The OpenDatabase method takes one required argument, the name of the database you want to open. (This name can also be the name of an ODBC data source; for more information on ODBC, see Chapter 5, "Client/Server.")

OpenDatabase also has several optional parameters. The following is the full syntax of OpenDatabase:

```
OpenDatabase(dbname, [options], [readonly], [connect])
```

Table 3.2 describes the optional parameters of the OpenDatabase method.

Table 3.2: Optional Parameters of the OpenDatabase Method

Parameter	Description
options	If this argument is True, the database opens in exclusive mode; no other users can open a database when you open it in exclusive mode. If the value is False, other users can open the database.
	When you're opening a database using ODBCDirect, this option can take other values. For more information, see Chapter 5.
readonly	If this argument is True, you can't make changes to the database.
connect	A string that specifies how to connect to the database; the string is usually used for client/server and ODBC data sources only. For more information on using the connect argument, see Chapter 5.

There are significant performance benefits to opening a database in read-only and exclusive modes. If you're building an application that is designed to analyze data, for example, it is appropriate for such an application to open the database in read-only mode.

> **For more information**   on multiuser access to databases, see Chapter 5 as well as Chapter 8.

> **Note:** Although the OpenDatabase method seems like it's really a function rather than a method, rest assured that it is, in fact, a method. It's a method of the DAO Workspace object. You don't have to refer to this Workspace object because Jet assumes you're using a default, invisible Workspace object if you don't explicitly refer to one. This is partly to maintain backward compatibility with previous versions of DAO, which did not contain the Workspace object, but also to make your code simpler. There is more information on the Workspace object later in this chapter.

Using the Execute Method to Run Action Queries   You use the Execute method of the Database object to execute a SQL command against the database. This method shouldn't be used in all cases, however. You use the Execute method to run SQL code that does the following:

- ▶ Updates, deletes, or copies records (an action query)
- ▶ Modifies the structure of the database (a data-definition language command)

> **Note:** *DAO 3.5* Previous versions of DAO called the Execute method ExecuteSQL.

Conventional select queries (the kind that return records) are typically run using the Database object's OpenRecordset method; for more on this, see the section on the OpenRecordset method later in this chapter.

Listing 3.4 demonstrates a typical use of the Execute method. This code runs an update query against the tblInventory table, increasing the retail price of items by 10 percent.

Listing 3.4: An Update Query that Alters all the Records in a Particular Table

```
' References: Microsoft DAO 3.5 Object Library
'
Dim db As Database
'


Private Sub Form_Load()

    Set db = OpenDatabase(App.Path & "\novelty.mdb")

End Sub

Private Sub Command5_Click()

    db.Execute "UPDATE tblInventory " & _
               "SET RetailPrice = [RetailPrice]*1.1"

End Sub
```

A DDL command using the Execute method works much the same way, as shown in Listing 3.5.

Listing 3.5: A DDL Command that Creates the Supplier Table Using the Execute Method

```
Private Sub Command6_Click()

    db.Execute "CREATE TABLE tblSupplier " & _
               "([Name] TEXT (50), [Address] TEXT (40))"

End Sub
```

When you run a query or DDL command using the Execute method of the database, it executes immediately. Note too that QueryDef objects have Execute methods as well; you use Execute in this context when the QueryDef is a stored update query or DDL command and you want to run it.

Note: Chapter 2 explains the different types of SQL queries, their syntax, and example.

Using the DBEngine Object to Control Database Access   Although you'd think that the Database object would be at the top of the object hierarchy of DAO, it isn't. (It's useful to think of the Database object as being at the top, because it's where you start coding most of the time.) But in fact, the highest-level object in the DAO object model is the DBEngine object.

Figure 3.3 shows the position of the DBEngine object in the DAO hierarchy.

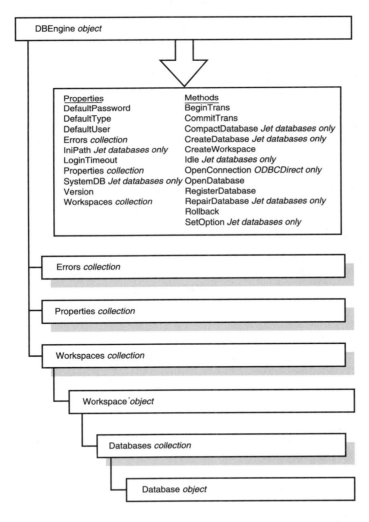

Figure 3.3: The DBEngine object and the objects beneath it in the DAO hierarchy.

The DBEngine object is a *singleton* object; there's only one such object available, and you can't create new instances of DBEngines.

You can use the DBEngine object to determine ahead of time which type of Workspace objects you create. You typically do this in situations where your application uses ODBCDirect (because Jet workspaces are the default). To set the default type of workspace to ODBCDirect, set the DBEngine's DefaultWorkspace property to dbUseODBC.

For more on ODBCDirect, see Chapter 5.

You can also use the DBEngine to set other types of defaults in your workspaces. For example, suppose that your application accesses a secured database, and it always accesses that database using the same username and password. For your application always to create Workspace objects based on a particular combination of user name and password, you can set the DBEngine's DefaultUser and DefaultPassword properties to whatever the user supplies. That way, every Workspace object you create starts with the same default username and password.

For more information on users, passwords, and databases, see Chapter 8.

Using the Connection Object to Open a Client/Server Connection The Connection object is new in DAO 3.5. It serves a purpose similar to that of the Database object, but for ODBCDirect databases only. For information on how to connect to an ODBC database using the Connection object, see Chapter 5.

Using the Recordset Object

You use the Recordset object to manipulate records in DAO. Recordset objects provide an object-oriented interface to the relational database model involving tables divided into records and fields.

Figure 3.4 shows the position of the Recordset object within the DAO hierarchy, as well as its properties and methods.

To create a recordset, you typically use the OpenRecordset method as described in the next section.

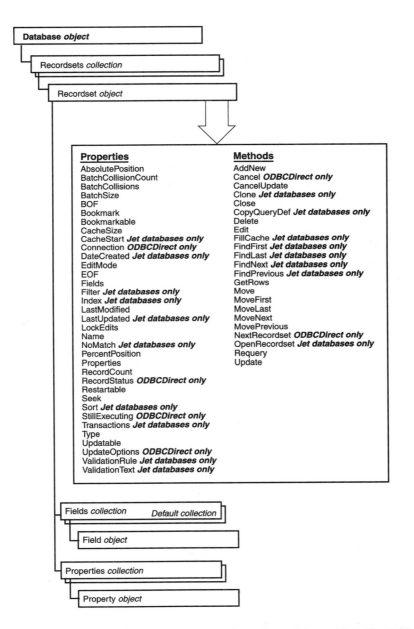

Figure 3.4: The Recordsets collection and the Recordset object within the DAO object hierarchy.

Creating a Recordset Object Using the OpenRecordset Method   You create a Recordset object by using the OpenRecordset method. In DAO, the Database, Connection, QueryDef, TableDef, and Recordset objects have OpenRecordset methods.

> **Note: *DAO* 3.5** The OpenRecordset method replaces the OpenSnapshot, OpenTable, and OpenDynaset methods that existed in previous versions of DAO. These methods are now obsolete; they still work, but you should use OpenRecordset instead. Additionally, the Snapshot, Dynaset, and Table objects are obsolete; to get access to a structure that contains data, you use the Recordset object.

Because the OpenRecordset method is really a function that returns a Recordset object, you need to dimension a Recordset object before you use OpenRecordset. The code to do this typically looks like Listing 3.6.

Listing 3.6: A Typical Example of an OpenRecordset Method Applied to a Database Object

```
Dim db As Database
Dim rs As Recordset

Set db = OpenDatabase(App.Path & "\novelty.mdb")
Set rs = db.OpenRecordset("tblCustomer")
```

The single required argument of the OpenRecordset method is the data source. This is typically the name of a table or a stored query definition, but it can also be a SQL SELECT statement, as demonstrated in Listing 3.7.

Listing 3.7: Creating a Recordset Object Using the OpenRecordset Method

```
Dim db As Database
Dim rs As Recordset

Set db = OpenDatabase(App.Path & "\novelty.mdb")
Set rs = db.OpenRecordset("SELECT * " & _
                          "FROM tblCustomer " & _
                          "ORDER BY [LastName]")
```

After creating a Recordset object, you can access the data in it by using code that accesses its properties and methods.

Avoiding the Great OpenDatabase Quotation Mark Caper   A common problem among programmers interested in using the OpenRecordset method with SQL statements is determining how to delimit a text string embedded in the SQL statement. For example, how do you submit the SQL statement in Listing 3.8 to the database engine using OpenRecordset?

Listing 3.8: A SQL SELECT Statement that Includes a Text Parameter in Quotations

```
SELECT *
FROM tblCustomer
WHERE [LastName] = "Smith"
```

The problem lies in the fact that you can't include double quotation marks in the parameter of an OpenRecordset method. If you did so, the code would look like Listing 3.9.

Listing 3.9: The Problem with Trying to Embed a SQL Statement that Includes Quotation Marks in an OpenRecordset Method

```
Dim db As Database
Dim rs As Recordset

Set db = OpenDatabase(App.Path & "\novelty.mdb")
Set rs = db.OpenRecordset("SELECT * " & _
                          "FROM tblCustomer " & _
                          "WHERE [LastName] = "Smith"")
```

This code would cause a compile error, because Visual Basic can't parse the double quotation marks within double quotation marks.

The solution to the problem is to change the double quotation marks to single quotation marks, as in Listing 3.10.

Listing 3.10: Code that Overcomes the Great OpenDatabase Quotation Mark Caper

```
Dim db As Database
Dim rs As Recordset

Set db = OpenDatabase(App.Path & "\novelty.mdb")
Set rs = db.OpenRecordset("SELECT * " & _
                          "FROM tblCustomer " & _
                          "WHERE [LastName] = 'Smith'")
```

If the value for the WHERE clause is not hard-coded (as is often the case), the solution gets even more complicated. For example, suppose that instead of the name Smith, you want to create a Recordset object based on the name the user enters in a text box Text1. Your code would then look like Listing 3.11.

Listing 3.11: A Query Generated from a SQL String Concatenated with User Input

```
Dim db As Database
Dim rs As Recordset

Set db = OpenDatabase(App.Path & "\novelty.mdb")
Set rs = db.OpenRecordset("SELECT * " & _
                          "FROM tblCustomer " & _
                          "WHERE [LastName] = '" & Text1.Text & "'")
```

The key here is not to forget that you must delimit string data in quotation marks, even when the data is part of a big, ugly concatenated expression.

Because this kind of code can be so difficult to read and debug, it makes more sense in such a situation to create a parameterized query stored in the database. (In addition to making this code easier to maintain, replacing SQL code in your Visual Basic code with stored queries in the database can make your queries run faster as well.) For information on how to do this, see the section "Manipulating Stored Queries Using the QueryDef Object," later in this chapter.

Setting Recordset Options   The Options argument of the OpenRecordset method determines several things about how the records can be manipulated. Table 3.3 outlines the legal values for this argument.

Table 3.3: Values for the Options Argument of the OpenRecordset Method

Constant	Meaning
dbOpenTable	In a Microsoft Jet workspaces, creates a Table-style Recordset object
dbOpenDynamic	In an ODBCDirect workspace, opens a dynamic-type Recordset object
dbOpenDynaset	Opens a Dynaset-type Recordset object
dbOpenSnapshot	Opens a Snapshot-type Recordset object
dbOpenForwardOnly	Opens a Recordset object whose cursor can scroll forward only

Chapter 5 covers dynamic recordsets in ODBCDirect.

Manipulating Fields Using the Field Object

The Field object represents a field in a data structure. TableDefs, Recordsets, Relations, and Index objects have collections of fields.

You can retrieve the value of a field by inspecting the Value property of a Field object. (Because the Value property is the Field object's default property, you need only make reference to the Field object.)

> **Note: *DAO 3.5*** The Fields collection replaces the ListFields method that existed in previous versions of DAO. This method is now obsolete; it still works, but you should use the Fields collection instead.

Figure 3.5 shows the Field object's place in the DAO hierarchy.

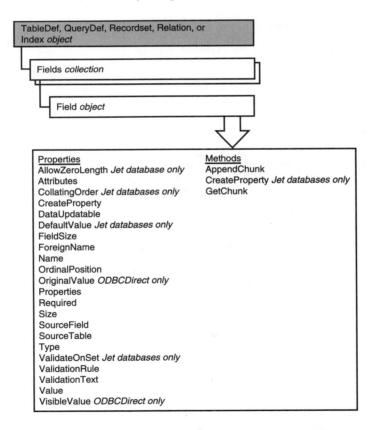

Figure 3.5: The Fields Collection and the Field Object in the DAO hierarchy.

Business Case 3.1: Creating a Database Browser The Jones Novelties customer database has begun to grow. The users of the database are now requesting a quick browser application that enables them to choose customers from a list, then view the complete details of the customer's data.

You can use a combination of the DAO Database, Recordset, and Field objects to create a database browser application. This application can consist of pure DAO code. The benefit is that the application does not require the Data control, so the application is fast.

This application consists of two forms: frmMain and frmSingle. The main form displays a list of all the customers in the database; the form frmSingle displays the details for a single customer.

Listing 3.12 shows the code that initializes the application's main form.

Listing 3.12: Code that Initializes the Database Browser Application

```
' References: Microsoft DAO Object Library 3.5

Dim db As Database
Dim rs As Recordset
'

Private Sub Form_Load()

    Set db = OpenDatabase(App.Path & "\novelty.mdb")
    Set rs = db.OpenRecordset("SELECT * FROM tblCustomer " & _
                              "ORDER BY [LastName], [FirstName]")

    ' Populate the list box
    Do Until rs.EOF
        lstCustomer.AddItem rs.Fields("LastName") & ", " & _
                            rs.Fields("FirstName")
        lstCustomer.ItemData(lstCustomer.NewIndex) = rs.Fields("ID")

        rs.MoveNext

    Loop

End Sub
```

Note that this code uses the ItemData property of the list box, which enables you to add an additional piece of numeric data to each item in the list box. In this case, you're adding the value of the ID field —the tblCustomer table's primary key —to the list box. This value populates the single-record form when the user double-clicks the list box.

After loading the form and running this code, the application looks like Figure 3.6.

Figure 3.6: The Data Browser application after DAO code populates its list box.

Listing 3.13 shows the code that reveals the detail of a record when a user double-clicks a name in the list.

Listing 3.13: Code that Causes a Form with Detailed Data to Appear when an Item in the User Double-Clicks the List

```
Private Sub lstEmployee_DblClick()

    Dim f As frmSingle
    Set f = New frmSingle

    rs.FindFirst "[ID] = " & lstEmployee.ItemData(lstEmployee.ListIndex)

    f.TextBox(0) = rs.Fields("FirstName")
    f.TextBox(1) = rs.Fields("LastName")
    f.TextBox(2) = rs.Fields("Address") & ""
    f.TextBox(3) = rs.Fields("City") & ""
    f.TextBox(4) = rs.Fields("State") & ""


    f.Show

End Sub
```

The concatenated empty strings ("") at the end of the field assignments are a trick designed to avoid ax common error: A text box's Text property must be a string, but a database field can potentially return a special value —Null, the value of a database field that has no data. When you attempt to assign a Null to a text box's Text property, an error occurs.

Even worse, the obvious solution to this problem doesn't work. When you use conventional means (for example, the CStr function) in an attempt to convert the Null field value into a string, the error still takes place, because by definition the product of nearly any operation involving a Null value is Null.

Concatenating Null to an empty string always returns an empty string, but concatenating a non-empty string to an empty string gives you the string you started with. So by always concatenating an empty string to a field value whose value could be Null, you avoid the error. It's a trick, but it works, and it's used commonly to weed out Null values in the world of Visual Basic database access programming.

Using Navigational Methods with the Recordset Object

After creating a Recordset object, you can use navigational methods to move from one record to the next in the recordset. You typically do this in situations where you need to retrieve data from every record in a recordset. The following are navigational methods of a Recordset object:

▶ The MoveFirst method moves to the first row in the recordset.

▶ The MoveNext method moves to the next row in the recordset.

▶ The MovePrevious method moves to the previous row in the recordset.

▶ The MoveLast method moves to the last row in the recordset.

Bear in mind that there are recordsets with cursors that enable you to move forward only; in such recordsets, the MovePrevious and MoveFirst methods trigger errors.

Using BOF and EOF to Navigate Through Recordsets   In addition to these methods, the Recordset object provides two properties that let you know when you've moved to the beginning or end of the recordset:

▶ The EOF (End Of File) propert y is True when you've moved beyond the last record in the recordset.

▶ The BOF (Beginning Of File) property is True when you've moved to a position before the first record in the recordset.

Instead of thinking of EOF and BOF as properties of the recordset, you might find it helpful to think of them as places, as shown in Figure 3.7.

The code you typically use to iterate through a recordset, then, combines navigation methods along with BOF and EOF. In general, such code involves a loop of the following form:

```
Do Until EOF
    ' Perform action on the data or
    ' read values from fields
    rs.MoveNext
Loop
```

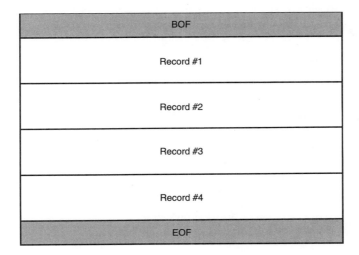

Figure 3.7: BOF and EOF in a recordset.

Business Case 3.2: Accessing Data in a Table Using Navigational Methods
Now that the Jones Novelties database system is beginning to shape up, you're realizing that it is somewhat lacking in performance. Rather than using the Data control, which can be somewhat inefficient and unwieldy to program, you decide to use pure DAO code to navigate through the recordset.

Listing 3.14 provides an example of navigational code that satisfies this requirement (and does something potentially useful). This code prints out the complete list of customers returned from a query of the tblCustomer table. (However, the code could just as well be sending this data to the printer or using it to populate a list box, for example.)

Listing 3.14: An Example of Iterating Through a Recordset Using Navigational Methods

```
' References: Microsoft DAO 3.5 Object Library
'
Dim db As Database
'

Private Sub Form_Load()

    Set db = OpenDatabase(App.Path & "\novelty.mdb")

End Sub

Private Sub Command10_Click()

    Dim rs As Recordset
    Set rs = db.OpenRecordset("tblCustomer")

    Do Until rs.EOF = True
        Debug.Print rs.Fields("FirstName") & _
                    " " & rs.Fields("LastName")
        rs.MoveNext
    Loop

End Sub
```

If you aren't sure whether a given recordset will return records or not, you might consider inspecting its EOF and BOF properties before performing actions on it; if EOF and BOF are true, the recordset has no records. This technique is discussed in the section "Using BOF and EOF to Determine Whether a Recordset Is Empty."

Iterating through a table by using a While loop is a *very* commonly used technique in the world of DAO programming. You can use such code to populate user-interface controls, output data to a file or the printer, or export data to a file.

However, it's usually not appropriate to use this kind of code to change the values of a particular field in all the records in a table, for example, or delete a particular set of records based on a particular criterion. You should use a SQL action query for those kinds of operations because using SQL for bulk update operations is usually faster than iterating through records using code.

Using BOF and EOF to Determine Whether a Recordset Is Empty   BOF and EOF are always available, even in a recordset that has no records. In fact, the best way to see whether a recordset retrieved zero records is to inspect the value of BOF and EOF. If BOF and EOF are both True, the recordset has no records. Figure 3.8 illustrates this.

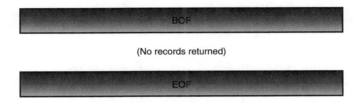

Figure 3.8: A recordset that has no records still has BOF and EOF properties.

Using the RecordCount Property to Determine the Number of Records in a Recordset   You use the RecordCount property to find out how many records are in a Recordset object. But it's important to remember that the value of the RecordCount property is not valid until you move to the end of the recordset.

This is the case because Jet handles queries in two stages. The first stage returns just enough data to enable your program to start performing action on the data. The second stage executes in the background, retrieving all the data required to execute the query completely. Jet does this for performance reasons, so your application's execution isn't blocked while it waits to retrieve a large result set. You don't have direct control over how this process works, but you do need to know that it exists and how to get around it when, for example, you want to know exactly how many records are in a recordset.

So, code to determine how many records are in a recordset looks like Listing 3.15.

Listing 3.15: Code that Determines the Number of Records in a Recordset Object

```
' References: Microsoft DAO 3.5 Object Library
'
Dim db As Database
'


Private Sub Form_Load()
                                                        continues
```

Listing 3.15: Code that Determines the Number of Records in a Recordset Object (Continued)

```
    Set db = OpenDatabase(App.Path & "\novelty.mdb")

End Sub

Private Sub Command7_Click()

    Dim rs As Recordset

    Set rs = db.OpenRecordset("tblInventory")

    rs.MoveLast
    MsgBox "There are " & rs.RecordCount & _
           " items in inventory.", vbInformation

End Sub
```

Remember that if you are simply trying to determine whether there are *zero* records in a recordset, it is much easier (and faster) simply to inspect the BOF and EOF properties of the Recordset object, as described in the previous section.

Understanding the Types of Recordsets It's important to understand that the OpenRecordset method can return several types of Recordset objects. The type of recordset has implications for what you can do with it (for example, Snapshot-style recordsets are usually read-only).

You can determine the type of a particular Recordset object by inspecting the value of its Type property. Table 3.4 summarizes the possible values for this property.

Table 3.4: Values of a Recordset's Type Property

Constant	Value	Type of Recordset
dbOpenTable	1	A Table-style recordset (Microsoft Jet only)
dbOpenDynaset	2	A Dynaset-style recordset
dbOpenSnapshot	4	A Snapshot-style recordset
dbOpenForwardOnly	8	A Snapshot-style recordset with a forward-only cursor

Constant	Value	Type of Recordset
dbOpenDynamic	16	A recordset with a dynamic cursor (ODBCDirect only)

How do you control which type of recordset returns when you execute the OpenRecordset method? By supplying the appropriate constant in the *type* argument of the OpenRecordset method. (For more on this, see the "Creating a Recordset Object Using the OpenRecordset Method" section in this chapter.)

Changing Values in a Record Using the Edit Method   You can edit the current record in an updatable Recordset object using the Edit and Update methods of the recordset. To edit the value of a field in a recordset:

1 Use the Recordset object's navigation methods to move to the record you wish to edit.

2 Execute the Recordset's Edit method.

3 Assign values to the fields in the record using the Fields collection of the Recordset object.

```
rs.Fields("LastName") = "Smith"
```

4 Alternatively, because Fields is the default collection of the Recordset object, you can omit the explicit reference to the field collection when you're assigning a value to a field.

```
rs!LastName = "Smith"
```

5 Save the record to the database using the recordset's Update method.

Creating New Records Using the AddNew and Update Methods   You can create a new record in any updatable Recordset object using the AddNew and Update methods of the recordset. Creating a new record in a recordset is a three-step process:

1 Execute the Recordset's AddNew method. This adds a new, blank record to the end of the recordset.

2 Assign values to the new record using the same kind of assignment statements you normally make to database fields.

3 Write the record to the database using the recordset's Update method.

Business Case 3.3: Creating a Data-Entry Application   Jones Novelties requires an application that enables employees to enter items into the product database. This application is written with DAO for maximum efficiency and flexibility. And because the application only needs to enter data, it requires only the Database and Recordset objects, along with the AddNew and Update methods.

The application's interface consists of text boxes, labels and buttons, not unlike the Data control applications described in the section "Using the Visual Basic Data Control" in Chapter 1, "Database Basics." Figure 3.9 shows the layout of the Inventory data-entry application.

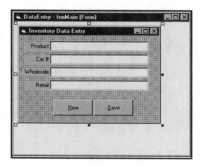

Figure 3.9: The user interface of the Inventory data-entry application.

Note, however, that this application does not require a Data control; all its functionality derives from DAO.

The code for the application starts with some module-level declarations, shown in Listing 3.16. The code defines indexes of a control array of text boxes, and declares the DAO Recordset and Database objects.

Listing 3.16: Module-Level Declarations for the Inventory Data-Entry Application

```
Option Explicit

' References Microsoft DAO Object Library 3.5

Private Enum TextBoxes
    txtProduct = 0
    txtCatalogNumber = 1
    txtWholesalePrice = 2
    txtRetailPrice = 3
End Enum
```

Listing 3.16: Module-Level Declarations for the Inventory Data-Entry Application (Continued)

```
Private db As Database
Private rs As Recordset
Private x As Integer
```

Next, the application's main form initializes the Database and Recordset objects when it is loaded, as shown in Listing 3.17.

Listing 3.17: The Database-Initialization Code that Runs when the Form Loads

```
Private Sub Form_Load()

    Set db = OpenDatabase(App.Path & "\novelty.mdb")
    Set rs = db.OpenRecordset("tblInventory")

    For x = txtProduct To txtRetailPrice
        TextBox(x).Enabled = False
    Next x

    cmdSave.Enabled = False
    cmdNew.Enabled = True

End Sub
```

The code that enables and disables the user-interface controls ensures that the user doesn't do anything inappropriate (such as hit the Save button when there's no data to save). So when the application first launches, the only thing the user can do is hit the New button. (This is a contrived example; you will certainly be able to come up with a more inspired user interface in your DAO applications.)

When the user hits the New button, the code in Code Listing 3.18 runs.

Listing 3.18: Code that creates a new record in the Recordset Object and Sets Up the User Interface for Data Entry

```
Private Sub cmdNew_Click()

    rs.AddNew

    For x = txtProduct To txtRetailPrice
        TextBox(x).Enabled = True
    Next x

    TextBox(0).SetFocus
```

continues

Listing 3.18: Code that creates a new record in the Recordset Object and Sets Up the User Interface for Data Entry (Continued)

```
    cmdSave.Enabled = True
    cmdNew.Enabled = False

End Sub
```

This code creates a new record in the Recordset object, enables all the text boxes on the form, and enables the application's Save button.

The only thing the user can do when the application is in this state is enter data and save a record. When the user is entering a record, the user interface looks like Figure 3.10.

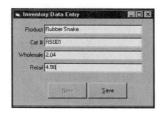

Figure 3.10: The Inventory data-entry application when a user is entering data.

Listing 3.19 shows the code for the Save button.

Listing 3.19: Code that Saves the Record Being Edited and Resets the User Interface

```
Private Sub cmdSave_Click()

    rs.Fields("Product") = TextBox(txtProduct)
    rs.Fields("CatalogNumber") = TextBox(txtCatalogNumber)
    rs.Fields("WholesalePrice") = TextBox(txtWholesalePrice)
    rs.Fields("RetailPrice") = TextBox(txtRetailPrice)

    rs.Update

    For x = txtProduct To txtRetailPrice
        TextBox(x).Text = ""
        TextBox(x).Enabled = False
    Next x

    cmdSave.Enabled = False
```

**Listing 3.19: Code that Saves the Record Being Edited and Resets the User
Interface (Continued)**

```
    cmdNew.Enabled = True

End Sub
```

Note: This code assigns values to the fields in the new record using the
Fields collection of the Recordset object. The Fields collection and Field
object are discussed in more depth later in this chapter.

Remember also that because of the database-engine-level validation rule for
the CatalogNumber field (set up in Chapter 1), the catalog number must
begin with the letters A through M.

This application isn't the most sophisticated in the world, but it's thoroughly
functional and reasonably bulletproof. You can probably think of several additions to add to the application, such as a procedure that automatically generates
a catalog number based on an algorithm applied to the name, and a setting that
enables a data-entry user to enter records one after another (without having to
go through the extra step of clicking the New button each time). All these additional features would be relatively trivial to add using Visual Basic code.

Appending Data to a Binary Field Using AppendChunk   You can store binary
data in your databases. Binary data includes such things as graphics or sound
files —anything you might need to store in a database that *isn't* a simple textual
or numeric value.

Note: Microsoft Access refers to binary fields as OLE Object fields. The rest
of the database universe, however, consistently refers to them as *binary
fields*, so that's the term used in this discussion. Also, you can use the
GetChunk technique described in this section to append data to a memo
field as well as a binary field.

When you assign a value to a binary field in code, you need to perform some
extra steps to get the data in the field. This is because binary data doesn't have a
fixed length as other data types do; a single piece of binary data could conceivably take up megabytes or more.

So, to put a piece of binary data in the database, you must first break it into
chunks. You do this using the GetChunk method of a recordset's Field object.

After reading a chunk of binary data, you append it to the field using the AppendChunk method of the recordset's Field object.

For example, suppose that your salespeople make sales calls on customers frequently. It might be helpful if the database stored a little graphical map for each customer that shows where the customer's office is located. You could create this graphic in a paint program and display it in a picture box control. Because the graphic resides in a field in the tblCustomer table, the user can browse it alongside other data pertaining to the customer.

The challenge here is to come up with a way to create and save the information to the database. You use GetChunk and AppendChunk to do this.

Using these methods still poses a problem, however. In an application with user-interface controls bound to a Data control, you can't use the PictureBox control to display the data; instead, you must resort to more creative tactics. See Chapter 11, "Using the DBGrid and ApexTrue DBGrid Controls," for more information on enabling your users to access binary data in an application of this kind.

Closing the Recordset Using the Close Method   You close a recordset using the Close method. You should do this when your code finishes using a Recordset object.

```
rs.Close
```

It's particularly important to close a Recordset object if the object places a lock on the table (as described in Chapter 8).

Note that in DAO, the Workspace, Connection, Database, and QueryDef objects also have Close methods.

Searching for Data in Recordsets and Tables

After creating a database and making provisions for entering data, you want a way to locate individual records within a recordset. The process of locating an individual record in a recordset according to criteria you specify in code is called a *search*.

A search is different than a query in that a query returns a recordset. A search scrolls through records in an existing recordset to find a single record that satisfies a specific criterion.

There are several techniques for searching for data. The method that is appropriate to use depends on the kind of data structure to which you have access:

▶ If you're working with a recordset, you're limited to the Find methods—FindFirst, FindNext, FindLast, and FindPrevious.

▶ If you have direct access to a table-style recordset, you can use the Seek method to locate records. This method is harder to code, but it can be faster, because you can use a table's index with the Seek method.

The following sections describe these two techniques for finding records.

Locating Records in a Recordset Using the Find Methods To find a record in a recordset, you use the one of the four find methods of the Recordset object:

▶ FindFirst

▶ FindLast

▶ FindNext

▶ FindPrevious

The syntax of these four methods is the same— to use a find method, you pass an SQL WHERE clause to the method specifying the information you wish to find. After executing the method, the current record in the Recordset object becomes the record that matches the WHERE criteria. If the find method doesn't locate a record that matches your criteria, the Recordset object's NoMatch property is set to true.

The type of method you use determines how the record is found. For example, if you use the FindFirst method, the database engine will move to the first record in the recordset that matches your criteria.

For example, suppose that you have a recordset composed of customers, and you're interested in finding the first customer whose last name is Smith. Use the following code:

```
rs.FindFirst "[LastName] = 'Smith'"
```

It's important to remember that unlike a SQL SELECT query, a search does not generate a recordset. When the database engine finds a match for the criterion you specify, it moves to that record; the record becomes the current record. If no match is found, the current record is unchanged and the Recordset object's NoMatch property is set to True.

Business Case 3.4: Creating a Customer Finder Application Jones Novelties needs a small application that will quickly retrieve a customer's contact information given his or her first and last names. You can use DAO to do this using a Dynaset-style Recordset object and the FindFirst method, or you can use a Table-style Recordset object and the Seek method. This business case demonstrates an application that uses both techniques.

You start developing the Customer Finder application by creating its user interface. This can be as simple as a few text boxes and a command button, as shown in Figure 3.11.

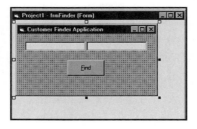

Figure 3.11: The design of the user interface of the Customer Finder application.

The application initializes its Database and Recordset objects when its main form loads, as shown in Listing 3.20.

Listing 3.20: The Initialization Code of the Customer Finder Application

```
' References MS DAO 3.5 Object Library

Private db As Database
Private rs As Recordset
'

Private Sub Form_Load()

    Set db = OpenDatabase(App.Path & "\novelty.mdb")

    ' Force this to be opened as a Dynaset
    ' so you can use FindFirst. (If you don't
    ' do this, it will be opened as a table-type
    ' recordset, and you won't be able to use
    ' FindFirst.)
    Set rs = db.OpenRecordset("tblCustomer", dbOpenDynaset)

End Sub
```

As the comment in the code indicates, you use the dbOpenDynaset argument of the OpenRecordset method to ensure that Jet opens the query as a Dynaset. This is required for the use of the FindFirst method.

After the application runs, the user types in a customer first and last name in the text boxes, then clicks the Find button. The button's Click event triggers a simple validation on the search criteria (ensuring that the user entered a first and last name), then performs the search. The event then returns the customer's name and address information in a message box. Listing 3.21 shows the code that does this.

Listing 3.21   Code that Performs the Search in the Customer Finder Application

```
Private Sub cmdFind_Click()

    If txtFirstName.Text <> "" And txtLastName.Text <> "" Then

        rs.FindFirst "[LastName] = '" & txtLastName.Text & "' " & _
                     "AND [FirstName] = '" & txtFirstName.Text & "'"

        If rs.NoMatch Then
            ' not found
            MsgBox "No customer by that name was found.", vbExclamation
        Else
            ' return info
            MsgBox rs!Address & vbCrLf & _
                   rs!City & ", " & rs!State & "  " & _
                   rs!Zip & vbCrLf & _
                   rs!Phone, _
                   vbInformation, _
                   rs!FirstName & " " & rs!LastName
        End If
    Else
        ' you must enter a first and last name
        MsgBox "Please enter a first and last name.", vbExclamation, "Error"

    End If
End Sub
```

When you run the application, enter a valid customer name, and click the Find button, the application returns that customer's address and phone number, as shown in Figure 3.12.

This application works well, but you could enhance it to use an index on the table. To do this, you must use the Seek method of the Recordset object, as described in the next section.

Figure 3.12: Output of the Customer Finder Application after it finds a customer.

Performing Indexed Searches Using the Seek Method   You can perform searches on a Table-type Recordset object more efficiently using the Seek method.

To perform a search on an index, the table first must have an index. (See "Creating Indexes Using the Index Object," later in this chapter, for information on how to create indexes using DAO code.) You also need to know the name of the index, which can be tricky, particularly if you created the database in Microsoft Access, because Access hides the names of indexes from you behind its graphical user interface.

For this example, just assume that you have a tblCustomer table with an index on the LastName field. The name of the index is LastNameIndex. Listing 3.22 shows the code to retrieve a piece of information from this table using the Seek method.

Listing 3.22: An Indexed Search Using the Seek Method

```
' References MS DAO 3.5 Object Library

Private db As Database
Private rs As Recordset
'


Private Sub Form_Load()

    Set db = OpenDatabase(App.Path & "\novelty.mdb")

    Set rs = db.OpenRecordset("tblCustomer", dbOpenTable)

End Sub

Private Sub cmdSeek_Click()
```

Listing 3.22: An Indexed Search Using the Seek Method (Continued)

```
    rs.Index = "LastNameIndex"
    rs.Seek "=", txtLastName.Text
    If rs.NoMatch Then
            ' not found
            MsgBox "No customer by that name was found.", vbExclamation
    Else
            ' return info
            MsgBox rs!Address & vbCrLf & _
                    rs!City & ", " & rs!State & "   " & _
                    rs!Zip & vbCrLf & _
                    rs!Phone, _
                    vbInformation, _
                    rs!FirstName & " " & rs!LastName
    End If

End Sub
```

Note that this code creates the Recordset object by using the dbOpenTable argument, instead of dbOpenDynaset, as in the previous examples. Opening a Table-type recordset enables you to use the Seek method to do a fast indexed search.

Figure 3.13 shows the result of a search using this technique.

Figure 3.13: The result of a seek on a Table-type recordset.

Bear in mind that the Seek method limits your options for searching on a field. In addition to the requirement that the field on which you're searching must be indexed, when you use Seek, the only operators you can use are listed in Table 3.5.

Table 3. 5: Operators Available with the Seek Method

Operator	Definition
<	Less than
<=	Less than or equal to
>	Greater than
>=	Greater than or equal to
=	Equal to

Unlike the Seek method, which restricts you to indexed fields and a limited set of operators, the Find methods enable you to use any operators available with the SQL WHERE clause, including Like and In. (For more information on the operators that you can use with a SQL WHERE clause, see Chapter 2, "Queries."

Iterating Through a TableDef's Indexes Collection   When you're performing a Seek operation on a Table-type recordset, you might not know what indexes are available. To determine which indexes exist in a given TableDef, and what their names are, you can iterate through the Indexes collection. The code in Listing 3.23 shows how to do this.

Listing 3.23: Listing the Names of the Index Objects Belonging to a Particular TableDef

```
' References MS DAO 3.5 Object Library

Private db As Database
Private rs As Recordset
'


Private Sub Form_Load()

    Set db = OpenDatabase(App.Path & "\novelty.mdb")

End Sub

Private Sub cmdShowIndexes_Click()

    Dim td As TableDef
    Dim ind As Index
    Dim f As Field
```

Listing 3.23: Listing the Names of the Index Objects Belonging to a Particular TableDef (Continued)

```
    Set td = db.TableDefs("tblCustomer")

    For Each ind In td.Indexes
        Debug.Print ind.Name

        For Each f In ind.Fields
            Debug.Print "   On field: " & f.Name
        Next

    Next

End Sub
```

Note: You can use code similar to this to iterate through other collections in DAO. For example, code like this might be useful to view all the databases in a Workspace, the QueryDefs in a database, or the Fields in a TableDef.

Figure 3.14 shows the output of this procedure.

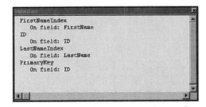

Figure 3.14: Output of the code that displays all the indexes in a TableDef.

Remembering Your Place in a Recordset Using the Bookmark Property

When you're performing operations on a Recordset object, it's common to move hither and yon in the recordset, only to return to your starting place later. You use the Bookmark property of the Recordset object to hold your place so you can return to a position in the recordset later.

The Bookmark property exists to give you an efficient way of scrolling back and forth between two or more records in a recordset. It's much faster to use a bookmark than it is to repeatedly use find methods to move through the database.

Every record in a bookmarkable recordset has its own unique bookmark that you can retrieve and store at any time. To use a bookmark, then, you follow these general steps:

1 Move to the position in the recordset you wish to bookmark.

2 Assign the value of the Recordset object's Bookmark property to a string variable. This saves the unique bookmark for the current record.

3 When you wish to move back to the record, assign the recordset's Bookmark property to the value of the string variable. The current record will be changed to the bookmarked record.

Business Case 3.5: Browsing a Database using Bookmarks Jones Novelties' customer service representatives have noticed that they spend much time querying and requerying the database for information as they attempt to handle orders that deal with more than one customer at a time. They ask you to build an application that enables them to browse the database and store bookmarks for up to two customers at a time. Users of the customer browser then can bounce back and forth between many customers quickly.

Figure 3.15 shows the user interface of this application.

Figure 3.15: The user interface of the enhanced Customer Browser featuring bookmarks.

This application provides a database browser interface, enabling the user to move forward and backward in the recordset without the use of a Data control. Listing 3.24 shows the code that initializes this application.

Listing 3.24: The Declarations and Load Event for the Enhanced Customer Browser

```
' References: MS DAO 3.5 Object Library

Private db As Database
Private rs As Recordset

Private Bookmark1 As String
Private Bookmark2 As String

Private Enum TextBoxes
    txtFirstName = 0
    txtLastName = 1
    txtAddress = 2
    txtPhone = 3
End Enum

Private Enum CommandButtons
    cmdSetBookmark1 = 0
    cmdSetBookmark2 = 1
    cmdGoToBookmark1 = 2
    cmdGotoBookmark2 = 3
End Enum

Private Sub Form_Load()

    Set db = OpenDatabase(App.Path & "\novelty.mdb")
    Set rs = db.OpenRecordset("tblCustomer")
    PopulateControls

End Sub
```

This code (and several other procedures in the application) call the PopulateControls subroutine. This subroutine simply takes text values from the current record in the recordset and uses the data to populate the application's text boxes. Listing 3.25 shows the code for this procedure.

Listing 3.25: The Code for the PopulateControls Subroutine

```
Private Sub PopulateControls()
On Error GoTo ErrHandler

    TextBox(txtFirstName).Text = rs!FirstName & ""
    TextBox(txtLastName).Text = rs!LastName & ""
    TextBox(txtAddress).Text = rs!Address & ""
```

continues

Listing 3.25: The Code for the PopulateControls Subroutine (Continued)

```
      TextBox(txtPhone).Text = rs!Phone & ""

Exit Sub
ErrHandler:
    If Err = 3021 Then ' no current record
        Exit Sub
    Else
        MsgBox Err.Description
    End If

End Sub
```

Note that this routine assigns values from the recordset to the Text properties of the text boxes on the form, but it doesn't assign those properties directly; instead, it concatenates those values to an empty string. The routine does this to coerce null values from the database into empty string values that the text box's Text property can accept. (If you didn't do this, an error would be generated every time the user scrolled to a record that contained no data in one of its fields.)

Listing 3.26 shows the code that enables the Next and Previous buttons.

Listing 3.26: DAO Code that Enables the User to Move Forward and Backward in the Recordset

```
Private Sub cmdNext_Click()
On Error GoTo ErrHandler

    rs.MoveNext
    PopulateControls

Exit Sub
ErrHandler:
    If Err = 3021 Then ' no current record
        rs.MoveLast
        Exit Sub
    Else
        MsgBox Err.Description
    End If

End Sub


Private Sub cmdPrevious_Click()
On Error GoTo ErrHandler
```

Listing 3.26: DAO Code that Enables the User to Move Forward and Backward in the Recordset (Continued)

```
    rs.MovePrevious
    PopulateControls

Exit Sub
ErrHandler:
    If Err = 3021 Then ' no current record
        rs.MoveFirst
        Exit Sub
    Else
        MsgBox Err.Description
    End If

End Sub
```

The error handlers in these procedures are predicated on the idea that errors occur when the user attempts to scroll outside of the boundaries of the record-set (that is, beyond BOF and EOF). It is possible to write another, more elegant version of these routines to inspect the values of BOF and EOF and disable the buttons when the values of these properties are True. But this version works for your purposes.

The bookmark-setting portion of the code is in Listing 3.27.

Listing 3.27: The Code that Sets Bookmarks in the Enhanced Customer Browser Application

```
Private Sub BookMark_Click(Index As Integer)

    Select Case Index
        Case cmdSetBookmark1
          Bookmark1 = rs.BookMark

        Case cmdSetBookmark2
          Bookmark2 = rs.BookMark

        Case cmdGoToBookmark1
          If Bookmark1 <> "" Then
              rs.BookMark = Bookmark1
              PopulateControls
          Else
              MsgBox "That bookmark has not been set.", _
                      vbExclamation, "Error"
          End If
```

continues

Listing 3.27: The Code that Sets Bookmarks in the Enhanced Customer Browser Application (Continued)

```
        Case cmdGotoBookmark2
            If Bookmark2 <> "" Then
                rs.BookMark = Bookmark2
                PopulateControls
            Else
                MsgBox "That bookmark has not been set.", _
                        vbExclamation, "Error"
            End If


        Case Else
            MsgBox "BookMark_Click: Something's terribly wrong.", _
                    vbExclamation, "Error"


    End Select

End Sub
```

To understand this code, remember that in this application, the command buttons (like the text boxes) are in control arrays. Based on which button in the control array the user clicked, either the application saves a bookmark (that is, the application reads the bookmark into a variable) or the recordset moves to a previously set bookmark. Anytime the recordset repositions itself, the PopulateControls subroutine is called to update the data displayed in the text box controls.

After entering the code or loading it from disk, to test the application, do the following:

1 Run the application. The database loads and the application displays the first record in the recordset.

2 Click the Next button a few times until you locate a record you like.

3 To bookmark the record, click the Set B1 button.

4 Move forward or backward a few more records, then click the Go to B1 button.

The previously bookmarked record is displayed.

Note: Not every type of Recordset object supports the Bookmark property. To determine whether you can bookmark a particular type of recordset, inspect the value of the recordset's Bookmarkable property. If the property is True, you can bookmark the recordset.

Accessing Session Information with the Workspace Object

You establish a user session with the database engine using the Workspace object. This object governs everything related to how an individual user interacts with the database engine; accordingly, the Workspace collection and Workspace object occupy a position in the DAO object model below the DBEngine object but above the Database object.

Figure 3.16 shows the Workspace object's place in the DAO hierarchy.

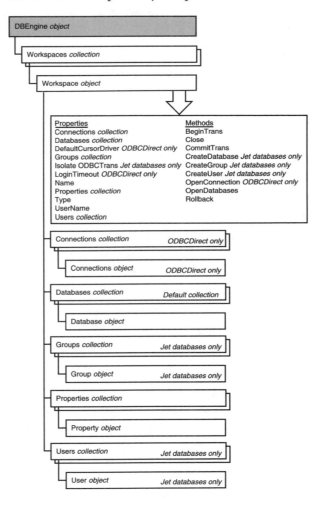

Figure 3.16: The position of the Workspace collection and Workspace object in the DAO hierarchy.

So far, you've seen plenty of code examples that don't require the use of the Workspace object. So why is the object necessary? One answer is that it's as necessary as your kidney—and you don't have to pay any attention to it, just as you don't have to pay any attention to your kidney. In other words, "there's always a Workspace object, even if you're not aware of it, and you don't code against it."

To verify this, try this fun experiment: In some code that creates a Recordset object, place a breakpoint on the line immediately after the one that contains the OpenRecordset method. Open the Immediate window and execute the following line of code:

```
Print Workspaces(0).Name
```

The Immediate window deftly responds with the following:

```
#Default Workspace#
```

Surprise! You're the unwitting parent of a bouncing baby Workspace object.

In DAO programming, you wittingly create Workspace objects in the following situations:

▶ You want to perform *transactions*—multiple database operations that are grouped together and executed as one operation. The next section describes transactions.

▶ You want to create or manipulate groups and users in the Microsoft Jet security system. The technique for doing this is coyly alluded to later in this chapter and described more fully in Chapter 8.

Creating Transactions Using the Workspace Object   A *transaction* is a unit of work performed by a database engine. Generally, transactions comprise two or more distinct operations, all of which much be successfully accomplished for any of the operations to be valid.

The oft-repeated (but effective) example of a typical transaction is a financial credit and debit. For money to be debited from someone's account, it must be credited to some other account, or the bank's books won't balance. If some error condition takes place between the time the money is credited and the time it is debited, you have a serious problem.

A transaction is used in this situation to ensure that one operation doesn't take place without the other. Either the debit and the credit are successful, in which case the transaction is successful and the change to the database is *committed*, or one of the operations fails, in which case the transaction is *rolled back*.

Note: You can use transactions only on Microsoft Jet databases and on ODBC data sources; you can't use transactions with "installable ISAM" data sources such as dBASE and Paradox.

In general, transactions are stored in memory until they are committed; however, for transactions composed of many operations, the transaction might need to write temporary data to disk. Jet handles this writing behind the scenes.

Note that in previous versions of Microsoft Jet, there was a performance benefit to wrapping intensive data access code in transactions. Transactions usually take place in memory, and coding against constructs stored in memory is orders of magnitude more efficient than coding against a database stored on disk. Jet 3.5, however, adds several performance enhancements to make this step unnecessary.

You follow these steps to create a transaction in DAO:

1 To initiate a transaction, use the Workspace object's BeginTrans method. This initiates a transaction and tells the database engine not to write to the database until the transaction is committed. Subsequent database operations are either cached in memory or stored in a temporary database.

2 If any of the database operations in your transaction fail, execute the Workspace object's Rollback method.

3 If all the database operations in the transaction succeed, execute the Workspace object's CommitTrans method.

When you initiate a transaction, that transaction is owned not by the database, but by the Workspace object, because the Workspace object manages your application's session with the database engine. (This makes sense, because if a Database object owned the transaction, you couldn't perform transactions across databases.)

This gives you an interesting capability—because the Workspace object owns a Databases collection, and the scope of a transaction spans every Database owned by a workspace, you can perform transactions against multiple databases, then commit or roll them all back as a group. This can be useful, but it can be a trap, especially when you consider that the Workspace object is often referenced implicitly. If you initiate a transaction, perform updates on one database, perform updates in another database, then roll back the transaction expecting only the changes to the second database to be rolled back, you're going to be in for a nasty surprise. Because both databases are part of the same workspace, everything gets rolled back.

If you want each database to be part of separate transactions, you create a new workspace for each database—using the CreateWorkspace method of the DBEngine object —and execute separate BeginTrans and CommitTrans methods against each workspace. That way, you can roll back a transaction against one database, but not against the other.

Business Case 3.6: Using Transactions to Impose Business Rules   Listing 3.28 is an example of code that runs a simple transaction. The business rule behind this transaction has to do with the awarding of bonuses to salespeople: Each salesperson gets a bonus based on total sales, but no salesperson receives an award unless each member of the team surpasses a sales goal of $10,000.

Listing 3.28: An Example of a Database Transaction Using the DAO Workspace Object

```
' References: Microsoft DAO 3.5 Object Library
'
Dim db As Database

Enum EmployeeType
    empSalesPerson = 1
    empEngineer = 2
    empAdmin = 3
    empManager = 4
End Enum
'


Private Sub Form_Load()

    Set db = OpenDatabase(App.Path & "\novelty.mdb")

End Sub


Private Sub Command9_Click()

    Dim rs As Recordset
    Set rs = db.OpenRecordset("SELECT * " & _
                              "FROM tblEmployee " & _
                              "WHERE [Type] = " & empSalesPerson & _
                              " ORDER BY [LastName], [FirstName]")
    Workspaces(0).BeginTrans

    Do Until rs.EOF
```

Listing 3.28: An Example of a Database Transaction Using the DAO Workspace Object (Continued)

```
        If rs!SalesToDate < 10000 Then
            Workspaces(0).Rollback
            Exit Sub
        Else
            rs.Edit
            rs!Commission = rs!SalesToDate * 0.1
            rs.Update
        End If


        rs.MoveNext

    Loop

    Workspaces(0).CommitTrans

End Sub
```

This is an extremely typical example of how transactions are used in database access applications. You can see that the transaction is tightly integrated into the If…Then…Else logic of the procedure. If the "If" conditions is satisfied, the transaction proceeds; otherwise, it's rolled back.

When using transactions, it's helpful to remember that you can refer to the default Workspace object implicitly. Consider the following code:

```
Workspaces(0).BeginTrans

    ' [vital earth-shaking code goes here]

Workspaces(0).CommitTrans
```

Instead of using this code, you can drop the references to Workspaces(0), and write code such as the following:

```
BeginTrans

    ' [really important mind-blowing code goes here]

CommitTrans
```

If you never use multiple workspaces, this technique can make your transactions easier to code.

Understanding Objects That Manage Users and Groups   In addition to handling transactions, Workspace objects are useful for managing users and groups. In a secured database, users identify individuals who have access to your database; groups contain collections of users.

User and group objects are only available with Jet databases; you can't use them with ODBCDirect. Figure 3.17 shows the position of the User and Group objects in the DAO object model.

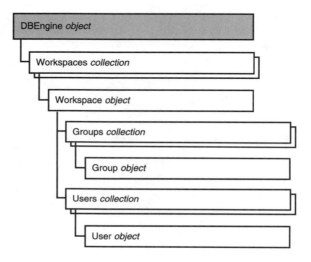

Figure 3.17: The User and Group objects in the DAO model.

Users and groups are part of the DAO object model for Microsoft Jet databases. But because users and groups aren't directly related to the construction of a database application, the DAO code that enables you to create users and groups is covered in more detail in Chapter 8.

Handling Errors Using the Errors Collection and the Error Object

Your application can deal with errors in DAO by using the Error object and the Errors collection. The Errors collection exists because in database programming, a particular operation can generate more than one error. (This is particularly true in client/server programming, in which, for example, an ODBC driver bites the dust because a piece of middleware is hosed because the server is toast. All three components might generate their own unique and lovely error messages, but you'd never see them all unless you had a nice collection to iterate through.)

Having a collection of errors instead of a single Error object, then, enables you to iterate through all the errors in an effort to determine what went wrong.

Figure 3.18 shows the Error object's place in the DAO object hierarchy.

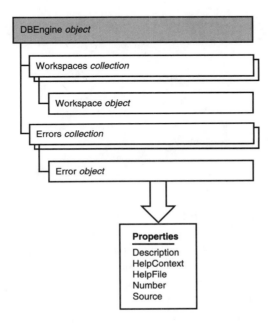

Figure 3.18: The Errors collection and the Error object in the DAO object hierarchy.

Note: You can't append or delete Error objects to the Errors collection.

Listing 3.29 gives an example of how to iterate through the DBEngine's Errors collection to see all the errors it generates.

Listing 3.29: Iterating Through the Errors Collection to See all the Error Descriptions

```
' References: MS DAO 3.5

Dim db As Database
```

continues

Listing 3.29: Iterating Through the Errors Collection to See all the Error Descriptions (Continued)

```
Dim rs As Recordset

Private Sub cmdBadFileName_Click()
On Error GoTo ErrHandler

    Set db = OpenDatabase(App.Path & "\slez.mdb")

Exit Sub
ErrHandler:
Dim DBError As Error
    Debug.Print "Contents of DBEngine Errors Collection"
    Debug.Print "----------------------------------------"
    For Each DBError In DBEngine.Errors
        Debug.Print DBError.Description
    Next
End Sub
```

Note that the last error generated by the DBEngine Errors collection is raised to the Visual Basic Err object. In this case, because the operation generates only one error ("Couldn't find file 'slez.mdb'"), the effect is the same as if you'd trapped the error at the Visual Basic level, using Visual Basic's Err object.

As you can imagine, it's tough to simulate a situation in which you'd generate multiple errors when you're working with a Jet database. However, it's quite easy to generate multiple errors in a client/server environment, because so many components work together to establish the connection between the client and server. For more information on error handling in the world of client/server programming, see Chapter 5.

CREATING OBJECTS THAT MANIPULATE THE STRUCTURE OF A DATABASE

DAO gives you a rich set of methods for creating databases, tables, fields, and query definitions. In addition, DAO 3.5 enables you to create new types of custom data in your application, such as custom properties of database objects and new types of database documents.

Creating a Database

You create a Microsoft Jet database using the CreateDatabase method of the DBEngine object in DAO.

When you create a database, you must supply a file name (typically containing an .MDB extension) and a *locale*. The locale is a function of the language used by users of your application; it sets the *collating order* for your database. The collating order determines how text values in your database are sorted.

Note: *DAO 3.5* The CreateDatabase method of the DBEngine object replaces the CreateDatabase statement that existed in previous versions of DAO. But because DBEngine is one of those DAO objects you never need to reference explictly in code, you can continue using CreateDatabase the old way, without a reference to a DBEngine object in front of it. However, if you want to be 100 percent correct, you use DBEngine.CreateDatabase instead of just CreateDatabase.

Listing 3.30 gives an example of code that creates a database. In addition to creating the database, the code also appends a single table with two fields to the database. The code used here is slightly different than the table-creating code listed in the next section on creating TableDefs.

Listing 3.30   Creating a New Database Using the CreateDatabase Method of the DBEngine Object

```
' References MS DAO 3.0

Private db As Database
Private td As TableDef
Private f As Field
'


Private Sub Command1_Click()

Set db = DBEngine.CreateDatabase(App.Path & "\newdb.mdb", dbLangGeneral)
Set td = New TableDef

Set f = td.CreateField("LastName", dbText, 50)
td.Fields.Append f

Set f = td.CreateField("FirstName", dbText, 50)
td.Fields.Append f

td.Name = "tblSupplier"
db.TableDefs.Append td

End Sub
```

Remember that you don't need to instantiate an instance of the DBEngine object. It's always available for your application to use.

Manipulating Tables Using the TableDef Object

You use the TableDef object to create and manipulate the structure of tables in your application. You can use the TableDef object to create new tables or change existing tables.

Figure 3.19 shows the position of the TableDef object in the DAO hierarchy, as well as the properties and methods of a TableDef object.

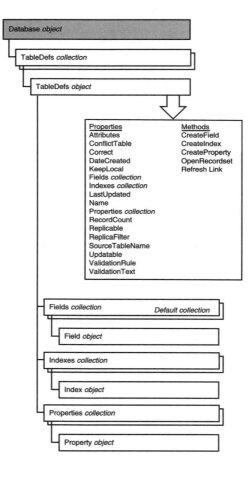

Figure 3.19: The TableDefs collection and TableDef object in the DAO object hierarchy.

Note: *DAO 3.5* In previous versions of DAO, you used the ListTables method of the Database object to get the names of the TableDefs in the database. This method is obsolete; you now use the TableDefs collection to access all the tables in a database.

Creating a New Table Using the TableDef Object　To create a new table, you instantiate an object of type TableDef, then append it to the TableDefs collection using the Append method. (This pattern is similar for many types of DAO objects that create persistent components of the database.)

Listing 3.31 shows an example of code that uses the TableDef to create a new table. This code uses the Field object and Fields collection; these are discussed later in this chapter. Note that if you use this code to create a table that already exists, you'll get a runtime error; accordingly, if your already have a table called tblEmployee, you may wish to set the Name property of the TableDef object to something like tblEmployee2.

Listing 3.31: Creating a New Table with a Single Text Field Using DAO Code

```
' References: Microsoft DAO 3.5 Object Library
'
Dim db As Database
'

Private Sub Form_Load()

    Set db = OpenDatabase(App.Path & "\novelty.mdb")

End Sub

Private Sub Command1_Click()

    Dim td As TableDef
    Dim f As Field

    Set td = New TableDef
    Set f = New Field

    f.Name = "FirstName"
    f.Type = dbText

    td.Name = "tblEmployee"
```

continues

Listing 3.31: Creating a New Table with a Single Text Field Using DAO Code (Continued)

```
    td.Fields.Append f

    db.TableDefs.Append td

End Sub
```

You might not find yourself using DAO to create tables and fields on a regular basis; you have Microsoft Access and Visual Basic's Visual Data Manager for that. However, because you can create tables in code, you can write applications that treat database tables as documents.

For example, consider an application that enables an engineer to create a new type of product. The product might have properties that no one has ever thought of before. If your application enables the engineer to build tables to represent data pertaining to the new product, she could then create fields to represent each property of the new product. Each prototype the engineer created would then be a distinct record in the table, so that when the engineer came upon the correct combination of properties, the new product could then be built. Such an application might require that the user be able to create custom fields and tables.

> **Note:** Remember that you can also use SQL to perform many of the same types of operations on tables as you would using the TableDef object in DAO. However, using DAO gives you an object-oriented programming interface that is usually more similar to Visual Basic. For more information on using SQL to create and alter tables, see "Using DDL" in Chapter 2.

Creating a Field Object Using the CreateField Method You can create a field object by using the TableDef's CreateField method. You typically do this to add a new field to a table or modify an existing field in a table. You can also create a field for other purposes, such as adding a field to an index.

Listing 3.32 demonstrates how to create a new field in an existing TableDef. (Note that attempting to create an existing field causes an error; if you want to try out this code and you already have a tblEmployee table with a LastName field, you'll want to change the name of the field to something like LastName2.)

Listing 3.32: Adding a New Field to an Existing TableDef Using the CreateField Method

```
' References: Microsoft DAO 3.5 Object Library
'
Dim db As Database
'

Private Sub Form_Load()

    Set db = OpenDatabase(App.Path & "\novelty.mdb")

End Sub

Private Sub Command2_Click()

    Dim td As TableDef
    Dim f As Field

    Set td = db.TableDefs("tblEmployee")
    Set f = td.CreateField("LastName", dbText)

    td.Fields.Append f

End Sub
```

In this example, you're adding a totally new field to the table's structure. The field is permanently appended to the table's structure when you append the Field object to the TableDef's Fields collection.

Note: The CreateField method works in Jet workspaces only.

Creating Relationships Between Tables Using the Relation Object

You use the Relation object to create a relationship in your database. You use this object with other DAO commands that create tables.

Figure 3.20 shows the place of the Relation object in the DAO hierarchy.

Recall from the discussion of relationships in Chapter 2 that a relation is a formal declaration of the relationship between two tables. For a relationship to exist, you must name two fields, one in each table: the primary key of one table and a foreign key in the related table.

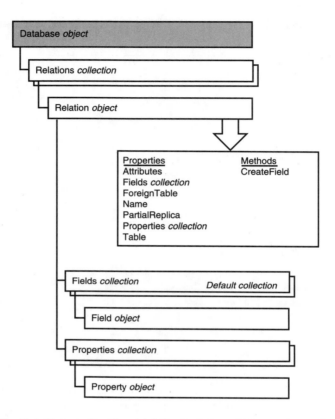

Figure 3.20: The Relations collection and the Relation object in the DAO hierarchy.

You create a new relationship between two tables using the CreateRelation method of the Database object. To create a new relationship, you must specify the name of the new relationship, the tables involved in the relationship, and the type of relationship; you then append fields to the Relation object to specify which fields are linked in the relationship.

The following is the syntax of the CreateRelation method:

```
Set relation = db.CreateRelation ([name], [table], [foreigntable], [attributes])
```

▶ *relation* is the name of an object variable of type Relation.

▶ *db* is a Database object.

▶ *name* is the name of the Relation object you're trying to create.

▶ *table* is the name of the primary table involved in the relationship.

▶ *foreigntable* is the name of the foreign table involved in the relationship.

▶ *attributes* specifies any attributes assigned to the relationship (for example, whether you want the database to enforce cascading deletes).

Listing 3.33 shows an example of a DAO procedure that creates a relationship in an existing database.

Listing 3.33: Creating a New Relation Object Using DAO Code

```
' References MS DAO 3.5 Object Library

Dim db As Database
Dim rel As Relation
'

Private Sub cmdMakeRelation_Click()

    Set db = OpenDatabase(App.Path & "\novelty.mdb")

    Set rel = db.CreateRelation("CustomerOrder", _
            "tblCustomer", _
            "tblOrder", _
            dbRelationUpdateCascade)

    rel.Fields.Append rel.CreateField("ID")
    rel.Fields("ID").ForeignName = "CustomerID"

    db.Relations.Append rel

End Sub
```

This code creates a relationship between the tblCustomer and tblOrder tables. It begins by creating a Relation object using the CreateRelation method of the Database object. It then creates a field object (called ID) using the CreateField method of the Relation object. It does not matter that this field does not derive directly from the underlying table definition, because the relationship requires only a Field object that contains the name of the field used in the relationship. You then set the ForeignName property of the Field object to the name of the foreign key, and finally append the whole works to the Relations collection.

Note: Creating relationships is something that you might not do often, and when you do, you don't use DAO code. (You'll typically use a utility such as the Visual Data Manager or Microsoft Access to create relationships.)

Creating Indexes Using the Index Object

You can create indexes on fields belonging to TableDefs by using DAO code with the Index object and the CreateIndex method of the TableDef object.

Figure 3.21 shows the place of the Index object in the DAO hierarchy.

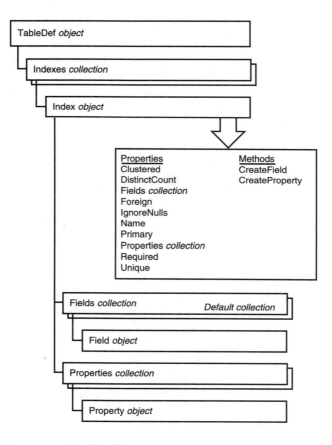

Figure 3.21: The Indexes collection and the Index object in the DAO hierarchy.

Note: *DAO 3.5* The Indexes collection replaces the ListIndex method that existed in previous versions of DAO. This method is now obsolete; it still works, but you should use the Indexes collection instead.

To create an index on the LastName field of the tblCustomer table, you use the code in Listing 3.34.

Listing 3.34: Creating an Index on a Field in DAO Using the Index Object

```
' References MS DAO 3.5 Object Library

Private db As Database
'

Private Sub Form_Load()

    Set db = OpenDatabase(App.Path & "\novelty.mdb")

End Sub

Private Sub cmdMakeIndex_Click()

    Dim td As TableDef
    Dim ind As Index

    Set td = db.TableDefs("tblCustomer")
    Set ind = td.CreateIndex("LastNameIndex")

    ind.Fields.Append td.CreateField("LastName")
    td.Indexes.Append ind

End Sub
```

Note that if another user, or another process in your application, has the table open while you attempt to create an index on it, the CreateIndex method generates an error. Also, if the index already exists, the method also fails.

Manipulating Stored Queries Using the QueryDef Object

You can create and alter stored queries using DAO's QueryDef object. In addition to creating stored queries, the QueryDef object also enables you to run parameterized queries; this is a common reason to access QueryDef objects using DAO code.

Note: *DAO 3.5* The QueryDefs collection replaces the OpenQueryDef method of the Database object that existed in previous versions of DAO. This method is now obsolete; you should use the QueryDefs collection to manipulate QueryDef objects instead.

As an alternative to creating stored queries using DAO, you can also create stored queries using Microsoft Access or Visual Basic's Visual Data Manager. For more information on creating stored queries this way, see Chapter 2.

Figure 3.22 shows the QueryDef object's place in the DAO hierarchy, along with its properties and methods.

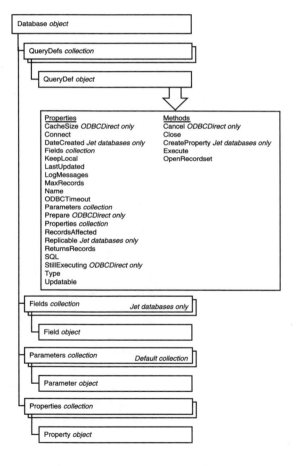

Figure 3.22: The QueryDefs collection and the QueryDef object within the DAO hierarchy.

In DAO, you create query definitions using DAO's QueryDef object. Such definitions can either be temporary, in which case they disappear as soon as you are done with them, or permanent, in which case they are permanently stored in the database.

You create a QueryDef object using code similar to that shown in Listing 3.35.

Listing 3.35: Creating a New QueryDef Object in DAO Code

```
' References: Microsoft DAO 3.5 Object Library
'
Dim db As Database
'

Private Sub Form_Load()

    Set db = OpenDatabase(App.Path & "\novelty.mdb")

End Sub

Private Sub Command3_Click()

    Dim qd As QueryDef
    Set qd = New QueryDef

    qd.Name = "qryCustomerZip"
    qd.SQL = "SELECT * " & _
             "FROM tblCustomer " & _
             "ORDER BY [Zip]"

    db.QueryDefs.Append qd

End Sub
```

You designate the name of the QueryDef you're creating using the QueryDef object's Name property. If you attempt to create a QueryDef that already exists, you trigger a trappable error (3021 - Object already exists).

Don't forget to give your new QueryDef a name; otherwise, you won't have a way to refer to it (and Jet won't be able to save it). Remember too that you can determine which queries exist in the database at any time by iterating through the QueryDefs collection.

Running Queries Using the QueryDef Object   You can run, or execute, a query by using the methods of the QueryDef object. You typically do this in situations where you need to do something unusual to the query before running it, such as specifying a parameter, or when you need to execute an action query that updates, deletes or changes records in the database. (To run a query normally, you use the OpenRecordset method of the Database object, as demonstrated earlier in this chapter.)

To execute a QueryDef, you use the OpenRecordset method of the QueryDef object (to run a SELECT query) or the QueryDef object's Execute method (to run an action query).

To execute a QueryDef, follow these steps:

1 Create an instance of a QueryDef object in code.

2 Create a SQL string that defines what the QueryDef will do when it is run.

3 Assign the SQL string to the QueryDef's SQL property.

4 Append the QueryDef to the Database object's QueryDefs collection.

Listing 3.36 demonstrates how to execute a QueryDef in a database.

Listing 3.36: Executing a QueryDef Object in DAO Code

```
' References MS DAO 3.5

Private db As Database
Private qd As QueryDef
Private rs As Recordset
'

Private Sub Form_Load()

    Set db = OpenDatabase(App.Path & "\novelty.mdb")
    Set qd = db.QueryDefs("qryCustomer")

End Sub

Private Sub cmdQuery_Click()

    Set rs = qd.OpenRecordset

    MsgBox rs!Address & vbCrLf & _
           rs!Phone, _
           vbInformation, _
           "Info for " & rs!FirstName & " " & rs!LastName

End Sub
```

This code example assumes you have a stored query in your database called qryCustomer; the procedure uses a message box to display the first customer it retrieves from the database.

Creating Parameterized Queries Using the Parameter Object   The Parameters collection of a QueryDef enables you to perform parameterized queries. These queries are built with one or more components (the parameter or parameters) intentionally omitted; these components must be filled in when the query is run.

You create parameterized queries because they execute much faster than queries you build in SQL on the fly in Visual Basic code. This is because the database engine compiles a query before you run it, applying optimizations to it.

Figure 3.23 shows the place of the Parameters collection and Parameter object in the DAO hierarchy, as well as the Parameter object's properties.

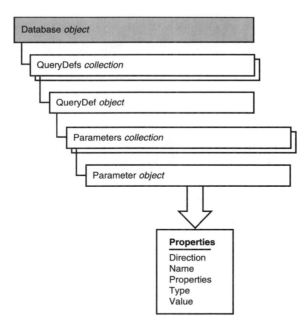

Figure 3.23: The Parameters collection and the Parameter object in the DAO object hierarchy.

Note: *DAO 3.5* The Parameters collection replaces the ListParameters method that existed in previous versions of DAO. This method is now obsolete; you should use the Parameters collection instead.

Chapter 2 describes the syntax of a parameterized query in SQL. To keep you from having to ruffle through pages to find it, Listing 3.37 contains an example of a parameterized query.

Listing 3.37: The SQL Code for a Parameterized Query

```
SELECT *
FROM tblCustomer
WHERE [LastName] = prmLastName
```

The parameter in this query is called prmLastName; it's defined as a parameter because it doesn't correspond to the names of any fields or tables in the database.

For the query to run, you must supply a value for this parameter (this is one of the few advantages of parameterized queries). You supply a parameter by assigning a value to the Value property of the appropriate Parameter object, as shown in Listing 3.38.

Listing 3.38: Returning a Recordset Object Using a Parameterized Query

```
' References MS DAO 3.5

Private db As Database
Private qd As QueryDef
Private rs As Recordset
'

Private Sub Form_Load()

    Set db = OpenDatabase(App.Path & "\novelty.mdb")
    Set qd = db.QueryDefs("qryCustomerParam")

End Sub

Private Sub cmdQuery_Click()

    qd.Parameters("prmLastName").Value = txtLastName.Text
    Set rs = qd.OpenRecordset

    rs.MoveLast
```

Listing 3.38: Returning a Recordset Object Using a Parameterized Query (Continued)

```
    If rs.RecordCount > 1 Then
        MsgBox "There are " & rs.RecordCount & " customers in " & _
               "the database with that last name.", _
               vbExclamation, _
               "Parameter too narrow"
    Else
        MsgBox rs!Address & vbCrLf & _
               rs!Phone, _
               vbInformation, _
               "Info for " & rs!FirstName & " " & rs!LastName
    End If

End Sub
```

This application is similar to the Customer Finder application used in previous examples in this chapter. The user enters the customer's last name in the text box; if the application determines that there's only one customer with that name in the database, it displays the customer's address and phone number (if the application determines that there is more than one record in the database matching the parameter supplied, it informs the user to use more specific criteria).

Note: Because a QueryDef's parameters are a function of the SQL statement that defines the query, you can't add new parameters to the Parameters collection of a QueryDef the way you add other objects to collections in DAO.

Compacting and Repairing a Jet Database

The DBEngine object gives you several methods that enable you to perform maintenance operations on Jet databases These operations include the following:

▶ *Compacting* the database, which removes deleted data from the database, causing it to take up less space on disk.

▶ *Repairing* the database, which is necessary when the database becomes damaged, usually as a result of something unusual, such as the computer losing power while trying to save data to the database.

Note: The database maintenance procedures described in this section work only on Microsoft Jet databases; they don't work on client/server or IISAM data sources.

Using the CompactDatabase Method   You use the CompactDatabase method to shrink the size of a database after it's been in use for a while. The reason that CompactDatabase is necessary has to do with how components of a database get deleted. When you delete a database object, instead of wiping out every bit and byte in the object you just deleted, Jet puts it in a bit bucket that's still stored in an inaccessible place in the .MDB file. Compacting the database empties this bit bucket.

Note: *DAO 3.5* The CompactDatabase method of the DBEngine object replaces the CompactDatabase statement that existed in previous versions of DAO. But because DBEngine is one of those DAO objects, you never need to reference it explictly in code; you can continue using CompactDatabase the old way, without a reference to a DBEngine object in front of it. However, if you want to be 100 percent correct, you'll use DBEngine.CompactDatabase instead of just CompactDatabase.

The complete syntax of the CompactDatabase method is as follows:

```
DBEngine.CompactDatabase olddb, newdb, [locale], [options], [password]
```

Executing the CompactDatabase method creates a new copy of your database. The *olddb* parameter is the current name of your database's .MDB file. The *newdb* parameter is the name of the file to which the Jet engine will copy the new, compacted database.

The *locale* parameter affects the sorting order of the database. (For example, text gets sorted in German differently than it gets sorted in English.) This parameter is relevant only if you're developing a database application for international use.

The *options* argument sets a locale for the database; it is the same as the *options* argument of the CreateDatabase method (discussed earlier in this chapter).

The database can't be open when you run CompactDatabase on it; if it's open (by any user), the database engine generates an error. Listing 3.39 gives an example of how to compact a database; this code traps any errors that occur in the compacting process and notifies the user that something went wrong.

Listing 3.39: Using the CompactDatabase Method of the DBEngine Object to Compact a Jet Database

```
'
'References MS DAO 3.5
'


Private Sub cmdRepair_Click()

On Error Resume Next

Dim strOldFile As String
Dim strNewFile As String

strOldFile = App.Path & "\novelty.mdb"
strNewFile = App.Path & "\novelty-compacted.mdb"

' Delete the compacted file, if it exists
    Kill strNewFile

    DBEngine.CompactDatabase strOldFile, strNewFile
    If Err Then
        MsgBox "The compact was not successful. " & _
               "Make sure the database is not open.", _
               vbExclamation, _
               "Database Compact Error"
    Else
        Err.Clear
        MsgBox "Database successfully compacted."
    End If

End Sub
```

This code also renames the file and includes error trapping that takes care of situations where the database can't be compacted (most likely because it's open).

Changing the Database's Version Using CompactDatabase   You can change the version of a Jet database using the CompactDatabase method. You do this in situations where you want to upgrade a database to a newer version of Jet.

Such a situation occurs when you want the new database file produced by the CompactDatabase method to be compatible with different versions of the Microsoft Jet database engine. Upgrading a database to a newer version gives you access to new features; for example, database replication (discussed in Chapter 8) became available in Jet 3.0.

However, you must be careful not to upgrade a database in situations where a client application (created in Visual Basic, Microsoft Access, or another development environment) uses an older version of the database engine. Doing so forces you to make changes to the application—at the very least, you'll need to set a reference to the new version of the database engine. (In Visual Basic 5.0, you do this in the Project References menu.)

For example, if you have a 16-bit application developed in Visual Basic 3.0 that uses a Jet 2.0 database created with Microsoft Access 2.0, and you convert the database to Jet 3.5 format using CompactDatabase, your application will break, and you won't be able to open the database in Microsoft Access 2.0. The moral of the story is that you should carefully prototype and test your client applications before converting and deploying a converted database.

> **Note:** Bear in mind that an application developed in an environment that uses Jet 3.5 (that is, Microsoft Access 97 and Visual Basic 5.0) can access data created in any previous version of Jet.

To convert a database using CompactDatabase, you assign a version constant to the *options* parameter of the CompactDatabase method. (To convert the database to Jet 3.0/3.5, use the dbVersion30 argument.)

In the following example, the DAO constant dbVersion30 tells CompactDatabase to convert the database to a format that is compatible with Jet 3.0 and 3.5:

```
DBEngine.CompactDatabase strOldFile, _
                         strNewFile, _
                         dbLangGeneral, _
                         dbVersion30
```

Repairing the Database   You can repair a damaged database by using the RepairDatabase method of the DBEngine object. The RepairDatabase method requires only the name of the database as an argument:

```
DBEngine.RepairDatabase App.Path & "\normal.mdb"
```

RepairDatabase, like the CompactDatabase method, cannot run if any user has the database open. But unlike CompactDatabase, RepairDatabase doesn't create a copy of the database.

You should consider running CompactDatabase after you run RepairDatabase, because the process of repairing the database can create the kind of useless temporary data chunks inside the database file that CompactDatabase gets rid of.

Working with Database Documents and Containers

Database documents are a DAO construct that enable you to refer to elements of the database generically. You access the properties of a database document through a Container object.

Figure 3.24 shows the position of the Containers collection and Container objects.

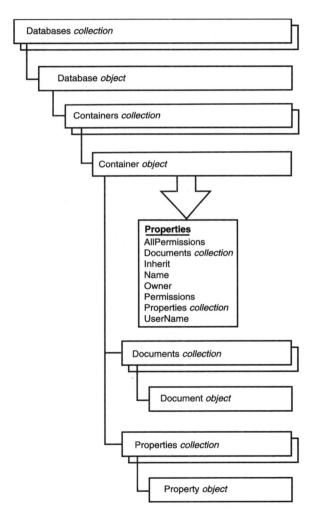

Figure 3.24: The Containers collection and the Container object in the DAO object hierarchy.

Container objects own sets of Document objects. Figure 3.25 shows the position of the Document object, along with its properties and methods.

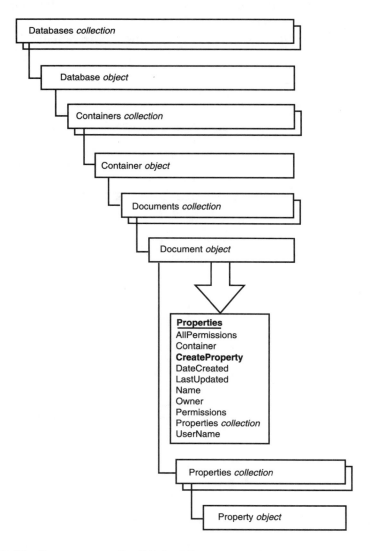

Figure 3.25: The Documents collection and Document object in the DAO object hierarchy.

As with the many other objects available in DAO, you can use DAO code to iterate through containers and documents. Listing 3.40 shows the code to iterate through the Collection and Document objects in a Jet database.

Listing 3.40: Code to Display the Contents of a Database's Containers and Documents Collections

```
' References DAO 3.5

Private db As Database
Dim con As Container
Dim doc As Document

Private Sub Form_Load()

Set db = OpenDatabase(App.Path & "\novelty.mdb")

    For Each con In db.Containers
        Debug.Print con.Name
        For Each doc In con.Documents
            Debug.Print "   " & doc.Name
        Next
    Next

End Sub
```

For the database novelty.mdb, this code should produce output similar to the following:

```
Databases
   AccessLayout
   MSysDb
   SummaryInfo
   UserDefined
Forms
Modules
Relationships
   tblCustomertblOrder
Reports
   rptEmployees
Scripts
SysRel
   Admin
Tables
   ~sq_rrptEmployees
   MSysACEs
```

continues

continued

```
MSysModules
MSysModules2
MSysObjects
MSysQueries
MSysRelationships
qryAppendCustomer
qryCustomer
qryCustomerParam
qryCustomerSortName
qryCustomerZip
qryNamesSorted
qryOrder
tblCustomer
tblEmployee
tblInventory
tblOrder
tblOrderArchive
tblRegion
```

(The elements highlighted in bold are Containers; the indented elements are Documents.)

It's important to understand the difference between database documents and DAO collections. A collection of TableDefs, for example, refers to all the TableDefs you've opened in your code. The Tables document, on the other hand, contains references to all the table documents in the database that you could open. In Jet, the Tables container includes documents such as stored queries and system tables (which begin with the prefix MSys).

You use Container and Document objects in these situations:

▶ You want to assign security permissions to an object in a secured database. (See Chapter 8, for information on how to do this.)

▶ You want to create or retrieve custom properties for all the components of a database by iterating through collections. (See "Creating and Using Custom Properties" later in this chapter for more information on how to do this.)

In addition to inspecting the contents of existing database documents, DAO also enables you to define and create your own documents, which are stored in the database alongside the default documents.

Custom documents are included in the Jet object model to support extensibility. The general idea is to prevent the existing object model from inhibiting new features.

One example of how custom documents give you access to additional database functionality is replication, the ability of Jet databases to copy their contents to replica databases over a network. Replication is introduced in Chapter 8.

Creating and Using Custom Properties of Database Objects

You can refer to the properties of Data Access Objects generically. This allows for extensibility, enabling you to add your own properties and read the properties of existing objects whether you know what they're called or not.

You access the generic list of properties of a Data Access Object through the Properties collection and Property object. You can create a new property by using the CreateProperty method of the Document object.

Note: Just as the Document object is available only in Microsoft Jet databases, the Properties collection and Property object are unique features of Jet databases. They aren't available in other types of databases.

As an example of how the Properties collection works, Listing 3.41 shows a procedure that generates the list of default properties available in a database.

Listing 3.41: Code that Exports the Current Database's Properties to the Immediate Window

```
' References: Microsoft DAO 3.5 Object Library
'

Dim db As Database
Dim pr as Property

Private Sub Command11_Click()
On Error Resume Next

    For Each pr In db.Properties
        With db.Properties
            Debug.Print Property.Name & ": " & Property.Value
        End With
    Next

End Sub
```

Running this code generates the output shown in Figure 3.26.

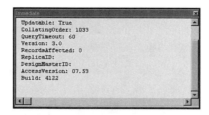

Figure 3.26: Output generated by code that iterates through the Properties collection of a Jet database.

There are 13 default properties of a Database object available through the Properties collection, including such perennial favorites as Name, Version, and Connect, but also including properties that can't be accessed directly, such as AccessVersion and Build (both of which are undocumented in Visual Basic and Microsoft Access, but presumably pertain to the exact version of the Jet database engine used to create the database).

You can just write code like this:

```
MsgBox db.Name
```

So why would you want to write code that accesses a database's properties like the following?

```
MsgBox db.Properties("Name")
```

The answer is that you can create your own custom properties and assign them to virtually any Data Access Object (not only the Database object). Listing 3.42 shows code that creates a new property in your database.

Listing 3.42: Creating a New Property in the Database Using the DAO Properties Object

```
' References: Microsoft DAO 3.5 Object Library
'

Dim db As Database
'


Private Sub Form_Load()

    Set db = OpenDatabase(App.Path & "\novelty.mdb")

End Sub
```

Listing 3.42: Creating a New Property in the Database Using the DAO Properties Object (Continued)

```
Private Sub Command12_Click()

    Dim prp As Property

    Set prp = db.CreateProperty("DateLastBackedUp", dbDate, Now)

    db.Properties.Append prp

End Sub
```

The following is the full syntax of the CreateProperty method:

```
obj.CreateProperty(propertyname, [datatype], [value], [ddl])
```

▶ The *propertyname* argument is a string that denotes the name of the new property.

▶ The *datatype* argument specifies the data type of the new property.

▶ The *value* argument supplies an initial value for the property.

▶ The *ddl* argument is a Boolean value that specifies whether the new property is a DDL object; if so, then users who lack permission to alter the database structure can't change the custom property.

To retrieve the value of your custom property after you've created it, you simply access it through the Properties collection of the Database object, as Listing 3.43 demonstrates:

Listing 3.43: Retrieving a Custom Property Through the Database Object's Properties Collection

```
' References: Microsoft DAO 3.5 Object Library
'
Dim db As Database
'
Private Sub Form_Load()

    Set db = OpenDatabase(App.Path & "\novelty.mdb")

End Sub

Private Sub Command13_Click()
```
continues

Listing 3.43: Retrieving a Custom Property Through the Database Object's Properties Collection (Continued)

```
    MsgBox "This database was last backed up on " & _
           db.Properties("DateLastBackedUp")

End Sub
```

You might think that you can access your custom property using this syntax:

```
MsgBox db.DateLastBackedUp
```

However, this syntax doesn't work, because custom database properties are stored differently than normal properties. You must go through the Properties object to set or retrieve your custom property.

Values of custom properties attached to Database objects are stored in the database permanently; code that sets a custom property looks like this:

```
db.Properties("DateLastBackedUp") = Now
```

SUMMARY

This chapter explained the grand, unified theory of DAO programming. If you have a good handle on the topics discussed in this chapter, you can perform most of the actions you will ever be called upon to do in the universe of Visual Basic database access.

That is, of course, until your zippy little two-user application needs to be scaled to be usable by everyone in your department or everybody in your company—in which case you'll need to graduate to the world of client/server programming. Fortunately, this book includes a nice, juicy chapter on that very subject—Chapter 5.

But before you take the plunge into the wonderful world of remote database access, there's one more major topic to cover: packaging and sending all this lovely data to some useful output format. Reporting and exporting data is covered in Chapter 4, "Reporting and Exporting Data."

QUESTIONS AND ANSWERS

Q: Is it appropriate to use DAO to do client/server programming?

A: It's possible to use DAO for client/server programming, but it's more appropriate to use Remote Data Objects (RDO), discussed in Chapter 5. RDO provides a programming interface similar to DAO, but with additional features (such as a Connection object and the capability to return multiple result sets) that are geared toward client/server programming. So if you learn DAO first, and spend some time experimenting on Jet databases, you will have a leg up on RDO, because many of the concepts are the same. Another bonus of learning both DAO and RDO is that you can create a prototype database design in a Microsoft Access/Jet database, then later use a client/server database for your production application. Chapter 5 gives some suggestions on how and when you'd want to do that.

Q: I'm upgrading to VB 5.0 and DAO 3.5 from a 16-bit version of Visual Basic. Are there any big changes I should know about?

A: The most important change you'll want to be aware of is the fact that support for different types of recordset objects is dropped. For example, in DAO 3.5, there isn't a Dynaset or Snapshot object like there is in DAO 2.0.

If you need to continue to support DAO 2.5, there is a "DAO 2.5/3.0 Compatibility Library" that lets you continue to use the old objects you're accustomed to using (such as the Dynaset object). You might consider using this library if you need to move existing DAO 2.5 code into VB5 and DAO 3.5.

Reporting and Exporting Data

How can I print data stored in a database?

How can I export data to a text file?

How can I use my data to create Web pages?

How can I send data in a database to a Microsoft Office application such as Word or Excel?

Chapter 4

After you've got your database up and running and you've populated it with data, you need a way to output information from it. This chapter discusses several options—some are easy to implement and will work with Visual Basic out of the box, some require third-party tools, and some are rather code-intensive. The method you use depends on your application's requirements, as well as how much flexibility you need (and how much code you're interested in writing).

Database reporting involves much more than simply printing data from your database. Most database reports involve additional operations on the data, including:

▶ **Querying** the data in order to retrieve, display and print just the data you want. In a report context, this is sometimes referred to as *filtering*.

▶ **Sorting** the data so it appears in an order that makes sense (this is another facet of querying).

▶ **Grouping** the data in order to display more concisely. For example, you wouldn't show your boss the cash register receipts for the entire year if she wanted to know how much money the company made; you'd instead show her the receipts grouped in some way—month-by-month or product-by-product, for example.

This chapter makes the distinction between *reporting*—which involves printing data as well as grouping and sorting it—and *exporting*, which involves converting the data in your database to another file format.

Taking Advantage of the Great Forward-Scrolling Cursor Caper

You haven't really learned about client/server systems in depth yet, but it's worth jumping ahead at this point. Visual Basic 5.0 gives you access to some new client/server technologies that enable you to perform database access more efficiently—particularly when it comes to exporting or reporting data.

This technique involves the use of *forward-scrolling cursors.* A forward-scrolling cursor is a type of recordset that enables you to move forward only (that is, you can only do MoveNexts—you can't use recordset methods such as MovePrevious or Find). This kind of record is much easier for the database engine to keep track of, and therefore much more efficient to work with. It's ideal for generating reports, because you almost never need to scroll backward when you're outputting data.

When you're using Remote Data Objects (RDO) (discussed in Chapter 5, "Client/Server"), you have the option of creating forward-scrolling recordsets.

Reporting Using Crystal Reports

Crystal Reports permits you to create database reports in your Visual Basic applications. It consists of two major parts—a report designer that lets you determine the data that will be included in a report and how it should look, and an ActiveX control that permits you to run, display and print the control at run time.

For many Visual Basic programmers, Crystal Reports is the be-all end-all when it comes to database reporting. This is because a version of Crystal Reports comes with Visual Basic and is extremely easy to use.

There are two steps to creating a report for your application using Crystal Reports: creating the report and adding the Crystal Reports ActiveX control to your project. You create the report using the Crystal Reports Designer application. This application creates report documents that you can run from within your Visual Basic applications. You open report documents in your Visual Basic application using the Crystal ActiveX control.

Creating a Report Using Crystal Reports

Before you can use a report in your Visual Basic application, you must first create it. You can't create reports in code; you must instead use Crystal Reports' own application for building reports. After building your report, you save it as a file on disk and distribute it to users along with your application.

To launch the Crystal Reports designer, follow these steps:

1 From the Visual Basic Add-Ins menu, choose Report Designer.

Note: If Report Designer isn't available, you might have neglected to install it when you set up Visual Basic; run Visual Basic's Setup program to install Report Designer.

2 The Crystal Reports designer launches.

3 From Crystal Reports' File menu, choose New. The Create New Report dialog box appears, as shown in Figure 4.1.

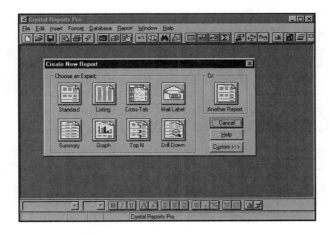

Figure 4.1: The Create New Report dialog box in Crystal Reports.

From this dialog box, Crystal Reports offers you several report templates you can use to output data; you can also use your own reports as templates, as well as create custom reports that aren't based on templates. Table 4.1 summarizes the different report types that are available.

Table 4.1: Report Experts Available in Crystal Reports

Report Type	Description
Standard	A report that lists information in rows and columns, enabling you to sort and total data.
Listing	A straight list of data with no summary or totaling fields. You might use this kind of report to print telephone directories.
Cross-Tab	A summary of data in two dimensions (see Chapter 2, "Queries," for information on crosstab queries).
Mail Label	A report designed to print data in columns for mailing labels.
Summary	A report showing only totals or other aggregate figures, without the detailed data.
Graph	A visual representation of data.
Top *N*	A report that enables you to specify a certain number of records to display.
Drill Down	A report that enables you to double-click summary data to see the detail behind that data.
Another Report	A report that uses as a template a report you've previously created as a template.

Business Case 4.1: Outputting Business Data Using Crystal Reports The sales force of Jones Novelties Incorporated has requested information on which products are selling well.

By using Crystal Reports, you decide to create a report that will show how much total revenue each item in inventory has generated. To do this, follow these steps:

1 Start Crystal Reports and create a new report. Choose the Standard expert.

2 In step one of the Standard expert, click the Data File button.

3 In the file dialog box, select the database NOVELTY.MDB on your disk. Click on Add to add the database's tables to your report, then click Done.

The list of tables is populated. The Standard expert moves to step two, which shows relationships among tables in your database. Figure 4.2 shows step two of the Standard expert.

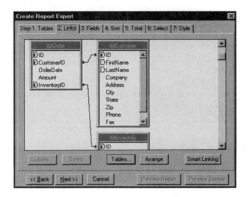

Figure 4.2: Step two of the Standard expert, which shows relationships among tables in your database.

Because predefined relationships for this database have been defined at the database engine level, you don't have to define them again here. But if you did need to establish or delete a relationship at the report level instead of the database engine level, you'd follow these steps:

1 Click the relationship line joining the tblOrder and tblInventory tables.

2 Click the Delete button. The relationship is deleted.

3 Click-drag from the ID field in the tblInventory table to the InventoryID field in the tblOrder table, then click-drag on the tables themselves to arrange them in the window. The Links step looks like Figure 4.3. The relationship is restored.

Note: It's easy to click-drag onto the wrong field when you're creating a relationship in this dialog. If Crystal gives you an error message to the effect that the field you dragged onto is "missing an index," try click-dragging again, making sure to drag-drop directly onto the foreign key field.

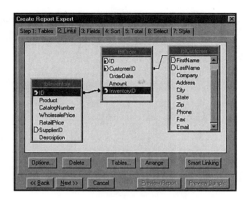

Figure 4.3: The Links dialog box after you establish relationships between the tables.

4 Click the Next button.

You're now in step three of the Standard expert. In this step, you determine which fields will appear in your report. From the tblInventory table, select the Product field. From the tblOrder table, select the Amount field.

5 Click the Sort tab. This step enables you to determine how to sort your data. Select the Product field.

6 Click the Total tab. The Total page enables you to determine how the report will sum up your data. It selects the Amount field by default because it's a numeric field.

Note: For this example, there's no need to go to the Select step because you want all the data to be reported. But if you wanted to limit the type of data to display, you could do so in this step.

7 Click the Style tab. The Style page enables you to determine how the report will look. Choose a report style that strikes your fancy (I like the Shading style).

8 In the Title text box, type **Product Summary Report**.

9 Click the Preview Report button.

The report previews. The screen looks like Figure 4.4.

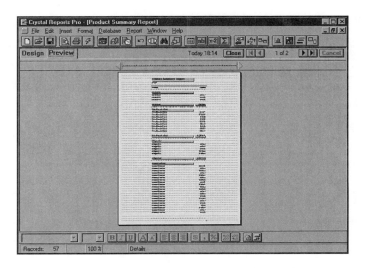

Figure 4.4: The report after you've gone though all the expert steps.

This example is intentionally simplified and designed to give you an idea of how easy it is to get started with Crystal Reports. Because creating reports is relatively straightforward, you don't need to go into much more detail here. However, at this point, you should save your report so you can incorporate it in your application later. To do this, follow these steps:

1 From the Crystal Reports File menu, choose Save.

2 The file dialog box appears. Give the report the file name **product.rpt**.

3 Click OK.

4 Exit Crystal Reports by choosing File, Exit.

In the next business case, you'll create a Visual Basic application that enables the user to run this report at will.

Running the Report in Your Application with the Crystal Reports ActiveX Control

After writing your report, you need a way to run it from within your application. The Crystal Reports ActiveX control provides a method to do this.

Enabling users of your applications to run Crystal Reports is quite simple; it involves adding the Crystal ActiveX control to your project and writing a few lines of code. To see how this works, follow these steps:

1 Create a new Visual Basic application with a single command button.

2 Add the Crystal ActiveX control to your project through the Project Components menu.

3 Create an instance of the Crystal Report control on your form by double-clicking it in the toolbar. The resulting control is called CrystalReport1.

4 In the command button's Click event, enter the following code:

```
Private Sub cmdReport_Click()

    CrystalReport1.ReportFileName = App.Path & "\product.rpt"
    CrystalReport1.PrintReport

End Sub
```

5 Run the application and click the Run button. The report runs, displaying its output to the user in a preview window. At this point, the user can output the report to a printer by clicking the Print button.

Note: By using the Crystal Report control's Destination property, you can send data directly to the printer, bypassing the preview window.

Obtaining and Using Newer Versions of Crystal Reports   The version of Crystal Reports that ships with Visual Basic 5 is 4.6. There is a newer version of Crystal Reports available; for information on it, check out the Seagate Software Web site at **http://www.img.seagate.com**.

The commercial version of the system, Crystal Reports 6.0, offers several new features. These include the following:

▶ *Subreports,* which are similar to the subreport feature in Microsoft Access that enables you to show one-to-many relationships

▶ *New formatting options,* including the capability to run reports in columns and display different types of reports side-by-side

▶ *Conditional reports,* which can display differently based on the status of your data

▶ *Direct database drivers* for many major platforms (including Oracle, Informix, and Microsoft SQL Server) that enable you to bypass conventional Open Database Connectivity (ODBC) drivers, eliminating the need to set up ODBC data sources on client computers

▶ *Export* to Microsoft Word and Microsoft Excel formats

▶ *Web support,* including the capability to export to HyperText Markup Language (HTML) Web pages

▶ *Support for nonrelational, server-side data sources* such as Microsoft Exchange Server activity and Windows NT event logs

▶ *Printed documentation* that is greatly superior to the manual for the version of Crystal Reports that comes with Visual Basic 5.0

Note: As this book was being completed, a new version of Crystal Reports was released. This release, dubbed Crystal Reports 6.0, adds a design-time server-side reporting component for Microsoft's Web server, a programmable Component Object Model (COM) interface, and permits users to "drill down" into reports to enable them to see the details behind data.

The new version sports a number of other neat features as well. You can get information on the latest version of Crystal Reports at **http://seagatesoftware.com.**

REPORTING USING MICROSOFT ACCESS

Microsoft Access enables you to write database reports. It sports an easy-to-use, visual interface that most Visual Basic programmers will feel very comfortable with. Like Crystal Reports, Microsoft Access' reports enable you to group and sort data, as well as include custom expressions in your reports.

This section is designed to give you an idea of Access' report-writing capabilities, but it's not a complete reference to reports in Access. Rather, this section is designed to give you an idea of how to integrate Access reports into your Visual Basic database access application.

This section describes two techniques for running Access reports in your Visual Basic application:

▶ Using Automation to launch an instance of Access, running the report directly from within that application

▶ Using the VideoSoft VSREPORTS product to enable users of your application to run Microsoft Access reports whether or not they have Access installed on their computers

Running Microsoft Access Reports from Visual Basic

You can use several techniques to run database reports that were created in Microsoft Access from within your Visual Basic application. These techniques include the following:

▶ Using Automation, a technology that enables interapplication communication in Windows, to run reports from Access. This technique uses Access as an Automation server.

▶ Using VideoSoft VSREPORTS, a third-party ActiveX control that converts reports from a Microsoft Access .MDB file into a format that you can redistribute along with your applications

You can also enable users to run Access reports by using the Microsoft Office 97 Developer Edition (formerly known as the Microsoft Access Developer's Toolkit) to distribute the run-time version of Microsoft Access to users.

With this technique, you build a reporting tool using Microsoft Access, and then install the tool on users' computers. Deploying the application requires installing an .MDB file and the Microsoft Access run-time libraries (which have significant size or resource requirements).

Because this solution transforms your project from a Visual Basic program to a Microsoft Access application, the technique goes beyond the Visual-Basic-centric scope of this book. However, much of what this book discusses—particularly the information about querying and Data Access Objects (DAO)—pertains to development in Microsoft Access.

Note: You can get more information on what's included in the Microsoft Office Developer Edition by visiting the Microsoft Office Developer Forum online at **http://www.microsoft.com/OfficeDev/Default.htm**.

Running Access Reports Using Automation   You can use a technology known as Automation to launch an instance of Microsoft Access from your Visual Basic application. Using this technique, you can program Microsoft Access the same way you program other objects (such as Data Access Objects or an ActiveX control) in Visual Basic.

The disadvantage of this technique is that it forces users to run an instance of Microsoft Access every time they want to view or print a report. It obviously also requires that they have Microsoft Access loaded on their machines. If you are interested in overcoming these drawbacks but you still want to use Access reports as part of your Visual Basic application, you might consider a reporting solution based on VideoSoft VSREPORTS, discussed later in the section "Running Access Reports Using VideoSoft VSREPORTS."

To program Microsoft Access through Automation, you begin by making a reference to Access in your Visual Basic application. Do this by using the Project References menu to make a reference to Microsoft Access 8.0 Object Library, as shown in Figure 4.5.

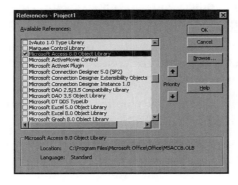

Figure 4.5: Making a reference to the Microsoft Access Object Library for Automation.

Bear in mind that the Microsoft Access 8.0 Object Library creates a reference to Microsoft Access 97. If you're using an earlier version of Access, you can still use Automation; however, the object library will be called something else.

Avoiding Early Binding with Automation   You might be familiar with Automation from the days when it was called OLE Automation; most of the techniques described in this section worked way back in the days of Visual Basic 3.0 and Microsoft Access 2.0.

If you've used Automation before, you should know that there is one important difference between the Automation technique described in this section and the Automation technique you might be familiar with: In Visual Basic 5.0, you want to avoid defining Automation objects as the generic Object data type. For example, in Visual Basic 3.0, you might write a ton of code that looks like this:

```
Dim appAccess As Object
Set appAccess = CreateObject("Access.Application")
```

This code worked fine in Visual Basic 3.0, and it still works, but there's a better way to do it now. Instead of using the generic Object data type, you should define the Automation object as whatever object data type the Automation server provides—*Access.Application*, in the case of Microsoft Access. Making an explicit reference to the object server's library, then explicitly creating objects using its data types is more efficient. This is because Visual Basic doesn't have to run a query on the Automation server each time you access it in an attempt to determine what kind of object you're trying to create. This technique, known as *late binding*, is now appropriate in only two situations:

▶ You don't know what kind of Automation server object your application is going to create when writing the code (a situation which will probably occur extremely rarely, if ever).

▶ You're using an application development environment that does not support early binding.

Because Visual Basic *does* support early binding, the use of late binding in modern Visual Basic applications happens very infrequently. In fact, it makes sense for you to upgrade your existing Visual Basic applications to take advantage of early binding—particularly for processor-intensive calls to Microsoft Office Automation servers—because of the performance benefits provided by early binding.

Note: For a more in-depth discussion on the difference between late and early binding in Automation, as well as a plethora of information on other aspects of interprocess communication in Windows, check out Dan Appleman's *Developing ActiveX Components with Visual Basic 5.0* (Ziff-Davis Press, 1997).

Running Automation Code to Control Microsoft Access   After creating a reference to Microsoft Access from within your Visual Basic application, you can start writing code to instantiate objects provided by it. You'll notice that after you make a reference to an external object server, Visual Basic integrates that server's object model into the Auto List Members feature.

Because programming against hostile, alien object models can be such a daunting task, integration into Auto List Members is a beautiful thing, as Figure 4.6 illustrates.

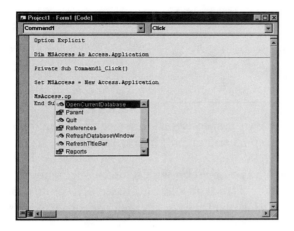

Figure 4.6: Viewing members of the Microsoft Access object model with Visual Basic's Auto List Members feature.

Note: Remember, too, that you can view all the members of a hostile, alien object model by using Visual Basic's object browser.

Listing 4.1 shows how to create an instance of Microsoft Access from within Visual Basic. This code uses Automation to execute methods of Access' DoCmd object; this object is used to issue commands to the Microsoft Access application through Automation.

Listing 4.1: Programming Microsoft Access from Visual Basic using Automation

```
' References MS Access 8.0 Object Library (this
' code will work with any version of Access that
' supports Automation)

Dim MSAccess As Access.Application
'


Private Sub Command1_Click()

    Set MSAccess = New Access.Application

    MSAccess.OpenCurrentDatabase (App.Path & "\novelty.mdb")

    MSAccess.DoCmd.OpenReport "rptEmployees", acViewNormal
```

continues

Listing 4.1: Programming Microsoft Access from Visual Basic using Automation (Continued)

```
    MSAccess.CloseCurrentDatabase
    Set MSAccess = Nothing

End Sub
```

Note that the acViewNormal constant passed to the OpenReport method tells Access to open the report and print it immediately.

Knowing When to Use Automation with Access   Remember to consider the advantages and disadvantages of solutions based on Automation. The disadvantage of such solutions is that they require that users have Access installed on their computer. There is also a significant performance hit associated with launching the entire Microsoft Access application.

As an alternative to running Access reports through Automation, you can run reports created in Microsoft Access by using the VideoSoft VSREPORTS product discussed in the next section.

Running Access Reports Using VideoSoft VSREPORTS

You can use the VSREPORTS tool to run database reports created in Microsoft Access in your Visual Basic application. VSREPORTS is implemented in two parts:

▶ A conversion utility that takes an Access .MDB file and creates a report file from report objects stored in the Access database

▶ An ActiveX control that is responsible for opening the report file and running it in your Visual Basic application

If this architecture sounds familiar, it's because VSREPORTS is similar to Crystal Reports; with both systems, you must first create a report file, then add a control and code to your application to make the report file print. Each time you make a change in the basic report, you must save and redistribute the report file to users.

There are many differences between Crystal and VSREPORTS, however—not the least of which is the fact that Crystal Reports has its own report-writing facility, whereas VSREPORTS uses that of Microsoft Access. The product that is best for you is a matter of personal preference and feature-set robustness.

If you want to use Microsoft Access reports, one advantage of using VSREPORTS over the Automation technique described in the previous section is that users don't have to start a new instance of Access each time they run reports. In fact, with VSREPORTS, users don't even have to have Access loaded on their computers. This fact can come in handy if you're responsible for managing a large, database-driven organization with all kinds of users. If you can't be certain that users will have the latest version of Access on their computers, you can give them a VSREPORTS file that will work no matter what the users have.

> ***For more information*** VideoSoft frequently releases maintenance updates to its products to fix bugs and add features. You can read about the latest version of VSREPORTS and download a trial version from VideoSoft's Web site at **http://www.videosoft.com**. A trial version of VSREPORTS is also on this book's companion CD-ROM.

Converting Microsoft Access Reports Using VSREPORTS To begin the process of integrating a Microsoft Access report in your application, you first create a report in Microsoft Access, then run the VSREPORTS translator on it. The product of the translator is a file that you can use with the VSREPORTS ActiveX control inside your application.

There are actually two translator utilities:

▶ TRANS95.EXE, for converting reports created in Microsoft Access 95

▶ TRANS97.EXE, for reports created in Microsoft Access 97

These utilities are installed into the folder you chose when you first installed VSREPORTS.

Business Case 4.2: Creating an Application Using VideoSoft VSREPORTS In its ever-widening search to create custom software systems incorporating as many different types of technologies as possible, the human resources staff of Jones Novelties has begun to generate reports using Microsoft Access. The staff approaches you with the department's work, asking whether you can integrate the staff's report-writing work with its existing custom employee-tracking application. Because not every person in the human resources department has Microsoft Access on his or her computer, you determine that VSREPORTS is the ideal way to give everyone in the department access to the employee information reports.

The version of the Jones Novelties database in the Chapter 4 folder on the CD-ROM accompanying this book contains a report called rptEmployees. You can use the VSREPORTS translator to convert this report into a file that you can use in a Visual Basic application. To do this, follow these steps:

1 Locate and launch the Access 97 translator utility TRANS97.EXE. This file can be found in the folder where you originally installed VSREPORTS.

The translator launches, as shown in Figure 4.7.

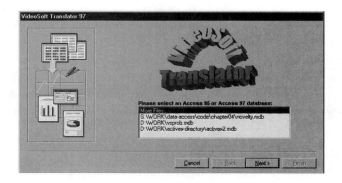

Figure 4.7: The VSREPORTS translator utility.

2 Double-click More Files to display a file dialog box.

3 From the file dialog box, select the version of the Jones Novelties database NOVELTY.MDB from the Chapter 4 folder on the CD-ROM that accompanies this book.

4 The translator opens the database and displays a list of reports. Choose rptEmployees, then click the Next button.

In the next step, the translator asks you to supply a path and file name for the output file. You can either choose the path and file name it suggests or choose your own. You can also change the output file name at this time.

5 Click Finish. The translator generates a .VSR file that contains the definition of your report.

Note: To run the translator under Windows NT 4.0, VideoSoft recommends that you apply Windows NT Service Pack 2 to your system (I applied Service Pack 3, which was the latest Service Pack as of this writing, and it worked fine for me). You can get the latest Windows NT Service Pack from the Microsoft Windows NT Server Web site, located at http://www.microsoft.com/ntserver/.

The VSREPORTS translator generates a *report definition file.* This file contains all the information used to print your report; you'll use the file in the next step to add the report to your Visual Basic application.

Running Microsoft Access Reports with the **VSREPORTS** ActiveX Control

Now that you've created a report file using the VSREPORTS converter, you can integrate it into your project. You do this by using the VSREPORTS ActiveX control. This control is invisible at run time; its sole purpose is to read and output .VSR files created with the VSREPORTS translator utility.

> **Caution:** It's important to understand that there are two versions of the VSREPORTS ActiveX control. The one that's installed on your computer by default, VSREPORT.OCX, is appropriate for use with Jet 3.0. Another version of the control, VSREP351.OCX, is appropriate for use with Jet 3.5. If you attempt to connect to a database and get the error message "ActiveX component can't create object," the problem is probably that you have the wrong flavor of the VSREPORTS control installed.

To install the DAO 3.5 version of the VSREPORTS control, do the following:

1 Obtain the VSREPORTS update files from the CD-ROM that accompanies this book, or from the VideoSoft Web site at **http://www.videosoft.com**.

2 Copy the file VSREP351.OCX to your Windows system directory.

3 Register the new OCX file using the regsvr32 utility. This utility is included with Visual Basic; it's on the Visual Basic 5.0 CD-ROM in the \TOOLS\REGUTILS folder. The command line to register the OCX file is as follows:

```
regsvr32 c:\windows\system32\vsrep351.ocx
```

You can execute this command line from the Run command located in the Windows Start menu. Also, note that the Windows system directory is not necessarily the same on all computers; for example, the file may be located in the \WINDOWS\SYSTEM directory if you're using Windows 95.

4 When you add the control to your project using the Project Components menu, you should see entries for two vsReport controls: one for the Jet 3.0 version, and another for the Jet 3.5 version. Choose the Jet 3.5 version.

For More Information   VideoSoft maintains an excellent and frequently updated Web page containing the latest technical information on VSREPORTS. The page is at **http://www.videosoft.com/faqrept.html**.

Business Case 4.3: Creating a VSREPORTS Solution   Now that you've created a report definition file from the Access report that the human resources department brought to you, you can integrate the file into your human resources application.

To do this, follow these steps:

1 In your Visual Basic project, use the Project Components menu to add the vsReport control to your project.

2 The vsReport control appears in your project's toolbox. Double-click the vsReport tool in the toolbox to add an instance of the vsReport control to your project's main form. This control will be invisible at run time, so it doesn't matter where you place it on the form.

3 Set the vsReport control's ReportFileName property to the name of the .VSR file you created previously. Then set the control's DatabaseName property to the name of your .MDB file. You can do this either in Visual Basic's property sheet or in code. Listing 4.2 shows how to do this with code.

Note: You'll notice that, annoyingly, the ReportFileName property does not provide a file name browse button, nor does the current version of the vsReport control provide a custom property page that enables you to browse files. Perhaps future versions of VSREPORTS will provide this functionality.

4 Execute the control's PrintReport method to run the report. You have the option of sending output either to the screen or to the printer, depending on the setting of the control's PrintDevice property.

When you've set up the application for print preview (that is, you've set the PrintDevice property to vsrPrintDeviceScreen), the report looks like Figure 4.8.

Figure 4.8: Example application containing the vsReport ActiveX control displaying a report written in Microsoft Access.

In this demonstration application, everything is done in code. Listing 4.2 shows the code behind the application's print and print preview features.

Listing 4.2: Code to Preview and Run Database Reports Using the VSREPORTS ActiveX Control

```
Option Explicit

' Requires Jet 3.5 version of VSREPORTS (vsrep351.ocx)

Private Sub Form_Load()

    vsReport1.ReportFileName = App.Path & "\rptEmployees.vsr"
    vsReport1.DatabaseName = App.Path & "\novelty.mdb"

End Sub

Private Sub cmdPreview_Click()

    vsReport1.PrintDevice = vsrPrintDeviceScreen
    vsReport1.Zoom = 50    ' Percent
    vsReport1.PrintReport

End Sub

Private Sub cmdPrint_Click()

    vsReport1.PrintDevice = vsrPrintDevicePrinter
    vsReport1.PrintReport

End Sub
```

Creating Advanced Reporting Applications with VSREPORTS   The VSRE-PORTS package has several other features that enable you to create more robust reporting applications. You can use these advanced features of the vsReport control to provide advanced functionality:

▶ *The Zoom property.* This property, demonstrated previously in Listing 4.2, enables you to zoom in and out by percentages. If your user interface allows it, you can let users determine the zoom percentage, giving them full flexibility to view the report the way they want.

▶ *Printer properties.* You can set the Collate, ColorMode, Copies, Duplex, Pages, PaperBin, PrintQuality, and PrintRange properties to control how the report is printed. You can also use the Device property to determine which printer will print the report, and the Port property to determine which printer port to use.

▶ *Support for browsing through multipage reports.* You can enable users to move from one page to the next in a multipage report by setting the PreviewPage property.

▶ *Integration with the DAO Database object.* Instead of assigning a DatabaseName to the control, you can assign a DAO Database object to the vsReport control. This solution might be appropriate if your application already uses DAO to get to a database and you don't want to make an explicit reference to the database from within the vsReport control. To assign a Database object to the vsReport control, you set the control's DatabaseAccessMode property to 1 - vsrDatabaseObject. You can then assign a DAO Database object to the DatabaseObject property of the vsReport control. Note that VSREPORTS version 1.0b includes the DatabaseAccessMode and DatabaseObject properties.

In addition to these properties, reports run with the vsReport control can trigger events, just like Microsoft Access reports do. This capability enables you to write code to respond to events that take place while the report is printing. The event model for the vsReport control is different than that provided by Access, however, so you'll want to prototype your existing Access reports carefully before attempting to port them to VSREPORTS.

> **Note:** Note that VideoSoft is hinting about providing support for HTML export in this product. As of this writing, the control's HTML export features were documented, but not actually supported in the control.

USING THE VISUAL BASIC PRINTER OBJECT

You can use the Visual Basic Printer object to print data from your database access application. This is the most code-intensive way of reporting database data, but it can give you more flexibility in situations where you need complete control over your printed output.

The Printer object is an intrinsic Visual Basic object; like the other Visual Basic intrinsic objects (such as the Clipboard, Screen, and Debug objects), the Printer object is always available to your applications. It is an abstract way to access the printer to which the user's computer is connected. It's helpful to think of the Printer object as a printed page; it has Width and Height properties, as well as other properties that enable you to print text and graphics.

Although it takes more code to create a database report using the Printer object, you gain access to your printer's entire feature set. You also don't have to distribute any additional files or purchase any third-party products, as you do with some of the other reporting solutions described in this chapter.

To create a custom output solution involving database access and the Visual Basic Printer object, follow these steps:

1 Determine the coordinate system you want to use with the Printer object.

2 Create a design layout for the report.

3 Use code to create a Recordset object.

4 Iterate through the records retrieved in the Recordset object, sending data to the Printer object using its properties and methods.

The following sections explore these steps in detail.

Setting Up the Printer's Coordinate System

You interact with the Printer object by assigning text and graphics to its coordinate system. The printer's coordinate system is an imaginary grid that divides a page into horizontal and vertical units.

You use the ScaleMode property of the Printer object to define the coordinate system used when you print. You can set the coordinate system to several English or metric-based measurement systems, or you can set it to a custom-defined system. The choice of measurement systems also determines the granularity of control you have over the page; a less granular system (such as centimeters or inches) gives you less control than a more granular system (such as twips or points).

By default, Visual Basic uses *twips* as the basis of its coordinate system; one twip is equivalent to 1/20 of a point, and 72 points equal one inch.

If you're an American who is familiar with desktop publishing software, you might be most comfortable using points to plot custom reports using the Printer object. If you're one of our international friends outside the Land of English Measurement, then you probably will prefer to use metric measurements. It doesn't matter what type of coordinate system you use, because the Printer object supports many different types through the ScaleMode property.

Table 4.2 shows the different settings for the ScaleMode property and what they mean.

Table 4.2: Settings for the ScaleMode Property of the Printer Object

Constant	Value	Meaning
vbUser	0	The coordinate system is user-defined
vbTwips	1	Twip (1/20 of a point or 1/1440 of (default) an inch)
vbPoints	2	Point (72 points to the inch)
vbPixels	3	Pixel (size varies according to the resolution of the user's screen)
vbCharacters	4	Character (120 twips per unit horizontally and 240 twips per unit vertically)
vbInches	5	Inch
vbMillimeters	6	Millimeter
vbCentimeters	7	Centimeter

Designing the Report

It's helpful to have an idea ahead of time about what your report will look like, because database reporting using the Printer object is the most code-intensive way to output data. So in addition to creating a written design that maps out what your report will look like (I've always been partial to graph paper for this kind of thing), you'll also want to create an *architectural* design for the report. The architectural design will determine exactly how your code will send data to the Printer object.

If you want to print your results in columns contained in boxes, you can create a subroutine (or, better yet, a class) that knows how to draw boxes exactly the way you like. Then you can call that subroutine or class each time you print a record. (For more information on classes and why they're useful, see Chapter 6, "Classes.")

Unless the code that you write always works right the first time it's run, you'll always find that devoting time to design pays off in the long run, when you have to debug and maintain your code. That goes for any software you write, but particularly for a code-intensive solution involving the Printer object.

Outputting a Recordset to the Printer Object

After you have your data in place and an idea as to how to construct it, creating the report becomes a matter of mapping data from a Recordset object to the Printer object.

The Printer object offers several properties and methods that can help you render data on the page and control the print job. These include the following:

▶ *The CurrentX and CurrentY properties* control the current print position on the page. CurrentX refers to the horizontal position on the page, whereas CurrentY refers to the vertical position. The position of everything you print is a function of these two values.

▶ *The Font object* of the Printer object controls the textual properties of text printed on the page.

▶ *The Print method* of the Printer object renders text on the page. Oddly, the *Visual Basic 5.0 Language Reference* doesn't list the Printer object's Print method, even though it's the Printer object's most important method; see business case 4.4 for an example of how to use it.

▶ *The NewPage method* inserts a page break in the print job; the *Page property* returns the current page of the print job; and the *KillDoc method* cancels a print job.

▶ *Graphics methods* such as Line, Point, and Circle can help you add organization and flair to the report.

▶ *The EndDoc method* sends the entire print job to the printer. You should execute this method at the end of a print job that uses the Printer object.

Note: The Printer object is an abstract way to communicate with the printer that the user has designated as his or her default printer (this setting is in the Printers control panel). If your application needs to get access to all the printers installed on a user's computer (for example, to present a list of available printers or to change the printer to which you're printing), use the Printers collection. However, as of this writing, there is a bug related to the Printers collection in Visual Basic 5.0; in some cases, when you try to change the current printer by using the Printers collection, the application prints to the default printer anyway. For more information on this bug and a (painful, involved, code-ridden) workaround, see the Microsoft Knowledge Base article at **http://support.microsoft.com/support/kb/articles/Q167/7/35.asp**.

Business Case 4.4: Creating a Custom Database Report Using the Printer Object   The database denizens of Jones Novelties have once again asked you to create a database report for the sales force. This time, they're interested in creating a report that prints data differently for every record. The report prints the names of salespeople who received a commission.

Because this job calls for a great deal of flexibility with respect to how data is presented, you decide to create a custom report using the Printer object.

To do this, follow these steps:

1 Start a Visual Basic project. On the project's main form, create a command button (or similar user-interface component). This button will enable the user to run the report. Use the Project, References dialog to create a reference to DAO 3.5.

2 In the Declarations section of the form, set up some module-level variables that will store some of the frequently used information in the project.

```
Option Explicit

' References DAO 3.5

' Printer object variables.
' All measurements are in *points*
' (72 points = 1 inch)

Private mlngTopMargin As Long
Private mlngLeftMargin As Long
Private mlngHeaderFontSize As Long
Private mlngBodyFontSize As Long
```

```
Private mstrHeaderFontName As Long
Private mstrBodyFontName As Long

' DAO variables
Private db As Database
Private rs As Recordset
```

3 In the form's Load event, initialize the module-level variables, set the Printer object's coordinate system to points, and create a DAO Database object. The Load event should look like the following:

```
Private Sub Form_Load()

    ' Set printer's coordinate system
    Printer.ScaleMode = vbPoints

    ' Set report defaults
    mlngTopMargin = 72
    mlngLeftMargin = 72
    mlngHeaderFontSize = 18
    mlngBodyFontSize = 12
    mstrHeaderFontName = "Arial"
    mstrBodyFontName = "Times New Roman"

    ' Open database
    Set db = Opendatabase(App.Path & "\novelty.mdb")

End Sub
```

4 Create a subroutine that prints the page header. This subroutine will be called at the beginning of each page of your report. The subroutine should look like the following:

```
Private Sub PrintHeader()

    ' Margins
    Printer.CurrentX = mlngLeftMargin
    Printer.CurrentY = mlngTopMargin

    ' Set font
    With Printer.Font
        .Name = mstrHeaderFontName
        .Size = mlngHeaderFontSize
        .Bold = True
    End With
```

continues

continued

```
Printer.Print "Employee Report"

' Draw a line under the title
Printer.Line (mlngLeftMargin, _
              mlngTopMargin + 24)-(Printer.ScaleWidth - 72, _
              mlngTopMargin + 24)

End Sub
```

5 Create a subroutine that opens a recordset and sends the data to the database one record at a time:

```
Private Sub PrintData()

    Set rs = db.OpenRecordset("tblEmployee")

    ' Set font
    With Printer.Font
        .Name = mstrBodyFontName
        .Size = mlngBodyFontSize
        .Bold = False
    End With

    Do Until rs.EOF

        Printer.CurrentX = mlngLeftMargin

        ' Note the semicolon here -- it tells the Printer
        ' object not to advance CurrentX and CurrentY to
        ' the next line
        Printer.Print rs!FirstName & " " & _
                      rs!LastName;

        Printer.CurrentX = mlngLeftMargin + 144

        Printer.Print Format(rs!SalesToDate, "$0.00")

        rs.MoveNext
    Loop

End Sub
```

6 In the Click event of the Print button, make references to all the subroutines you created, ending the code by executing the EndDoc method of the Printer object. The Click event should look like the following:

```
Private Sub cmdPrint_Click()

    ' Print page header
    PrintHeader

    Printer.CurrentY = Printer.CurrentY + 24

    ' Print data
    PrintData

    Printer.EndDoc

End Sub
```

To earn extra credit, you might modify this code by enabling it to print multipage reports. To do so, monitor the state of the Printer object's CurrentY property. When CurrentY gets to be within an inch or so of the ScaleHeight property, you execute the NewPage method of the Printer object, execute your PrintHeader subroutine again, and continue outputting records.

One of the obvious shortcomings of the Printer object technique for database reporting is that it's difficult to determine what the report will look like—or even how many pages it will take up—before it's printed. You might solve this problem by writing a print preview facility for your reporting application. Instead of developing a print preview feature from scratch, though, it makes more sense to use an off-the-shelf tool that is suited to the job. The vsPrinter control, described in the next section, fits that bill nicely.

REPORTING USING VIDEOSOFT VSVIEW

You can use VideoSoft VSVIEW to create reports using code similar to that which you'd use with the Printer object, but with a more robust programming interface and more features, including print preview.

VSVIEW is a suite of ActiveX controls that includes vsPrinter. Although the vsPrinter control is similar in some ways to the Visual Basic Printer object, it offers several additional features, including the following:

▶ Automatic text wrapping

▶ Printing headers and footers on each page

▶ Printing in columns

▶ The capability to arrange data in tables

▶ Automatic page numbering

▶ Print preview, including zooming

▶ The capability to save a previewed document to a file

For more information VideoSoft frequently releases maintenance updates to its products to fix bugs and add features. You can read about the latest version of VSVIEW and download a trial version from VideoSoft's Web site at **http://www.videosoft.com**. (The current version of VSVIEW as of this writing was version 3.0.) A trial version of VSVIEW is also on the CD-ROM that accompanies this book.

Printing Tables with vsPrinter

The vsPrinter control is well suited to printing database tables because it has explicit support for printing data in a row-and-column format. You can print data in this table by assigning data to the vsPrinter object's Table property.

To create a vsPrinter table, you first create a string that contains formatting information that determines how to print the table. This string determines the number of columns in the table, the alignment of text within each cell in a column, and the width of each column.

To denote the number of columns in a vsPrinter table, you supply the columns' widths in twips, or 20ths of a point (there are 1,440 twips to the inch). To denote the number of columns in a table, you separate the column measurements with a pipe character (|). You end the formatting string with a semicolon (;)—this is also the way you tell vsPrinter that you've come to the end of a row.

Note: You can change the meaning of the semicolon and pipe characters by altering the vsPrinter control's TableSep property. You might do so if you want your data output to display actual pipe characters or semicolons.

Table 4.3 lists the formatting characters you can use to set up a vsPrinter table.

Table 4.3: Formatting Characters Used in vsPrinter Tables

Character	Effect
<	Left-align the column
>	Right-align the column
^	Center the column
=	Justify the text
+	Center the column vertically
_	Align the text vertically along the bottom of the cell.
~	Don't wrap text in cells
!	Set a vertical border

For example, to set up a table that has three centered columns that are one inch wide, you use this formatting string:

```
^1440¦^1440¦^1440;
```

Business Case 4.5: Printing Data Using VideoSoft VSVIEW   The marketing staff of Jones Novelties wants to print a catalog of the company's rapidly growing inventory regularly, but lacks the ability to do so. Asking for your help, the marketing department requests a utility that is fast, easy to use, and flexible, envisioning that the company's needs could change over time. The department is also interested in saving the reports that it generates to a file for future reference.

You decide to address the problem by creating a printing utility using the vsPrinter control, contained in the VSVIEW package.

To create a printing utility using the vsPrinter control, follow these steps:

1 Create a new Visual Basic project.

2 Add the VSVIEW tools to your project by choosing Project, Components. Add a standard command button and an instance of the vsPrinter control to the project's main form. The interface should look like Figure 4.9.

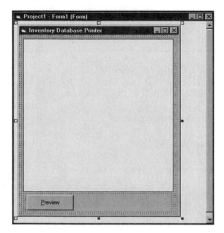

Figure 4.9: The user interface of the vsPrinter database reporting application.

3 By choosing Project, References, make a reference to the Microsoft DAO 3.5 Project Library.

4 In the form's Declarations section, create the object variables you'll need to access the database:

```
Dim db As Database
Dim rs As Recordset
```

5 In the main form's Load event, establish the connection to the database:

```
Private Sub Form_Load()

    Set db = OpenDatabase(App.Path & "\novelty.mdb")

End Sub
```

6 In the Preview button's Click event, enter code that renders the page on the vsReport control. Listing 4.3 shows this code.

Listing 4.3: Viewing Data in the Print Preview Window of the vsPrinter Control

```
Private Sub cmdPreview_Click()

  Set rs = db.OpenRecordset("tblInventory")
  vsPrinter1.Preview = True

  vsPrinter1.StartDoc
```

Listing 4.3: Viewing Data in the Print Preview Window of the vsPrinter Control (Continued)

```
vsPrinter1.MarginTop = 720   ' twips
vsPrinter1.MarginLeft = 720

With vsPrinter1.Font
   .Bold = False
   .Name = "Arial"
   .Size = 18
End With

' This is formatting information
strTable = "<2880¦<1440¦<4880;"

Do Until rs.EOF
   strTable = strTable & _
             rs!Product & "¦" & _
             rs!RetailPrice & "¦" & _
             rs!Description & ";"
   vsPrinter1.Table = strTable
   rs.MoveNext
Loop

vsPrinter1.EndDoc

End Sub
```

7 Run the application and click the Preview button. The data appears on the vsPrinter control, as shown in Figure 4.10.

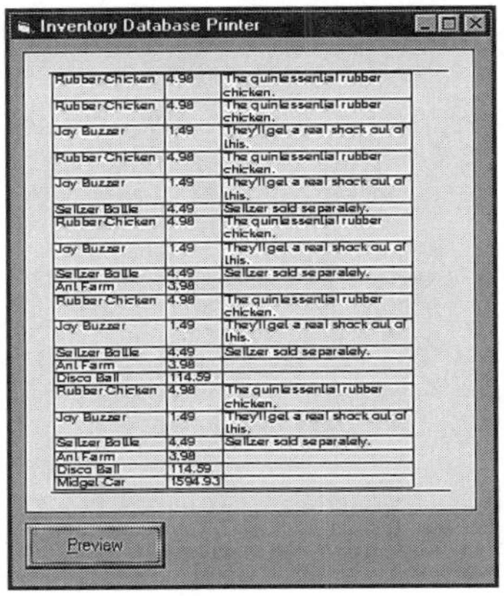

Figure 4.10: The print utility after the application populates it with data from the database.

8 To give your application the capability to save the documents it creates, add two command buttons to the form. Label one command button **Save**, the other **Load**.

9 In the Save button's Click event, add the following code:

```
Private Sub cmdSave_Click()

    vsPrinter1.SaveDoc App.Path & "\myreport.rep"

End Sub
```

10 In the Load button's Click event, add the following code:

```
Private Sub cmdLoad_Click()
On Error GoTo ErrHandler

    vsPrinter1.LoadDoc App.Path & "\myreport.rep"

Exit Sub

ErrHandler:
    MsgBox "The file 'myreport.rep' was not found.", _
           vbExclamation, _
           "File Load Error"
    Resume Next

End Sub
```

In the applications you build with the vsPrinter control, you'll probably want to give the user some way to choose the file name to save to, most likely by using the Windows file common dialog control.

Note also that when you save a report with the vsPrinter control, it's saved in a proprietary format that can be reloaded only through the vsPrinter's LoadDoc method.

EXPORTING TO TEXT FILES

Exporting database data to a text file in Visual Basic involves the following steps:

1 Use the Open statement to open a file.

2 Use the OpenRecordset method to create a recordset.

3 Loop through a recordset one record at a time.

4 Use the Print # statement to send data from the recordset to the text file.

5 Use the Close statement to close the file.

The next few sections give details on how you accomplish these steps.

Using the Open Statement to Create a File

To create a file on disk, you use the Visual Basic Open statement. The Open statement has many forms, including forms that enable you to read files and write binary files. But in this case, you're interested only in outputting text, so you use this form of the Open statement:

```
Open filename For Output As #filenumber
```

The argument *filename* is any valid file name, enclosed in double quotation marks.

The argument *filenumber* can be any number between 1 and 511; it's used as shorthand to identify the file later when you send information to it using the Print # statement.

> **Note:** In previous versions of Visual Basic, you could open only files numbered 1 to 255. See the discussion on the FreeFile function later in this chapter for information on how to access file numbers in the range 256 to 511.

For example, to create a file called CHEESE.TXT, you use the following code:

```
Open "cheese.txt" For Output As #1
```

At this point, the file is created and you can send data to it; in code, you refer to this file as file #1.

Using FreeFile to Determine the Next Available File

If your application outputs information in a somewhat linear fashion, you probably can design it so that it has a definite number of files open at a time. This is often the case in reporting and exporting applications, because the user probably won't want to export more than one file at a time.

However, your application might need to do file input and output for other reasons, so it's quite possible that it will have more than one file open at a time. In this case, you cannot use Print #1 for every file to which you write; you'll need to have a way of determining which file number is available.

The FreeFile function accomplishes this. When you call FreeFile, it returns the next available file number. If your application hasn't opened any files, this number will initially be 1.

Listing 4.4 shows an example of how to open a file with a file number generated by FreeFile.

Listing 4.4: Determining the Next Free File Number Using the FreeFile Function

```
Dim intFile As Integer
intFile = FreeFile()
Open "export.txt" For Output As intFile
```

Note that if you call FreeFile with its optional argument (the number 1), the function returns the next free file number in the range 256 to 511, as shown in Listing 4.5.

Listing 4.5: Using FreeFile's Optional Argument to Access Higher-Numbered Files

```
Dim intFile As Integer
intFile = FreeFile(1)
Open "export.txt" For Output As intFile
```

The two forms of the FreeFile function exist to maintain backward compatibility with previous versions of Visual Basic.

Using Print # to Loop Through a Recordset and Output

After you have opened a file for output using the Open statement, the next step is to create a recordset and send data from the recordset to the file using the Print # statement. Listing 4.6 gives a minimal example of how you can use this technique to print the names of all the items in your inventory.

Listing 4.6: Sending Information from a Recordset to a File Using Print #

```
Dim db As Database
Dim rs As Recordset

Private Sub Form_Load()

Set db = OpenDatabase(App.Path & "\novelty.mdb")
Set rs = db.OpenRecordset("tblEmployees")

Open App.Path & "\items.txt" For Output As #1

Do Until rs.EOF
    Print #1, rs!FirstName & " " & rs!LastName
    rs.MoveNext
Loop

Close #1

End Sub
```

Note: The syntax of the Print # statement is a little weird because Print # has been part of the BASIC language since the dawn of time. The key thing to remember about Print # is not to forget the comma between Print # and its textual argument.

Using Print # to Format Output   You have several options that enable you to format textual output with the Print # statement. Table 4.4 lists these options.

Table 4.4: Formatting Options Used with Print #

Setting/Operator	Meaning
Spc(*n*)	Insert a fixed number of spaces
Tab(*n*)	Insert the text at a fixed point in the row
Semicolon (;)	Do not break a line after the print expression

So, for example, if you want to print several database fields delimited by spaces, you might use code like this:

```
Print #1, rs!FirstName; Spc(1); rs!LastName
```

This can, in some cases, be more clear than doing the same thing with standard Visual Basic concatenation, which looks like this:

```
Print #1, rs!FirstName & " " & rs!LastName
```

If you want fields to start at a particular column in the exported text file, you use code like this:

```
Print #1, Tab(5); rs!FirstName; Tab(20); rs!LastName
```

This formatting expression exports the FirstName field at column 5 and the LastName field at column 20. (This means that there are five blank spaces at the beginning of each line.)

Using the Tab(*n*) expression to export data to a particular column in the text file should not be confused with embedding delimiter characters in the exported text. You use concatenation to embed delimiter characters in an exported text file.

For example, to create a tab-delimited text file, you use Print # expressions that look like this:

```
Print #1, rs!FirstName; Chr(9); rs!LastName
```

The expression Chr(9) is the BASIC way to denote the tab character; you must use the Chr function to do this because you can't type a tab directly into a concatenated expression.

One advantage of tab-delimited output is the fact that it can be readily imported into many applications. For example, when you open a tab-delimited text file in Microsoft Excel, it will recognize and convert the text file into spreadsheet format. If you need to send data to an Excel spreadsheet, creating a tab-delimited text file is far less processing-intensive than sending the data directly to Excel using Automation (which is described in detail later in this chapter).

Using the Close Statement to Close the File

You close a file using the Close statement. Closing a file indicates to the system that you're done sending output to it.

To close a file, you simply use the Close statement, followed by the number of the file you want to close.

```
Close #1
```

When your code is done sending output to a text file, it's important for the sake of efficiency to close the file explicitly using the Close statement. Visual Basic buffers the output you send to an open file using the Print statement; this buffer is not "flushed" (or completely written to the disk) until you execute a Close statement. So, in cases where you write a small text file to the disk and forget to use the Close method, the data in the file might not appear at all; the file will be created, but it will have a length of zero bytes.

Business Case 4.6: Exporting Data to a Text File   Jones Novelties is interested in saving "snapshots" of its sales data from one week to the next, so that the company's chief financial officer can create trend reports that show the company's performance over time.

However, other managers in the company use several different applications for creating reports; some choose to format and print data in Excel, some only care to view it in Word, and so on.

So, to provide the information in a format that is easy to understand and that makes everyone happy, you choose to create a utility that exports sales data to a text file. Because virtually any application understands how to read a text file, everyone has access to the data.

To do this, follow these steps:

1 Create a new Visual Basic application.

2 Add a command button labeled Export to the application's main form.

3 Make a reference to DAO 3.5.

4 In the form's Declarations section, include the following DAO declarations:

```
Option Explicit

' References DAO 3.5

Private db As Database
Private rs As Recordset
```

5 In the Click event of the command button, write the code that exports the text. Listing 4.7 shows this code.

Listing 4.7: Code to Export Sales Information from the Database to a Tab-Delimited Text File

```
Private Sub cmdExport_Click()

    Dim curProfit As Currency

    Set db = OpenDatabase(App.Path & "\novelty.mdb")
    Set rs = db.OpenRecordset("qryOrder")

    Open App.Path & "\output.txt" For Output As #1

    Do Until rs.EOF

        curProfit = rs!RetailPrice - rs!WholeSalePrice

        Print #1, rs!OrderDate; Chr(9); _
                rs!Product; Chr(9); _
                rs!WholeSalePrice; Chr(9); _
                rs!RetailPrice; Chr(9); _
                curProfit

        rs.MoveNext
    Loop

    Close #1

End Sub
```

Note that in addition to simply sending this file to a tab-delimited text file, this code performs a calculation on the data (creating a column that indicates the profit made on each sale). The query used in retrieving the data from the database is based on a join between the Order and Inventory tables; this enables the recordset to include price information and names of products, as well as information pertaining to the order itself.

To view the text file generated by this application, you can open it in Microsoft Excel. The latest versions of Microsoft Excel include a Text Import Wizard that recognizes text files and enables you to specify data types of information in delimited text files.

To do this, follow these steps:

1 Use the Visual Basic application you just created to generate the text file OUTPUT.TXT.

2 Launch Microsoft Excel.

3 In Excel, choose File, Open.

4 In the Open dialog box, change the Files of Type combo to Text Files, so the file dialog box displays text files.

5 Locate and select the file OUTPUT.TXT.

6 Click the Open button.

The Text Import Wizard runs, as shown in Figure 4.11.

Figure 4.11: Microsoft Excel 97's Text Import Wizard, which enables you to import text files intelligently.

7 The Text Import Wizard recognizes that this is a delimited text file and provides a preview of your data. Click the Next button.

8 The wizard recognizes that your data is delimited with tabs. (Pretty smart, this wizard.) Click Next.

9 The wizard displays your data in columns. At this step, you have the option to denote data types for each column. The first column, which contains dates, should be stored in Excel's date format. To do this, select the column by clicking it (if it hasn't been selected already), then choose Date from the Column data format panel. The wizard should look like Figure 4.12.

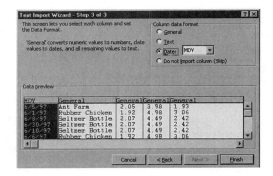

Figure 4.12: Using the Text Import Wizard to import a text file with a column containing dates.

10 Click Finish. Excel creates a new spreadsheet with your data in it. You can work with this spreadsheet the same way you work with any other Excel worksheet.

Exporting to HTML Web Pages

You can export from a database to an HTML file to produce Web pages from your database application. Because Web pages are really just text files, the technique you use to export to HTML is similar to the method you use for exporting to text (as explained in previous sections in this chapter).

You write procedures to export to static HTML files in the following situations:

▶ Several different types of users—potentially with different operating systems—are interested in viewing the data in a Web browser.

▶ You're interested in taking advantage of the features of a Web browser that are not offered by a plain text file, such as formatting, embedded graphics, and hyperlinks.

▶ You want to display information that does not become obsolete very often, such as an employee phone directory or the catalog of a company's products.

▶ You are uninterested in or unable to deploy Active Server Pages on your Web server—either because you're not running a Microsoft Web server, or because Active Server Pages just don't fit into your organization's scheme for presenting data to users.

HTML Export Versus Active Server Pages If you are interested in providing up-to-the-minute accuracy—that is, you want to give users access to "live" data through a Web browser—then the HTML export procedure described in this section might not be a good choice for you. You might instead consider a solution based on Active Server Pages (ASP), which does have facilities for enabling users to query data.

For example, if your company has a catalog of products to which you add new products once a month, you might consider exporting the whole catalog to HTML whenever you enter new data. Alternatively, you might write code that dumps only new or changed database records to HTML files; this solution is trickier to implement, but more efficient. Either way, with monthly updates, your data is probably stable enough to warrant using HTML export rather than ASP.

The biggest advantage of using ASP is that it can generate on-the-fly output in pure HTML, so that any user on any platform with any Web browser can view query results. The drawback is that you need to be using a Microsoft Web browser to use ASP. Additionally, users can update information only if you're running Microsoft SQL Server on the back end, and the development tool of choice for creating ASP (Visual InterDev) isn't very mature. (One drawback for developers who are accustomed to Visual Basic is that Visual InterDev is decidedly *un*-visual.)

For more information on developing Active Server Pages that connect to your databases, see Chapter 9, "Internet Database Applications and ActiveX Data Objects."

Creating an HTML Template To write a procedure that exports to HTML, it's helpful to have an idea of what you're shooting for before you write Visual Basic code. This is because when you export to HTML, you're using a query language (SQL) within a programming language (Visual Basic) to export to a document-markup language (HTML). When you live in this complicated world, things can get confusing quickly.

To reduce the confusion, start by creating an HTML file the way you normally would. This file will become the pattern, or template, that your Visual Basic program will attempt to re-create—in effect, a prototype.

When you're creating your template, use whatever HTML editing tools you feel comfortable with. There is no shame in using Notepad to create HTML files, particularly if you know what you are doing. In fact, Notepad's popularity as an HTML editor has caused it to garner the name "Visual Notepad." (The people who call it this are, of course, making a little joke.)

> **For More Information**   If you are new to this Web stuff and you don't understand how HTML works, never fear. It's not difficult to learn, and there are a million books out there that can help you get started. The best are written by the fabulous Laura Lemay; her Sams' *Teach Yourself Web Publishing with HTML 4.0 in 14 Days* (Sams.net, 1997) is a beautiful, thousand-page behemoth of HTML goodness.

Listing 4.8 displays the code for a typical HTML report template. Note that the parts of the data generated by your Visual Basic application, such as the date and time the page was exported as well as the actual sales data taken from the database, are inserted in the template in all uppercase letters. You'll replace these when you translate the template into Visual Basic code.

Listing 4.8: An HTML Template that Serves as the Design Prototype of Your Export Procedure

```
<html>
<head>
<title>
Sales Report - OUTPUT DATE
</title>
</head>

<body bgcolor="white">
<font face="Arial, Helvetica">
<p align=right><b>Jones Novelties Incorporated</b><br>
                                   Sales Report<br>
                    Last updated: OUTPUT DATE<br>
</font>

<hr>
<center>
<font face="Courier New, Courier">
```

continues

Listing 4.8: An HTML Template that Serves as the Design Prototype of Your Export Procedure (Continued)

```html
<table border>
<tr>

<!- these are column headers->

    <td>
    <b>Catalog #</b>
    </td>

    <td>
    <b>Product</b>
    </td>

    <td>
    <b>Units sold</b>
    </td>

    <td>
    <b>Wsle price</b>
    </td>

    <td>
    <b>Retail price</b>
    </td>

    <td>
    <b>Total profit</b>
    </td>
</tr>

<tr>

<!- database data goes here ->

    <td>
    CAT#
    </td>

    <td>
    PRODUCT
    </td>

    <td>
    UNITS
    </td>
```

Listing 4.8: An HTML Template that Serves as the Design Prototype of Your Export Procedure (Continued)

```
        <td>
        WHOLESALE
        </td>

        <td>
        RETAIL
        </td>

        <td>
        PROFIT
        </td>

    </tr>
    </table>

    </font>
    </center>

    </body>
    </html>
```

Figure 4.13 shows the template as viewed in a Web browser.

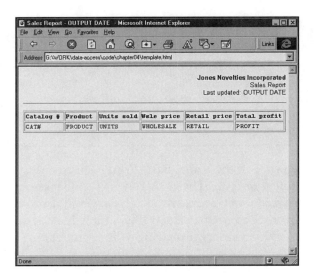

Figure 4.13: The HTML template file as viewed in a Web browser.

Writing Visual Basic Code to Export Data to HTML   After you have an idea of what you want your HTML file to look like, you can write the Visual Basic code to write it to disk. This is a process of dismantling the HTML file and putting Visual Basic code around it; the Visual Basic application you create takes care of everything having to do with database access and file handling.

> **Note:** As with most things, there is no one "right" way to write a procedure like this. However, if you export to HTML frequently, you'll find it helpful to place the HTML export code in a Visual Basic class module. Putting frequently used code into a class makes it extremely easy to re-use. You haven't learned about classes yet, so the following example doesn't use that technique. However, for more information on using classes to create export functions, see "Using Export Classes" in Chapter 6.

Listing 4.9 shows the code to create a minimal HTML file. This code contains everything except the part that involves database access.

Listing 4.9: Exporting a Minimal HTML File from Within a Visual Basic Application

```
Open "my-basic-file.html" For Output As #1

Print #1, "<html>"
Print #1, "<head>"
Print #1, "<title>"
Print #1, "Welcome to my HTML world."
Print #1, "</title>"
Print #1, "</head>"
Print #1, "<body bgcolor=#ffffff>"
Print #1, "This is my first HTML page created using Visual Basic."
Print #1, "</body>"
Print #1, "</html>"


Close #1
```

The default behavior of the Visual Basic Print # statement is to add a line break after each line it outputs. The HTML export code takes advantage of this behavior, producing files that are easy to read. However, if you want to include an additional line break after a particular line, simply include an additional Print # statement with an empty text string as an argument:

```
Print #1, "<html>"
Print #1, "<head>"
Print #1, ""
```

```
Print #1, "<title>"
Print #1, "Welcome to my HTML world."
Print #1, "</title>"
```

Similarly, if you don't want a line break, you include a semicolon after the Print # statement's textual argument:

```
Print #1, "<html>"
Print #1, "<head>"
Print #1, ""
Print #1, "<title>";
Print #1, "Welcome to my HTML world.";
Print #1, "</title>"
```

HTML ignores white space characters such as tabs and spaces. So if you use the formatting techniques described in the section "Using Print # to Format Output," the Web browser will ignore them when displaying your exported page. This is not to say that you shouldn't format your exported HTML code—white space in your HTML code can make it much easier to read. But remember that such formatting has no bearing on how the page displays.

Business Case 4.7: Publishing HTML Database Reports to the Web   Jones Novelties' chief financial officer likes the work you've done on exporting data to text files. But he's beginning to realize that this data is difficult for him to reach all the time. He travels a lot, and he works from home. He's now interested in seeing weekly financial report data on a Web page, so he can access it from anywhere, at any time, on any computer.

You decide to create an HTML export function that automatically copies its output to an HTML file that can be stored on the company's Web server. To do this, follow these steps:

1 Start a Visual Basic project. To the project's main form, add the Export button.

2 In Project References, make a reference to DAO 3.5.

3 In the Declarations section of the form, create the variable declarations:

```
Option Explicit

' References MS DAO 3.5

Private db As Database
Private rs As Recordset
```

4 In the form's Load event, open the database:

```
Private Sub Form_Load()

    Set db = OpenDatabase(App.Path & "\novelty.mdb")

End Sub
```

5 Create a subroutine that sets up the HTML page. This subroutine takes a string parameter that specifies the title of the document (which the browser's title bar usually displays). Because it is parameterized, this subroutine can be used with any HTML export procedure.

```
Private Sub HTMLPageStart(strTitle As String)

    Print #1, "<html>"
    Print #1, "<head>"
    Print #1, "<title>"
    Print #1, "<h1>"
    Print #1, strTitle
    Print #1, "</h1>"
    Print #1, "</title>"
    Print #1, "</head>"

    Print #1, "<body bgcolor=#ffffff>"
    Print #1, "<font face=Arial, Helvetica>"

End Sub
```

(This procedure works only if a file is open; you'll open the file later, in the Click event of the form's command button.)

6 Create a subroutine that takes data from a recordset and outputs HTML to the text file. Listing 4.10 shows the code that does this.

Listing 4.10: Code that Exports Data from the Orders Query to an HTML Table

```
Private Sub HTMLDataExport()

    Set rs = db.OpenRecordset("qryOrder")

    Print #1, "<table border>"

    ' Column headers
    Print #1, "<tr>"
```

Listing 4.10: Code that Exports Data from the Orders Query to an HTML Table (Continued)

```
Print #1, "   <td bgcolor=CCCCCC>"
Print #1, "   <b>Order Date</b>"
Print #1, "   </td>"

Print #1, "   <td bgcolor=CCCCCC>"
Print #1, "   <b>Product</b>"
Print #1, "   </td>"

Print #1, "   <td bgcolor=CCCCCC>"
Print #1, "   <b>Wholesale Price</b>"
Print #1, "   </td>"

Print #1, "   <td bgcolor=CCCCCC>"
Print #1, "   <b>Retail Price</b>"
Print #1, "   </td>"

Print #1, "   <td bgcolor=CCCCCC>"
Print #1, "   <b>Profit</b>"
Print #1, "   </td>"

Print #1, "</tr>"

' Export the data
Do Until rs.EOF
    Print #1, "<tr>"
    Print #1, "   <td>"
    Print #1, "   " & rs!OrderDate
    Print #1, "   </td>"

    Print #1, "   <td>"
    Print #1, "   " & rs!Product
    Print #1, "   </td>"

    Print #1, "   <td>"
    Print #1, "   " & rs!WholesalePrice
    Print #1, "   </td>"

    Print #1, "   <td>"
    Print #1, "   " & rs!RetailPrice
    Print #1, "   </td>"

    Print #1, "   <td>"
```

continues

Listing 4.10: Code that Exports Data from the Orders Query to an HTML Table (Continued)

```
        Print #1, "  " & rs!RetailPrice - rs!WholesalePrice
        Print #1, "  </td>"

        Print #1, "</tr>"
        rs.MoveNext
    Loop

    Print #1, "</table>"

    Set rs = Nothing

End Sub
```

7 In the Click event of the form's command button, write code that opens a file, calls the HTML-exporting subroutines, and closes the file:

```
Private Sub cmdExport_Click()

    Open App.Path & "\orders.html" For Output As #1

    HTMLPageStart "Jones Novelties - Orders"

    HTMLDataExport

    Print #1, "</center>"
    Print #1, "</body>"
    Print #1, "</html>"

    Close #1

End Sub
```

8 Run the application and click the command button. The HTML file ORDERS.HTML is created. When you open the file in a Web browser, it looks like Figure 4.14.

You could add many cosmetic and functional adornments to this application. For example, you could include hyperlinks with each product, so that when you click a product name, the browser loads a page of information on sales of that product; you could do the same thing with customer information.

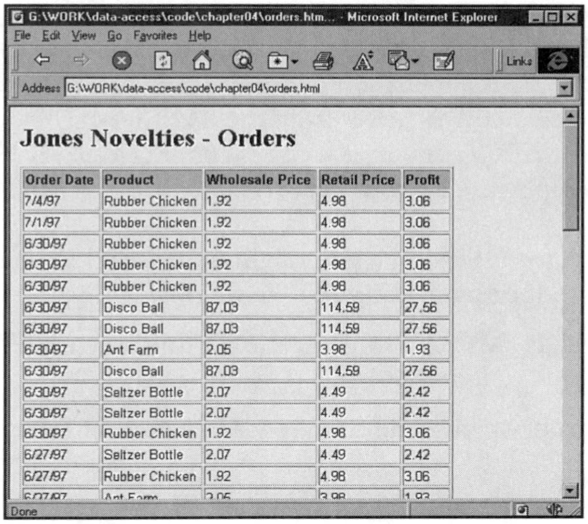

Figure 4.14: Database information exported to an HTML file viewed in a Web browser.

Sending Your Files to the Web Server If you are using the same local area network (LAN) as the computer you use, then putting your exported HTML files on the Web requires only that you copy them to the Web server's direcory. (For Microsoft Internet Information Server, this directory is any directory under the \WWWROOT directory.)

But if you don't own the server, you'll need to take a few extra steps to publish your exported HTML files on the Web. These steps usually entail sending the files to the Web server using Internet File Transfer Protocol, or FTP. You can use the Internet Transfer Control that comes with Visual Basic for this purpose; because it suffered from some bugs (that have since been fixed in Visual Basic Service Packs), I chose instead to use a third-party tool (the Mabry FTP Control) to upload exported HTML files to the Web server.

> **Note:** The Microsoft Knowledge Base has more information on the problems with the Internet Transfer Control. In a nutshell: upgrade to the latest VB service pack to resolve the problems. In the meantime, check out the Knowledge Base articles on the control at **http://support.microsoft.com/ support/kb/articles/Q168/7/66.asp** and **http://support.microsoft.com/ support/kb/articles/Q167/7/06.asp**.

Business Case 4.8: Publishing HTML Database Reports to the Web   Now that you have an application that exports data from your database to HTML, you can add a feature to your application that uploads it to a Web server.

If you have access to a Web server from the LAN to which your computer is connected, or if the computer you're using is running Web server software, this process is easy: Simply modify your export procedure so it sends data to a Web server directory.

But if you don't own the server, you might need to upload your exported HTML Web files to the server using FTP. To do this, follow these steps:

1 Start with the HTML export application in the previous HTML export example.

2 In Project Components, add a reference to Microsoft Mabry Internet FTP 5.0.

Note: A shareware copy of the Mabry Internet Control Pack, which contains the Mabry FTP Control, is on the CD-ROM that accompanies this book. You can also download the Mabry FTP Control from Mabry Software's Web site at **http://www.mabry.com.** You'll need to download and install the control before you can add it to your project.

3 Add an instance of the Mabry FTP Control to the application's form. This control is invisible at run time, so it doesn't matter where you put it.

4 Create a subroutine that uses the Mabry FTP Control to upload the file ORDER.HTML to your Web server. Listing 4.11 shows the code to do this.

Listing 4.11: Code to Upload the Exported Web Page to a Server Using FTP

```
Private Sub UploadFile()

    mFTP1.LogonPassword = "YOUR_PASSWORD"
    mFTP1.LogonName = "jeffreyp"   ' replace with your logon name

    mFTP1.Host = "ftp.sirius.com"   ' replace with a reference to your server
    mFTP1.SrcFilename = App.Path & "\orders.html"
    mFTP1.DstFilename = "orders.html"
    mFTP1.Connect
    mFTP1.ChangeDir "/public_html/orders"
    mFTP1.PutFile
    mFTP1.Disconnect

End Sub
```

5 Place a call to the UploadFile subroutine in the Click event of the Export button. The modified UploadFile subroutine should look like Listing 4.12.

Listing 4.12: The Code Behind the Export Button's Click Event, Modified so It also Uploads the Exported File

```
Private Sub cmdExport_Click()

    Open App.Path & "\orders.html" For Output As #1

    HTMLPageStart "Jones Novelties - Orders"

    HTMLDataExport

    Print #1, "</center>"
    Print #1, "</body>"
    Print #1, "</html>"

    Close #1

    UploadFile

End Sub
```

Now when the user clicks the Export button, the file is exported and uploaded to the Web server at the same time.

Exporting to Microsoft Office Applications

You can send database data to Microsoft Office applications from your Visual Basic application. You do this through a Windows technology known as Automation. Automation is a process that enables applications to communicate and exchange data with each other.

Note: Automation was formerly known as OLE Automation, in the days before OLE became a four-letter word.

To target an Automation server for database output, you go through the following steps:

1 In your Visual Basic project, set a reference to the object library of the Automation server you want to use.

2 Create an instance of the Automation server object in your Visual Basic application using the Dim and Set statements.

3 Dimension and set any subordinate objects (such as documents) provided by the Automation server.

4 Create a Recordset object that retrieves that data you're interested in exporting.

5 Send data from the Recordset object from your application to the Automation server using the properties and methods of its objects.

The exact code you use to create documents, enter data, and do formatting in a document depends on the Automation server's object model. This chapter gives examples for Word, but if you're creative, you should be able to set up procedures that will send data to any Automation server at all. Other Automation servers include all the Microsoft Office applications as well as some third-party applications (such as the drag-and-drop graphics application Visio).

Exporting to Microsoft Word

Because Microsoft Word is an Automation server, you can write Visual Basic code to send database data to it. The product of an Automation session with Microsoft Word is typically a Word document, although you can also use Word as a sort of print engine—creating a document with data stored in the database, then printing it. Through Automation, you can also use Word from within your Visual Basic application to perform nearly any task Word can handle.

You can access Word's programmable features because it is an *Automation server*. An Automation server exposes a set of objects (which in turn have properties and methods) that you can program. The way you do this is similar to programming against Visual Basic's own database object model, DAO, discussed in Chapter 3, "Data Access Objects."

To program Word as an Automation server, you begin by making a reference to Word in Project References.

Note: The examples in this section use the latest version of Word, Microsoft Word 97. Automation has been a feature of Word for a while, but only recently has it supported a robust object model. Previous versions of Word exposed a single object, the WordBasic programming language, which is similar to, but not 100 percent compatible with, Visual Basic. Word 97, on the other hand, has Visual Basic for Applications as well as a far more robust object model. The point is that if you're using an older version of Word, you might have trouble adapting the examples in this section to work with the version of Word you're using.

Business Case 4.9: Exporting Data to Word Through Automation In an effort to run you completely through the wringer, your taskmasters at Jones Novelties have asked that you once again reformulate the order reporting system so that it can generate Word documents.

To do this, follow these steps:

1 Create a new Visual Basic project. In Project References, make references to DAO 3.5 and the Microsoft Word 8.0 Object Library.

2 Create a command button on the application's main form.

3 In the Declarations section of the form, declare the following variables:

```
Option Explicit

' References DAO 3.5
' References Microsoft Word 8.0 Object Library

Private WordApp As Word.Application
Private doc As Word.Document
Private sel As Word.Selection
Private db As Database
Private rs As Recordset
```

4 In the Click event of the command button, include code to instantiate the object variables and send data to Word:

```
Private Sub cmdExport_Click()

    Set db = OpenDatabase(App.Path & "\novelty.mdb")
    Set rs = db.OpenRecordset("qryOrder")
    Set WordApp = New Word.Application

    WordApp.Documents.Add
    Set doc = WordApp.ActiveDocument
    Set sel = WordApp.Selection

    doc.Tables.Add Range:=sel.Range, NumRows:=1, NumColumns:=4

    Do Until rs.EOF
```

continues

continued

```
            sel.TypeText Text:=rs!OrderDate
      sel.MoveRight Unit:=12                ' 12 = next cell

      sel.TypeText Text:=rs!Product
      sel.MoveRight Unit:=12

      sel.TypeText Text:=rs!WholesalePrice
      sel.MoveRight Unit:=12

      sel.TypeText Text:=rs!RetailPrice
      sel.MoveRight Unit:=12

      rs.MoveNext
   Loop

   WordApp.Visible = True

   Set WordApp = Nothing

End Sub
```

You'll notice that many of the assignment statements in this code use *named arguments*. Named arguments are useful in programming complicated object models that have many properties and methods with a large number of arguments; instead of having to remember which argument comes in which order, you can instead name the argument directly.

When looking at Automation code, you might ask yourself how anyone is expected to garner information on the complicated object models exposed by Automation server, considering how many Automation servers there are in the world and how many interrelated objects they expose. There are two answers to this question:

▶ The least time-intensive solution is simply to make a reference to the Automation server and start writing code, allowing Visual Basic's Auto List Members feature to show you the objects, properties, and methods of each object in its drop-down list. This method is rather hit-and-miss, but it certainly works, particularly in a situation where you know what you want to do but you simply can't remember the proper syntax.

▶ If you're just experimenting, or if you want a fast track to a solution, you can do what you did when developing the code for business case 4.9, which is to run Word's Macro Recorder. The versions of Visual Basic for Applications that exist in the Microsoft Office applications today are so similar to the code used in Visual Basic 5.0, it's easy to exchange code between the two development environments. (The changes between the Macro Recorder version of this code and the version you see in this chapter mostly involve the declaration of object variables.)

For More Information If you're the kind of person who has to know simply everything about a component before you incorporate it into your application, you'll want to get your hands on the *Microsoft Office 97 Visual Basic Language Reference* (Microsoft Press, 1997). This reference has information on programming Visual Basic for Applications in Word, Access, Excel, and PowerPoint. Because the book weighs in at 4,192 pages, you can either use it to build cool applications or use it to bludgeon your neighbor to within an inch of his life; it's your choice.

SUMMARY

This chapter was designed to give you (hopefully) all the solutions you'll ever need for extracting data from database applications. The chapter didn't cover many new database concepts; rather, it provided practical applications of the existing database concepts introduced in previous chapters.

Bear in mind when reviewing the database solutions in this chapter that although the examples were all written using DAO, they'll work with minimal modification with other database technologies (such as RDO, introduced in the next chapter). This is because both DAO and RDO expose recordsets in a navigational model that enables your applications to iterate through recordsets from beginning to end.

QUESTIONS AND ANSWERS

Q. This chapter seems like quite the *tour de force.* It seems as if it has included information on virtually every kind of reporting and exporting technique available to a Visual Basic programmer. Are there any others?

A. No.

Q. Really?

A. Well, pretty much. Perhaps the chapter missed some things, such as graphing. (Most of the top third-party graphing packages provide database-aware ActiveX implementations, however, so they don't require code.)

After you see five or six different examples of iterating through a recordset, you pretty much get the idea of how to do it in any situation.

Q. I think Automation is the greatest thing since hairless cats. What are some drawbacks?

A. There are three main drawbacks: slow performance, unacceptably slow performance, and, occasionally, mind-bogglingly slow performance. I've done a bunch of work with Visual Basic applications that send data to Word through Automation (this was how my last book, *The Visual Basic Components Sourcebook*, was formatted; I've also used Automation to provide solutions for clients). Nearly every time I've attempted to write a serious application using Automation, though, I've run into situations where Word runs out of memory (complaining that there are "too many edits" in the document, even though the document I was creating seemed ridiculously small). The moral of the story is that when you're creating solutions involving Automation, be sure to test rigorously and save your work frequently.

Q. Can I use Automation with older versions of Microsoft Office applications?

A. Yes, although not all of the older Office applications support Automation in the same way. For example, Word didn't include Visual Basic for Applications until the current version, Word 97; to interact with Word, you had to create an instance of its procedural macro language, WordBasic. And the current version of Microsoft Outlook doesn't include Visual Basic for Applications at all (although you can program it as an Automation server). As Microsoft licenses Visual Basic for Applications to more and more vendors (which it is doing aggressively), your options for providing solutions involving third-party applications will continue to grow. You'll want to consult the documentation for the application you're interested in using so that you can determine the robustness and functionality of the object model it exposes.

Client/Server

How can I create a client/server database system that supports multiple users and a high level of traffic with good performance?

What tools can I use to maintain and work with a client/server database?

How can I use object-oriented programming methods to communicate with such a database from Visual Basic?

What special programming considerations must I take into consideration when taking my small-workgroup system and scaling it to client/server?

M any Visual Basic programmers' first exposure to database programming is through the Data control or Data Access Objects. As soon as
your database application grows beyond a few hundred records or a
few users, it's common to run into limitations. Multiuser contention for data,
poor performance, and lack of advanced data and server-management features cause many programmers to turn to a more heavy-duty architecture to
resolve their database problems. That architecture is *client/server computing.*

Client/server is not to be confused with multiuser computing, which Jet
supports just fine. In a multiuser architecture, a number of users share the
same data over a LAN.

In order to have a client/server architecture, you have to have some sort of
back end. This doesn't refer to the body part of a programmer who sits in a
chair for 18 hours a day; rather, it refers to a piece of software responsible for
retrieving and caching data, arbitrating contention between multiple users,
and handling security. While Microsoft Access supports multiple users, it's not
a client/server system because all requests for information are processed by
individual client computers. There's no intelligence on the other side of the
network that is responsible for processing requests and returning data.

If you have the Enterprise Edition of Visual Basic 5.0, then Microsoft SQL
Server 6.5, is your most obvious choice for a database back end, since SQL
Server comes along with VB. But bear in mind that most, if not all, of the
information in this chapter pertains to you, even if you aren't using SQL
Server. This is the case for two reasons:

▶ Most database back ends use a common language, known as Structured Query Language, or SQL, to access data.

▶ In Visual Basic, you most commonly access a database back end through Remote Data Objects—a database-independent method of performing client/server programming.

This chapter focuses on getting started with SQL Server and Remote Data Objects. It intentionally overlooks the emerging client/server trend known as three-tier architecture. This chapter's intention is to give you a whirlwind introduction to client/server using Visual Basic and SQL Server; the three-tier material is covered in Chapters 6, "Classes," 7, "Remote Database Access," and 8 "Multiuser Issues."

Also bear in mind that nearly all the techniques described in this chapter are exclusively for use with the Enterprise Edition of Visual Basic 5.0. The one exception to this is the ODBCDirect technique for database access, which is in some ways on the cusp between Data Access Objects' ease of use and Remote Data Objects' efficiency. ODBCDirect is specifically designed for developers who don't have the Enterprise Edition of VB5, or who are creating solutions in non-VB development environments (such as Microsoft Office VBA). This technique is covered in the section "Configuring and Using Open Database Connectivity (ODBC)" in this chapter.

THE DRAMA OF THE GIFTED SERVER PROGRAMMER

Here's a typical scenario: You're working as the member of a client/server development team. You have a database server that is 95 percent functional—which is to say that it isn't really functional at all. You still need to get your work done, but the server component of the application just isn't happening at the moment.

What's more, you may only have one or two server-side programmers at your disposal. Because server-side programmers tend to have the most rarefied set of skills, this tends to happen often in client/server development organizations. They're the hardest kind of programmer for companies to hire and retain, and as a consequence, they can be the most stressed-out bunch of people you'd ever see. Consequently, they are the hardest to get hold of when something goes wrong.

A big problem with this situation is that client-side programmers often can't get their work done until server-side programmers fix what's wrong with the server.

This is The Drama of the Gifted Server Programmer.

If you've ever been in a client/server development project involving more than two developers, you'll understand The Drama of the Gifted Server Programmer. One solution to The Drama is to prototype your client-side application using a mocked-up Jet data source first, then hook up your application to the server when the server is ready.

Placing one or more layers of abstraction between the client and the server is another tactic that keeps your client-side programmers from overburdening the server-side programmer. For the server-side programmer, that means exposing views or stored procedures that provide data services to clients; for VB programmers, it means creating ActiveX code components that do much the same thing. For information on strategies involving stored procedures and views, see the section "Using Stored Procedures" in this chapter; for more on ActiveX code components, see Chapter 7.

SETTING UP AND RUNNING MICROSOFT SQL SERVER

Running a true database server is a significant departure from sharing a Microsoft Jet database file. You have new things to worry about, new concepts to get your head around, and you don't get as much help from friendly user interfaces. (Although to its credit, Microsoft SQL Server is much easier to set up and maintain than its competitors.)

This section is intended to get you started with the bare minimum required to get a database up and running under SQL Server.

> **Note:** A development version of Microsoft SQL Server 6.5 comes with the Enterprise Edition of Visual Basic 5.0. This version gives you a full installation of SQL Server 6.5, but restricts you to 15 client connections. To create a production application using SQL Server, you'll need to obtain licenses for additional connections. For more information on upgrading your SQL Server installation to increase the number of connections, see the SQL Server Web site at **http://www.windows.com/sql/default.asp**.

Determining Installation Requirements for SQL Server

To install SQL Server 6.5, Microsoft says you'll need a Windows NT computer with a 486 processor, 16MB of memory, 80MB of hard disk space, a CD-ROM drive, and Windows NT 3.51 or later.

If you've actually tried to run SQL Server on a 486 computer with 16 MB of memory, you have my permission to stop laughing and resume reading now. The fact of the matter is that these specifications are minimum requirements for running SQL Server. SQL Server may very well run on a machine this anemic, but in the real world, the minimum requirement is the biggest, baddest computer you can realistically afford. This is supposed to be the computer that runs your entire business; scrimping on the hardware will only cause you grief later.

If there's one area you want to consider maxing out your computer, it's memory. Here's a totally anecdotal and unscientific example: The Windows NT Server used to build some of the examples in this chapter started with 56MB of memory. By the time the chapter was completed, I'd dropped an additional 128MB into the machine and it was running in a much perkier manner. This is definitely not to say that you need 184MB for development on an SQL Server machine; rather, you may want to experiment with different configurations and consider upgrading if the performance on your machine isn't what you'd like.

Note: Because this book is designed to be a survey of database-oriented solutions in Visual Basic, it doesn't drill down every possible SQL Server feature. If you're looking for a book that goes into more detail about how to use SQL Server with Visual Basic, check out Bill Vaughn's *Hitchhiker's Guide to Visual Basic and SQL Server* (Microsoft Press, 1997).

Installing SQL Server

After you've designated a computer for use with SQL Server, you can proceed with installation. The installation of SQL Server is fairly straightforward (double-click the program **setup.exe** in the **\i386** folder on the CD-ROM, if you're working with an Intel box). That is, the process is straightforward with a few minor exceptions:

▶ It takes a really long time.

▶ It asks you a lot of really weird questions that most conventional applications don't ask.

This book can't help you with the fact that it takes a long time, but it can give you some pointers about the questions posed by SQL Server's setup application.

First, the setup application asks you for location of the directory where you want to install SQL Server. This can be any directory on the server.

Next, setup asks you where you want to create a file called master.dat. This is a database file SQL Server uses to keep track of all of the databases it manages.

Accordingly, you want to install this file in a place normal users can't get to it (use Windows NT security to ensure this) and on a disk that is not coming close to running out of disk space (because 25MB is the minimum size for the master database).

The setup application then asks you about the code page and sort order you want to use. The *code page* refers to the set of alphabetic characters available to the application. Choose the code page that's appropriate for your international locale.

Sort order determines how data is sorted when it's queried from SQL Server. Unless you have some unusual requirement for sorting, choose the default case-insensitive sort order.

SQL Server supports a number of network protocols. In this step, simply choose the network protocol that your LAN users will be utilizing. If you're not sure which choice to make, you'll need to get in touch with your LAN administrator or check your network's settings yourself in the Network control panel.

You next determine whether SQL Server should start automatically when Windows NT is started. If you select this option, bear in mind that SQL Server will be started as a service from Windows NT. Services act as if they're part of the operating system; they don't appear in the Task Manager, and they can't be shut down like normal applications can. The next section gives more information on how to manage a service running under Windows NT, but you might also see "Controlling the Way SQL Server Starts Up" later in this chapter.

Starting and Stopping SQL Server Using SQL Service Manager

You use the SQL Service Manager to start and stop SQL Server. You do this in situations where you need to take down the server to perform certain tasks, or if you just don't want to run SQL Server on a particular machine (on a development machine, for example).

You don't have to stop SQL Server under normal circumstances. This goes along with SQL Server's role as an *enterprise* database system—the idea is that you're supposed to start it up and leave it running, come heck or high water.

Yet there are certain rare situations where you must stop the server to perform certain tasks, such as changing configuration options on the server or performing a hardware upgrade to the computer on which the server resides. When one of these situations comes up, you use SQL Service Manager to take down SQL Server and bring it back up again.

SQL Service Manager does not have to be running in order for SQL Server to do its work. The SQL Service Manager exists merely to give you control over the activation and deactivation of your server. After your server is in production mode, you probably won't often use SQL Service Manager.

When you launch it (by selecting its icon in the SQL Server program group), SQL Service Manager looks like Figure 5.1.

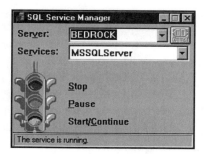

Figure 5.1: SQL Service Manager in its pristine state, in which SQL Server is running and all is well with the universe.

If SQL Server is running, the traffic light is green; if it's not running, the light is red. To start SQL Server, double-click the green light; to stop it, double-click the red light. It's really easier than making toast.

Controlling the Way SQL Server Starts Up   After you set up SQL Server, the operating system automatically launches SQL Server when your server computer is started. Through the Services control panel, you can control whether SQL Server always starts when your computer starts. To view the current state of SQL Server and control how it runs when your computer is started, follow these steps:

1 Launch the Windows Control Panel. Select Services from the Control Panel.

2 The Services control panel appears. Scroll through the list of services until you find MSSQLServer.

If you just installed SQL Server on your machine, the MSSQLServer service status is Started and its startup is Automatic. To stop the MSSQLServer service from the Services control panel:

1 Click the Stop button.

2 The control panel asks if you really want to stop SQL Server. Click Yes.

3 After a few seconds, SQL Server is stopped.

4 To restart SQL Server, click the Start button in the Services control panel.

Note: Starting and stopping SQL Server using the Services control panel is essentially the same thing as starting and stopping it from the SQL Service Manager, although you don't get to see the festive traffic light provided by the Service Manager.

Also notice that another SQL Server-related service, SQLExecutive, appears in the Services control panel. This service exists specifically to support the SQL Enterprise Manager application described later in this chapter. It's only activated when needed, so if you're not using SQL Server, you don't have to worry about it consuming memory on your computer.

Getting Started with SQL Server: The Basics

After it's installed, you have a number of minimum tasks to complete before SQL Server begins storing and retrieving data.

These basic steps are:

▶ Creating one or more disk devices

▶ Creating one or more databases on a particular disk device

▶ Creating tables in a database

▶ Creating views and stored procedures that govern how data is retrieved from a database

▶ Setting up user accounts and security groups

All the tasks you need to perform are described in this section; most can be handled without writing code by using the SQL Enterprise Manager utility in SQL Server 6.5.

Running SQL Enterprise Manager   You can perform many of the most common database configuration and setup tasks in SQL Server using a utility called SQL Enterprise Manager. Because of its power and ease of use, SQL Enterprise Manager is one of the most important additions to Microsoft SQL Server 6.5. The utility makes the database administrator's task easier by putting an easy-to-use graphical interface on a number of chores that were formerly accomplished (and can still be accomplished) using arcane SQL commands.

You launch SQL Enterprise Manager from its icon in your SQL Server program group. After you've launched it, you'll gain access to the SQL Server(s) available on your network. The following sections in this chapter describe some of the most common tasks you perform with SQL Enterprise Manager in a production application.

Creating a New Database Device Using SQL Enterprise Manager   Before you can start creating databases in SQL Server, you must first create a database device. A *disk device* is where databases reside in the SQL Server universe.

SQL Server makes you create disk devices in part because it's possible for a SQL Server disk device to span more than one physical hard disk. So you can have one *logical* disk device that spans multiple *physical* disks. This is an advantage because you can have a database that spans dozens of gigabytes; it also means that if one disk drive fails, you can still have access to data stored on other disk drives.

While it's possible to create database devices using SQL code, in SQL Server 6.5 it's far easier to create them using Microsoft SQL Enterprise Manager. To do this:

1 Select SQL Enterprise Manager from the SQL Server 6.5 Program Group.

2 The first time you run SQL Enterprise Manager, you must register your SQL Server installation. This lets SQL Enterprise Manager know which SQL Server you want to work with; it also lets you administer more than one SQL Server installation.

Note: In a new SQL Server installation, you have only one username, SA, and it has no password. You'll obviously want to change this situation at your earliest convenience, because a username without a password is like a Buick without a back seat. For more information on how to manage user accounts and security in SQL Server, see the section "Managing Users and Security" later in this chapter.

You register a SQL Server in the Register Server dialog box, shown in Figure 5.2. You only need to register a particular server once.

Note: If you're attempting to register a SQL Server running on the machine you're working on, use the server name (*local*), including the parentheses. If you're trying to connect to a SQL Server located over a LAN, it's easiest to use the Servers button to browse the servers available on your network.

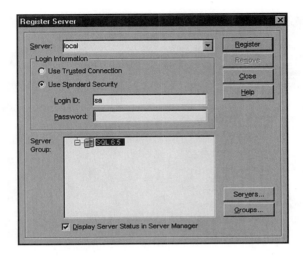

Figure 5.2: Microsoft SQL Enterprise Manager's Register Server dialog.

3 When you've registered the server you want to work with, click the Close button in the Register Server dialog. (You only have to do this once; after you've registered the server, SQL Enterprise Manager remembers how to connect to the server you want to work with.)

After you've registered your server, it appears in the Server Manager window (along with any other servers you may have also registered). On a machine with a connection to a local SQL Server, the Server Manager window looks like Figure 5.3.

Now that you've launched Enterprise Manager, you can proceed to create a database device. To do this:

1 In SQL Enterprise Manager's Server Manager window, open the Database Devices folder underneath your SQL Server.

2 You should see a number of default database devices (such as master and temp_data) that were created for you by SQL Server's setup application.

3 Right-click the Database Devices folder, then select New Device from the pop-up menu.

4 The New Database Device dialog appears, as shown in Figure 5.4.

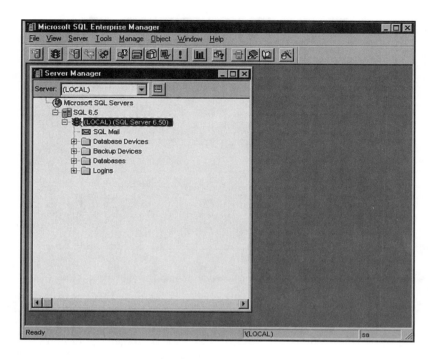

Figure 5.3: Server Manager window with a local SQL Server in SQL Enterprise Manager.

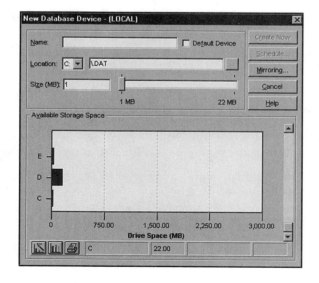

Figure 5.4: SQL Enterprise Manager's New Database Device dialog, which lets you create new database devices.

To create a new database device from the New Database Device dialog, follow these steps:

1 In the Name dialog box, type in a name for the new device; this can be any valid filename.

2 From the Location combo box, choose a disk drive on which the new database device will be stored. The graph at the bottom of the New Database Device dialog shows you which disks are available to you and how much free space each one has.

3 In the Size text box, select the size of the database device you want to create (in megabytes). Using the slider control (to the right of the Size text box) gives you an idea of how large your database device is going to be in relation to the amount of free disk space you have on the drive.

4 To create the database device immediately, click the Create Now button.

5 The database device is created. When you close the dialog, you should be able to see the new database device in the Database Devices folder of the Server Manager window.

Note: The Server Manager window of the SQL Enterprise Manager makes it easy to change how SQL Server runs. For example, if you want to make a database device smaller or larger, it's easy to do—simply double-click the device and change it in the dialog.

Scheduling the Creation of a Database Device   Because the creation of a new database device—particularly a very large database device—can take a lot of time, you may want to put off the creation of the new device for another time. If you don't want to create the new database device immediately, you can schedule it to take place automatically at a time you choose (for example, during a time when few or no users are accessing the database).

To schedule the creation of the database device for another time:

1 Click the Schedule button. The Schedule Database dialog appears, as shown in Figure 5.5.

2 Click the One Time button.

3 In the text boxes, specify the date and time you want SQL Server to create the database device, then click OK.

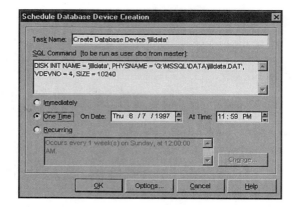

Figure 5.5: Scheduling the creation of a new database device in SQL Enterprise Manager.

Note: The Schedule dialog has an interesting side-effect: It displays the SQL command that will be executed to create the new database device. Does this mean that it's possible to create new database devices by issuing SQL commands to the server in ISQL/w? Yes, but even experienced database administrators tend to forget the syntax of the SQL DISK INIT command. Unless you have a photographic memory for arcane SQL syntax, or you want to create a more sophisticated type of database device (such as the kind that spans multiple physical disks) you'll probably want to stick with the graphical way of creating database devices provided by SQL Enterprise Manager.

Designating a Database Device as the Default   It's important to designate a particular database device as the *default database device*. This is because the default database device is initially master, which is the device SQL Server uses for its own administrative purposes. If you don't change this, it's possible your new databases will accidentally be created on the master device. Changing the default database device from master to a database device of your own should be one of your first orders of business in a new SQL Server installation.

At any time during the device's existence, designate it as the default database device.

To create a new database device and designate it as the default, click the Default Device check box in the New Database Device dialog.

Or, to designate an existing database device as the default:

1 Double-click the database device in the Server Manager window.

2 The Edit Database Device dialog appears, as illustrated in Figure 5.6.

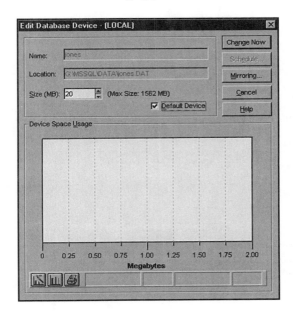

Figure 5.6: The Edit Database Device dialog box in SQL Enterprise Manager.

3 Click the Default Device check box, then click Change Now. The database device is set to be the default.

Creating a Database Using SQL Enterprise Manager

After you've installed SQL Server and created a database device, you're ready to get down to business. The next step is to create a database on a database device and begin populating it with database objects—tables, views, stored procedures, and so forth.

Although you can create databases using SQL code, it's easier to create them using SQL Enterprise Manager. This is because SQL Enterprise Manager lets you design the most common types of database objects graphically, shielding you from the complexity of SQL code.

To create a new database using SQL Enterprise Manager:

1 Right-click the Databases folder in the SQL Enterprise Manager's Server Manager window.

2 Select New Database from the pop-up menu.

3 The New Database dialog appears, as shown in Figure 5.7.

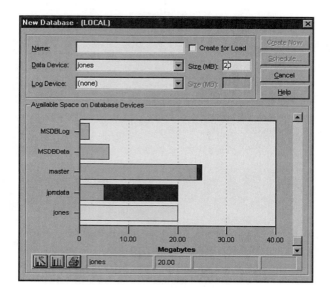

Figure 5.7: SQL Enterprise Manager's New Database dialog, showing the available database devices and how much space they contain.

4 Type the new database's name in the Name text box.

5 In the Size dialog, enter the size you want the new database to be in megabytes. The database can be as large as the database device it is stored on, but no larger. For your production databases, you'll want to make the database as large as you can to comfortably accommodate the data you're ever likely to store. You can increase the size of the database later, but it requires the intervention of the database administrator, which might prove inconvenient.

6 Click Create Now.

7 The new database is created and the New Database dialog closes. You should be able to see your new database in the Databases folder of the Server Manager window.

Note: You can schedule the creation of a database for an off-peak period the same way you can schedule the creation of a database device (as discussed in the previous section). You schedule the creation of a database by clicking the Schedule button in the New Database dialog.

Creating Tables in a SQL Server Database

In Microsoft SQL Server, you can create tables two ways. To create a table in a SQL Server database, you can:

▶ Use SQL data-definition commands (a technique introduced for Microsoft Jet databases in Chapter 2 and reintroduced here).

▶ Use a graphical utility included in SQL Server called SQL Enterprise Manager.

Both techniques have advantages and disadvantages. SQL commands are somewhat more complicated, particularly if you haven't worked with SQL extensively in the past; using SQL forces you to write and maintain code to create your database. Using the SQL Enterprise Manager, on the other hand, enables you to create a database structure quickly and easily, using all the graphical user interface advantages.

But some server programmers prefer using SQL code to create their databases, because they always have a written record (in the form of their SQL code) of what went into creating the database. The technique you use is a function of your personal preference, your organization's standards for development, and the kinds of database applications you're likely to create.

Using SQL Enterprise Manager to Create Tables in SQL Server   After you've created a database in SQL Server, you can use SQL Enterprise Manager to create tables in the database.

To create a table in a database:

1 In SQL Enterprise Manager's Server Manager window, click the database in which you want to create a table.

2 Two folders appear: Groups/Users and Objects. Right-click the Objects folder.

3 Choose New Table from the pop-up menu.

4 The Manage Tables dialog appears, as illustrated in Figure 5.8.

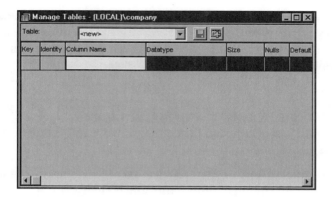

Figure 5.8: SQL Enterprise Manager's Manage Tables dialog, which lets you create tables in a database.

5 Start by creating a table to store customers. To do this, click in the column labeled Column Name in the Manage Tables dialog. Then type the name of the first field for this table: **FirstName**.

6 Press Tab to move to the next column, Datatype. In this column, make the data type a varchar. The varchar data type is generally used in SQL Server to store relatively small, variable-length string data.

7 In the next column, enter the number **50**. This limits the number of characters in a FirstName field to 50.

8 The Nulls column determines whether a field allows null values. If the box is checked, then null values can be entered into the field. For the FirstName field, the Nulls box should be *unchecked*.

Note: At this point, you might want to create a field that acts as a unique identifier for each record in the table. (In SQL Server, this type of field is referred to as an *identity column*.) Now is the time if you want to do this, because you can't create an identity column for the table after the table has already been created. This is because key fields cannot store null values, and you can only designate non-null fields in a table at the time the table is created. It's not as flexible as Microsoft Access in this respect, but it's the price you pay for the increased performance and scalability of SQL Server.

For more information on creating identity columns at the time the table is created, see "Creating Identity Columns" later in this chapter.

9 Enter field definitions and datatypes into the grid one at a time. When the table definition is done, it should look like Figure 5.9.

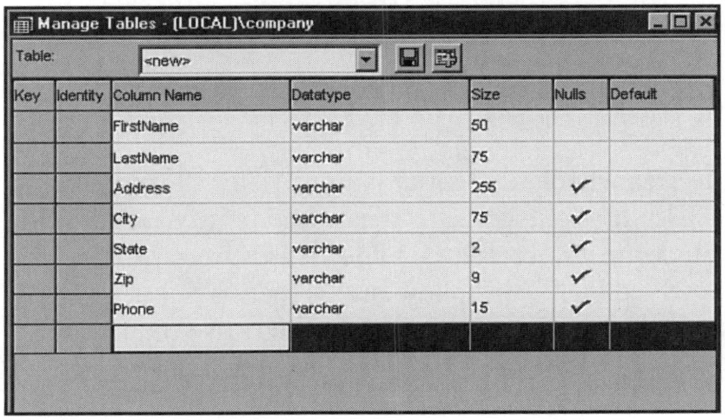

Figure 5.9: The Manage Tables dialog containing the field definitions for the new table.

10 When you're done designing the table, click Save at the top of the dialog.

11 The Specify Table Name dialog appears. Type the table's name in the box, then click OK.

12 The new table is created. You should be able to see the new table appear in the Server Manager window.

Creating an Identity Column to Uniquely Identify Records It's useful (although not required) for every record to have a piece of information that uniquely identifies it. Often, this unique identifier has nothing intrinsically to do with the data represented by the record. For example, nobody knows your driver's license number by looking at your face; it's a bogus number assigned to you to differentiate you from all the other Brad Joneses in the world.

The concept of an auto-numbering field in Microsoft Jet databases is introduced in Chapter 1, "Database Basics." SQL Server has an analogous concept known as an *identity column.* An identity column automatically assigns a unique numeric value for each record as the record is created.

A SQL Server identity column is in some ways more flexible than a Microsoft Jet AutoNumber field. Identity columns in SQL Server have the following properties:

▶ They can be of any numeric data type (in Jet, they can only be long integers).

▶ They can increment themselves by an amount you specify (in Jet, they can only increment themselves by one).

▶ They can start at a value you specify (in Jet, they always begin at the value 1).

There is one area where an identity column is less flexible than a Jet AutoNumber field: If you're going to create an identity column for a table, you must do it at the time you create the table. This is because SQL Server requires that any field created later must allow null values.

To create an identity column using SQL Enterprise Manager:

1 Open the database table's design by locating the table and double-clicking it.

2 The Manage Tables dialog appears; create a new field called ID. Make its data type int (remember that SQL Server integers are four bytes long, just like Visual Basic variables of the Long data type, so a SQL Server int is really a long integer).

3 Uncheck the Nulls box. This ensures that null values can't be inserted into this column; it also makes this column eligible to act as an identity column.

4 Click the Advanced Features button at the top of the Manage Tables dialog. This causes the bottom of the dialog to pop open.

5 In the Identity Column combo box, select the name of the field you want to serve as the identity column. Optionally, you can set values in the Seed Value and Increment boxes; these boxes govern where automatic numbering starts and by what value each successive number increases.

When your identity column has been set, the Manage Tables dialog looks like Figure 5.10.

Bear in mind when using identity columns in SQL Server that they're not guaranteed to be sequential. For example, if Kevin tries to create a record that is designated ID number 101, then Laura creates the next record (ID number 102), and Kevin's insert transaction fails, a record with ID number 101 is never created.

This may not be such a big deal, especially in a database application that never exposes the value of a primary key to the user, but remember that it is a possibility. If you use identity columns to give each record uniqueness, don't be surprised if you browse your data someday and you discover that there's no invoice number 101.

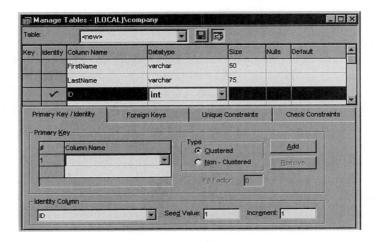

Figure 5.10: Creating an identity column in the Manage Tables dialog in SQL Enterprise Manager.

Using Other Methods to Generate Primary Keys   There's nothing that says you have to use Identity fields to generate primary keys in your database applications; in fact, there's nothing that says your tables have to have primary keys at all. You'll probably find, however, that having a primary key—even if it's a bogus value made up by the server at the time the record was created—is a really good idea. (This is because, as discussed in previous chapters on database design and querying, you need a primary key to do important things like joining multiple tables in queries.)

Some of the alternate tactics for generating primary keys include:

▶ Generating a completely random value in the primary key field for each record as it is created. This is the tactic used by tables containing AutoNumber fields that have been converted, or *upsized*, from Microsoft Access to SQL Server. This chapter's "Upsizing Databases to SQL Server" describes this in more detail.

▶ Storing a counter value in a temporary table, using that value to seed each new record's primary key column as the record is created. This involves creating a transaction that reads the counter table's current value and increments it in one swift operation. This technique has the advantage of providing a sequential numbering system that you have complete control over; the disadvantage (when compared to the simpler technique of creating an identity column) is that you need to write a stored procedure and add tables to your database to implement it.

▶ Deriving a key from cues given by the data; for example, the key for a record for a person named Richard Polito might be RP001. If another person with the initials RP comes along, the system would give that record the key RP002, and so forth. This tactic has the advantage of providing a key that isn't totally dissociated from the data, but it does require more coding on your part (in the form of a stored procedure executing as a trigger).

Marking a Column as the Primary Key   When you create an identity column, you'll almost certainly want to designate that column as your table's primary key. You can do that in SQL Enterprise Manager's Manage Tables dialog.
To designate a column as a table's primary key:

1 If you haven't done so already, open the Advanced Features section of the Manage Tables dialog by clicking the Advanced Features button.

2 In the Primary Key panel of the Primary Key/Identity tab, select the name of the column you want to serve as the table's primary key.

Note: You have the capability to designate multiple fields as a table's primary key; this is known as a *concatenated key*. You do this in situations where, for example, you want the first and last names of every person in the table to be unique. This would prevent the name "Amy Rosenthal" from being entered in the table twice, but it wouldn't prevent other people named Amy from being entered into the table.

3 Click Add. The primary key index is added to the table definition. The Manage Tables dialog looks like Figure 5.11.

You can only designate a primary key for a table once; if you change your mind, you have to drop the table and start over. Therefore, you want to designate a primary key at the time you create the table.

Note also that any field can serve as a table's primary key, not just an identity column.

Using ISQL/w to Access a Database

Microsoft SQL Server enables you to issue SQL commands to SQL Server through a utility called ISQL/w. With ISQL/w, you cannot only run queries, but perform updates, deletions, and other actions on records; you can also perform sophisticated database and server management tasks such as creating database devices, databases, views, and stored procedures.

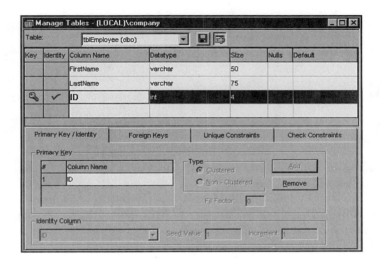

Figure 5.11: Designating a column as a table's primary key in SQL Enterprise Manager.

If you're familiar with the SQL syntax, getting started with ISQL/w is easy. (Mastering it, on the other hand, can be tricky—which is why many of the more complicated examples in this chapter rely on ISQL/w's more graphical little brother, SQL Enterprise Manager.)

To issue commands to the database using ISQL/w:

1 Launch ISQL/w from the SQL Server 6.5 program group.

2 ISQL/w launches, displaying the Connect Server dialog.

3 Choose the server you want to connect to, type in a username and password, and then click Connect.

4 The ISQL/w main window appears, as illustrated in Figure 5.12.

After ISQL/w has launched, you can begin issuing commands to the database in SQL. To make sure this is working properly, though, it makes sense to test the connection to the database before attempting to do anything else. You can do this by accessing the pubs database that ships with SQL Server. To do this:

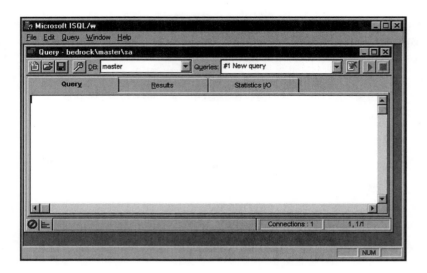

Figure 5.12: The main window of ISQL/w, which contains tabs for creating queries, returning results, and metering performance.

1 Tell SQL Server which database you want to use. To do this, use the USE command followed by the name of the database you want to use. In ISQL/w's Query tab, type the following command:

```
USE pubs
```

2 Execute the command by selecting **Query**, **Execute**, or by using Ctrl+E.

3 ISQL/w switches to the Results tab so you can view SQL Server's response. If everything worked properly, SQL Server responds with the terse message:

```
This command did not return data, and it did not return any rows
```

4 Return to the Query window by clicking it (or by using the keystroke shortcut Alt+Y).

5 You should be able to see the previous command you issued to SQL Server. Clear the window by selecting **Query**, **Clear Window** (or by using the keystroke shortcut Ctrl+Shift+Delete).

Next, you run a simple query against the pubs database to make sure it's returning data. To do this:

1 Type the following SQL code in the Query window:

```
SELECT *
FROM authors
```

2 Execute the query by pressing Ctrl+E.

3 If everything worked correctly, ISQL/w shows you the results of the query in the Query window, as illustrated in Figure 5.13.

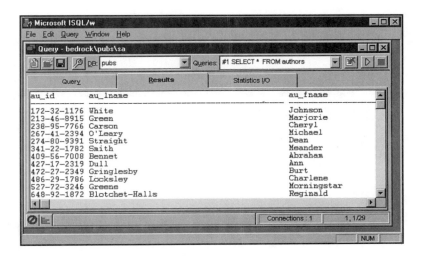

Figure 5.13: Results of a test query against the pubs database as displayed in the ISQL/w window.

Viewing All the Objects in Your Database Using sp_help   SQL Server enables you to see all the objects available in any database. The system gives you this capability through a *stored procedure*—a bit of code stored and executed on the server.

> **Note:** You can write your own stored procedures in SQL Server. For more information on this, see "Using Stored Procedures" later in this chapter. Also, while the stored procedures you create are usually local to an individual database, there are a number of other stored procedures provided by the system and available to every database in a SQL server. For another example of such a system-provided stored procedure, see "Displaying the Text of an Existing View or Stored Procedure" later in this chapter.

sp_help is the stored procedure that enables you browse databases. You execute sp_help the same way you execute any SQL query—entering it using ISQL/w's Query tab.

To get a road map to the objects in your database using sp_help:

1 Switch to the Query tab in ISQL/w; clear the query box using Ctrl+Shift+Delete if necessary.

2 In the query box, type the following:

```
sp_help
```

3 Execute the command. SQL Server responds by generating a listing of database objects similar to Figure 5.14.

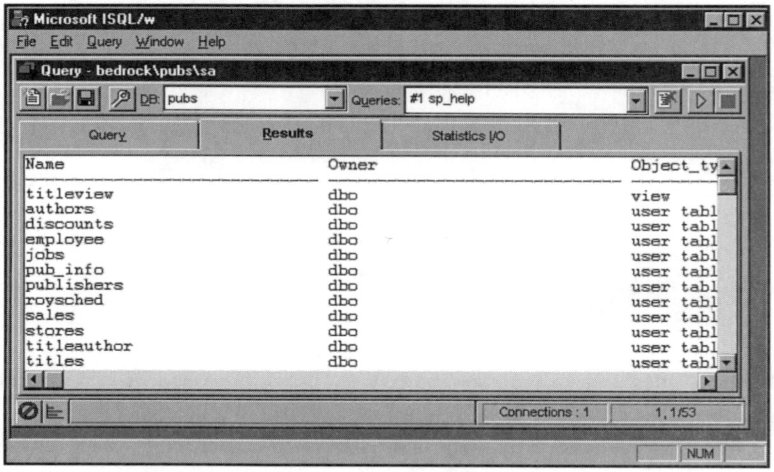

Figure 5.14: Typical response to an sp_help command for the pubs database.

Using an Existing Database   You can work with a particular database by executing the USE command in ISQL/w. When you designate a particular database with USE, all the subsequent SQL commands you issue are performed against that database. This is important to remember, because it's easy to inadvertently issue commands against the wrong database if you're not careful.

Note: Inadvertently issuing commands against the wrong database is one reason you should designate a database other than master to be your server's default database. (This is because only server configuration data should go into the master database.) You can change the default database at the time you create the database or anytime thereafter; the technique for accomplishing this is described earlier in this section.

For example, to switch from the master database to your company database:

1 In ISQL/w's Query window, enter the following code:

```
use company
```

2 If the company database exists, SQL Server responds by issuing this message:

```
This command did not return data, and it did not return any rows
```

3 If the database doesn't exist, you receive:

```
Msg 911, Level 16, State 2
Attempt to locate entry in Sysdatabases for database 'company' by name failed
- no entry found under that name. Make sure that name is entered properly.
```

Issuing SQL Commands to ISQL/w   You can execute any type of SQL command against a database by using ISQL/w. Using ISQL/w has a few advantages over other methods of sending commands to SQL Server. While it can be more difficult to remember SQL syntax than using SQL Enterprise Manager—particularly when using seldom-executed commands like creating databases—ISQL/w has the advantage of being interactive. It responds immediately to commands you issue. ISQL/w also has a number of features not offered by SQL Enterprise manager, such as the capability to run queries and stored procedures.

Chapter 2 discusses the syntax of most basic SQL commands you're ever going to want to issue against a SQL Server database.

Business Case 5.1: Writing a SQL Batch that Creates a Database
When a client/server database design is in development mode, it's common to write a SQL batch to create (and re-create) the database. Although writing a database batch to create your database design prevents you from taking advantage of the easier-to-use interface of SQL Enterprise Manager, it gives you a complete look at every command used to create every aspect of the database.

The intrepid developers of Jones Novelties, Incorporated have decided to take this approach to create the client/server version of their company database. The script they develop makes but a single assumption: that a database called company exists on the server.

Note: If you want to create the database under a name other than company, change the first line of code (the USE command) of the batch described here.

The database schema that comprises the company database is illustrated in Figure 5.15.

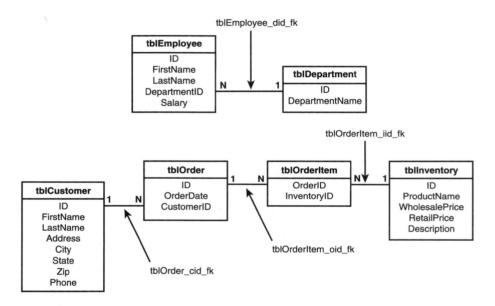

Figure 5.15: The schema of the Jones Novelties company database.

The batch that creates the database is executed in ISQL/w. In order to minimize bogus error messages, the batch destroys any old database objects each time it's run. This means that whenever you make a change in the design of the database in design mode, you can re-create the entire database from scratch by simply executing the entire batch again. This ensures that all the changes you've made in the database design get applied to the database each time you rebuild it.

The drawback of this technique, of course, is the fact that if you're not careful, the batch will wipe out all the tables in the database, and the data contained in the tables as well. You may want to consider disabling or deleting such scripts from your system after you have put your database server into production. Alternatively, you can simply let the script check to see if a table already exists before deleting and re-creating it.

> **Note:** While this section introduces the batch in chunks, the idea behind writing a SQL batch is to execute it as one big procedure. Accordingly, when you're writing batches in real life, dump the whole thing into ISQL/w's Query window (either by loading it from a text file or by copying and pasting) and hit the Execute button to run the batch. When you're developing SQL batches for use with ISQL/w, you can use that time-tested development environment known as Notepad to edit your batch. When you need to run it, copy it from Notepad and paste it into ISQL/w's Query window, then hit Execute.

To begin, your batch should switch to the company database. You do this with the USE command. Because this command is executed as part of a batch, you use the go command after it to indicate that this command should be executed before anything else happens:

```
use company

go
```

Next, begin creating tables. Before you create a table in a batch, however, it's a good idea to see whether the table you're about to create already exists. This gives you the ability to minimize bogus error messages when you run and re-run your database-creating batch. You can check to see whether a table already exists by querying the sysobjects table using the SQL EXISTS statement. If the name of the table is returned in the query on the sysobjects table, the table exists in the database, and should be dropped.

This batch checks to see if tblCustomer exists. If it exists, it checks to see whether it has a foreign key. If so, the batch destroys it.

```
if exists (select * from sysobjects
            where name = 'tblCustomer')
    begin
        if exists (select * from sysobjects
                    where name = 'tblOrder_cid_fk')
            begin
            alter table tblOrder
            drop constraint tblOrder_cid_fk
            end
    drop table tblCustomer
    end

go
```

Note: You can turn the EXISTS test around to prevent yourself from dropping a database that contains data. You typically do this in a production database where you don't want to inadvertently destroy a table that contains data. For a database that's in development mode, however, it's appropriate to drop the database unconditionally if it exists.

The code in this section of the batch checks for the foreign key definition tblOrder_cid_fk; the code attempts to destroy the foreign key constraint in another table, if it exists. This is done because referential integrity dictates that you can't destroy a table if a foreign key in another table refers to it.

Next, the batch actually creates the tblCustomer table:

```
create table tblCustomer
(
    ID               int identity,
        constraint tblCustomer_IDPK primary key (ID),
    FirstName        varchar(50)  not null,
    LastName         varchar(70)  not null,
    Address          varchar(100) null,
    City             varchar(50)  null,
    State            varchar(2)   null,
    Zip              varchar(9)   null,
    Phone            varchar(20)  null
)

print 'Creating tblCustomer.'

go
```

This code does a number of things in addition to simply creating the table. First, the batch declares the ID field as an identity column, meaning that it generates a unique number for each record. Next, it declares the ID column as the table's primary key. This provides an index for queries on the ID column.

The FirstName and LastName columns are declared with the not null qualifier; this ensures that it is impossible to insert null values into these columns.

Finally, use a print command to display a piece of text to the ISQL/w Results window telling you how far the batch has proceeded. This is a debugging tool that can help you determine where errors in your batch might be. Using the PRINT command has no direct bearing on the creation of the database.

Now that the first table has been created, create the other five tables in the database roughly the same way, using the code in Listing 5.1.

Listing 5.1: The Remainder of the SQL Batch that Creates the Tables in the Company Database

```
if exists (select * from sysobjects
          where name = 'tblEmployee')
    begin
    drop table tblEmployee
    end

go

create table tblEmployee
(
  ID            int identity,
    constraint tblEmployee_IDPK primary key (ID),
  FirstName     varchar(50) not null,
  LastName      varchar(70) not null,
  DepartmentID int         null,
  Salary        money       null
)

print 'Creating tblEmployee.'

go

if exists (select * from sysobjects
          where name = 'tblDepartment')
    begin
    if exists (select * from sysobjects
              where name = 'tblEmployee_did_fk')
        begin
        alter table tblEmployee
            drop constraint tblEmployee_did_fk
        end
    drop table tblDepartment
    end

go

create table tblDepartment
(
  ID               int identity,
    constraint   tblDepartment_IDPK primary key (ID),
  DepartmentName  varchar(75) not null
)

print 'Creating tblDepartment.'
```

continues

Listing 5.1: The Remainder of the SQL Batch that Creates the Tables in the Company Database (Continued)

```
go

if exists (select * from sysobjects
           where name = 'tblInventory')
    begin
    if exists (select * from sysobjects
               where name = 'tblOrderItem_iid_fk')
       begin
       alter table tblOrderItem
          drop constraint tblOrderItem_iid_fk
       end
    drop table tblInventory
    end

go

create table tblInventory
(
  ID               int identity,
     constraint    tblInventory_IDPK primary key (ID),
  ProductName      varchar(75) not null,
  WholesalePrice   money        null,
  RetailPrice      money        null,
  Description      text         null
)

print 'Creating tblInventory.'

go

if exists (select * from sysobjects
           where name = 'tblOrder')
    begin
    if exists (select * from sysobjects
               where name = 'tblOrderItem_oid_fk')
       begin
       alter table tblOrderItem
          drop constraint tblOrderItem_oid_fk
       end
    drop table tblOrder
    end

go

create table tblOrder
(
```

Listing 5.1: The Remainder of the SQL Batch that Creates the Tables in the Company Database (Continued)

```
   ID              int identity,
      constraint tblOrder_IDPK primary key (ID),
   OrderDate       datetime  null,
   CustomerID      int       not null
)

print 'Creating tblOrder.'

go

if exists (select * from sysobjects
           where name = 'tblOrderItem')
drop table tblOrderItem

go

create table tblOrderItem
(
   OrderID       int not null,
   InventoryID   int not null
)

print 'Creating tblOrderItem.'

go
```

Now that the tables have been created, your batch creates four referential integrity constraints on the tables. You use the alter table command to do this, as shown in Listing 5.2.

Listing 5.2: Referential Integrity Constraints Among Tables in the Company Database

```
alter table tblEmployee add
   constraint tblEmployee_did_fk
   foreign key (DepartmentID)
   references tblDepartment (ID)

alter table tblOrder add
   constraint tblOrder_cid_fk
   foreign key (CustomerID)
   references tblCustomer (ID)
```

continues

Listing 5.2: Referential Integrity Constraints Among Tables in the Company Database (Continued)

```
alter table tblOrderItem add
   constraint tblOrderItem_oid_fk
   foreign key (OrderID)
   references tblOrder (ID)

alter table tblOrderItem add
   constraint tblOrderItem_iid_fk
   foreign key (InventoryID)
   references tblInventory (ID)
```

Next, the batch creates a view that prevents unauthorized users from retrieving employees' salary information. The view accomplishes this by simply not returning the contents of the Salary column from the Employee table.

```
if exists (select * from sysobjects
            where name = 'qryEmployee')
drop view qryEmployee

go

create view qryEmployee
as
   select ID, FirstName, LastName, DepartmentID
   from tblEmployee

go

print 'Creating qryEmployee.'

go
```

Next, another view is created. This view simplifies the process of retrieving employees in situations where you want to retrieve both employees and department.

```
if exists (select * from sysobjects
            where name = 'qryEmployeeDepartment')
drop view qryEmployeeDepartment

go

create view qryEmployeeDepartment
as
   select e.ID, FirstName, LastName, DepartmentName
```

```
   from tblEmployee e, tblDepartment t
   where e.ID = t.ID

go

print 'Creating qryEmployeeDepartment.'

go
```

Next, the batch creates a view that enables you to access records in the tblCustomer table.

```
if exists (select * from sysobjects
            where name = 'qryCustomer')
drop view qryCustomer

go

create view qryCustomer
as
   select *
   from tblCustomer

go

print 'Creating qryCustomer.'

go
```

Finally, the batch populates the tblDepartment table with the names of the four departments in the Jones Novelties organization.

```
insert tblDepartment
   (DepartmentName)
values
   ("Administration")

go

insert tblDepartment
   (DepartmentName)
values
   ("Engineering")

go

insert tblDepartment
```

continues

continues

```
  (DepartmentName)
values
  ("Sales")

go

insert tblDepartment
  (DepartmentName)
values
  ("Marketing")

go
```

Remember, when you're using batches like this, feel free to run and re-run them whenever you want. The batch is written in such a way that it completely destroys and re-creates the database when it is executed—if you load sample data into your database during testing, you don't have to worry about that data inadvertently hanging around when you put your database into production mode. In addition, creating a database from a batch lets you easily migrate your database design to multiple servers. This enables you to have two physically distinct database servers, one for development and another for production.

Using Database Views to Control Access to Data

A *view* is a query definition stored in a database. It is conceptually similar to a query definition in the Microsoft Jet database engine, in the sense that it is a stored definition that resides in the database and gives client applications access to data.

You use views in situations where you want to give users access to data, but don't want to give them direct access to the underlying tables. The fact that a view looks exactly like a table to a client application gives you a number of advantages.

For example, when users access data through views rather than through direct access to tables:

▶ You can change the table's design without having to change the views associated with it.

▶ You can restrict the number of rows or columns returned by the view.

▶ You can provide simple access to data retrieved from multiple tables through the use of joins contained in the view.

Note that in order to take full advantage of views, you need to have a security strategy for your database. Security is discussed in this chapter's "Managing Security with Users and Groups."

Creating Views in SQL Enterprise Manager   As with many of the database objects you can create in SQL Server, you have an option to create views in either ISQL/w or SQL Enterprise manager. Both techniques are fundamentally similar; SQL Enterprise Manager's technique is slightly more graphical, while ISQL/w's technique is interactive, permitting you to test a view as soon as you create it.

To create a view in SQL Enterprise Manager:

1 From the Server Manager window, right-click the Views folder in the database you want to create a view.

2 Select **New View** from the pop-up menu.

3 The Manage Views window appears, as shown in Figure 5.16.

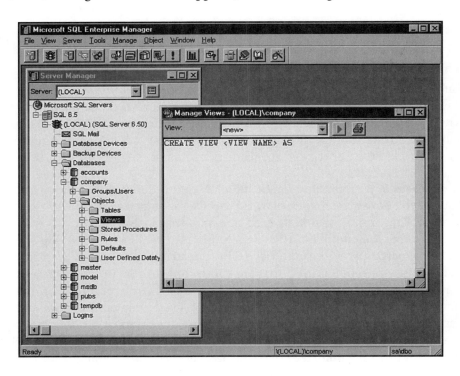

Figure 5.16: Creating a new view in SQL Server's SQL Enterprise Manager.

4 Replace the text <VIEW NAME> with the name of the view you want to create.

Note: If you're accustomed to dealing with Microsoft Access query definitions, you might want to use Access' naming conventions (prefixing the name of a stored query that returns records with the letters 'qry'). This makes it clearer to the client that what they're working with is a view rather than a table. Of course, you can use any naming convention you want, or none at all.

5 Enter the query statement shown in Listing 5.3 in the window.

Listing 5.3: A Basic Select Query that Sorts by Two Fields

```
CREATE VIEW qryEmployee AS
    SELECT *
    FROM tblEmployee
```

6 Click the Save button. The view is saved into your database and the Manage Views form is cleared.

The Save buttons in the Manage Views window and the other database object windows are different for your convenience—it isn't an inconsistency. The Manage Views window is set up to let you create a number of views rapid-fire. When you're done with one view, you can start creating another one immediately. When you're done with the Manage Views dialog, close it by clicking on its close button in the upper-right corner of the window.

Using Views in a Production Application   A view is designed to be a construct that lets you have greater control over the retrieval of data in your SQL Server database. This control manifests itself in a number of ways.

By limiting the number of rows or columns retrieved by the view, you control the data a particular user can retrieve. This can enable you to do neat tricks, such as create selection criteria that are known only to you, or lock out users from particular subsets of your data based on their security permissions. You can do this because each object in the database—including tables, views, and stored procedures—can be associated with individual users or security groups. In a database that takes advantage of views and stored procedures, direct access to tables is generally limited to the database administrator; client applications are limited to accessing views or stored procedures that are, in turn, responsible for retrieving data from base tables.

A Hide column is one of this technique's common applications. If the Hide column of a record is set to True, that row is never returned to a user; it's filtered out by the view that is responsible for retrieving the data from the database. Client applications never know that anything has changed, because they're always issuing requests to the same view.

Accessing databases through views, rather through direct access to tables, is an important component of any robust production SQL Server database installation. In addition to enabling you to limit the number of rows and columns retrieved, shielding your database tables with views gives you the capability to change things without breaking client applications.

This process of inoculating your database design from the change brought on by changing business rules can be taken a step further by introducing *middle-tier components*. Such components are philosophically similar to views and stored procedures in that they shield your database design from changes in your software application's mission, but they have advantages over views and procedures stored in SQL Server. Among these are the fact that they're easier to program, they return data in the form of objects instead of rows and columns, and they aren't tied to any one database management system or programming language. See Chapter 6, "Classes," for more information on such middle-tier components.

Creating Views Using an ISQL/w Batch   You have the capability to create views in ISQL/w. The process for doing this is similar to creating views in SQL Enterprise Manager, but in ISQL/w you have the advantage of being able to test your view immediately by running it.

To create a query in ISQL/w:

1 Enter the code in Listing 5.4 in the ISQL/w Query window.

Listing 5.4: A SQL Batch that Creates and Selects Records from a SQL Server View

```
use company
go

drop view qryEmployee
go

create view qryEmployee as
    SELECT *
    FROM tblEmployee
go

SELECT * FROM qryEmployee
```

2 Either click the Execute Query button, or select the menu command **Query Execute**.

3 The view is created and executed.

In addition to being an example of how to create a view using ISQL/w, this code also demonstrates another powerful technique you can use in ISQL/w—that of the batch. A *batch* is a series of SQL commands grouped together with the go command. You can see from the previous code example that the batch not only creates the view, but switches to the correct database and runs the view when it's done creating it. This confirms that the view is doing what you think it's supposed to be doing.

You create batches to simplify the process of creating database objects using ISQL/w; in most cases when you're creating database objects, you want to do more than one thing at a time. Dropping a table, creating a table, and then populating that table with sample data is a typical use for a SQL batch; checking to see if a user account exists, then creating that user account with a default password is another. There are many other uses.

Using Stored Procedures

While views give you a great deal of control over how data is retrieved from your SQL Server database, an even more powerful technique involves the use of *stored procedures*. A stored procedure is similar to a view, except that it gives you the capability to perform more complex operations on data.

For example, stored procedures let you:

▶ Sort data

▶ Perform calculations on data

▶ Take or return parameters

▶ Return data in a way that is easy and more efficient to program from the client side

None of these advantages are available with traditional views.

While this section is by no means an exhaustive description of all the commands available to you in the world of stored-procedure programming, it should give you enough information on how stored procedures work, why they're useful, and how you can incorporate them into your applications built on SQL Server.

Creating Stored Procedures in SQL Enterprise Manager You have the ability to create stored procedures in SQL Server's Enterprise Manager. To do this, follow these steps:

1 In SQL Enterprise Manager's Server Manager window, right-click on the Stored Procedures folder under the database with which you're working.

2 From the pop-up menu, select **Create Stored Procedure**. The Manage Stored Procedures dialog appears.

3 Replace the text <PROCEDURE NAME> with the name of the procedure you want to create.

4 Write the text of the procedure, as illustrated in Figure 5.17.

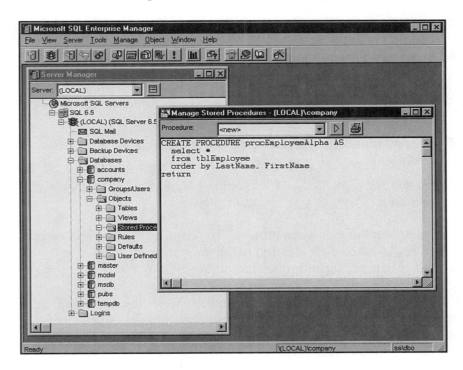

Figure 5.17: Creating a stored procedure in SQL Enterprise Manager.

5 When you're done with the procedure, click the Save Object button at the top of the Manage Stored Procedures window. As in the Manage Views window, saving a stored procedure doesn't close the window; instead, it clears the window so you can enter another stored procedure.

6 When you're done with the Manage Stored Procedures window, click on its close button in the upper-right corner.

Running a Stored Procedure from SQL Enterprise Manager   You can run stored procedures (as well as views and other SQL commands) from within SQL Enterprise Manager. This is helpful in situations where you want to test procedures or views you've created.

To test a stored procedure in SQL Enterprise Manager:

1 Select **SQL Query Tool** from SQL Enterprise Manager's Tools menu.

2 The Query window appears; it looks nearly identical to ISQL/w's command interface.

3 In the Query tab, type the name of the stored procedure you want to execute. For example, to execute the stored procedure you created in the last example, type:

```
procEmployeeAlpha
```

4 Execute the query by selecting the menu command **Query Execute** or using the keystroke shortcut Ctrl+E.

5 The procedure executes and (if there is any data in the table) returns a result set.

When you're done with the SQL Enterprise Manager Query window, click on its close button.

Creating Stored Procedures in ISQL/w   The steps to creating stored procedures in ISQL/w are nearly identical to the way you create them in SQL Enterprise Manager. The only difference is that ISQL/w doesn't set up the procedure's syntax the way SQL Enterprise Manager does.

To create a stored procedure in ISQL/w, you execute the create proc command. This command creates a procedure that returns data when given a numeric argument.

To do this, follow these steps:

1 In ISQL/w, enter the following code in the Query window:

```
create proc GetCustomerFromID
    @custID int
    as
    select * from tblCustomer
    where ID = @custID
```

This code creates a stored procedure called GetCustomerFromID. The procedure takes an argument, @custID, and returns a record for the customer that matches the @custID argument. (Because the ID field is tblCustomer's primary key, this procedure will always return either zero or one records.)

2 Execute the command. The stored procedure is created.

3 Return to the Query tab and test your stored procedure by running it. To run it, try to retrieve the first record in the table. Do this by typing the code:

```
GetCustomerFromID 1
```

SQL Server responds by returning the record for customer ID 1, as illustrated in Figure 5.18.

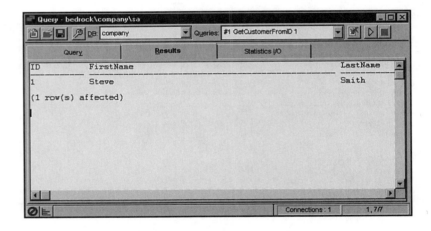

Figure 5.18: A single customer record returned by the stored procedure GetCustomerFromID in ISQL/w.

The procedure obviously only returns data if there is data in the table to retrieve.

Note: Be sure you've created the stored procedure in the company database. It's easy to forget to switch to the correct database (using the USE command in ISQL/w) before issuing commands against it. Creating stored procedures in SQL Enterprise manager makes it harder to commit this error.

Displaying the Text of an Existing View or Stored Procedure

You can use the stored procedure sp_helptext to display the code for a view or stored procedure. In order to display this data, you issue the command sp_helptext, followed by the name of the database object you're interested in viewing. The SQL Server processor then returns the full text of the view or stored procedure.

For example, to see a code listing of the view qryEmployee you created in the previous section on views:

1 In ISQL/w's Query box, type this command:

```
sp_helptext qryEmployee
```

2 Execute the stored procedure by using the menu command **Query Execute** (or the shortcut key Ctrl+E).

3 The query processor returns the code that comprises the view, as illustrated in Figure 5.19.

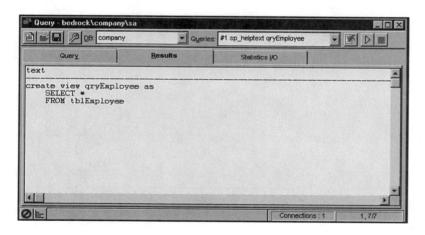

Figure 5.19: Displaying the text of a view using the stored procedure sp_helptext.

Creating Triggers

A *trigger* is a special type of stored procedure that's executed when data is accessed in a particular table. As a Visual Basic programmer, you can think of triggers as event procedures that execute when data is updated, deleted, or inserted into a table.

You generally use triggers when you need to do something complicated to your data in response to some kind of data access. For example, you might use a trigger to keep a log every time certain information in the database is changed, or you might use one to create a complicated default value for a field in a new record based on queries of one or more tables.

You shouldn't use triggers for simple defaults—instead, you should use rules. You shouldn't use them to maintain referential integrity—you should use SQL Server's inherent referential integrity constraint features for that. When you need to do something that goes beyond what's possible using SQL Server's feature set, you should consider using a trigger.

For example, you can use triggers to provide a unique value in a column to serve as a record's primary key; this tactic is used by Microsoft Access Upsizing Tools, which generate a random primary key for each record using a trigger. (Although you can use identity columns for this purpose, as discussed later in this chapter.) An example of the code generated for such a trigger by the Upsizing Tools is shown in code Listing 5.5.

Listing 5.5: A Trigger that Provides a Random Value for the Primary Key of a Record at the Time the Record is Created

```
CREATE TRIGGER tblCustomer_ITrig ON dbo.tblCustomer
FOR INSERT
AS
DECLARE @randc int, @newc int

SELECT @randc = (SELECT convert(int, rand() * power(2, 30)))
SELECT @newc = (SELECT ID FROM inserted)
UPDATE tblCustomer SET ID = @randc WHERE ID = @newc
```

Creating a random number to uniquely identify a record is by far the simplest technique for generating a primary key. This technique, however, suffers from two drawbacks. First, the primary keys are generated in no discernable order. This may seem like a cosmetic problem, but if you're trying to create an invoicing system, it's helpful to know that invoice 20010 follows invoice 20009.

The other, and potentially more serious problem, is the fact that there's no guarantee that the randomly generated primary key is actually going to be unique. This is because the trigger doesn't check to see if the random number it came up with has been used by some other record in the database. Granted, a random integer has a very small chance of being generated twice by the system (because a SQL Server integer data type is equivalent to a Visual Basic Long data type; that is, it is a four-bit whole number that can store values in the range of about negative 2.1 billion to about positive 2.1 billion).

Business Case 5.2: Creating a Trigger that Enables Soundalike Searches

In databases that involve queries on peoples' names, it can be difficult to deal with the problem of misspellings and homophones. Are you searching on Smith when the person spells it Smythe? Was it McManus or MacManus? If you have a last name that's the least bit unusual, you know what a problem this can be.

The intrepid database developers of Jones Novelties, Incorporated realize that they're going to run into this problem as well, so they decide to take advantage of a SQL Server function to resolve this problem. This function, soundex( ), converts a word into an alphanumeric value that represents its basic sounds. If you store the soundex value of a name at the time you create it, you can then search on the soundex value of the name in a query. The query returns more records, but it returns all the records that match the criterion.

Implementing this feature in the Jones Novelties company database requires several steps:

▶ Altering the tblCustomer table to accommodate a new LastNameSoundex field

▶ Running an update query to supply soundex values for existing records in the tblCustomer table

▶ Creation of a trigger that populates the LastNameSoundex field at the time the record is created or changed

▶ Creation of a stored procedure that returns all the customers whose last name sounds like a particular value

Begin by altering the tblCustomer table to accommodate a soundex value for each record in the database. Do this by issuing the following command to ISQL/w:

```
alter table tblCustomer add
   LastNameSoundex varchar(4) null
```

Next, run an update command that gives soundex values to records that are already in the database. You only have to do this once. Run the update by issuing the following SQL command to ISQL/w:

```
update tblCustomer
set LastNameSoundex = soundex(LastName)
go
select LastName, LastNameSoundex
from tblCustomer
go
```

Including the select statement in the batch after the update isn't necessary, but it's there if you want to confirm that the operation worked and see what data it changed.

Now you can create the trigger that will insert a soundex value for each customer as they're entered into the database. The code for this trigger should be entered in ISQL/w; it is listed in Listing 5.6.

Listing 5.6: An Insert/Update Trigger that Uses Soundex

```
create trigger trCustomerI
on tblCustomer
for insert, update
as
    update tblCustomer
    set tblCustomer.LastNameSoundex = soundex(tblCustomer.LastName)
    from inserted
    where tblCustomer.ID = inserted.ID
```

The reason this trigger seems a bit more complicated than it needs to be has to do with how triggers are executed. The rule with triggers is that they're executed once and only once, even if the insert, update, or delete that caused the trigger to execute is some kind of crazy batch process involving thousands of records. As a result of this rule, the triggers you write must be capable of handling a potentially unlimited number of records.

The key to handling the appropriate set of records in a trigger is to perform an update based on all the possible records that were changed by the procedure that caused the trigger to execute in the first place.

How does a trigger know what records were affected by this procedure? Triggers have access to this information through virtual tables called inserted and deleted. The *inserted* virtual table contains the record(s) that are inserted (or updated) by the procedure that launched the trigger; the *deleted* virtual table contains the data that is deleted by the procedure that launched a delete trigger.

Because the trigger you're building in this example is both an insert and an update trigger, referencing the records in the inserted virtual table sufficiently covers all the inserted or updated records, no matter how they were inserted or updated. Every record is assured to have a soundex value generated for it by the trigger.

Now that you have a bulletproof trigger that creates a soundex value for any record in your tblCustomer table, test it by inserting a record that fools a conventional query. Assuming you have a number of people named Smith in your database, the following insert command should suffice:

```
insert into tblCustomer (FirstName, LastName)
  values ('Abigail', 'Smythe')
```

You can confirm that the trigger created a soundex value for this record by immediately querying it back from the database:

```
select LastNameSoundex, LastName
from tblCustomer
where LastName = 'Smythe'
```

Now that you've confirmed that your trigger works, you can create a stored procedure that takes advantage of the LastNameSoundex column. This procedure takes a parameter—the last name of the person you're looking for—and returns all the people in the tblCustomer table whose names sound like the name for which you're looking. The code to create the stored procedure is in Listing 5.7.

Listing 5.7: Code to Create the LastNameLookup Stored Procedure

```
create proc LastNameLookup
  @name varchar(40)
as
select * from tblCustomer
where soundex(@name) = LastNameSoundex
```

Finally, you're ready to retrieve records from the database based on their soundex values. To do this, execute the LastNameLookup stored procedure:

```
LastNameLookup 'smith'
```

After executing this procedure, ISQL/w returns a result set composed of every person whose last name is similar to Smith in the database, including Abigail Smythe, as shown in Figure 5.20.

Managing Users and Security in SQL Enterprise Manager

One of the most important reasons you use SQL Server is to manage multiple users attempting to access the same data at the same time. Although a number of problems arise from this situation (such as users accessing privileged information and two users attempting to update the same record at the same time), you can resolve many of these problems with server-side settings.

Through its security features, SQL Server gives you a great deal of flexibility in determining who gets access to data.

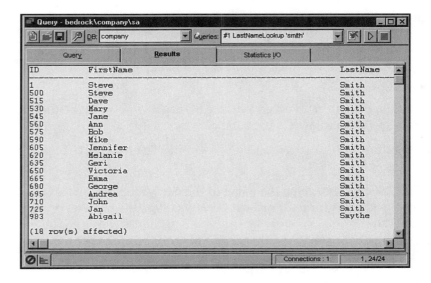

Figure 5.20: Result set returned by the LastNameLookup stored procedure.

Each database can have its own set of users, and each user can have his or her own set of permissions. A *permission set* gives users the capability to access and change data, and (if you choose) potentially create and destroy database objects themselves.

SQL Server's security also enables you to put individual users into groups to more easily facilitate the assignment of permissions. For example, you may choose to create a developers group that has permission to access all the objects in the database, a managers group that has the capability to access sensitive information about the company such as sales and salary information, and a users group for normal users without extrordinary permissions in the database. How you divide users into groups is up to you, but you should use groups even in a simple database in order to make it easier to manage access.

> **Note:** Another important multiuser issue pertains to *locking*, the process whereby no two users may access the same data in a table at the same time. For information on how locking works, see Chapter 8, "Multiuser Issues."

Managing Groups Using SQL Enterprise Manager   You can create groups in SQL Enterprise Manager, then assign permissions to the groups you create. After you create groups, you have the ability to add users to the group; any user added to a group inherits the permissions of that group. Changing the permissions of a group changes the permissions of all the users assigned to that group. That way, in order to add or revoke a large number of permissions for a particular user, you simply change which groups the user belongs to.

To create a group in SQL Enterprise Manager:

1 In SQL Enterprise Manager's Server Manager window, right-click on the Groups/Users folder for the database you want to alter.

2 From the pop-up menu, select New Group. The Manage Groups dialog appears.

3 In the Group box, type the name of the new group. The group you create here will be a group for ordinary users, so type the name **users**, then click on Add.

4 The new group is added to your database. Close the Manage Groups dialog by clicking on its Close button.

5 In the Server Manager window, you should be able to see your new group, as shown in Figure 5.21.

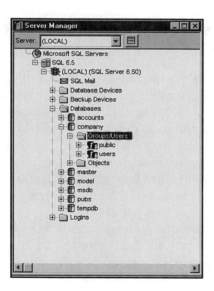

Figure 5.21: A new group in the Server Manager window of SQL Enterprise Manager.

Now that you've created a group, you need to assign permissions to it. To do this:

1 In the Server Manager window, right-click on the group you want to assign permissions to.

2 From the pop-up menu, choose Permissions. The Object Permissions dialog appears, as shown in Figure 5.22.

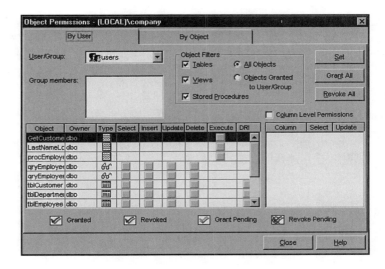

Figure 5.22: Using SQL Enterprise Manager's Object Permissions dialog to assign permissions to a group.

You'll recall from the discussion of views and stored procedures earlier in this chapter that it's a bad idea to give users direct access to tables. Accordingly, you'll use the Object Permissions dialog to revoke all permissions for the table objects in the database from members of the users group. To do this:

1 Scroll down the list of objects in the company database until you get to the table objects.

2 Click twice on each column (select, insert, update, delete) for the six table objects (Customer, Department, Employee, Inventory, Order, and OrderItem) in the database. Clicking on the permission column once grants the permission; clicking on it a second time revokes the permission (although the permission is currently "pending;" it isn't officially revoked until you click on the Set button).

3 Grant select, insert, update, and delete permissions to all the views in the database.

4 Grant execute permissions to the stored procedures in the database.

5 Click on the Set button to execute your permission changes.

6 The permission changes are executed. The Object Permissions dialog should look like Figure 5.23.

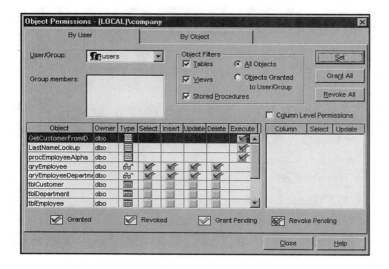

Figure 5.23: The Object Permissions dialog after you've secured the database.

7 When you're done with the Object Permissions dialog, click on its close button.

There are currently no users in the users group, so the permissions you've just applied don't mean anything yet. You'll create users and add them to the user group in the next section.

Creating and Maintaining Logins and Users   In order to have a security system that is robust and flexible, it's important to give users their own identities. SQL Server gives you this ability by letting you designate logins and users.

A *login* represents an individual human being who has access to your SQL Server.

You use logins to create *users.* Creating a user permits you to give a login specific permissions for a particular database. You can also add users to groups, in order to give them a broad group of permissions all at once.

If the difference between a login and a user doesn't make sense to you, think about it this way: A login is created at the server level. A user is created at the database level. You must have a login before you can become a user of a particular database.

Note: This chapter covers what SQL Server refers to as *standard security*; that is, security that is managed by SQL Server as opposed to the operating system. Standard security has the advantage of working in all types of SQL Server installations, and it is the default security mode for SQL Server. However, if your users utilize Windows NT, you have the option of using *integrated security*, in which users and groups are managed by Windows NT rather than SQL Server. This has the advantage of only requiring users to log on once—when they first turn their computers on each day. This type of security can also be easier to administer because it gives you a single place to manage everything having to do with users and groups.

You can use a utility called SQL Security Manager to make it easy to map Windows NT users and SQL Server users using integrated security. For more information on integrated security, see Chapter 8 in the *SQL Server Administrator Companion*.

To begin creating a user, create a login for an individual:

1 In SQL Enterprise Manager, right-click on the Logins folder at the very bottom of the Server Manager window. (Logins don't belong to any individual database; instead, they belong to the server itself.)

2 Select **New Login** from the pop-up menu.

3 The Manage Logins dialog appears.

4 In the Login Name box, type the name the person will use to log in. Optionally, enter a password and select a default language.

Note: In the client applications you build, consider establishing a procedure whereby a person can establish and change his or her password. You can implement this through the use of the sp_password stored procedure.

5 You can add this login as a user to a particular database at this time. To do this, click in the Permit column of the Database Access grid at the bottom of the Manage Logins dialog. The user is given permission to access the database in the public group, as shown in Figure 5.24.

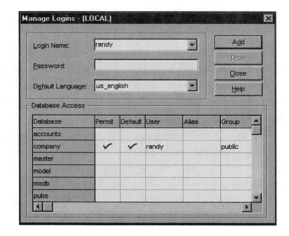

Figure 5.24: Creating a new login and adding user access to a database.

6 To add this user to a particular group other than public, select the group from the drop-down list in the Group column.

7 Click Add when you're done assigning this login to users in databases. The login is created, and any users you created for the login are added to the appropriate database. This is displayed immediately in SQL Enterprise Manager's Server Manager window, as shown in Figure 5.25.

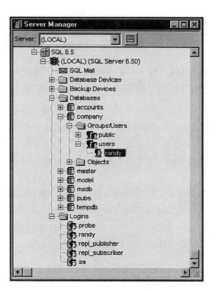

Figure 5.25: A new login and a new user displayed in the Server Manager window.

Testing Security Features in ISQL/w   You might be curious to see what happens when a "civilian" user attempts to use database objects for which he or she doesn't have permissions. Because ISQL/w lets you log in as any user, you can test how this works in the Query dialog of ISQL/w:

1 Log out of ISQL/w by choosing the menu command **File Disconnect**.

2 Use the menu command **File Connect** to log back in to SQL Server through ISQL/w. This time, rather than logging in as sa, log in as the user you created in the previous demonstration.

Rather than starting in the master database as you do when you logged in as sa, you're in the company database (or to whatever database your login defaults).

3 Execute the stored procedure sp_help. ISQL/w gives you a list of all the database objects in the company database.

4 Now try to run a query on a table you don't have permission to access. Execute the query:

```
select *
from tblCustomer
```

SQL Server responds with this message:

```
Msg 229, Level 14, State 1
SELECT permission denied on object tblCustomer, database company, owner dbo
```

5 Now try executing a stored procedure. Execute the procedure:

```
LastNameLookup 'smith'
```

SQL Server responds by retrieving all the names that sound like Smith in the tblCustomer table.

Applying Security Attributes in ISQL/w

You can perform operations related to database security in ISQL/w. You generally do this in situations where you want a database's security features to be created by the same SQL batch that creates the database. If you always append the commands pertaining to security to the same SQL batch that creates the database object, it's less likely you'll forget to apply security features to new database objects you create.

Create a login in ISQL/w using the sp_addlogin stored procedure. For example, to create a login for the user randy (as you did in SQL Enterprise Manager in the previous example), you execute the command:

```
sp_addlogin randy
```

To give the login randy the password prince, add the password as an additional argument to the sp_addlogin procedure:

```
sp_addlogin randy, prince
```

To make the login randy a user of the company database, use the sp_adduser procedure:

```
use company
go
sp_adduser randy
go
```

To show a list of all the logins in your SQL Server installation in ISQL/w, use the SQL command:

```
use master
go
select suid, name
from syslogins
```

To create a group, you use the sp_addgroup stored procedure:

```
sp_addgroup users
```

You can display a list of all the groups in the database using the stored procedure sp_helpgroup.

You apply and remove permissions for a particular database object using the SQL grant and revoke commands. The grant command permits a user or group to have access to a database object, while the revoke command removes a permission.

For example, to grant members of the users group complete access to the tblCustomer table, use the SQL command:

```
grant all
on tblCustomer
to users
```

To restrict members of the users group to the ability to select data from the tblCustomer table, qualify the grant command with the Select option:

```
grant select
on tblCustomer
to users
```

To revoke permissions on a database object, use the revoke command. For example, to revoke permissions to access the tblCustomer table from members of the users group, use the SQL command:

```
revoke all
on tblCustomer
to users
```

You can grant or revoke permissions for update, select, delete, and insert on tables and views. You can grant or revoke permissions for execute on stored procedures.

Determining Who Is Logged In with sp_who You have the capability to determine which users are logged into a database at any time by using stored procedure sp_who. This procedure returns information on the users who are logged into the system as well as what database they're working in.

To use sp_who, execute it in ISQL/w's Query window. ISQL/w returns a list of current users, as shown in Figure 5.26.

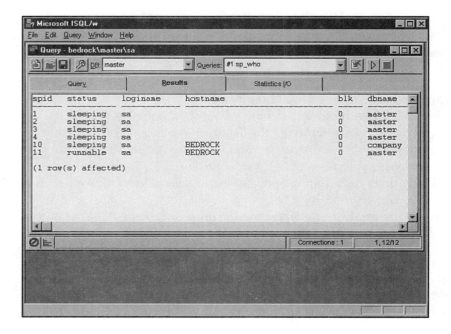

Figure 5.26: Results of running the sp_who stored procedure.

Viewing a list of currently logged-in users gives you the ability to do a number of things, such as terminate user sessions from the server; that is described in the next section.

Ending a Process with the kill Command

In SQL Server, the system administrator has the ability to kill a process—such as a user session or a database lock—with the kill command. You generally do this in a situation where a user's session terminated abnormally and you want to get rid of their *hung* session, or when a client procedure has initiated lock on a piece of data and won't let go. (These situations are rare, but they do happen.)

To use the kill command, you must first run the sp_who stored procedure (if you're trying to kill a user session) or the sp_lock procedure (if you're trying to kill a database lock). Both procedures return a column called spid, the procedure ID of the process. After you know the spid, you can kill the process by using the kill command.

For example, say you run sp_who and notice that there's a hung session from a user who you know for certain won the lottery three weeks ago and won't be returning to work. Notice that the bogus session's spid is 10. To kill spid 10, you issue the following command in ISQL/w. The bogus session is immediately killed.

```
kill 10
```

> **Note:** It's a good idea to run sp_who periodically, particularly during development, just to see what's going on in your database.

Removing Objects from the Database

The SQL Server term for removing an object from the database is to *drop* the object. When you drop an object from the database, it is deleted permanently. For tables that contain data, the structure and the data is deleted permanently.

To drop a database object—a table, for example—in SQL Enterprise Manager, simply right-click it. In the pop-up menu, select Delete. The object is deleted.

To drop a database object in ISQL/w, use the drop command. For example, to drop the tblCustomer table, use this command:

```
drop table tblCustomer
```

Publishing Results of SQL Server to the World Wide Web

New to SQL Server 6.5 is a utility that enables you to run queries against SQL Server and output the data in HTML, the format used by World Wide Web pages.

Because it is governed by a wizard called SQL Server Web Assistant, this technique is simpler to use than some of the other Internet-related techniques described in this book. It's also specifically geared for use with SQL Server, so it knows about server stuff like login ID and server names.

For information on how to use SQL Server Web Assistant, see Chapter 9, "Internet Database Applications and ADOs."

MIGRATING FROM MICROSOFT ACCESS TO SQL SERVER

If you're a psychic software developer, you'll always have a good idea of how big your database application needs to be, how many users it needs to support, and what kind of performance it needs to provide. If you're like most people, you need a way out when confronted with a situation in which your database needs to grow outside of the window box you planted it in.

For many Visual Basic developers, this means scaling a database application from a Microsoft Access/Jet-style database into SQL Server. Microsoft recognized early on that developers would have a need to do this, so they provided a wizard known as Microsoft Access Upsizing Tools. They have diligently upgraded the upsizing tools for each version of Access as new versions are released.

Because the tools are written as a Microsoft Access add-in, the Upsizing Tools aren't available to you if you're using straight Visual Basic. In this section, it's assumed that if you have Visual Basic and SQL Server, you'll likely also have Microsoft Access. (If you don't have Access, you should get a copy—it's a great tool for bridging the gap between VB and SQL Server.) Whether you have Access or not, the following sections give you some ideas for easing the transition from Jet to SQL Server.

Using Microsoft Access Upsizing Tools

To use the Microsoft Access Upsizing Tools to move your Access database to SQL Server, you must first download and install the tools. You can obtain the Microsoft Access Upsizing Tools for Access 97 as a free download from Microsoft. The tools are at **http://www.microsoft.com/AccessDev/ ProdInfo/Exe/AUT97.EXE**.

After you've downloaded and installed the add-in, you can launch it from Microsoft Access. Perform the following steps to run the Upsizing Tools:

1 First make sure that a database for storing the exported data exists on the SQL Server.

2 Make sure that the SQL Server database has a valid ODBC data source associated with it. (If you don't choose to create an ODBC data source at this time, you can create one using the Upsizing Tools.)

3 Select **Add-Ins** from Microsoft Access' Tools menu. Select **Upsize to SQL-Server** from the submenu.

4 The Upsizing Wizard launches, giving you the choice of creating a new database or migrating the current database to SQL Server. Choose **Use existing database**, then click Next.

5 The ODBC Select Data Source dialog box appears. Select the ODBC Data Source that corresponds to your SQL Server database, then click OK.

6 If your ODBC Data Source requires that you log in, you see the SQL Server Login dialog. Log in, then click OK.

7 The Upsizing Wizard displays a list of the tables in your local Access database. Double-click each table you want to export to SQL Server. Click Next when you're done.

8 The next step allows you to choose a number of options that control how your data is exported to SQL Server. These options include:

▶ Which elements of the table, besides the field structure, you want to export to SQL Server. This includes indexes, validation rules, default values, and relationships.

▶ Whether the exporter should create a Timestamp field in your exported table. (Timestamp fields let you keep multiple generations of data in the same table; to retrieve the most recent generation of data, you retrieve the one with the most recent timestamp. Timestamp fields also give you an audit trail that let you know when a record was last changed.)

▶ Whether the exporter should export the entire table, including its data, or merely its structure.

▶ Whether the exported table should be linked back to your Access database.

Choose the option you want, then click Next.

9 In the final step, decide whether you want the Upsizing Wizard to create a report explaining what it did. You should always do this. Check the box, then click Finish.

10 The table is exported to SQL Server. The Upsizing Wizard report appears, giving you a summary of what the Upsizing Wizard did. (Because it isn't automatically saved in your Access database, you should print this report.)

You should be aware that there are certain situations in which the Upsizing Wizard won't be able to convert your table to a structure that SQL Server likes. It creates fields you might not want in your table and gags on OLE Object fields. Additionally, it doesn't export AutoNumber fields the way you might expect; instead, it tries to create a trigger that generates a random value in the field, which might not be what you'd expect.

The Upsizing Wizard is fine when you want a quick way to send data to SQL Server from Access, but you shouldn't have to rely on it (and suffer under its limitations) as long as you have a handle on the SQL Server topics presented in this chapter.

Exporting Data from Access to SQL Server Using Linked Tables

If you prefer to have more control over how data is moved from your Microsoft Access tables to SQL Server, you have the option of linking SQL Server tables into your Access database, then exporting data to the SQL Server tables by using an append query in Access.

You need to perform this activity in Microsoft Access because Access uses the Jet database engine, which is singularly adept at integrating data from disparate database engines. Because this technique assumes that you've already created tables on a SQL Server database, it's more time-consuming than using the Access Upsizing Tools. However, because you have complete control over the table design, you can bypass some of the questionable decisions made by the Upsizing Tools, such as converting AutoNumber fields to a field populated with a random number (rather than a column designated as an identity column).

Note: In order for this technique to work, you need to have a handle on how to create an ODBC data source, because Access connects to SQL Server through ODBC. For information on how to do this, see "Configuring and Using Open Database Connectivity" later in this chapter.

Transferring data from Access to SQL Server involves three steps:

1 Creating tables on a SQL Server database to store your Access data

2 Linking those SQL Server tables to your Access database

3 Running an append query to transfer the data from Access to SQL Server

The first step in this technique is described in "Creating Tables in a SQL Server Database," earlier in this chapter. The second two steps are described in the following sections.

Linking SQL Server Tables to Microsoft Access　One of the easiest ways to transfer data from Access to SQL Server (or to simply use SQL Server data in an Access applications) is through the use of linked tables. *Linked tables* are a Microsoft Access feature that enables you to use and browse data from an ODBC database (such as SQL Server) as if the table were stored locally in the Access database.

Perform the following steps to transfer data in a particular table from Access to SQL Server using this technique:

1　In Microsoft Access 97, open the database from which you want to export data.

2　Select **Get External Data** from the File menu. Select **Link Tables** from the submenu.

3　The Link dialog appears, as shown in Figure 5.27.

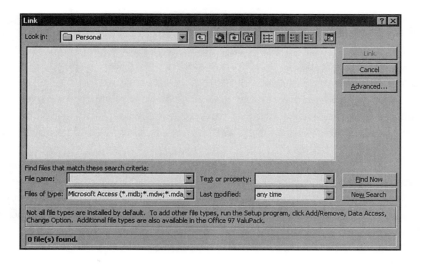

Figure 5.27: Using the Link dialog in Microsoft Access to attach SQL Server tables.

4　Select ODBC Databases in the Files of Type combo box.

5 The ODBC Select Data Source dialog appears. In this dialog, select the data source for your SQL Server database, then click OK.

6 The SQL Server Login dialog appears. Log in to SQL Server with your username and password, then click OK.

7 The Link Tables dialog appears. In this dialog, select the table (or tables— the dialog accepts multiple selections) you want to link to, then click OK.

8 The SQL Server table you've linked to appears in the Database window, as shown in Figure 5.28.

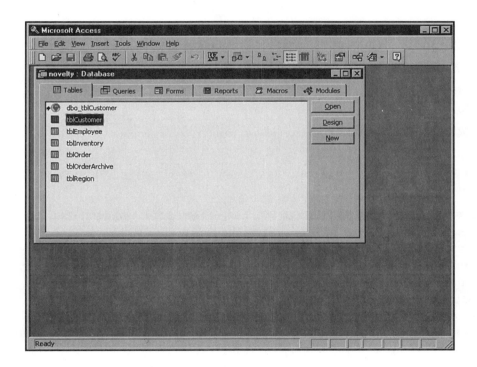

Figure 5.28: A SQL Server table linked into Microsoft Access.

Creating an Append Query to Transfer Access Data to SQL Server   Now that you've linked a table from SQL Server to your Access database, you can construct an action query to export Access data to your SQL Server database:

1 In Microsoft Access' database window, click once on the local (not linked) version of your database table to select it.

2 Select **Query** from the Insert menu.

3 Choose **Design View** from the New Query dialog, then click OK.

4 A new query definition window appears. Your local table should appear at the top of the window.

5 Select **Append Query** from the Query menu. This changes the query you're creating from a select query to an append query.

6 The Append dialog appears. In the Table Name combo box, select dbo_tblCustomer (or whatever you named your linked SQL Server table). Leave the Current Database button highlighted (although the tables are stored in another database, since they're linked, they're treated as if they exist in the current database for the purposes of this query).

7 Click OK.

8 In the Field row of the query design grid, select all the fields you want to export to the SQL Server database.

9 Select the menu command **Query, Run**. Access tells you how many records will be copied from the Access table to the SQL Server table. Click on OK.

10 The append query executes, and data is copied into the SQL Server table.

Problems Exporting Null Data to SQL Server with Access Append Queries

Access 97 has difficulty communicating the concept of a null value to SQL Server in an append query. This is probably a bug in Access 97, because this same thing has been successfully accomplished in previous versions of Access. However, our friends at Microsoft have nothing to say about whether this is a bug. Details of some encountered problems are provided here, as well as a workaround for you.

In a situation where you are attempting to export data to SQL Server through a Microsoft Access append query (as described in the previous section), when Access attempts to send a field that contains null data to SQL Server, you may get an error message that says "You tried to assign a null value to a variable that isn't a variant data type."

The workaround for this is to change the query so any field that might contain a null value is treated explicitly as a string value. The way to do this is to concatenate the contents of the field to empty strings.

Use the following expression in the Field row of the query grid in Access, instead of denoting the field name Address:

```
Address & ""
```

Access will prepend an expression label to the left of this expression when you enter it into the grid, which you can then ignore.

Never generate a null value when expressing fields this way; always pass an empty string. The even more perplexing and fascinating thing about this shortcoming in Access 97 is the fact that SQL Server does not make this distinction between an empty string and a null value; when you pass SQL Server an empty string, it stores it as a null.

An example of a Microsoft Access append query that has been modified to be null-safe is shown in Figure 5.29.

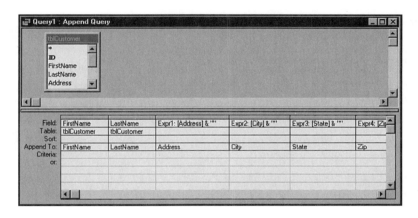

Figure 5.29: An append query that has been converted to be null-safe.

Exporting AutoNumber Fields to Identity Columns   One tricky thing about the process of exporting data from Access is the fact that there's no easy way to export an Access AutoNumber field to a SQL Server identity column. However, you can hot-wire a SQL Server identity column so that it will accept any value. This allows you to insert rows into a table with an identity column set to a specific value you choose.

You do this by using the identity_insert option in a SQL Server insert command. This option, which can be set to on or off, determines whether you're allowed to specify the value in a table's identity column. This value is set to off by default; you should only turn it on in a transaction specifically involving setting a value in an identity column.

For example, the SQL code to perform an insert involving an identity column in the tblCustomer table is shown in Listing 5.8.

Listing 5.8: Inserting a Value into an Identity Column Using the identity_insert Setting

```
set identity_insert tblCustomer on

insert tblCustomer (ID, FirstName, LastName)
       values (60559, "Mikki", "Halpin")

set identity_insert tblCustomer off

go
```

This batch inserts a record into the tblCustomer table with a customer ID of 60559.

Note: Overriding an identity column this way resets the identity column's internal counter. For example, after you've run the command in Listing 5.8, the next record you insert into the Customer table (assuming you don't override the counter again) has an ID of 60560.

CONFIGURING AND USING OPEN DATABASE CONNECTIVITY (ODBC)

Open Database Connectivity (ODBC) is a Windows technology that lets a database client application connect to a remote database. ODBC is a client-side technology that seeks to make every back-end data source generic. This means that your application doesn't need to know about what specific type of database it's connecting to, giving you the ability to write client applications against one standardized version of SQL.

Note: Because it's a client-side technology, ODBC doesn't require that you do anything to your database server.

ODBC is composed of three parts:

▶ A driver manager

▶ One or more drivers

▶ One or more data sources

The architecture of ODBC is illustrated in Figure 5.30.

Figure 5.30: ODBC architecture showing the connection between the client application and the server database through the ODBC Driver Manager.

Creating an ODBC Data Source

In order for a client application to connect to a client/server database using ODBC, you must first supply information about an ODBC data source on the client. This gives client applications the capability to refer to a combination of a driver, a database and optionally, a username and password—using a single name. This name is a *data source name* or DSN.

To create an ODBC data source name on the client:

1 Make sure you have a SQL Server database up and running, and make sure it's accessible from the client computer. In other words, before you proceed, you want to rule out any non-ODBC–related problems having to do with network connectivity, security, and so forth.

2 Launch Control Panel from your computer's Start menu.

3 From Control Panel, launch the ODBC control panel applet. The ODBC Data Source Administrator dialog appears, as shown in Figure 5.31.

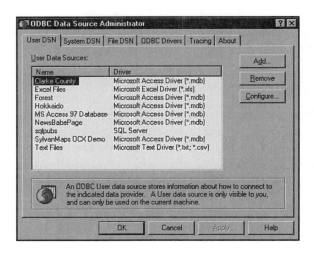

Figure 5.31: Creating an ODBC data source using the ODBC Data Source Administrator dialog.

At this point, you can create one of three types of ODBC data source names:

▶ A *user DSN*, which is usable only by you and only on the machine you're currently using.

▶ A *system DSN*, which anyone using your machine can use. Additionally, this is the kind of data source you need to create if you're setting up a Web database application (for more information on this, see Chapter 9).

▶ A *file DSN*, which is similar to a system DSN, except that it can be used by other users on other computers.

Because user DSNs are a bit easier to manage for some of the examples you run though later, you create one of those. To do this:

1 If it isn't selected already, click the User DSN tab in the ODBC Data Source Administrator window.

2 Click the Add button.

3 The Create New Data Source dialog appears. Click on the name of the database driver (in this case, SQL Server) you want to use.

4 Click Finish. The ODBC SQL Server Setup dialog appears.

5 In the Data Source Name box, enter the name of your data source. This name can be (essentially) anything you want. Because this is the name you use to refer to your database in your client applications, make it something memorable and consistent. Using the name of the database as the name of the DSN isn't a bad idea.

6 Filling in the Description box is optional. This gives you the ability to supply additional information pertaining to the ODBC data source name.

7 In the Server combo box, choose the SQL Server upon which your database resides.

   If your computer is connected to the SQL Server, it should appear in the drop-down list; if you're configuring an ODBC connection from the same computer on which your SQL Server resides, you can use the old reliable (local) to stand in for the name of your server. If necessary, you can also supply network connectivity information in this dialog.

8 Click the Options button. The dialog expands to expose additional options.

9 Type the name of the database you want this data source name to connect to in the Database Name box. Although this step is technically optional, you should generally always associate a database name with an ODBC data source name. Your screen should look like Figure 5.32.

Figure 5.32: Creating an ODBC data source name using the ODBC control panel.

10 Click OK. The new data source name appears in the ODBC Data Source Administrator window.

One easy way to confirm that your ODBC data source is operational is to create a small Visual Basic application to test it, as described in the next section.

Testing a Database Connection with odbcping

You can use the ODBC odbcping utility to determine whether you can connect to a database from a client computer. This command-line utility instructs the ODBC Driver Manager to create a connection to the back-end database and return information about whether the connection was successful. This can be helpful in situations where you're attempting to determine whether a problem with your client/server connection lies is on the server, in the network connection, in ODBC, or in your client application. The odbcping utility won't solve your problems for you, but it will at least tell you if you have connectivity to the server through ODBC.

The syntax of odbcping is:

```
odbcping /Uusername /Ppassword /Sserver
```

Use this command line in order to ping the SQL Server called BEDROCK using the login name randy and the password prince:

```
odbcping /Urandy /Pprince /SBEDROCK
```

To use odbcping to test your connectivity to the server:

1 From the Start menu, launch a new MS-DOS command prompt.

2 The Command Prompt window appears. In the Command Prompt window, type:

```
odbcping /Urandy /Pprince /SBEDROCK
```

3 The odbcping utility establishes a connection to the server and then exits. If everything functions properly, your command prompt window should look like Figure 5.33.

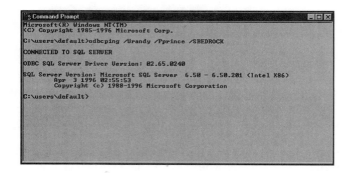

Figure 5.33: Results of a successful odbcping against a SQL Server.

Accessing a Client-Server Data Source with the Visual Basic Data Control and ODBCDirect

After you've created a data source name, test it immediately to make sure everything's working properly. Creating a Visual Basic application with the Data control makes this easy; in fact, it doesn't require any code at all to set up.

In previous versions of Data Access Object, your application loaded the Jet database engine when using client-server data—even if you weren't using an Access database. In VB5, you can now use ODBCDirect to access client-server data. ODBCDirect is simply a switch that tells DAO to access the server directly through DAO without loading the Jet database engine. This saves you memory and load time on the client computer.

To set up a VB application that tests a SQL Server data source name, do the following:

1 Make sure you've created an ODBC data source name as described in the previous section.

2 Launch Visual Basic and create a Standard EXE project.

3 From the Project Components menu, add a reference to the Microsoft Data Bound Grid Control to your project.

Note: In this demonstration, you use the DBGrid control simply as a way to browse data. It has a myriad of other uses. For more information on how to program the DBGrid control, see Chapter 11, "Using the DBGrid and Apex True DBGrid Controls."

4 The DBGrid control appears in your project's toolbox. Add an instance of the DBGrid control and a standard Data control to your project's form.

5 Change the Data control's DefaultType property to **1 - Use ODBC**. This causes the text application to bypass the Microsoft Jet engine, which makes your application start more quickly and consume less memory.

6 In the Data control's Connect property, enter the following text:

```
ODBC;UID=sa;PWD=mypassword;DSN=JonesCompany;
```

Replace the string *mypassword* with your password. If necessary, replace the username *sa* with your username.

Note: ODBC connect strings are expressed this way to give maximum flexibility to the particular database driver you're using; some database drivers use ODBC connect string settings that others don't. The order in which you pass the elements of an ODBC connect string is irrelevant; however, the `ODBC;` clause should come first.

7 In the Data control's RecordSource property, enter the following SQL string:

```
select * from tblCustomer
```

8 Set the DBGrid control's DataSource property to **Data1**.

9 Run the application. The grid should display all the data in the
tblCustomer table (assuming there is data in the table). The running
application is shown in Figure 5.34.

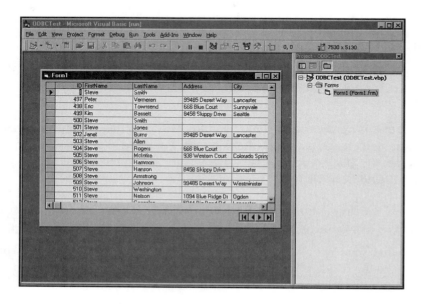

**Figure 5.34: A Visual Basic application using the DBGrid control to test an ODBC
database connection.**

ACCESSING DATA USING THE REMOTE DATA CONTROL

The Remote Data Control is another way to access remote data in a Visual Basic
application. This control uses a programmable interface similar to that of the
Visual Basic Data control (introduced in Chapter 2 and reintroduced in the previous section of this chapter).

The process of hooking your VB user interface up to a client/server data
source is startlingly similar to the process of using the Data control for the same
purpose. It's meant to be that way. With a few minor exceptions, the Remote
Data Control works the same way a Data control works—you give it some
information about where the data is stored and it retrieves data and supplies it
to other data-aware user interface controls. The user can then interact with the

data through these user interface controls—browsing data, performing updates, and adding records—and you don't have to write a single line of code to make it happen.

Using the Remote Data Control in Your Project

To use the Remote Data Control in your Visual Basic project, do the following:

1 In Visual Basic, select the menu command **Project, Components**.

2 From the list of components, select Microsoft RemoteData Control 2.0. Also add a reference to the Microsoft Data Bound Grid Control.

3 Click OK. The Remote Data and Databound Grid controls appear in the Visual Basic toolbox, as illustrated in Figure 5.35.

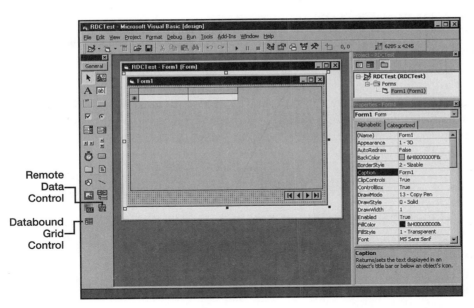

Figure 5.35: The icon for the Microsoft Remote Data Control as it appears in the Visual Basic toolbox.

4 Use the toolbox to create instances of the Remote Data control and the Databound Grid on the form in your project.

5 Change the Remote Data Control's UserName property to your username.

6 Change the Remote Data Control's Password property to your password.

7 Set the Remote Data Control's SQL property to:

```
select * from tblCustomer
```

8 In the DataSourceName property of the Remote Data Control, pick the DSN for your SQL Server database.

9 Set the DBGrid control's DataSource property to MSRDC1, the name of the Remote Data Control.

10 Run the application. The application retrieves the contents of the tblCustomer table and displays it in the data grid.

If you are perusing this chapter you've probably gotten the impression that using the Data control with the ODBCDirect option and the Remote Data Control to access data is essentially the same thing. Both controls give you access to an ODBC database without writing Visual Basic code. That's the whole point: The Remote Data Control was designed to work exactly like the standard Data control.

In addition to providing conveniently distinct properties for the different pieces of information comprising the Data control's Connect property (such as username, password, and data source name), the Remote Data control offers another important advantage: It uses Remote Data Objects to communicate with the database. Remote Data Objects are the client/server analog of Data Access Objects in Visual Basic.

Bugs in the Remote Data Control Fixed in the Visual Studio Service Packs

A number of issues specifically related to the functionality of the Remote Data Control were fixed in Service Packs for Microsoft Visual Studio (which includes patches for Visual Basic 5.0). These Service Packs were released as patches to VB after the main product shipped; they are freely downloadable from the Microsoft Web site.

Specifically, the resolved issues are:

Bug	For More Information, See:
A DBGrid control bound to the Remote Data Control displays small result sets incorrectly.	**http://www.microsoft.com/kb/articles/ Q168/1/56.htm**

Bug	For More Information, See:
More than one control bound to a Remote Data Control causes the control to stop updating data.	**http://www.microsoft.com/kb/articles/ Q168/1/57.htm**
You can't close a resultset if a DBGrid control is bound to the Remote Data Control.	**http://www.microsoft.com/kb/articles/ Q168/1/58.htm**
The DBCombo control does not update correctly when it is bound to a Remote Data Control.	**http://www.microsoft.com/kb/articles/ Q168/1/59.htm**
After adding a row, subsequently navigating through the resultset may generate a bogus error.	**http://www.microsoft.com/kb/articles/ Q168/1/60.htm**

Note: As of this writing, the latest service pack available was Visual Studio Service Pack 3. You can obtain the latest Visual Studio Service Pack for free by downloading it from **http://www.microsoft.com/msdownload/vs97sp/ vb.asp.**

Using Remote Data Objects to Access Client/Server Data

Remote Data Objects (RDO) are an object-oriented way to access client/server data sources. RDO was introduced in Visual Basic 4.0; it was enhanced in Visual Basic 5.0 to include a number of new features and enhance performance. Among these new features are changes in the way certain objects are instantiated and support for data objects that trigger events. These features are introduced in detail in the remainder of this chapter.

The basic idea behind Remote Data Objects is to give you an object-oriented, implementation-independent way of getting access to client/server data.

Because RDO is object-oriented, you can use the same type of code you use to program other objects in Visual Basic to access data.

Because RDO is implementation-independent, you can create solutions without regard for the specific vagaries of individual database vendors—as long as your application knows about RDO, it doesn't care what's on the back end.

Note: Remote Data Objects aren't just a VB thing; they're shared across a number of Microsoft development tools. Currently, you can use RDO in the Enterprise Edition of Visual Basic (versions 4.0 and 5.0), Visual C++, Visual InterDev, and Visual J++.

Remote Data Objects are arranged in an object hierarchy similar to that of Data Access Objects. Figure 5.36 illustrates this hierarchy.

Notice that RDO's object model is simpler than that of DAO's. This reflects the fact that much of DAO's functionality (such as responsibility for security and the capability to make changes in the database schema) is handled by the database engine itself. In RDO, on the other hand, this functionality is handled by the server.

This means that you can't use RDO to create database objects such as tables, views, and stored procedures (at least, you can't do it in the same object-oriented way you're accustomed to in Data Access Objects. You can, however, pass SQL commands directly to the server in RDO, which means that almost anything you're able to do in ISQL/w, you can do in RDO in Visual Basic).

In order to get started with Remote Data Objects, you must first make a reference to them in your Visual Basic project:

1 Select **References** from Visual Basic's Project menu. The References dialog appears.

2 Select **Microsoft Remote Data Object 2.0** from the list.

3 Click OK. Remote Data Objects are now available to your application.

Remember to perform these steps any time your application needs to access Remote Data Objects. If your application uses the Remote Data Control, you must add a reference to RDO and add the Remote Data Control to your project, as described in this chapter's "Using the Remote Data Control in Your Project."

Setting Database Engine Properties with the rdoEngine Object

The rdoEngine object is the highest-level object in the RDO object model. You generally use the rdoEngine object to set default properties for the other RDO objects your application creates.

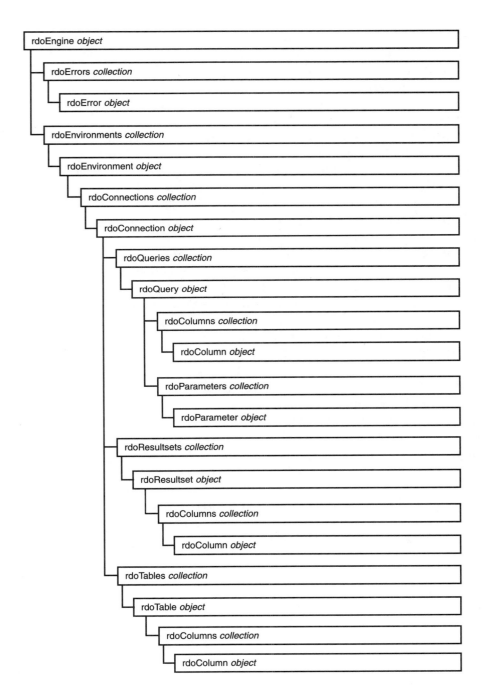

Figure 5.36: The complete structure of Remote Data Objects 2.0.

The rdoEngine object is also useful in situations where you want to set or inspect the type of cursors used by the database engine. A cursor is a way of accessing a row in a result set one row at a time. Different cursors have different capabilities; for example, a forward-scrolling cursor permits you to access rows, one after the other, but it doesn't permit you to go backwards and reference rows in the result set you've moved past.

The rdoEngine object is equivalent to the DBEngine object in Data Access Objects. In addition to representing the data source, it also contains an rdoErrors collection that lets you iterate through all the error messages generated by a particular database transaction (more on this in "Handling Errors with the rdoErrors Collection and the rdoError Object," later in this chapter).

The rdoEngine object belongs to no collection; it is a singleton object that can't be instantiated by your application. (It just simply exists, in a Zen-like sort of way: It comes into existence the first time your application accesses RDO.)

The rdoEngine object contains a collection of Environment objects, as well as a collection of rdoError objects, as illustrated in Figure 5.37.

For example, if your application needs to create a number of data objects based on a common user login and password, you can specify these when you start using remote data objects in your application. The defaults you set (using the rdoDefaultPassword and rdoDefaultUser properties) are in force for any rdoEnvironment objects created in your application.

You can also use the rdoEngine object to control how cursors are created and maintained by your application.

In addition to supplying defaults for other objects created in RDO, the rdoEngine object automatically creates an rdoEnvironment object. You can refer to this object in code as rdoEnvironments(0).

Note that the properties of the rdoEngine object aren't used often, because by the time you have access to the rdoEngine object, it's already created the only rdoEnvironment object you're ever likely to need—rdoEnvironments(0). If you want to change the database environment, you're probably better off simply adjusting the properties of rdoEnvironments(0), as described in the next section.

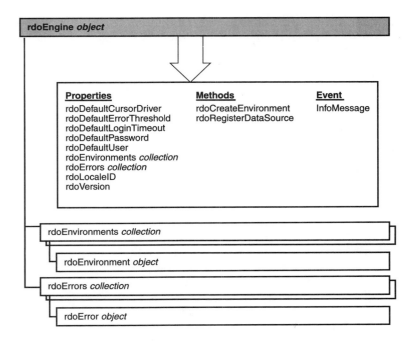

Figure 5.37: The Environments collection and Environment object in the Remote Data Object hierarchy.

Accessing the Environment with the rdoEnvironment Object

The rdoEnvironment object represents the database environment. It is a way to refer to a set of database connections (in the form of rdoConnection objects, discussed in the next section).

The rdoEnvironment object is analogous to the Workspace object in Data Access Object programming.

As with the rdoEngine object, it is unlikely that your application would ever need to create more than one instance of an rdoEnvironment object. It wouldn't need to unless your application needed to support multiple simultaneous transactions or multiple simultaneous logins to a database. Rather than instantiating a new instance of the rdoEnvironment object, it's more likely that you'll access the existing rdoEnvironment object, rdoEnvironments(0), created for you by the rdoEngine object when you initally make a reference to Remote Data Objects in your VB application.

The rdoEnvironment object belongs to an rdoEnvironments collection and contains a collection of rdoConnection objects, as illustrated in Figure 5.38.

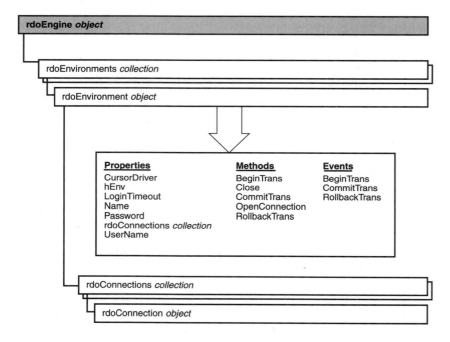

Figure 5.38: The rdoEnvironments collection and rdoEnvironment object in the Remote Data Object hierarchy.

Establishing a Connection with the rdoConnection Object

You use the rdoConnection object to establish a connection to a database server. This is the object that you start with most of the time when writing code to create a connection to a remote database. After you have a valid rdoConnection object, your application can begin interacting with the database in earnest.

The rdoConnection object is analogous to the Database object in Data Access Objects programming.

rdoConnection objects belong to an rdoConnections collection and contain collections of rdoQuery objects, rdoResultSets, and rdoTables, as illustrated in Figure 5.39.

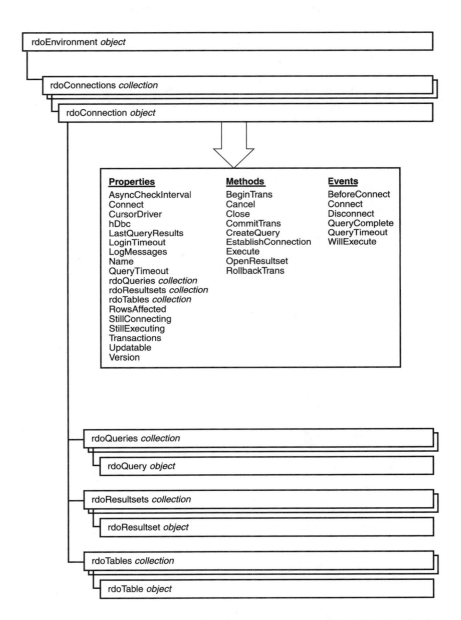

Figure 5.39: The rdoConnections collection and rdoConnection object in the Remote Data Object hierarchy.

To create a connection using the rdoConnection object, you begin by creating an ODBC connect string. This string is similar to the Data control's Connect property (as described in "Accessing an Client-Server Data Source with the

Visual Basic Data Control and ODBCDirect," earlier in this chapter). Unlike the Data control, for an rdoConnection object you omit the ODBC; clause of the connect string.

An rdoConnection connect string minimally consists of a data source name, a login, and a password. The actual elements of the ODBC connect string are dictated by your database's ODBC driver; you may have to provide more information, particularly if your back-end data source isn't SQL Server. Table 5.1 provides a summary of the typical ODBC connect strings's elements.

Table 5.1: Typical ODBC Connect Strings

Argument	Description	Required?
UID=	The user's login name	Yes
PWD=	The user's password	Yes
DSN=	Your data source's data source name as defined in the ODBC Driver Manager	Only if no DRIVER is specified
DRIVER=	The data source driver's name	Only if there is no DSN; for Microsoft SQL Server, the driver name is {SQL Server}
DATABASE=	The name of the database the user is connecting to	No (if no database is specified, defaults to the default database designated for the user; shouldn't be relied on in your application)
APP=	The name of the application connecting to the database	No
LANGUAGE=	The language used by SQL Server	No
SERVER=	The name of the SQL Server the application is connecting to	No
WSID=	The name of the client computer (or workstation ID)	No

Again, bear in mind that this isn't necessarily a complete list of connect string arguments; your database may provide (or require) more arguments, particularly if you're using a non-Microsoft database back-end.

Note: In order to connect to an ODBC data source using a data source name, the data source name must first be properly configured in the ODBC Control Panel. For information on how to do this, see "Configuring and Using Open Database Connectivity," earlier in this chapter.

For example, to connect to the database called company with the login name randy and the password prince, you use this connect string:

```
UID=randy;PWD=prince;DATABASE=company;DSN=JonesCompany
```

Bear in mind that if you bungle something in the connect string—forgetting to supply a login or password, for example—your user is greeted with a potentially unpleasant surprise. The ODBC Driver Manager displays a dialog box asking the user to supply the missing information, as shown in Figure 5.40.

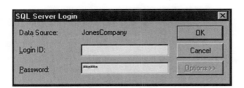

Figure 5.40: SQL Server Login dialog box displayed when your application neglects to supply a login name when attempting to connect.

Although you might be tempted to take advantage of this login dialog, there's a problem. Displaying the ODBC login dialog means that the Options button becomes available. This enables the user to muck around with the stuff that should normally be hidden, such as the name of the database he or she is connecting to and the workstation ID. You want to take steps to ensure that your applications never display this dialog box, if possible.

In addition to creating a connect string that takes advantage of a preconfigured ODBC data source name, you have the option of creating a connect string that does not require a DSN. To create a connection string that doesn't require a DSN (a so-called "DSN-less connection"), you use a connect string that looks like this:

```
SERVER=BEDROCK;UID=randy;PWD=prince;DATABASE=company;DRIVER={SQL Server}
```

Note: Using a DSN-less connection is useful in situations where you don't have complete control over the configuration of a client computer; for example, when you're sending data to an Internet browser. For more information on this, see Chapter 9.

After you have the information you need to establish the connection to the database, you have two options to establish the connection:

▶ Use the OpenConnection method of the rdoEnvironment object.

▶ Use the EstablishConnection method of the rdoConnection object.

Both methods do exactly the same thing although they work in slightly different ways. To demonstrate, Listing 5.9 shows an example of the rdoEnvironment's OpenConnection method.

Listing 5.9: Creating a Database Connection Using the OpenConnection Method

```
Option Explicit

' References RDO 2.0

Private MyConn As rdoConnection

Private Sub Form_Load()

Dim strConnect As String

strConnect = "UID=randy;" & _
             "PWD=prince;"

Set MyConn = rdoEnvironments(0).OpenConnection("JonesCompany", , , strConnect)

End Sub
```

As you can see, the OpenConnection method has the disadvantage of being rather procedural; you have to pass one or more parameters to the method in order to get it to work. The EstablishConnection method, on the other hand, is more object-oriented, as you see in the next example.

Note also that this code uses the implicitly created rdoEnvironment object, rdoEnvironments(0), as described in the previous section on the rdoEnvironment object.

Instead of using the OpenConnection method, you may want to instead use the rdoConnection object's EstablishConnection method. This technique can be somewhat simpler to use, as demonstrated in Listing 5.10.

Listing 5.10: Connecting to the Database Using the EstablishConnection Method

```
Option Explicit

' References RDO 2.0

Private MyConn As rdoConnection

Private Sub Form_Load()

Set MyConn = New rdoConnection

MyConn.Connect = "DSN=JonesCompany;" & _
                 "UID=randy;" & _
                 "PWD=prince;"

MyConn.EstablishConnection

End Sub
```

Though Remote Data Objects 2.0 makes it easier to establish a connection using the EstablishConnection method, there's an even easier way—using a UserConnection designer. This is demonstrated in "Creating a Connection with UserConnection Designers" later in this chapter.

Responding to Events in RDO

New to RDO 2.0 is the objects's event-generating capability. This gives you a great deal of flexibility for writing code that is associated with the object, like you do with other types of objects in Visual Basic.

To cause a particular data object to generate events, you must declare it in a special way: using the WithEvents keyword. For example, to declare a rdoConnection object called MyConn that generates events, you use the following code:

```
Private WithEvents MyConn As rdoConnection
```

After you've declared an object using WithEvents, its events become available in the Visual Basic code window, as shown in Figure 5.41.

After you have an object that generates events, you can then write event procedures that perform actions based on the events generated by the object in question.

One of the easiest ways to demonstrate how RDO events work is to write an event procedure that displays a message when a connection to the database is established. An example of a complete procedure that displays such a message in response to the rdoConnection object's Connect event is shown in Listing 5.11.

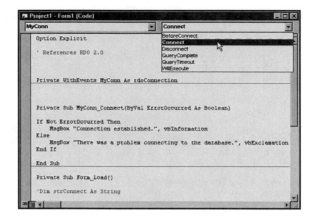

Figure 5.41: Accessing an event procedure of an RDO object declared with the WithEvents keyword.

Listing 5.11: Using the Connect Event of the rdoConnection Object

```
Option Explicit

' References RDO 2.0

Private WithEvents MyConn As rdoConnection

Private Sub Form_Load()

Set MyConn = New rdoConnection

MyConn.Connect = "DSN=JonesCompany;" & _
                "PWD=prince;" & _
                "UID=randy;"

MyConn.EstablishConnection

End Sub

Private Sub MyConn_Connect(ByVal ErrorOccurred As Boolean)

If ErrorOccurred Then
    MsgBox "There was a problem connecting to the database.", vbExclamation
Else
    MsgBox "Connection established.", vbInformation

End If

End Sub
```

Creating a Connection with UserConnection Designers

UserConnection designers make it easier for your VB applications to connect with a client/server database using RDO. Their purpose is to give you a design-time, graphical, reusable way to maintain information pertaining to a connection to a client/server database. The ultimate purpose of a UserConnection designer is to generate an rdoConnection object with a minimum of code.

UserConnection designers behave similarly to forms in VB projects; you add a UserConnection designer to your project and use it as you'd use a form. When you compile an executable file in VB, the UserConnection designer is compiled along with it, just as forms are.

> **Note:** If you're accustomed to writing code in Visual Basic with class modules, you have a leg up on UserConnection designers. UserConnection designers are actually a type of class module. If you're unfamiliar with how to use class modules to make your code more reusable and easier to maintain, check out Chapter 6, "Classes."

To use a UserConnection designer, follow these general steps:

1 Add a new UserConnection designer to your project.

2 Using the UserConnection's graphical interface, indicate which ODBC data source you want to connect to and how you want to connect to it.

3 In code, create an instance of an rdoConnection object from the UserConnection designer.

For example, to use the UserConnection Designer to connect to a particular ODBC database:

1 In a VB5 project, choose the menu item Project, Add ActiveX Designer. From the submenu, choose Microsoft UserConnection.

2 A new UserConnection designer is created, and the UserConnection Properties dialog is displayed, as illustrated in Figure 5.42.

3 In the Connection tab, choose a Use ODBC Datasource or build a DSN-less Connection String.

4 Click the Authentication tab and enter a valid username and password. Check the boxes labeled Save Connection Information for New Run-Mode Class and Save Connection Information for Design Time.

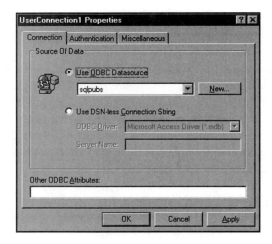

Figure 5.42: The Properties dialog of a new UserConnection designer.

Note: You have the option of leaving out information pertaining to authentication. Leaving out the authentication information means that your username and password won't be compiled into the application and it won't be saved along with the UserConnection designer. Remember, though, that if your UserConnection designer stores no authentication information and you don't provide that information in code at runtime, the ODBC driver will display a login dialog every time your application attempts to connect to the database.

In your applications, you might want to approach the problem of user authentication in a different way—by retrieving the user's name and password at the time a user starts your application or (for decision-support applications) creating a special read-only user account expressly for the purpose of browsing data.

5 Click OK.

6 The Properties dialog closes. You are left with the UserConnection designer, as shown in Figure 5.43.

7 In the Visual Basic Properties window, give the UserConnection designer a name. You use this name to refer to the UserConnection designer in code. For example, you might want to name a UserConnection designer that connects to the company database conCompany.

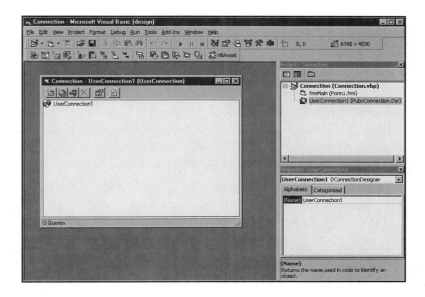

Figure 5.43: The UserConnection designer after you've set its initial properties.

Accessing Queries with a UserConnection Designer

After you've created a UserConnection designer, you can use it to retrieve data based on views or stored procedures on the server. You can also use the designer to generate client-side SQL queries on-the-fly; although if you have control over both the client and server, it's preferable for performance and maintainability reasons to restrict your client applications to accessing stored procedures that reside on the server.

You can create queries stored in the UserConnection designer in one of three ways:

▶ Call a stored procedure or view on the database server that returns records.

▶ Issue a command to the database server in the form of a SQL-string–generated on-the-fly.

▶ Build a query in the UserConnection designer using Microsoft Query. This technique is similar to the on-the-fly query technique, but it's graphical, so it's a bit easier to construct at design time.

Calling a Stored Procedure in a UserConnection Designer   In order to call a stored procedure from a connection object created from a UserConnection designer, you must add the stored procedure to the UserConnection designer at design time. After you've done this, you can access the stored procedure as a method of the connection object.

In this example, you add a reference to the LastNameLookup stored procedure in the company database:

1 In the toolbar of a UserConnection designer, click the Insert Query button. (Query in this context refers to either a SQL string you generate on the client side or a stored procedure or view that resides on the server. In this case, you add a reference to a stored procedure.)

2 The Query Properties dialog appears. In the Query Name box, give the query a name; it can (and probably should) be the same name as the stored procedure to which you're referring.

3 The Based on Stored Procedure combo box provides a list of all the stored procedures in the company database. In this combo box, select the name of the LastNameLookup procedure.

4 Click the Parameters tab. Note that the LastNameLookup procedure takes a name parameter that corresponds to the name of the person you're trying to look up.

5 Click OK. The LastNameLookup stored procedure is added to your UserConnection designer, as shown in Figure 5.44.

To see how to call a query referenced in a UserConnection, you must create an instance of the UserConnection in code and then execute the stored procedure as a method of the rdoConnection object created by the UserConnection.

1 Add a standard list box, a standard command button, and a standard text box to the form in your project containing the UserConnection. You use the text box to enter a parameter for the query, while the list box stores the results of the query. The code to run the query is triggered by a click on the command button.

2 In the Declarations section of the form, declare a variable that stores the rdoConnection and a rdoResultSet. (The rdoConnection is created from the UserConnection designer, as the code in Listing 5.12 demonstrates.)

```
Private Conn As conCompany
Private rs As rdoResultset
```

3 In the command button's Click event procedure, write code that creates an instance of the UserConnection, connects to the database, and runs the stored procedure. The code is in Listing 5.12.

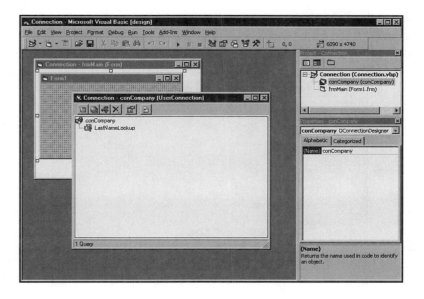

Figure 5.44: The conCompany UserConnection with a Reference to the Stored Procedure LastNameLookup.

Listing 5.12: Code that Runs a Stored Procedure and Returns Its Results to a Standard List Box

```
Private Sub Command1_Click()

Set Conn = New conCompany

Conn.EstablishConnection

Conn.LastNameLookup Text1.Text

Set rs = Conn.LastQueryResults

List1.Clear

Do Until rs.EOF
    List1.AddItem rs!LastName & " " & rs!FirstName
    rs.MoveNext
Loop

Conn.Close

End Sub
```

Notice that when you type a period after the Conn object, the stored procedure referenced by the UserConnection appears in the drop-down list of members of the object, as shown in Figure 5.45.

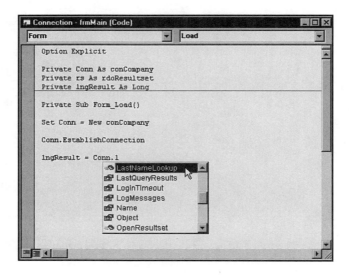

Figure 5.45: Running a stored procedure referenced by a UserConnection as a method of the rdoConnection object.

4 Run the application. Type a name such as Smith in the text box, and then click the command button. The list box is populated with a list of names that match what you typed, as shown in Figure 5.46.

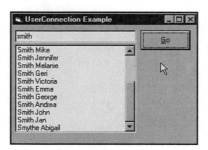

Figure 5.46: Results of a query in the application based on the UserConnection designer.

Using Microsoft Query to Build a SQL String in a UserConnection Designer

You've seen how easy it is to refer to a query stored on the server side using the UserConnection designer. In some cases, the query you want to run doesn't exist on the server, in which case you may want to generate the SQL on the client side and submit it to the server. The query is then executed on the server; the results are returned to the client.

To build a SQL string to submit to the server, you can either hand-code the SQL (the hard way) or use one of a number of client-side graphical query tools (the easy way). Microsoft Query is the tool most closely integrated with the UserConnection designer.

Note: Microsoft Query doesn't provide access to stored procedures stored in SQL Server, only access to tables and views.

To add a SQL query in the UserConnection designer using Microsoft Query:

1 Click the Insert Query button on the UserConnection designer's toolbar.

2 The Query Properties dialog box appears, as shown in Figure 5.47.

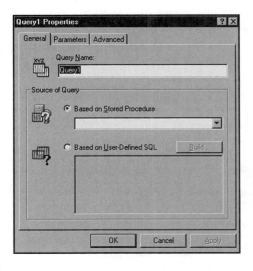

Figure 5.47: The UserConnection designer query's Query Properties dialog.

3 Type the name of the query you want to build in the Query Name text box. The query you're building retrieves everyone in the database named Jones, so call this query **qryJones**.

4 Select the **Based on User-Defined SQL** option, and then click **Build**.

5 Microsoft Query launches and displays a Choose Data Source dialog. Locate the data source you want to connect to, and then click OK.

Note: It might seem silly that you have to designate a data source again when you've already done so in the UserConnection designer. To make matters worse, you may have trouble getting Microsoft Query to recognize that you have a user DSN set up for the company database. For some reason, it really seems to want a file-based DSN rather than a user DSN or a system DSN. Fortunately, MS Query gives you the ability to create a DSN from within the program, so it's no major problem. It might, however, make you wish you could set up the whole shebang from one place.

Another problem you might have with MS Query stems from the fact that it's set up to look in the \Program Files\Common Files\Microsoft Shared\Vba directory for DSN files, and for some reason the ODBC applet creates file-based DSNs in \Program Files\Common Files\ODBC\Data Sources. In MS Query's Choose Data Source dialog, you can resolve this problem by clicking the Options button to specify which directory to search for DSNs in. To do this, in the Data Source Options dialog, click Browse, select the correct directory, click OK, and then click Add. The new directory is then recognized by MS Query in the future.

6 The Query Wizard runs, displaying the data available in the data source you just selected. The first dialog in the Query Wizard is illustrated in Figure 5.48.

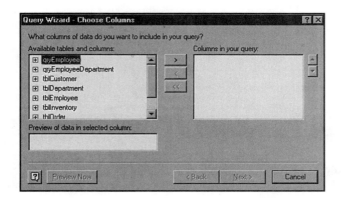

Figure 5.48: The initial screen of the Query Wizard, which lets you pick data to retrieve.

7 Double-click on the query or view you want to use (for this demonstration, select the view qryCustomer). The query or view expands to show a list of the fields contained in the view or table.

8 Double-click on each field you want to retrieve. Select the FirstName and LastName fields, as well as any other fields you want to retrieve.

9 Click the Next button.

10 The Filter Data step appears. In this step, you can determine how the query filters out records. To retrieve only those customers named Jones, select the LastName field from the list of fields. Then, in the combo box to the right of the list of columns, choose equals. In the next combo, choose Jones (the combo box performs a query on the data to determine the data that exists in the column you choose). The Filter Data dialog should look like Figure 5.49.

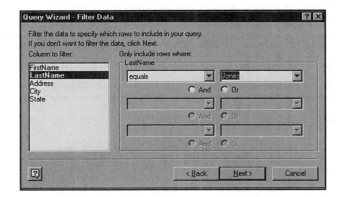

Figure 5.49: Filtering out data according to a particular criterion in Microsoft Query.

11 Click the Next button. The next step enables you to sort data. In the Sort combo box, choose FirstName.

12 Click the Next button. When you're done, you have the option of viewing the data you've retrieved or going back to the UserConnection designer. (If you choose to view the data in Microsoft Query, you can still return to the UserConnection designer later.) Choose View Data or Edit Query in Microsoft Query, then click Finish.

13 The data you've retrieved appears in Microsoft Query, as shown in Figure 5.50.

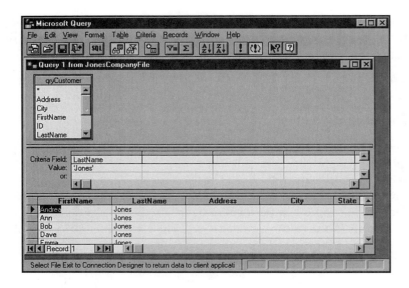

Figure 5.50: Data retrieved by the Query Wizard displayed in Microsoft Query.

When you're done viewing the data in Microsoft Query, select the menu command File, Exit to Connection Designer. Microsoft Query exits and return the query you built to the UserConnection designer's Query Properties dialog in the form of a SQL string. The Query Properties dialog looks like Figure 5.51.

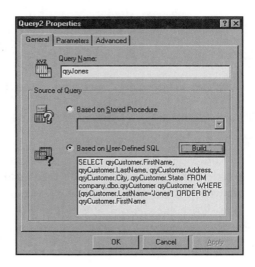

Figure 5.51: Query Properties dialog of the UserConnection designer, after it's been populated with a query string built in Microsoft Query.

When you're done with the Query Properties dialog, click OK. The query is stored in the UserConnection designer for your use in code.

There are several advantages to storing SQL queries in UserConnection designers. Among these is the fact that you can reuse designers across multiple projects and multiple developers without having to make changes on the server side.

Additionally, queries stored in UserConnection designers help you manage complexity in your application because there is less code to maintain—after you have the query working and have stored it in the UserConnection designer, you can put it out of your way and work on something else.

However, the problem with incorporating SQL strings in UserConnection designers is the fact that they're not universally accessible from every client application. This can lead to a situation where different client applications access server data in different ways, potentially leading to inconsistencies, especially in situations where the design of the database evolves over time. If you find yourself creating custom SQL queries on the client side, you may want to consider migrating that code to the server if you can.

After you've created a query in a UserConnection designer, you refer to it the same way you refer to a stored procedure—as a method of the connection object created by the UserConnection designer. This technique is described in this chapter's previous section.

Utilizing Data with the rdoResultset Object
You use the rdoResultset object to manipulate data returned by an interaction with the server.

Each rdoResultset object belongs to an rdoResultsets collection. The rdoResultset object contains a collection of rdoColumn objects, as illustrated in Figure 5.52.

The rdoResultset object is nearly identical to the Recordset object provided by Data Access Objects. You can create a rdoResultset object a number of ways; typically it's created as the result of a query (which can include a SQL string generated on the client, or the execution of a stored procedure or view on the server).

The following sections on queries and parameters give examples of the use of the rdoRecordset object in conjunction with queries generated on both the client- and server side.

Running Queries with the rdoQuery Object
You can run queries in RDO using the rdoQuery object. You typically do this in situations where the query in question is a parameterized query or an action query (a query that updates or deletes data).

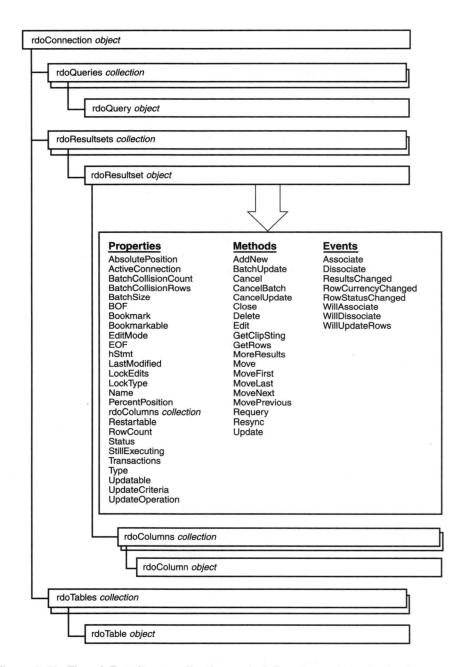

Figure 5.52: The rdoResultsets collection and rdoResultset object in the Remote Data Object hierarchy.

Note: In RDO 2.0, the rdoQuery object is a replacement for the rdoPreparedStatement object that existed in RDO 1.0. You can still use rdoPreparedStatement objects in your RDO 2.0 code; rdoPreparedStatement objects were included in RDO 2.0 for backward compatibility. However, for new RDO code you should use rdoQuery objects.

Each rdoQuery object belongs to an rdoQueries collection. The rdoQuery object contains collections of rdoColumn objects and rdoParameter objects, as illustrated in Figure 5.53.

You can use the rdoQuery object to create a SQL query on-the-fly without the use of the UserConnection designer or any other outside assistance. Listing 5.13 gives an example of how to do this, using an example application composed of a text box, a list box, and a command button.

Listing 5.13: Generating a Parameterized Query On-the-Fly Using the rdoQuery Object

```
Option Explicit

' References RDO 2.0

Dim Conn As New rdoConnection
Dim qy As New rdoQuery
Dim rs As rdoResultset

Private Sub Form_Load()

With Conn
    .Connect = "uid=randy;pwd=prince;dsn=JonesCompany"
    .EstablishConnection rdDriverNoPrompt, True
End With

End Sub

Private Sub Command1_Click()

    qy.SQL = "select * from qryCustomer " & _
            "where LastName = '" & txtValue.Text & "'"

    Set qy.ActiveConnection = Conn
    Set rs = qy.OpenResultset

    lstResult.Clear
```

continues

Listing 5.13: Generating a Parameterized Query On-the-Fly Using the rdoQuery Objects (Continued)

```
    Do Until rs.EOF
        lstResult.AddItem rs!LastName & " " & rs!FirstName
        rs.MoveNext
    Loop

End Sub
```

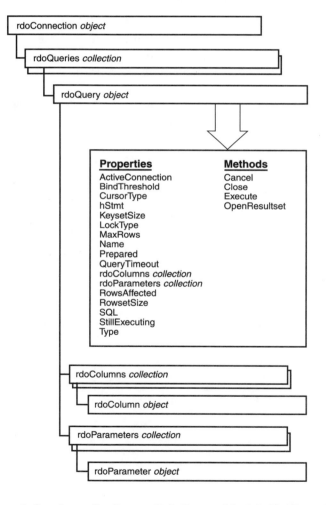

Figure 5.53: The rdoQueries collection and rdoQuery object in the Remote Data Object hierarchy.

You can see that this code is quite similar to the code you'd write in Data Access Objects to generate SQL queries at runtime. The only difference between this code and DAO code is that you'd encounter this code somewhat less frequently in RDO. This is because RDO applications generally make greater use of server-based queries.

> **Note:** Remember that even though the SQL command is generated on the client, it's executed on the server. This is an important, fundamental difference between RDO and DAO; in DAO with Jet, all queries are processed on the local computer, which is generally much less efficient.

The code also demonstrates that the rdoQuery object can be instantiated independently of its connection. (This is in contrast to DAO, where you instantiate a Recordset or QueryDef object from a Database object.) The capability to dissociate the rdoQuery object from its connection can lead to more flexibility in the code you write, because you're not forced to establish a database connection before you construct an rdoQuery object; instead, you can associate a query with a database connection at any time by assigning its ActiveConnection property.

There is another way to create parameterized queries on-the-fly in RDO: through the use of the rdoParameter object. This provides a more object-oriented way to create parameterized queries on-the-fly in your client applications. The rdoParameter object is introduced in the next section.

Creating Parameterized Queries Using the the rdoParameter Object   You can write parameterized queries using the rdoParameter object. Using rdoParameter objects gives you the ability to generate SQL queries on-the-fly and assign values to them in a manner that is neater and more object-oriented than generating a long concatenated SQL string (as described in the previous section).

Each rdoParameter object belongs to an rdoParameters collection. The position of the rdoParameter object in the RDO object-model hierarchy is illustrated in Figure 5.54.

Listing 5.14 demonstrates a query that uses an rdoParameter object. The parameter is set up in the query's SQL string through the use of the question mark character; in SQL Server, the question mark is a placeholder for a parameter.

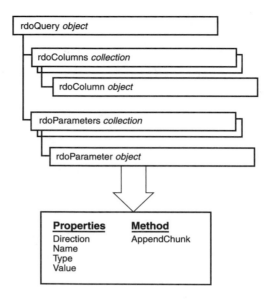

Figure 5.54: The rdoParameters collection and rdoParameter object in the Remote Data Object hierarchy.

Listing 5.14: Creating a Parameterized Query Using the rdoParameter Object

```
Option Explicit

' References RDO 2.0

Dim Conn As New rdoConnection
Dim qy As New rdoQuery
Dim rs As rdoResultset

Private Sub Form_Load()

With Conn
    .Connect = "uid=randy;pwd=prince;dsn=JonesCompany"
    .EstablishConnection rdDriverNoPrompt, True
End With

End Sub

Private Sub Command1_Click()

qy.SQL = "select * from qryCustomer " & _
         "where LastName Like ?"
```

Listing 5.14: Creating a Parameterized Query Using the rdoParameter Object (Continued)

```
    Set qy.ActiveConnection = Conn
    qy.rdoParameters(0) = "%" & txtValue.Text & "%"
    Set rs = qy.OpenResultset

    lstResult.Clear

    Do Until rs.EOF
        lstResult.AddItem rs!LastName & " " & rs!FirstName
        rs.MoveNext
    Loop

End Sub
```

One difference between this version of the query test application and the versions described previously in this chapter is the fact that this version uses the SQL LIKE operator to retrieve data. (The LIKE operator is introduced in "Operators in WHERE Clauses," in Chapter 2.) Remember that when you use the LIKE operator, the query retrieves data that partially matches the criterion you specify ("sm" retrieves all the customers named Smith, for example).

Note that in SQL Server, you use the percent sign as the wildcard with the LIKE operator. This is in contrast to DAO's dialect of SQL, which uses an asterisk.

Retrieving Values Using the rdoColumns Collection The rdoColumns collection gives you access to the columns involved in an rdoResultset or rdoQuery object.

Each rdoColumn object belongs to an rdoColumns collection. The position of the rdoColumn object in the RDO object model hierarchy is illustrated in Figure 5.55.

Because the rdoColumns collection is the default property of an rdoQuery or rdoResultset object, you don't often refer to the rdoColumns collection or rdoColumn object directly. More frequently, you refer to it implicitly; in fact, the query and resultset in this chapter's previous examples have made implicit reference to the rdoColumns collection in order to retrieve values from individual columns.

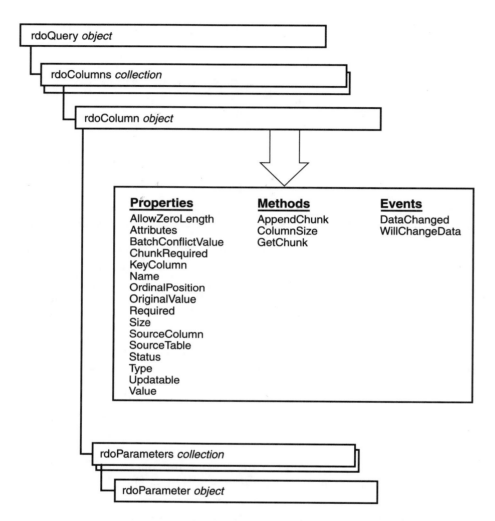

Figure 5.55: The rdoColumns collection and rdoColumn object in the Remote Data Object hierarchy.

For example, if you've queried the database and retrieved an rdoResultset object called rs, you use this code to populate a list box with its data:

```
Do Until rs.EOF
    List1.AddItem rs!FirstName & ? ? & rs!LastName
    rs.MoveNext
Loop
```

This code is actually shorthand for a reference to the rdoColumns collection contained in the rdoResultset object. If you were to write out the code without any shortcuts, it would look like this:

```
Do Until rs.EOF
    List1.AddItem rs.rdoColumns("LastName") & " " & _
                  rs.rdoColumns("FirstName")
    rs.MoveNext
Loop
```

You can see that using the default conserves a significant amount of code, and doesn't make the code less readable.

Accessing Tables with the rdoTable Object

You have the ability to access tables and views in RDO using the rdoTable object. You do this to map the *schema*, or structure, of your database.

The position of the rdoTable object in the RDO object hierarchy, as well as its properties and methods, is illustrated in Figure 5.56.

You can use the rdoTables collection to iterate through all the tables available in a particular database. To do this, use the code in Listing 5.15.

Listing 5.15: Retrieving a List of Objects in the Database Using the rdoTables Collection

```
Option Explicit

' References RDO 2.0

Dim Conn As New rdoConnection
Dim rs As rdoResultset
Dim t As rdoTable
Dim qry As rdoQuery

Private Sub Form_Load()

With Conn
    .Connect = "uid=randy;pwd=prince;dsn=JonesCompany"
    .EstablishConnection rdDriverNoPrompt, True
End With
```

continues

Listing 5.15: Retrieving a List of Objects in the Database Using the rdoTables Collection (Continued)

```
End Sub

Private Sub cmdTable_Click()

Conn.rdoTables.Refresh

lstResult.Clear

For Each t In Conn.rdoTables
    lstResult.AddItem t.Name
Next

End Sub

Private Sub cmdSys_Click()

Set qry = New rdoQuery

qry.SQL = "select * from sysobjects"

    Set qry.ActiveConnection = Conn
    Set rs = qry.OpenResultset

    lstResult.Clear

    Do Until rs.EOF
        lstResult.AddItem rs!Name
        rs.MoveNext
    Loop

End Sub
```

Remember that it's impossible to alter the structure of the database using RDO; consequently, the rdoTable object is read-only. This means that the rdoTable object is much less important and less frequently used than the TableDef object of Data Access Objects.

Furthermore, Microsoft has stated that the rdoTable object and rdoTables collection may be written out of the next version of Remote Data Objects. In that case, use rdoTable objects sparingly, if at all. If you need a procedure that inspects the structure of a database, it's probably better to reference a stored procedure that queries the sysobjects table of your database. In Listing 5.15 you saw an example of how to do this (in the Click event of the command button cmdSys).

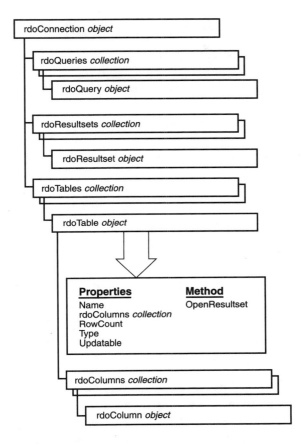

Figure 5.56: The rdoTables collection and rdoTable object in the Remote Data Object hierarchy.

Handling Errors with the rdoErrors Collection and the rdoError Object

The rdoErrors collection is used to identify and handle errors in Remote Data Object programming.

Each rdoError object belongs to an rdoErrors collection, as illustrated in Figure 5.57.

It's important to utilize the rdoErrors collection (as opposed to conventional Visual Basic error-handling) to evaluate and act on errors that take place in your application. This is because it's possible (quite likely, in fact) that your application will generate many errors when performing a single operation. Iterating through the rdoErrors collection gives you a complete picture of what went wrong.

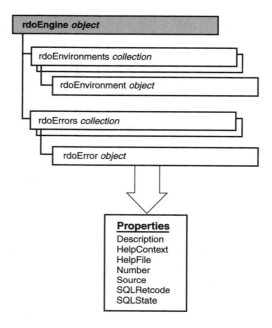

Figure 5.57: The rdoErrors collection and rdoError object in the Remote Data Object hierarchy.

This has to do with the bucket-brigade nature of client/server computing. When your application does something, it passes that something on to the ODBC driver, which then passes it on to middleware, which passes it on to the server. An error can be generated at any (or all) of these stages, so having access to a collection of errors instead of a single error (such as the type generated by VB) can go a long way toward helping you figure out exactly what went wrong. The code to implement this involves iterating through the rdoErrors collection, as shown in Listing 5.16.

Listing 5.16: Iterating Through the rdoErrors Collection in Response to a Data Access Error

```
Option Explicit

' References RDO 2.0

Dim Conn As New rdoConnection
Dim rerr As rdoError
```

Listing 5.16: Iterating Through the rdoErrors Collection in Response to a Data Access Error (Continued)

```
Private Sub Form_Load()

    On Error GoTo ErrHandler

    With Conn
        .Connect = "uid=randy;pwd=prince;dsn=JonesCompany"
        .EstablishConnection rdDriverNoPrompt, True
    End With

Exit Sub

ErrHandler:
    lstResult.Clear
    For Each rerr In rdoEngine.rdoErrors
        lstResult.AddItem rerr.Number & " - " & rerr.Description
    Next

End Sub
```

In this code example, any error generated by the process of creating a connection is placed in the rdoErrors collection; at the same time, a Visual Basic error is raised. In order to display all of the errors that may have been generated as a result of the problem, iterate through the rdoErrors collection using a For Each. . .Next loop.

Bugs in Remote Data Objects Fixed in Visual Studio Service Packs

A number of issues specifically relating to the functionality of Remote Data Objects were fixed in Service Packs for Microsoft Visual Studio. These Service Packs include patches for Visual Basic 5.0.

Specifically, the resolved issues are:

Bug	For More Information, See:
A distributed transaction fails after it is run repeatedly, stating that the connection is invalid.	**http://www.microsoft.com/kb/articles/ Q168/1/61.htm**
Executing a Move 0 method fails to refresh a record as documented.	**http://www.microsoft.com/kb/articles/ Q168/1/62.htm**

WRITING YOUR OWN JET SERVER

Using Visual Basic, it's possible for you to create a kind of database server application from scratch. You can do this using a combination of ActiveX and the Microsoft Jet database engine. This solution is as close as you can come to a true client/server database application without having to use an actual server such as Microsoft SQL Server.

Why would you want to do this? Performance on the client side, for one thing—if your clients don't have to load Jet, then each client conserves memory. This also means that you don't have to distribute Jet or configure ODBC drivers or other middleware on each client. Database access solutions that seek to minimize the amount of business logic, processing, and software components on the client side are sometimes referred to as *thin client* solutions. Such solutions are seen as desirable because in a corporate environment, the client computer is typically (but not always) the least powerful computer in the organization. Thin clients are also desirable because it makes it easier for organizations to standardize technology and business logic—the fewer changes you need to install on individual client computers, the easier it is to maintain and upgrade a system.

In order to create a solution like this, you must have a handle on programming with classes and objects in Visual Basic. This is introduced in Chapter 6. For more details on how to build a thin-client solution based on ActiveX servers, see Chapter 7, "Remote Database Access."

SUMMARY

This chapter gives you everything you need to get started doing client/server applications using the tools available in the Enterprise Edition of Visual Basic 5.0.

You should bear in mind that although this chapter focuses on client/server programming using SQL Server, the sections in the chapter on Remote Data Objects are applicable to any client/server system—Oracle, Sybase, Informix, whatever. As long as there is an ODBC driver that can get to your back-end data, you should be able to use Remote Data Objects.

In Chapter 6, you take the idea of accessing databases in an object-oriented environment a step further by introducing the concepts of classes and ActiveX servers—database objects you create yourself.

QUESTIONS AND ANSWERS

Q. **I've always been petrified to fool around with SQL Server. It always seemed like a black art to me. I once knew a guy whose brain exploded after doing a week of constant server-side programming. Will the topics covered in this chapter enable me to create serious database applications using SQL Server and keep my brain from exploding?**

A. Yes and no. This chapter wasn't designed to cover hard-core day-to-day database administration, performance tweaking, or anything like that, and it's definitely not designed to be a comprehensive guide to SQL Server— it's an introduction. The summary of getting started with SQL Server in the first half of this chapter was designed specifically so you can feel comfortable with the SQL Server. Migrating from the single-user and small-workgroup computing world up to client/server isn't trivial, but it shouldn't be a black art, either. That fear is what this chapter is designed to dispel. (As for your brain exploding, that's between you and your psychiatrist.)

Q. **I'm accustomed to writing applications using Data Access Objects. Because DAO supports client/server data sources, I'm having trouble finding a compelling reason for changing my existing code to use RDO. Can you give me a good reason?**

A. Performance, for one thing. Robustness, for another. Because Remote Data Objects is designed to be a thin layer around the ODBC API, it's capable of bypassing the Jet database engine entirely. Unless you're using ODBCDirect (which you should start doing unless you need to do something tricky, like link server data with a local Jet database), your existing application must load the Jet database engine whenever it makes a call to the SQL Server database. This doesn't make sense anymore, especially because DAO and RDO are so conceptually similar.

Beyond its performance benefits, RDO provides support for a number of compelling new features (establishing asynchronous connections, batch updates, and more) that go particularly well with client/server systems. You may be able to get by with existing code when you upgrade to a client/server system, but start using RDO as soon as you can for new client/server applications you write.

You should know that there is a third emerging object model for client-server computing, known as ActiveX Data Objects (or ADO). This object model is introduced and described in Chapter 9.

Q. Should I use the Remote Data Control or the Data control with ODBCDirect to create data-bound controls?

A. My first instinct is to avoid the whole thing entirely if you can, since the Data control and Remote Data Control can cause architectural and performance problems in database applications. If you must have data-bound controls in your user interface, the trade-off is between the slightly increased performance of the Remote Data Control versus the better reputation for stability provided by the Data control with ODBCDirect (the Remote Data Control in Visual Basic 4.0 had a particularly bad reputation for bugginess). Depending on the architecture of your application, consider prototyping with both types of data controls to determine which gives you the best combination of performance and stability. While we're on the topic—if you're going to use the conventional Data control with client/server data, don't make the mistake of forgetting to use ODBCDirect. There's no point in loading Jet in situations where your Data control is going after data on a server.

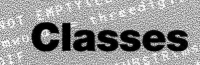

Classes

WORK WITH CLASSES AND OBJECTS

USE CLASSES AND OBJECTS WITH DATABASE ACCESS

CREATE CLASSES THAT EXPORT DATA

DEPLOY CLASSES AS ACTIVEX SERVERS

Chapter 6

Database access applications can be complicated—much more so than other types of applications. One reason Visual Basic gives you access to technologies such as Data Access Objects, Remote Data Objects, and Open Database Connectivity is to help you manage this complexity.

Yet these database access technologies only go part of the way in helping you deal with complicated issues that arise in software development. A database object model such as DAO, for example, helps you by abstracting the database and therefore making it easy for you to update a record or change a table definition in code. It doesn't help you calculate tax on a sale of merchandise or reject a piece of customer data because it isn't associated with a valid customer ID.

These types of operations go beyond the bare minimum of what's required to get your data from point A to point B; they go even further than what is traditionally known as validation, in which your application checks a piece of data before it is committed to the database. These operations instead fall into a category known as *business rules*.

Visual Basic lets your applications enforce business rules through the use of *classes*. A class is a special kind of code module that enables you to create *objects*. The objects you create with classes are similar to the data access objects you use to communicate with databases, except they can be used for any purpose. In the context of database access, you typically use classes along with database objects to create a database access application.

For example, say you're creating an application to deal with orders and customers. In a non-object–oriented, or *procedural* application, you'd attack the problem by writing functions that record customer and order information, retrieve such information from the database, print the information, and so forth. If you're writing the code in Visual Basic, it's likely that the code will be scattered hither and yon across perhaps a dozen or more event procedures. Each procedure would be hooked up to some esoteric function in your user interface such as a button click or dragging and dropping an icon on a form.

An object-oriented programmer, on the other hand, would begin by analyzing and designing components, or objects, that abstract the problem of dealing with customers and orders. He or she would determine what information a customer owns and what actions that customer object performs with that data; likewise with the order object. After the basic objects involved in the business problem are analyzed and expressed as classes, it becomes a simple matter (most of the time) to express customers and orders as objects in the application. You can then reuse the customer and order object in any application that requires them in the future. Because the source code of these objects exists in an easy-to-access container—the class module—rather than in a dozen event procedures scattered throughout the application's source code, you can more easily debug and maintain these objects.

In addition to making for good organization and reuse, classes and objects permit you to take advantage of powerful language features in Visual Basic. For example, there is a relationship between customers and orders—you can say that a customer "belongs" to an order, or more accurately, that a collection of orders belongs to a customer. As you see later in this chapter, there is support in the Visual Basic language for collections—a set of objects that can be handled elegantly and efficiently in code.

Were it not for the fact that these concepts were represented by objects, it would be much more difficult for you to conceptualize the problem, discuss it with others, and create a software application that solves the problem.

Object-oriented systems, then, help you conceptualize problems by letting you work backward—starting at the solution, proceeding to the objects involved in that solution, and then on to the business rules that govern those objects. You may find that working this way represents a bit of a mental stretch if you're accustomed to procedural programming, but in time you'll likely find that focusing on the problem rather than the solution is a more natural way to program.

An object-oriented system contains language elements that provide these elements:

▶ **Abstraction**   Entails reducing a problem to an easy-to-understand metaphor.

▶ **Polymorphism**   Involves enabling an object to perform the same actions or store the same data as other objects. This eases your programming tasks because you don't have to re-learn how to program each new object that comes along.

▶ **Encapsulation**   The mechanism by which program logic and data are grouped together.

▶ **Inheritance**   The idea that a new object can be created from existing objects. The feature of inheritance as implemented in Visual Basic is limited; it's provided in the form of interfaces and through delegation.

Note: There are a number of books that can help you go further with classes and objects. Deborah Kurata's *Doing Objects in Visual Basic 5.0* (Ziff-Davis Press, 1997) is a great reference to object-oriented programming in Visual Basic; Kurata's book also contains a one-of-a-kind design methodology geared toward object-oriented development in VB. There's a Web page for this book at **http://www.insteptech.com/Books.htm**.

Daniel Appleman's *Developing ActiveX Components with Visual Basic 5.0* (Ziff Davis Press, 1997) provides a wealth of information on the underpinnings of ActiveX objects and how you can access them from your VB5 projects. You can get more information on Appleman's book on the Web at **http://www.desaware.com/desaware/axgtp.htm**.

Finally, my *How to Program Visual Basic 5.0 Control Creation Edition* (Ziff-Davis Press, 1997) is a step-by-step guide to creating ActiveX user-interface controls using any edition of Visual Basic 5.0. The book also contains a chapter on creating data-aware controls. The Web page for this book is **http://www.redblazer.com/cce**.

WORKING WITH CLASSES AND OBJECTS

Because working with classes represents a serious departure from traditional Visual Basic programming, for this section you don't concentrate on accessing the database; instead, the intention is to get you started creating your own custom classes, then to worry about integrating them with the database later.

If you've never used classes before, don't be surprised if some of the topics discussed in this section feel a little wrong to you. It's the instinct of every VB programmer to want to reduce the amount of code in his or her application; on the face of things, classes seem to run counter to that instinct, adding what appear at first glance to be pointless additional lines of code to your project.

Remember as you start working with classes that it's all about encapsulation and reusability. The code you write in a class module today is more maintainable because it's encapsulated into one logical structure (the class module itself) and it's more reusable because you can utilize class modules in more than one project (as is discussed in "Deploying Classes as ActiveX Servers" later in this chapter).

Building Custom Classes

You start creating an object-oriented application in Visual Basic by adding a class module to your application. After you've done that, you define the interface of objects to be created by that class. An object's *interface* comprises its properties and methods.

Classes can be composed of:

▶ *Private member variables*, which store data

▶ *Property Let procedures*, which let users of your classes assign and change private member variables

▶ *Property Get procedures*, which let users of your classes read the values of private member variables

▶ *Methods*, which cause your classes to perform actions

▶ *Events*, which allow your classes to broadcast messages to host applications

▶ *Collections*, which allow you to store references to groups of objects

All the basic elements of classes are discussed in this section. Later in this chapter, you see how to utilize database objects with classes.

> **Note:** The capability of a class to generate events is new to Visual Basic 5.0. The other features of programming with classes and objects are available in both Visual Basic 4.0 and 5.0.

Creating Custom Properties　Any time you create a public data element in your class, the objects created in that class expose the data element as a *property* of the object.

Properties are the bread and butter of classes; very few classes without properties exist. You have two options for exposing properties in the classes you write:

▶ Declare a public variable in your class.

▶ Declare a private variable in your class, then expose it publicly using Property Get and Property Let procedures.

The public variable technique has the advantage of being easy to program; however, it's extremely inflexible because you have no control over what values get assigned to a public variable.

With a private variable and Property Let and Get, on the other hand, you have complete control over what gets assigned to a property. Your code can elegantly reject invalid values that users of your class attempt to assign, and it can spindle data as it is retrieved from the property of your class.

> **Note:** Property Let and Property Get procedures in Visual Basic are sometimes referred to in other languages as *writer* and *reader functions*.

Creating a Class with Properties   To give you an example of how to set up and use a class, start with something easy—an Order class that stores all the information required to take and process an order for a single item. (For this example, you ignore the fact that an order can be composed of more than one product, as well as the fact that the order needs to be stored in the database—you want to focus on the order itself, for now.) After you create the Order class in code, you can create and use Order objects in the application.

To create the Order class, do the following:

1 In Visual Basic, create a new Standard EXE project. The project, called Project1, is created. Initially, it contains a single form.

2 Close Form 1; you won't need it for right now.

3 In the Visual Basic Project Explorer, right-click on Project1. From the pop-up menu, select Add. From the submenu, select Class Module.

4 The Class Module dialog appears; Class Module is selected. Click Open.

5 A new class module appears, as illustrated in Figure 6.1. Note that the class module is composed of code only; unlike a form, it has no visible user interface.

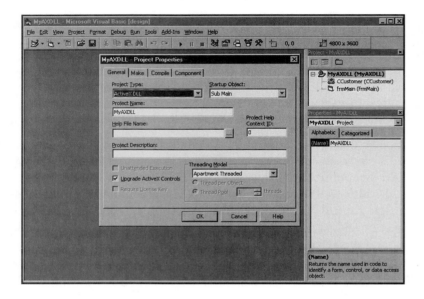

Figure 6.1: A new Visual Basic project containing a new class module.

6 Finish creating the class by giving the class a name, and typing it in the Visual Basic properties window. Change the name of the class from Class1 to COrder. (Prepending the letter C before the name of the object is a standard convention for naming classes.)

The Order object needs to store a number of data items pertaining to orders—order date, customer ID, item ordered, and total cost of the order. These data items are stored by the Order object in the form of properties, which you create in the form of code.

To add properties to the COrder class:

1 Add four private member variables to the Declarations section, as shown in Listing 6.1.

Listing 6.1: Code to Declare Private Member Variables in the Order Class

```
Option Explicit

' Private member variables
Private mdatOrderDate As Date
Private mlngCustomerID As Long
Private mstrItemOrdered As String
Private mcurPrice As Currency
```

2 Next, write code to expose the first private member variable, mdatOrderDate, as a public property called OrderDate. You do this with a Property Let and Property Get code, as shown in Listing 6.2.

Listing 6.2: Code to Implement a Public OrderDate Property in the Order Class

```
Public Property Get OrderDate() As Date
    OrderDate = mdatOrderDate
End Property

Public Property Let OrderDate(ByVal datNew As Date)
    mdatOrderDate = datNew
End Property
```

This is how the code works: The variable mdatOrderDate stores the actual date of the order in the object. The Property Get procedure is executed whenever the application needs access to the order date; it returns the value of mdatOrderDate. The Property Let, on the other hand, is executed when the application needs to assign a value to the order date property.

Using Property Get and Let gives you more control over how data is stored in objects you create from classes. What if you want to make a property read-only? Simple—delete the Property Let. What if you want to perform validation on date values assigned to the OrderDate property to make sure they're not four years in the past? No problem—write code in the Property Let to reject date values that are less than the current date.

To round out the properties of the Order class, add the code shown in Listing 6.3. This provides objects created by this class the properties of CustomerID, ItemOrdered, and Price.

Listing 6.3: Implementing the Remaining Property Procedures in the Order Class

```
Public Property Get CustomerID() As Long
    CustomerID = mlngCustomerID
End Property

Public Property Let CustomerID(ByVal lngNew As Long)
    mlngCustomerID = lngNew
End Property

Public Property Get ItemOrdered() As String
    ItemOrdered = mstrItemOrdered
End Property
```

continues

Listing 6.3: Implementing the Remaining Property Procedures in the Order Class (Continued)

```
Public Property Let ItemOrdered(ByVal strNew As String)
    mstrItemOrdered = strNew
End Property

Public Property Get Price() As Currency
    Price = mcurPrice
End Property

Public Property Let Price(ByVal curNew As Currency)
    mcurPrice = curNew
End Property
```

Your class is now fully functional; you can begin creating objects from it immediately. To test your new class, use the Immediate window to instantiate an object from it:

1 From the View menu, select Immediate window (or use the keystroke shortcut Ctrl+G).

2 The Immediate window appears. In the window, type this code:

```
Set MyOrder = New Order
```

After you type the keyword New, you should be able to see the list of objects in your current project drop-down box; you should be able to choose Order from the list.

Note: The Auto List Members feature seems to work inconsistently in the Immediate window; sometimes it doesn't display a list of properties and methods for an object unless the project you were working on is actually running.

After you enter this line of code, the Immediate window instantiates an Order object, MyOrder, from your class. To assign a property to it, execute the following code in the Immediate window:

```
MyOrder.OrderDate = #6/5/98#
Print MyOrder.OrderDate
```

The Immediate window should respond by printing the date value you stored in the Order object.

Note: Using the Immediate window in this manner is a new Visual Basic 5.0 feature; in previous versions you needed to run code before testing it interactively. The Immediate window's capability to permit you to interactively test code like this is a very powerful feature.

You expand and modify the Order class in the next few sections.

Creating Custom Methods   In addition to public properties, most classes contain methods. Your component's users execute methods to get objects created by your classes to do work.

When you create a procedure in a class that is declared Public, it becomes a method of that class.

Methods can be implemented as either functions or subs; a method declared as a function can return a value. You run into methods that return values every so often in the world of object-oriented programming. The OpenDatabase method in DAO is an example of a method that returns a value; this method opens a Jet database and returns a Database object. For more on how you can use such methods in your own classes, see "Using Factory Methods" later in this chapter.

For an example of how you can create a method in the Order class, add a method that calculates sales tax for an order.

Perform the following steps to add the AddSalesTax method to the Order class:

1 In the Order class, enter the code in Listing 6.4.

Listing 6.4: Code to Add the AddSalesTax Method to the Order Class

```
Public Function AddSalesTax() As Currency

    ' Adds sales tax to the price and
    ' returns the amount of sales tax.

    Dim sngSalesTaxRate As Single
    Dim curTax As Currency

    sngSalesTaxRate = 0.085

    ' Figure out what the tax is
    curTax = Price * sngSalesTaxRate

    ' Add sales tax to the price
    Price = Price + curTax

                                        continues
```

Listing 6.4: Code to Add the AddSalesTax Method to the Order Class (Continued)

```
    ' Return the sales tax you added
    AddSalesTax = curTax

End Function
```

2 In the Immediate window, enter the following code to test your new method:

```
Set MyOrder = New Order
```

This creates a new instance of the Order class.

3 Next, type the following code to set the value of the Price property of the Order object:

```
MyOrder.Price = 3.98
```

4 To add the sales tax, enter the code:

```
Print MyOrder.AddSalesTax
```

This returns the value of the sales tax computed on a $3.98 order, which is 0.3383.

5 Finally, enter the code:

```
Print MyOrder.Price
```

The Immediate window should respond with the new price of the item ordered, which is $4.3183.

After you interact with an object this way, you begin to see why programming with objects makes your job simpler—objects hide *complexity* from you, letting you concentrate on the problem instead of the details of how that problem is solved. When you're calculating a sales tax using the Order object, you don't need to know that the sales tax rate is 0.085; instead, you simply tell the object to add sales tax, and are done with it.

Creating Collections and Collection Classes

A *collection* is a special data type designed to store references to other objects. You can use collections to easily manage a number of related objects all at once. The Visual Basic language provides support for manipulating objects in collections. This makes it easier for you to perform operations that affect all the objects in a collection; this can involve anything from changing one or more properties of the objects in a collection to saving objects to a database as a group.

For example, if you have an Orders collection that contains a collection of Order objects, you can calculate the order's total by using the following code:

```
Dim curTotal As Currency

For Each Order in Orders
    curTotal = curTotal + Order.Price
Next
```

If you've already been through the chapters in this book on Data Access Objects and Remote Data Objects, you've seen examples of how to use collections to elegantly handle data. For an example of this, see "Working with Collections in Code," in Chapter 3, "Data Access Objects."

In addition, using collections is easier than using arrays, because collections provide a predefined set of methods for manipulating data. For example, when you have an array of five elements and you want to add a sixth element, you have to write several lines of code, redimensioning the array and then adding the new element. The collection, in contrast, has an Add method; to add a new element to the Orders collection, you simply use this code:

```
Orders.Add MyOrder
```

You don't have to write any code to implement the Add method of a collection, so adding a new element to the collection requires a grand total of one line of code. Adding new elements to collections using the collection's Add method is also far more efficient than redimensioning and adding a new element to an array.

There are a number of ways to implement a collection in the classes you build.

The easiest (yet least flexible) method is to declare a public variable of the data type Collection in your class. Like public member variables (described in "Creating Custom Properties" earlier in this chapter), this ease of programming comes at a cost of control and flexibility.

The more flexible method of working with collections in your projects is to build *collection classes*. The collection class is to collections what Property Let and Get procedures are to properties; they protect the data from unauthorized access, permit you to control and extend your object's functionality, and enable you to perform additional processing (such as validation) when data is stored or retrieved.

The relationship between your application, a collection class, and the private collection object it contains is illustrated in Figure 6.2.

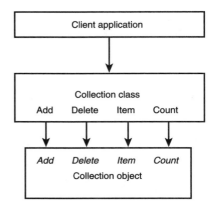

Figure 6.2: Relationship between an application and a collection class.

In order to implement a class that wraps a collection, follow these general steps:

▶ **Create a class** with a private member variable declared as the Collection data type.

▶ **Create property procedures** for the four elements of the interface of the collection objects: Add, Delete, Item, and Count. These trigger the Add, Delete, Item, and Count methods of the private collection member variable.

▶ **If you want, add any additional code** your collection class needs. This can include modifications to enhance the default behaviors of the Add, Delete, Item, and Count methods of the collection, for example, as well as any additional properties or methods the collection class needs to expose. For example, in a collection class, the Add method typically performs type validation, preventing inappropriate objects from being added to the collection.

If the idea of writing code in order to wrap a collection doesn't appeal to you, check out the Class Builder utility. In addition to generating code for classes (including Property Let and Get procedures), this VB5 add-in automatically writes the basic code for wrapping a collection; all you have to do is tell it what objects belong in the collection. There is an example of building an object hierarchy with Class Builder in the next section.

Creating Class Hierarchies with VB Class Builder Utility

When you're setting up classes that contain other classes—particularly classes that wrap collections—the code can be tedious to write and difficult to keep track of. You can use Visual Basic's Class Builder Utility to make the task of setting up and managing the relationship between a collection and its class wrapper easier.

For example, to create a collection class that enables you to work with collections of Order objects, do the following:

1 Start Visual Basic and load the project that contains the Order class.

2 Choose Add-In Manager from Visual Basic's Add-Ins menu.

3 Choose VB Class Builder Utility from the Add-In Manager dialog.

4 Click OK. The Class Builder Utility loads and becomes available to you.

5 To launch the Class Builder Utility, select Class Builder Utility from the Add-Ins menu.

6 The Class Builder Utility gives you a warning that the current project contains existing classes not built with the Class Builder Utility. Click OK.

7 The Class Builder Utility window appears, as shown in Figure 6.3.

8 Now use the Class Builder Utility to create a collection class. To do this, start by clicking the New Collection button in the toolbar, as shown in Figure 6.3. The Collection Builder dialog appears.

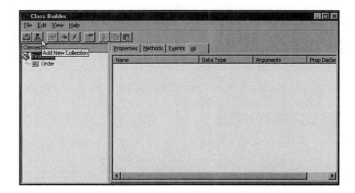

Figure 6.3: Using the Class Builder Utility's New Collection button to create a collection class.

9 In the Name box, type the name of your collection class—Orders.

10 Select Order in the Collection Of panel to indicate that this collection class is a collection of Order objects.

11 Click OK. The collection class is built, as shown in Figure 6.4.

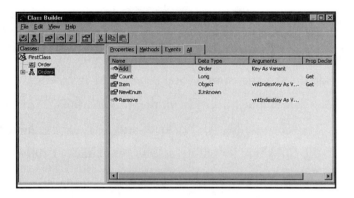

Figure 6.4: The Class Builder Utility window after it's created a collection class.

12 You can see that the Class Builder Utility has generated properties and methods to support the four methods of the collection (Add, Count, Item, and Remove) as well as NewEnum.

Note: The NewEnum property is created by the Class Builder Utility to enable your collection class to support iteration through the collection using the For Each...Next code construct. It's not usually necessary to do anything with the NewEnum property in your code.

13 Now that you've defined your collection class, you can tell the Class Builder Utility to write its code for you. To do this, choose File Update Project (or use the keystroke shortcut Ctrl+S).

14 The Class Builder Utility silently constructs the collection class in the background. Close the utility by choosing File, Exit. You should be able to see the Orders class that was created by the Class Builder utility.

The collection class isn't quite ready to use—you have to make one adjustment to the code it has written before it will work. In the Add method of the collection class, notice that the Class Builder Utility wrote an incorrect, erroneous line of code:

```
Public Function Add(, Optional sKey As String) As Order
```

The Class Builder Utility did this because it wants to give you the option of adding a parameter to the Add method of your collection class, to make it work just like the Add method of the collection object. This isn't strictly necessary; in fact, depending on the architecture of your object model, it can make more sense to permit the Add function to serve the dual purpose of creating the object and adding it to the collection simultaneously. In fact, that's the way a number of DAO and RDO methods that create objects work—the data access object is created and simultaneously added to a collection in case you need to access it later.

To resolve this problem, delete the first comma from the Add method's declaration so that it looks like this:

```
Public Function Add(Optional sKey As String) As Order
```

Now your collection class is ready to go. You need to build a test application in order to test your collection class. That is described in the next section.

Business Case 6.1: Manipulating Data Items Using a Collection Class Hard at work in their dank basement cubicles, the intrepid programmers of Jones Novelties, Incorporated are busy converting the entire corporation's business rules to objects. They're ready to build their first prototype—an order-entry application that transfers data from the user interface to an Order object stored in a collection. Storing the object in a collection enables the application to easily calculate a total on demand.

To build an application that prototypes the Order class and the Orders collection, do the following:

1 Start a project containing the Order and Orders classes you created earlier in this chapter. (If you didn't follow along with the demonstrations earlier in this chapter, you can load the classes from the CD-ROM that accompanies this book; they're in the Chapter 6 folder.)

2 In the project, create a form that enables the user to enter Date, Customer ID, Item, and Price. Additionally, add two command buttons to the interface—the first button enters data, while the second one calculates a total of all the orders entered so far. The interface should look like Figure 6.5.

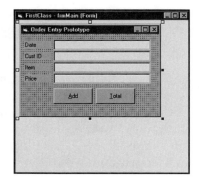

Figure 6.5: Interface of the prototype object-oriented order-entry system.

3 In the code for the form, begin by declaring two module-level variables, one corresponding to a single Order object, the other for the Orders collection:

```
Option Explicit

Private ThisOrder As Order
Private AllOrders As Orders
```

4 Instantiate an Orders object in the form's Load event:

```
Private Sub Form_Load()

    Set AllOrders = New Orders

End Sub
```

5 In the Add button's Click event, write code that adds the order to the collection and resets the application's user interface.

```
Private Sub cmdAdd_Click()

    ' Creates a new order and adds
    ' it to the collection
    Set ThisOrder = AllOrders.Add

    ThisOrder.OrderDate = txtOrderDate.Text
    ThisOrder.CustomerID = txtCustomerID.Text
```

```
ThisOrder.ItemOrdered = txtItemOrdered.Text
ThisOrder.Price = txtPrice.Text

' Reset the user interface
txtOrderDate.Text = ""
txtCustomerID.Text = ""
txtItemOrdered.Text = ""
txtPrice.Text = ""
txtOrderDate.SetFocus

End Sub
```

6 Finally, in the Click event of the Total button, write code that returns the total value of the orders that have been entered so far using a For Each...Next loop.

```
Private Sub cmdTotal_Click()

Dim TotalSales As Currency

    For Each ThisOrder In AllOrders
        TotalSales = TotalSales + ThisOrder.Price
        MsgBox "The total is " & TotalSales, vbInformation
    Next

End Sub
```

One cool thing about this code is the fact that it doesn't change when the internal procedures involved in the Order object and Orders collection class change. Even if you build your classes out to support features such as database access, the programmable interface of your objects remains the same.

Referring to Items in a Collection Remember that iterating through the collection with a For Each...Next loop isn't the only thing you can do with a collection. After you have the collection set up and populated with data, you can retrieve individual items from the collection as well. If you add objects to the collection with a key or with a unique text value, you can retrieve the objects without having to know which position in the collection the object occupies—another distinct advantage over arrays.

For example, in the previous business case example, you created a collection of Order objects. To retrieve the fourth Order object in the collection of Orders, use this code:

```
Set MyOrder = AllOrders(4)
```

To refer to a property of the fourth Order object in the collection, simply make a reference to it by its index in the collection, as this line of code demonstrates:

```
AllOrders(4).OrderDate = #6/5/98#
```

This works because the default procedure of a collection returns a reference to the numbered item. This default procedure is the Item method. Because Item is the default method of a collection, you never have to explicitly write it out. If you choose to, though, the previous line of code would look like this:

```
AllOrders.Item(4).OrderDate = #6/5/98#
```

> **Caution:** The first item in a collection is item number one. This is different than arrays, which begin numbering their members at zero. Confusingly, it's also different than Visual Basic collections of things like Form and Control objects—these collections begin numbering their items at zero. The rule is that collections you create are one-based, while collections VB creates are zero-based. This is also the case for collections of data access objects, such as the TableDefs collection of the Database object.

To retrieve an item from the collection using a key, you must first add it to the collection with a key. To do this with a collection class, pass a unique string value to the Add method:

```
AllOrders.Add "ORD1193"
```

You get a run-time error if this string value is not unique. To refer to a property of this object after it's been created in the collection, use the code:

```
MsgBox AllOrders("ORD1193").Price
```

It's important that you don't use a numeric value for an object's key value, even if you pass it to the Add method in the form of a string. This is because the Item method can return an object from the collection by key or by ordinal position; it determines whether to return an object by key or by ordinal position by what data type it gets. If the Item method gets a number n, it returns the nth item in the collection. If it receives a string, it returns the object with a key equal to that string. If your strings can be cast as numbers, though, you're setting yourself up for a problem.

Using Forms as Classes

You can use forms in your application the same way you use classes. This is useful in situations where you want to create instances of the same form repeatedly. It's also useful in situations where a particular data value or procedure is tightly bound to the user interface.

The login form is an example of this in the database access world. This form allows the user to enter a login name and password. There's no reason why that user-interface component can't also store the information pertaining to the user, making that information available to other procedures in the application. Such a form would also be reusable across other applications that required the user to log in to the same database.

To create and use a login form that exposes custom properties, do the following:

1 In a VB project, right-click the Project Explorer.

2 Select Add from the pop-up menu. Choose Form from the submenu.

3 The Form dialog appears. Choose Login form, as shown in Figure 6.6.

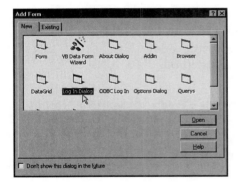

Figure 6.6: Visual Basic's form dialog, which lets you choose from a variety of predefined form templates.

4 In the Form dialog, click Open. A new form is created.

5 In the form's code, enter the property procedures in Listing 6.5.

Listing 6.5: Code to Supply Custom Properties and a Method to the Login Form

```
Public Property Get UserName() As String
    UserName = txtUserName.Text
End Property

Public Property Let UserName(ByVal strNew As String)
    txtUserName.Text = strNew
End Property

Public Property Get Password() As String
    Password = txtPassword.Text
End Property

Public Property Let Password(ByVal strNew As String)
    txtPassword.Text = strNew
End Property

Public Sub Login()
    MsgBox "Code to log in user " & UserName & " goes here."
    End Sub
```

6 The standard Visual Basic login form contains code in the Click events of the OK and Cancel buttons to log the user in to the system. Remove this code and replace it with code in Listing 6.6; it takes advantage of your custom properties and method.

Listing 6.6: Code for the Click Events of the Login Form's OK and Cancel Buttons

```
Private Sub cmdCancel_Click()
    Me.Hide
End Sub

Private Sub cmdOK_Click()
    UserName = txtUserName.Text
    Password = txtPassword.Text
    Login
End Sub
```

Although expressing this code in terms of properties and methods may not seem like a radical departure from the default code provided by Visual Basic's login form template, it has a number of important advantages. Among these are the fact that the login form can be more easily reused across multiple applications. It's also easier to get information out of this form; you can use code like frmLogin.Password and frmLogin.UserName from anywhere in the application. Finally, placing a single public Login method in your login form means that it can be called from anywhere in your application. Having a single point of access to a database is very important when you're trying to conserve resources in a client-server application, as discussed in "Using Factory Methods," later in this chapter.

Creating Multiple Instances of Forms You can create multiple instances of forms just as you create multiple instances of objects from classes. Each additional instance of the form has its own identity in the context of your application, with a copy of all the properties, methods, and user-interface controls that exist on the original design of the form.

It doesn't make sense to have more than one instance of a user login form, but it's common to have multiple instances of other types of forms. To do this, create a new instance of the form using the same code you'd use to create new instances of objects from a class. Listing 6.7 shows an example of how to do this.

Listing 6.7: Creating Multiple Instances of a Form Using Object-Oriented Code

```
Dim f as frmMain
Set f = New frmMain
f.Show
```

You can execute this code as many times as you want. Each time you create a new instance of frmMain and show it using its Show method, a new form—with its own interface, controls, properties, and methods—appears.

USING CLASSES AND OBJECTS WITH DATABASE ACCESS

Creating your own objects can go a long way toward managing complexity and leveraging reusability of code. Using object-oriented techniques for accessing databases, however, can be tricky. Developers who how to create their own custom classes and collections in Visual Basic, often have the initial instinct to take all the database access code they currently have and convert it into collections.

To a certain extent, this strategy makes sense; if you have a single object or set of objects that manage database access in your application, your application is easier to debug and modify, because you always know where the database access portion of your program is. You don't have to reinvent the wheel repeatedly, in order to simply retrieve data and write it back to the data store.

The problem with database access in classes has to do with the fact that the object model and the relational model are at odds with each other. In many cases, treating a database record as an object is like sticking a round peg in a not-so-round hole. Most databases you're likely to use in the foreseeable future don't have the capability to store and retrieve custom-made objects (although database vendors are hard at work creating such "object-oriented databases").

To let your objects do database access using the mainstream database engines available to you today, you have to write code to *translate*, or *map*, data stored in a database to the set of properties exposed by the objects you create.

There are a number of techniques for applying object-oriented techniques to database access in VB. These include:

▶ **Mapping a single record to an object.** This is the simplest technique, requiring the least amount of code. Each field in the record becomes a property of the object; retrieving and saving the data to and from the database is handled by the object itself.

▶ **Delegating the handling of data to a Recordset object owned by your object.** This is the best technique to use when you have to deal with a potentially unlimited number of records. This technique can also be a bit easier to code, because much of the data management functionality is provided for you by the object model (either DAO or RDO) your class utilizes.

▶ **Mapping a small group of records to a collection.** This is more difficult to code than mapping one object to one record at a time, but it's more useful if you have to deal with small related groups of records at a time. You can run into performance problems with this technique if you aren't careful to limit the number of records you handle at one time.

There are various methods of mapping relational data to objects; different methods are appropriate for different situations. The examples in the remainder of this chapter give you an idea of which technique to use, and under what circumstances each method is most appropriate for your application's goals.

Using Single Record-Handling Classes

A *record-handling class* retrieves a single record from the database and makes it available to your application in the form of an object. The fields in the record are exposed as the object's properties; any actions performed by the data (such as saving its data back to the database, printing, or performing calculations) are exposed as methods of the record-handling object.

You can perform the actual retrieval of the database data in a number of ways. You can provide a method that retrieves the data from the database on demand, or you can set up your class so it populates its properties with a record from the database automatically when the record is created.

To implement a record-handling class that populates its properties on demand, give the class a method (named something like GetData) that knows how to perform a single-record query from the database. When the GetData method queries the data from the database, it uses the fields in the record it retrieves to populate the properties of the object.

To create a record-handling class that automatically populates its properties with data from the database at the time an object is created, write code in the class's Initialize event. The code in this event is triggered whenever an object is instantiated from a class; it's the perfect place to insert code that performs a database call to retrieve the object's data.

In either case, when you give the object the responsibility of retrieving a record from a database, you'll need to give that object something to uniquely identify that record—preferably that record's primary key. The easiest way to do this is to make the primary key a property of the record-handling object; the object's GetData method (or the code in its Initialize event) uses this key data to retrieve the record it needs.

In addition to retrieving data from the database, you probably also want to give your record-handling class a method—most likely called Save—that enables the user of component to save the record back to the database. Business Case 6.2 gives a more detailed example of such a class.

Business Case 6.2: Using a Single-Record–Handling Class   Jones Novelties has expanded its Information Services division. New applications are being planned monthly in response to increasing demand for data services by managers and users.

The intrepid database programmers of Jones Novelties decide to meet the need for reusable components that provide access to the corporate database by creating a class library that gives standardized access to the corporate database.

As with any database access in Visual Basic, you must begin by making a reference to a database object library—either Data Access Objects or Remote Data Objects. This technique works equally well with DAO or RDO, but because you've already set up a SQL Server database for Jones Novelties (the company database described in Chapter 5), use that for this example.

To start, create a Customer class that enables your applications to deal with customers in an object-oriented way. Each Customer object will have all the properties a customer has, including first name, last name, address, city, state, and zip code. These values correspond to fields in the tblCustomer table in the company database, but in the object-oriented world, they are expressed as properties of the Customer object.

In order to provide connectivity to the company database, the Customer class uses a UserConnection designer named conCompany. (UserConnection designers are introduced in Chapter 5.) All the database access code involved in retrieving and manipulating customers is kept away from the user of the Customer class, however—the gory details are "under the hood," in the guts of the Customer class.

Mapping a single record to an object requires that you write code to retrieve and store the record in the database; each field in the record becomes a property of the object created from your class. Single-record-handlers (like recordset handlers) also contain Database and Recordset objects, which are stored as private member variables and are responsible for database access. In a single-record-handler object, these private member variables are not exposed to the user of the class; in the recordset-handler object, the Recordset object is exposed.

Additionally, the Customer object needs to know how to save itself to the database (through the execution of a Save method) and perform other tasks related to accessing the database.

Listing 6.8 shows the properties of a single-record-handler in a class called CCustomer.

Listing 6.8: A Single-Record Handler Class that Exposes Fields in a Record as Properties of an Object

```
Option Explicit

' Private member variables for
' object properties
Private mstrFirstName As String
Private mstrLastName As String
Private mstrAddress As String
Private mstrCity As String
Private mlngCustomerID As Long    ' Primary key
Private mstrState As String
Private mstrZip As String
Private mstrPhone As String

' Private variables for RDO
Private Conn As rdoConnection         ' Connection to the database
```

Listing 6.8: A Single-Record Handler Class that Exposes Fields in a Record as Properties of an Object (Continued)

```
Private qy As rdoQuery
Private rs As rdoResultset

' Error constants
Const srCouldNotGetData = vbObjectError + 512 + 2
Const srCouldNotSaveData = vbObjectError + 512 + 3
'

Private Sub Class_Initialize()

    Set Conn = New conCompany
    Conn.EstablishConnection

End Sub

Public Property Let Address(ByVal strNew As String)
    mstrAddress = strNew
End Property

Public Property Get Address() As String
    Address = mstrAddress
End Property

Public Property Let City(ByVal strNew As String)
    mstrCity = strNew
End Property

Public Property Get City() As String
    City = mstrCity
End Property

Public Property Get CustomerID() As Long
    CustomerID = mlngCustomerID
End Property

Public Property Let CustomerID(ByVal lngNew As Long)
    mlngCustomerID = lngNew
End Property

Public Property Let FirstName(ByVal strNew As String)
    mstrFirstName = strNew
End Property
```

continues

Listing 6.8: A Single-Record Handler Class that Exposes Fields in a Record as Properties of an Object (Continued)

```
Public Property Get FirstName() As String
    FirstName = mstrFirstName
End Property

Public Property Let LastName(ByVal strNew As String)
    mstrLastName = strNew
End Property

Public Property Get LastName() As String
    LastName = mstrLastName
End Property

Public Property Let Phone(ByVal strNew As String)
    mstrPhone = strNew
End Property

Public Property Get Phone() As String
    Phone = mstrPhone
End Property

Public Property Let State(ByVal strNew As String)
    mstrState = strNew
End Property

Public Property Get State() As String
    State = mstrState
End Property

Public Property Let Zip(ByVal strNew As String)
    mstrZip = strNew
End Property

Public Property Get Zip() As String
    Zip = mstrZip
End Property

Public Sub GetData()

    If CustomerID <> 0 Then
        qy.SQL = "select * from qryCustomer " & _
                 "where ID = " & CustomerID
        qy.MaxRows = 1
        Set qy.ActiveConnection = Conn
        Set rs = qy.OpenResultSet
```

Listing 6.8: A Single-Record Handler Class that Exposes Fields in a Record as Properties of an Object (Continued)

```
        ' Populate properties with
        ' results of the query.
        FirstName = rs!FirstName
        LastName = rs!LastName
        Address = rs!Address & ""    ' cheesy null-safe trick
        City = rs!City & ""
        State = rs!State & ""
        Zip = rs!Zip & ""
        Phone = rs!Phone & ""
    Else
        Err.Raise srCouldNotGetData, _
                "Customer - GetData", _
                "You must supply a Customer ID to retrieve a customer."
        Exit Sub
    End If

End Sub

Public Sub Save()

    Set qy = New rdoQuery
    Set qy.ActiveConnection = Conn

    qy.SQL = "update qryCustomer set " & _
            "FirstName = ?, " & _
            "LastName = ?, " & _
            "Address = ?, " & _
            "City = ?, " & _
            "State = ?, " & _
            "Zip = ?, " & _
            "Phone = ? " & _
            "where ID = ?"

    qy.rdoParameters(0) = FirstName
    qy.rdoParameters(1) = LastName
    qy.rdoParameters(2) = Address
    qy.rdoParameters(3) = City
    qy.rdoParameters(4) = State
    qy.rdoParameters(5) = Zip
    qy.rdoParameters(6) = Phone
    qy.rdoParameters(7) = CustomerID

    qy.Execute

End Sub
```

The initialization of the database connection happens in the class's Initialize event, but the class's real work can't be performed until the user sets the CustomerID property. CustomerID, which is the tblCustomer table's primary key, allows the record-handler class to look up all the information in the database pertaining to the wonder requested by the user. This is actually performed by the GetData method.

The real benefit of placing database access in a single-record-handler class becomes evident when you look at the class's Save method. This method requires quite a bit of code to perform a simple update—and the method shown here (a parameterized SQL update command) isn't even the most sophisticated way to perform updates in RDO.

What if you decide to be ambitious and revise the Save method to take advantage of RDO's features that let you manage multiuser contention (described in more detail in Chapter 8)? Does your application care that you changed the code? Heck, no. All your application cares about is the fact that the data was actually saved in the database. The code used to call the class's Save method remains the same regardless of the code involved to perform the save.

The point here is that the technique used to save the data shouldn't matter to your application. Separating the functionality of your application from its specific implementation is an important object-oriented technique that can go a long way toward making your programs easier to maintain and improve over time without breaking related code.

To use this class, write code in the project's form that retrieves a record and permits the user to save it back to the database:

1 Add eight text boxes to the project's form. The first text box stores the customer's ID number and is used for querying; the other seven text boxes display the customer's properties. Add two command buttons, one for retrieving data, the other for saving data.

2 Declare a Customer object variable in the form's Declarations section. In the form's Load event, instantiate the object, as shown in Listing 6.9.

Listing 6.9: Code to Declare an Object Variable and Create an Instance of the Customer Object

```
Option Explicit

Private CurrentCustomer As Customer

Private Sub Form_Load()
```

Listing 6.9: Code to Declare an Object Variable and Create an Instance of the Customer Object (Continued)

```
Set CurrentCustomer = New Customer

End Sub
```

3 Next, add code to retrieve data for the Customer object according to the ID entered by the user, as shown in Listing 6.10.

Listing 6.10: Mapping Properties of User-Interface Controls to Properties of the CurrentCustomer Object

```
Private Sub cmdGet_Click()

    CurrentCustomer.CustomerID = txtCustomerID.Text
    CurrentCustomer.GetData

    txtFirstName.Text = CurrentCustomer.FirstName
    txtLastName.Text = CurrentCustomer.LastName
    txtAddress.Text = CurrentCustomer.Address
    txtCity.Text = CurrentCustomer.City
    txtState.Text = CurrentCustomer.State
    txtZip.Text = CurrentCustomer.Zip
    txtPhone.Text = CurrentCustomer.Phone

End Sub
```

4 Enter code to save the record after the user changes it, as shown in Listing 6.11.

Listing 6.11: Saving a Customer Object from Within a Form

```
Private Sub cmdSave_Click()

    CurrentCustomer.FirstName = txtFirstName.Text
    CurrentCustomer.LastName = txtLastName.Text
    CurrentCustomer.Address = txtAddress.Text
    CurrentCustomer.City = txtCity.Text
    CurrentCustomer.State = txtState.Text
    CurrentCustomer.Zip = txtZip.Text
    CurrentCustomer.Phone = txtPhone.Text

    CurrentCustomer.Save

    MsgBox "The current customer has been saved.", vbInformation

End Sub
```

5 Finally, add code to destroy the Customer object when the form is unloaded, as shown in Listing 6.12.

Listing 6.12: Destroying the Instance of the Customer Object Used by the Form

```
Private Sub Form_Unload(Cancel As Integer)

    Set CurrentCustomer = Nothing

End Sub
```

Now the advantage of using classes to access records in a database really becomes apparent. The code in the form is so straightforward, looking at it makes you sleepy.

Creating Classes that Handle Recordsets

Single-record-handling classes are an effective way to access data, but they don't provide a number of features you might want when working with data. For example, single objects that represent database records don't let you easily iterate through a large number of records. Even if you place such objects in a collection as described earlier in this chapter, performance and memory limitations make this technique prohibitive.

The database access object models DAO and RDO provide a rich set of features for handling information stored in a database. You can take advantage of these features by creating a recordset-handling class. This type of class is responsible for doing everything necessary to access the database, assembling or accessing a query, and returning a recordset.

The recordset generated by a recordset-handling class is typically a property of the class (although you can create a recordset handler that generates recordset objects with a factory method, as described later in this chapter).

Unlike the single-record-handling class, the recordset-handling class doesn't require the calling application to supply any information about what data is to be returned; instead, the class knows what data to return and exactly how to access it. Placing the database access code in a class of its own means that it's much easier to call; the calling application only has to instantiate the object in order to retrieve the data.

After your application has instantiated an object that contains its own Recordset, you can use that object just as you'd use any other Recordset object. This includes assigning the recordset object to the Recordset property of a Data control, as described later in this chapter.

Business Case 6.3: Creating an Application that Uses a Recordset-Handling Class Those wacky software developers of Jones Novelties, Incorporated want to channel access to their database through a set of classes. However, they have a problem—they need to use database-aware controls, such as the database grid and others.

At first glance, it would seem that the Visual Basic Data control doesn't lend itself to the types of object-oriented data access techniques described in this chapter. This is because the Data control connects to the database procedurally (through the assignment of its DatabaseName and RecordSource properties).

However, it's possible to incorporate the Data control in a solution that involves a recordset-handling class. The trick is to use the recordset-handler to generate a recordset, then assign that Recordset object to the Recordset property of the Data control at run-time. When you do this, you don't need to set the Data control's DatabaseName and RecordSource properties; the Data control uses the existing Recordset object created by your class.

The recordset-handling class called CrsCustomer is designed to return a recordset rather than a single record. This gives users of the class full object-oriented access to the data, as well as the ability to maintain a common interface into the database, even if elements of the database change over time.

The reference to the Database and Recordset objects are set in the class's Initialize event, as demonstrated in Listing 6.13.

Listing 6.13: The Recordset-Handling Class CrsCustomer

```
Option Explicit

' References DAO 3.5

Private db As Database
Private rs As Recordset

Public Property Get Recordset() As Recordset

' Read-only.

    Set Recordset = rs

End Property

Private Sub Class_Initialize()

    Set db = OpenDatabase(App.Path & "\novelty.mdb")
    Set rs = db.OpenRecordset("tblCustomer")


End Sub
```

As you can see, the code for this class is relatively simple; that's because most of the functionality is delegated to Data Access Objects.

You instantiate and utilize this class in a form the way you'd create any other type of object. The only difference is the fact that the class's Recordset property is an object, so you must assign it using the Set keyword. You can see an example of this in Listing 6.14.

Listing 6.14: Creating an Instance of the CrsCustomer Class and Using It in an Application

```
Option Explicit

' References DAO 3.5

Private Customers As CrsCustomer

Private Sub Form_Load()

    Set Customers = New CrsCustomer
    Set Data1.Recordset = Customers.Recordset
    Data1.Refresh

End Sub
```

One way to test this code is to create a DBGrid control on the form and assign its DataSource property to Data1 at design time. When you run the application, the Customers object is created and the grid is populated with data from its recordset, as illustrated in Figure 6.7.

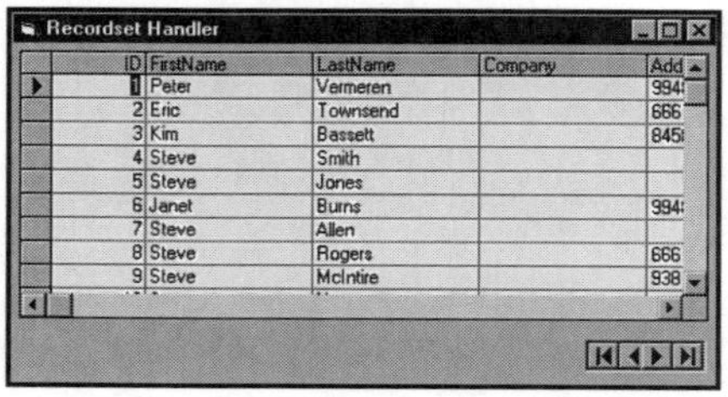

Figure 6.7: A user interface based on a data-aware control whose data is populated with a Recordset Handler class.

In a recordset-handling class, you have the ability to use the properties and methods of the Recordset object embedded in your class. For example, in an object produced by the CrsCustomer class, you'd use the following code to determine the number of customers in the database:

```
Customers.Recordset.RecordCount
```

This works because RecordCount is a property of the DAO Recordset object. You should also be able to see another advantage of the delegated Recordset object—you get access to the entire set of properties and methods of the Recordset object created by your class through Auto List Members feature of VB5.

Similarly, if you want to obtain the name of the first customer returned by the CrsCustomer class, you'd use this code:

```
Customers.Recordset.Fields("FirstName")
```

These are only examples; remember that you have access to the full interface of the delegated Recordset object when you include a Recordset property in a class you build.

Using Array-Handling Classes

You can create classes that query the database, then pass arrays back to client applications in the form of arrays. The advantage to this technique is that if your array-handling class is compiled to an ActiveX server DLL or EXE, it's possible to create a client application that requires no references to the database engine. All the client requires is a reference to your ActiveX server component. This makes the footprint of your client-side application much smaller; it also makes the application much easier to distribute and configure.

For more information on creating ActiveX components that pass data in the form of arrays, see "Using GetRows to Return Data in an Array" in Chapter 7, "Remote Database Access."

Using Factory Methods

An *object factory* is a method that creates other objects. You use object factories in situations where one object takes responsibility for creating other objects. Objects create other objects through the use of methods; such methods are called *factory methods*.

Although this might seems like one of those alien object-oriented concepts, you've probably used it already—in Data Access Objects, for example. The DAO Database object has factory methods that can produce a number of objects. By way of example, Table 6.1 lists all the factory methods of the Database object in DAO.

Table 6.1: Factory Methods of the Database Object in DAO

Method	Description
CreateQueryDef	Creates a QueryDef object
CreateRelation	Creates a Relation object
CreateTableDef	Creates a TableDef object
OpenRecordset	Creates a Recordset object
CreateProperty	Creates a Property object

In addition to using the factory methods provided by Visual Basic, you can create factory methods in the classes you build yourself. You do this in a number of situations, generally pertaining to simplifying and extending the capabilities of object instantiation in your application.

One common reason to use factory methods has to do with the way objects are created in VB. Other programming languages that use objects (such as C++) have constructors responsible for creating instances of the object from the class; these constructors can also perform other tasks, such as supply initialization data for the class.

There's no direct correlation, however, to constructors in Visual Basic. Instead, VB classes have an Initialize event. You can run code in the Initialize event like you can in a C++ constructor. Unfortunately, you can't pass arguments to the VB Initialize event. This makes the usefulness of the Initialize event extremely limited for all but the most basic, hard-coded default values.

Business Case 6.4: Using a Factory Method to Create Record-Handling Objects The stalwart developers of Jones Novelties Incorporated have really taken to using record-handling classes. Now they wish to simplify the process of working with the Customer object by creating a factory method, CCustomerFactory, to produce Customer objects whenever the applications require them.

The CCustomerFactory object has one method: CreateCustomer. This factory method takes an optional argument. If the argument is present, CreateCustomer retrieves an existing customer from the database. If it is missing, it creates a new Customer object. The code for the CCustomerFactory class is shown in Listing 6.15.

Listing 6.15: Code for the CCustomerFactory Class

```
Option Explicit

' Requires Customer class
' References DAO 3.5

Public Function CreateCustomer(Optional lngID As Variant) As CdaoCustomer

Dim cust As CdaoCustomer

    If IsMissing(lngID) Then
        ' Create new customer
        Set CreateCustomer = New Customer
    Else
        ' Retrieve customer from DB
        Set cust = New Customer
        cust.CustomerID = lngID
        cust.GetData
        Set CreateCustomer = cust
    End If

End Function
```

Note: This project uses the a Customer class similar to that introduced in Business Case 6.2, "Using a Single-Record–Handling Class." The only difference between the Customer class used in that business case and the CdaoCustomer class used here is the fact that the CdaoCustomer class uses DAO instead of RDO for simplicity.

Another reason for using factory methods in Visual Basic database programming is to conserve connection resources in RDO. It's in your interest to make as few connections to the database as possible, because connecting to the database is computationally expensive; it requires time and memory resources on the client and on the server.

If you use a class that acts as an object factory, it's easier to limit the number of connections you make to the server. In this scenario, the only connection to the database is the single rdoConnection object maintained by the class that contains the factory method. The factory method's job is to produce rdoResultSet objects based on the rdoConnection object.

Note: The concept of the factory method introduced in this section is described in more detail in *Design Patterns: Elements of Reusable Object-Oriented Software* (Addison-Wesley, 1995). This book provides a number of scenarios for using objects in your applications in addition to the concept of the factory method. While not all the concepts introduced in the book are applicable to Visual Basic because of limitations in the language, many of the OOP concepts in the book can help you grasp the Zen of OOP.

CREATING CLASSES THAT EXPORT DATA

When you have a good general idea of how you want to export data, it makes sense to take that export logic and place it in a class. This is because classes make it easy to reuse code, and export code is among the most reused in the world of database programming.

Chances are that if you write one procedure that takes a database table and converts it into a delimited text file, you're going to have to do it again at some point in your life. This section shows you how to create such procedures once, get them right the first time, and never have to worry about them once you've deployed them.

This section builds on the HTML export function described in Chapter 4 to demonstrate how easy it is to provide a programmable export object using classes. In that chapter, you built a function to take a database and map its fields to the properties of an object. The product of this process was the Customer class.

To give the Customer class export capabilities, you add one additional property and one method to the class. The property, HTMLText, takes properties of the Customer object and formats them as an HTML page. This property procedure calls a private function, HTMLTableRow, that formats each individual row of the table. This code is shown in Listing 6.16.

Note: The functions described in this section work with either the RDO or DAO versions of the Customer class introduced in this chapter.

Listing 6.16: The HTMLText Property of the Customer Class

```
Public Property Get HTMLText() As String
Dim str As String
```

Listing 6.16: The HTMLText Property of the Customer Class (Continued)

```
    str = "<html>" & vbCrLf
    str = str & "<head>" & vbCrLf
    str = str & "<title>" & "Customer: " & _
                FirstName & " " & _
                LastName & _
                "</title>" & vbCrLf

    str = str & "<body bgcolor=#ffffff>" & vbCrLf
    str = str & "<font face=Arial,Helvetica>" & vbCrLf

    str = str & "<table border>" & vbCrLf

    str = str & HTMLTableRow("First name:", FirstName)
    str = str & HTMLTableRow("Last name:", LastName)
    str = str & HTMLTableRow("Address:", Address)
    str = str & HTMLTableRow("City:", City)
    str = str & HTMLTableRow("State:", State)

    str = str & "</table>"

    str = str & "</font>" & vbCrLf
    str = str & "</body>" & vbCrLf
    str = str & "</html>" & vbCrLf

    HTMLText = str

End Property

Private Function HTMLTableRow(strLabel As String, vValue As Variant) As String

' Returns a row of a two-column HTML table

Dim str As String

    str = str & "<tr>" & vbCrLf
    str = str & "  <td>" & vbCrLf
    str = str & "  " & strLabel & vbCrLf
    str = str & "  </td>" & vbCrLf
    str = str & "  <td>" & vbCrLf
    str = str & "  " & vValue & vbCrLf
    str = str & "  </td>" & vbCrLf
    str = str & "</tr>"

HTMLTableRow = str

End Function
```

You'll notice that this code doesn't actually export the HTML to a file, it simply formats it. This is done because you want the flexibility to do anything with the HTML data, not necessarily just export it to a file. The process of exporting is really two things: first, formatting the data in HTML, and second, writing it to a file. Accordingly, you write one procedure to perform each task.

The SaveHTML method of the Customer object actually saves the HTML data to a file. Its code is shown in Code Listing 6.17.

Listing 6.17: The SaveHTML Method of the Customer Object, which Saves the HTML-ized Customer Data to a File

```
Public Sub SaveHTML(strFileName As String)

Dim intFile As Integer
intFile = FreeFile

Open strFileName For Output As intFile

Print #intFile, HTMLText
Close #intFile

End Sub
```

It's important to note that these procedures should be part of the Customer class. This has to do with the object-oriented concept of encapsulation. Classes whose functionality is properly encapsulated are trivially easy to re-use in other projects.

To use the export functionality of the Customer class, create an application that allows the user to supply a Customer ID and an export filename. When the user clicks on a command button, the selected customer is exported to the HTML file specified by the user, as shown in Listing 6.18.

Listing 6.18: Code in a Form that Calls the Export Functionality of the Customer Class

```
Option Explicit

Private Cust As CdaoCustomer

Private Sub Form_Load()

Set Cust = New CdaoCustomer

End Sub
```

Listing 6.18: Code in a Form that Calls the Export Functionality of the Customer Class (Continued)

```
Private Sub cmdExport_Click()

Cust.CustomerID = txtID.Text
Cust.GetData
Cust.SaveHTML App.Path & "\" & txtFilename.Text

MsgBox "File saved.", vbInformation

End Sub
```

The important thing to note about this code is its brevity, as well as the fact that it doesn't have to communicate with the database directly in order to perform its work.

The result of the code executing is illustrated in Figure 6.8.

Figure 6.8: Application that uses the enhanced Customer class to export HTML data.

The HTML file created by the export method is illustrated in Figure 6.9.

DEPLOYING CLASSES AS ACTIVEX SERVERS

You can use Visual Basic to compile class-based projects as ActiveX components. These components, which can take the form of either DLLs or EXEs, give you the ability to provide the functionality of objects without having to redistribute or duplicate the source code of your classes. This makes it easier for you to reuse code across multiple projects as well as multiple developers. Creating ActiveX components from the classes you build also lets you take advantages of other technologies such as remote distribution of objects, as described in Chapter 7.

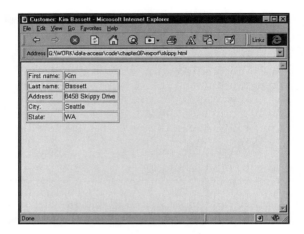

Figure 6.9: Exported HTML data as viewed in Microsoft Internet Explorer.

To create an ActiveX component project In Visual Basic, you start by creating a new project. When Visual Basic asks you what kind of project to create, choose ActiveX DLL or ActiveX EXE. A new project is created with a single class module. You can then add additional classes to the project if you wish and write code for the classes. The final step is to compile the project into an ActiveX DLL or EXE.

You compile an ActiveX project the same way you compile a conventional project. The difference between compiling an ActiveX project and a standard EXE is that for ActiveX DLL, the product of the compilation is (obviously) a DLL rather than an EXE. However, ActiveX DLLs and EXEs are used differently than conventional executables. ActiveX components are object servers, designed to be used (and reused) with other applications.

While both ActiveX DLLs and EXEs can provide objects to other applications, ActiveX EXEs have the capability to execute on their own, a feature that ActiveX DLLs lack. For this reason, ActiveX EXEs are sometimes called "out-of-process servers Conversely, ActiveX servers are sometimes called "in-process servers" because they can only run in the context of some other process.

To compile an ActiveX component, select the File Make menu command as you would with a standard EXE. The project is then compiled to an ActiveX DLL or an ActiveX EXE, as appropriate. Additionally, after it is compiled, the component is registered on your computer, so you have the ability to use objects created from its classes in other applications. The technique you use to accomplish this is described in the next section.

Using an ActiveX Server in a Standard EXE Project

After you've compiled an ActiveX component, you can make a reference to it from another Visual Basic project. When you do this, you can use the classes contained in the ActiveX component to create objects in your project. This permits you to take advantage of the functionality of the ActiveX component in a simple, consistent way, without having to bother yourself with the code that went into the component.

To do this, begin by making a reference to the ActiveX server component from your project. This technique is exactly the same as making a reference to a database access library such as DAO or RDO—you use the menu command Project References.

To compile an ActiveX server and use it in a standard EXE application, do the following:

1 Create a new Visual Basic project. When VB asks you which type of project to create, select ActiveX DLL.

2 In the Properties window, change the Name property of the ActiveX DLL project from Project1 to CustomerServer.

3 Visual Basic added a blank class, called Class1, to the ActiveX DLL project by default. Remove it by right-clicking on it, then selecting Remove Class1 from the pop-up menu.

4 Because the class you're going to add to this project will use DAO, use the Project References menu to add a reference to Microsoft Data Access Objects 3.5.

5 Next you'll add the classes you created previously to the ActiveX DLL project. To do this, right-click on the ActiveX DLL project CustomerServer. Select Add from the pop-up menu. Choose Class Module from the sub-menu.

6 The Add Class Module dialog appears. Click the Existing tab. Locate the CdaoCustomer class and select it.

7 In the Properties for the CdaoCustomer class, set the Instancing property to 5—Multiuse.

Note: The Instancing property of a class controls how users of an ActiveX component can instantiate objects from it. Only classes within an ActiveX project have the Instancing property.

8 The DLL project is now ready to be compiled. To compile it, select File, Make CustomerServer.dll.

9 The Make Project dialog appears. Choose a folder in which to save the DLL and click OK.

The ActiveX DLL is now compiled and registered on your computer. You can use the server from any of your projects.

Note: Not only can you use an ActiveX server from any Visual Basic project, you can use it from any development environment that knows about ActiveX components. This includes Visual C++ and most of the Microsoft Office applications.

Perform the following steps to see how to use an ActiveX server from a Visual Basic project:

1 Start a new Standard EXE project.

2 Locate and check the CustomerServer in the Project References menu, as illustrated in Figure 6.10.

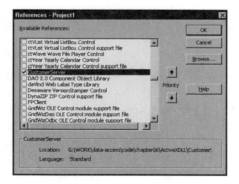

Figure 6.10: Adding a reference to an ActiveX server you created in a standard EXE project.

3 In the form, enter the code in Listing 6.19. This instantiates an object from the ActiveX server and returns a record from the database in the form of an object.

Listing 6.19: Creating an Object from the ActiveX Server and Displaying Data from It

```
Option Explicit

' References CustomerServer

Private Cust As CdaoCustomer

Private Sub Form_Load()

Set Cust = New CdaoCustomer
Cust.CustomerID = 3
Cust.GetData

End Sub

Private Sub Command1_Click()

    MsgBox Cust.FirstName & " " & _
           Cust.LastName & " " & _
           Cust.Address & " " & _
           Cust.City & " " & _
           Cust.State
End Sub
```

4 Run the application. It should display data from the database.

The important thing to note about this application is that it doesn't need to know anything about the database—in fact, to function, it doesn't even need to know that there's a relational database on the other end. Additionally, the client application doesn't need to have a reference to Data Access Objects or any other database engine—that's taken care of by the ActiveX component. That's not a very significant benefit when you're creating single-user, stand-alone applications, but when you enter the world of distributed systems, it can be a very significant benefit.

Distributed systems using ActiveX components are discussed at length in Chapter 7.

Registering ActiveX Components on Users's Computers

An ActiveX component must be registered on a particular computer in order to be usable on that computer. Registration ensures that the operating system is aware of the existence of the component whenever an application attempts to instantiate objects from it.

When you're working with ActiveX servers on a development computer, the concept of registration is no problem. That's because components are registered automatically by Visual Basic at the time they are compiled. When you distribute a component to a user, you must ensure that the ActiveX component is registered on the user's computer. There are a few methods you can use to accomplish this.

If you use the Visual Basic Setup Wizard to distribute your applications, registration of ActiveX components on a user's machine is done automatically by the Setup application. When you build a Setup application, the wizard adds any ActiveX components referenced by your project to your Setup application. When the user runs the Setup application created by the Setup Wizard, the components are registered transparently.

> **Note:** You can also register (and unregister) ActiveX components manually using the regsvr32.exe utility. You can find this command-line utility in the \TOOLS\REGUTILS directory of the VB5 CD-ROM.

Converting Standard EXE Projects to ActiveX Projects

You have the ability to convert a conventional project into an ActiveX component. You do this in a situation where you've built a project based on classes and you realize that you want to compile it as an independently compiled ActiveX component.

Additionally, you can convert between the two types of ActiveX components (ActiveX DLL and ActiveX EXE) by changing a property of the project:

1 In Visual Basic, open the project you want to convert.

2 Select Project Properties.

3 Choose the project type you want your project to be, as illustrated in Figure 6.11.

Using ActiveX Components Remotely

The ability to compile sets of classes independently as ActiveX components is an important element of remote database access. In a client-server environment, you can use ActiveX servers to mediate the interaction between client applications and database servers.

For more information on how this works, see Chapter 7.

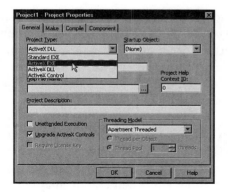

Figure 6.11: Changing a standard EXE project to an ActiveX project using the Project Properties dialog.

Creating Multithreaded Components Using Visual Basic 5.0 Service Pack 2 or Greater

Visual Basic 5.0 has the capability to create multithreaded ActiveX components. With multithreading, your components execute in a more responsive way. This is because the operating system can allocate processor resources to individual threads; if your component is running on multiple threads, it's less likely that the functions your component is responsible for will be blocked by other threads (some of which may be assigned higher priority by the operating system).

Additionally, on a multiprocessor machine, the operating system has the capability to assign particular threads of execution to separate processors. Giving your components multithreading capability is one way to maximize the power of a computer with multiple processors.

> **Note:** The ability to assign multithreading capabilities to ActiveX components is greatly expanded beginning in Visual Basic 5.0 Service Pack 2; in fact, the discussion of multithreading in this section assumes you have SP2 or greater installed.
>
> As of this writing, the most recent patch for Visual Basic was Service Pack 3, which contains all the features of Service Pack 2 as well as some additional bug fixes. To obtain the latest Visual Basic Service Pack, you download it from the Visual Studio site, then install it. This page is located on the Web at **http://www.microsoft.com/msdownload/vs97sp/vb.asp.**

Visual Basic 5.0 introduced support for multithreaded ActiveX components, but the multithreading was limited to certain types of components—the components had to be marked for unattended execution, meaning they were the kind of components designed to run on a server box in a closet somewhere, and could not, therefore, contain any user-interface elements such as forms. (In SP2 and later, the option for running an ActiveX component now has nothing do with its multithreading capabilities.)

Visual Basic 5.0 Service Pack 2 adds support for multithreading across all the types of ActiveX components you can build with Visual Basic, including ActiveX DLLs, ActiveX EXEs, and ActiveX controls. The multithreading features work whether your ActiveX component is marked for unattended execution or not (this is a restriction of multithreaded components in VB5 prior to SP2).

For client-server development, SP2 also adds support for multithreaded components based on the UserConnection designer (introduced in Chapter 5).

Adding support for multithreading in your components requires only that you change a project property at compile time. To add support for multithreading to a component project:

1 In Visual Basic 5.0, open a component project (an ActiveX EXE, ActiveX DLL, or ActiveX control project).

2 Select Properties from the Project menu.

3 Select Apartment Threaded in the Threading Model panel.

4 Click OK. When the project is compiled, it will take advantage of multithreading.

You have an additional option for ActiveX EXEs: Thread per Object or Thread Pool. Thread per Object means that your ActiveX EXE will spawn one thread for every object that is instantiated from it. This provides the best performance, but can consume more computational resources.

Thread Pool, on the other hand, enables you to control how many threads your ActiveX component is capable of instantiating at once, enabling you to limit the amount of resources consumed by the component. However, if the number of object requests exceeds the number of threads in a component server's thread pool, subsequent requests for objects from that server will be blocked until a client process frees up a thread. In other words, when a thread is no longer needed by a client process, control over the thread is returned to the pool of threads managed by the component server.

Note: Setting a thread pool ActiveX server with one thread is the same as making the component single-threaded.

The option you choose for your ActiveX component depends a great deal on the power of the computer it will run on and your application's behavior; you should perform extensive prototyping before making a decision about which route to take when deploying components based on this technology.

Restrictions on Multithreaded Components in VB5 SP2 Although they've made it easy to create multithreaded components in VB5, there are a number of considerations to keep in mind. Among them:

▶ **No language support for multithreading.** It's a compiler switch, and that's it. You can't write code to do anything with them except through Windows API calls, an extremely dicey proposition.

▶ **No debugger support for multithreading.**

▶ **No support for multithreading in multiple-document interface (MDI) applications.**

▶ **No support for single-threaded ActiveX controls in multithreaded applications.** This restriction is imposed by Visual Basic because of big performance problems created by the combination of a single-threaded control in a multithreaded container. This means that if you're attempting to create a multithreaded ActiveX control that uses single-threaded constituent controls, you're out of luck—it won't work.

The good news is that most of the controls that come with Visual Basic were updated in SP2 to take advantage of multithreading.

▶ **Properties and methods declared Friend can't be called across threads.** In order to call a property or method of a particular object, the property or method must be declared Public.

▶ **ActiveX EXE projects that support ActiveX documents need to have the Thread per Object or Thread Pool options (with a thread pool greater than one).** You do this if you're interested in taking advantage of the capabilities of a multithreaded container (such as Internet Explorer 4.0).

▶ **When a component displays a modal form, that form is modal in the context of that component.** This prevents a particular thread from blocking execution of another thread.

▶ **You can only exchange information between forms using dynamic data exchange (DDE) if both forms are on the same thread.** This is only an issue for you if you're still using DDE, that dawn-of-time method of inter-process communication, but it's an important issue nevertheless.

Note: You can get more detailed information on the new features of VB provided by Service Pack 2 at **http://www.microsoft.com/msdownload/ vs97sp/vb.asp**. Additionally, Visual Basic Books Online contains a deeper discussion of what multithreading is and how it relates to ActiveX component creation (in the topic "Designing Multithreaded Out-of-Process Components"). When reviewing the information in Books Online, just remember that what Books Online says about multithreading in ActiveX EXEs now applies to ActiveX DLLs and ActiveX controls as well.

SUMMARY

The world of classes and objects represents a whole new frontier in Visual Basic programming—a frontier that many experienced VB programmers resist. "My procedural code works just fine," some programmers say. "I have a good handle on what's going on in my projects. Why should I spend the extra time writing Property Let and Get procedures?"

This chapter gives you the information to put advanced object-oriented techniques into action, not only to take advantage of technologies such as multi-threading and ActiveX, but to make your life simpler and more stable over time. The techniques discussed in this chapter—including classes, objects, collections and ActiveX components—are key to this strategy.

QUESTIONS AND ANSWERS

Q. **All these issues about class modules and objects seems like a lot of work. It seems counterintuitive to me that you could make an application simpler by adding more code and more modules to it. The object information seems like it's a lot to get my head around. Am I missing something?**

A. You're right that building an application with objects and classes takes more time—the first time you build it. Remember one of the main goals of programming with objects—reusability. The implication here is that if you create a widget-handling application, you'll almost certainly have to deal with widgets again at some point in your career. If you already have an ActiveX DLL lying around that knows what widgets are, what information they use, and how they work, then you've saved yourself an enormous amount of time.

The fact of the matter is that it does take more work—and more planning—to write code in classes than it does to write it the old procedural way. The payoff in the long run, however, is easier maintainability, ease of debugging, and the ability to reuse code. In a sense, it's fair to say that while using classes and objects is a bigger time investment up front, it can save you an enormous amount of time in the long run if utilized properly.

Even if you don't foresee an obvious opportunity for reusing your code, it makes sense to use classes and objects for reasons of maintainability. If you find a bug having to do with customers in your application, the fact that you have a CCustomer class in your application means that you know just where to start looking in code for the problem.

If this stuff seems abstract and pointless to you, give it a try and stick with it. It is counterintuitive to the typical Visual Basic programmer. At first glance it seems backward to add more modules and more code to your application in the name of control, flexibility, and simplicity. After adopting the mindset of object-oriented programming over the course of a few projects, you'll likely wonder how you got along without it.

Q. **I think that objects are spiffy. If I had my way, all the developers in my organization would be using them, reusing them, and sharing them with each other. Only problem is, I'm not sure how we'd go about sharing them—especially since everybody has different ideas about how the objects we create should be documented, shared, and integrated across different applications. Is there a software tool that can help me with that?**

A. The technology is called Microsoft Repository, and the tool that exploits it in Visual Basic 5.0 is called Visual Component Manager. Repository is designed to permit developers to share object resources across enterprises. The idea is that a bunch of development tools will be built on the Repository API (including Visual Component Manager, but eventually encompassing a number of third-party tools) so that everyone's object-management system will be interoperable with everyone else's system.

Visual Component Manager is on the VB5 CD-ROM; you can download an updated version from the Microsoft Visual Basic Owners Only Web site at **http://premium.microsoft.com/vbasic/updates/vcmanager.asp**. You must register your copy of Visual Basic online before you are granted access to this site.

Remote Database Access

How can I access database information over a network?

What's the best way to isolate and maintain the portions of my program logic that are most succeptible to change?

How can multiple users across a network share program code written in a class module?

How can I allow users who are not connected to my network to continue working with the database?

Chapter

7

This book has given you insights into how database access works in Visual Basic. However, until now, you haven't delved into the architectural issues surrounding how data gets from point A to point B in a networked environment.

You've been able to skirt this issue because, by and large, you don't have to take very much into account when accessing a database over a network. The database object models (and, to a greater extent, the operating system) mask the complexity of remote database access from you. In general, it does not matter if your database resides on a machine across the network or on your own local machine.

However, Visual Basic does give you a few ways to move data from a database across a network that involves a bit more preparation and planning. Those topics are the subject of this chapter.

This chapter covers two major topics: three-tiered client-server database access using remotely-deployed ActiveX servers, and database replication with Microsoft Jet databases. The objective of these topics is to let you maintain reliable, consistent access to data across a network, and to enable you to set up systems that intelligently duplicate records in Jet databases to multiple computers in your organization.

Note: ActiveX servers were originally introduced in Chapter 6. You revisit them again in Chapter 9, "Internet Database Applications and ADOs."

This chapter is sort of an advanced version of the basic client-server technologies introduced in Chapter 5, "Client/Server," and in order to understand it, you also must have the object-oriented programming concepts discussed in Chapter 6 under your belt. If you aren't at least somewhat familiar with the concepts introduced in those chapters, go back and take a look at them first. Don't worry, this chapter will still be here when you get back.

ABOUT CLIENTS, SERVERS, AND CODE COMPONENTS

The terminology surrounding middle-tier components has changed since these techniques were originally introduced—not only because Microsoft has this funny habit of changing its jargon every few months, but because of confusion surrounding how the technologies are applied.

For example, if you adhere strictly to the terminology used by Visual Basic, you could say that it's possible to create an ActiveX control embedded in a client application that talks to an ActiveX server component that resides on the client, which in turn talks to an ActiveX server that resides on a middle-tier machine, which in turn talks to a database server located on a Windows NT server. If you're shooting electric beams of hate at my brain for having just written that sentence, then you understand the extent of the problem. Here's a little micro-primer that should help you sort things out.

▶ *ActiveX* is a broad term that generally pertains to software objects that communicate with each other. It's not a product, and it's not a technology—it's more of a blanket term for a bunch of (ostensibly) related technologies generally having to do with objects and inter-process communication.

▶ An *ActiveX control* is a visual component—usually (but not always) a user interface component. The database grid component that ships with VB5 (introduced in Chapter 1, and described in more depth in Chapter 11, "Using the DBGrid and Apex True DBGrid Controls") is an example of an ActiveX component; as you're doubtless aware, many other such components ship with the Professional and Enterprise Editions of Visual Basic. Most Visual Basic programmers are familiar with ActiveX controls, although ActiveX means much more than simple user-interface controls.

▶ An *ActiveX server* (also called an *ActiveX code component* and, in Visual Basic 4.0, an *OLE server*) is a component that exposes one or more classes in a compiled package. Your applications can use objects provided by the classes contained in the ActiveX component. The compiled package can also be accessed over a network through a technology known as Distributed Component Object Model (DCOM).

This chapter focuses on using ActiveX servers in a remote context and focuses even more specifically on setting up an ActiveX server on a network so that client computers can instantiate objects from it.

> **Note:** This book does not cover the topic of creating ActiveX controls. You should know that you can use VB to create your own controls, however. There's a super book on the topic of ActiveX control creation written by a fine, hard-working author named Jeffrey P. McManus. It's called *How to Program Visual Basic Control Creation Edition* (Ziff-Davis Press, 1997). It gives you all the information you need to create controls in any edition of VB (not just the Control Creation Edition). There's a Web page for the book at **http://www.redblazer.com/books/**.

Encapsulating Business Rules with a Three-Tier Client/Server Architecture

As described in Chapter 6, the Drama of the Gifted Server-Side Programmer dictates certain dynamics that any client/server developer is always going to contend with. These dynamics include:

▶ Maintaining a stable system in the face of business rules that change from time to time.

▶ Providing a single, consistent entry point into data, while at the same time protecting the database from client-side applications—and, conversely, protecting client-side applications from the complexity and mutability of the server.

▶ The desire to build business rules in any programming language, not just SQL.

▶ The desire to deploy business rules onto a machine other than the database server, in order to conserve the database server's processing power.

▶ The desire to deploy some business rules onto the client, in order to minimize network traffic.

▶ Deploying business rules to a single point in the system (as opposed to having to deploy them to every client computer every time a change is implemented).

A *three-tier client-server* architecture solves this problem. In three-tier architecture, business rules are encapsulated in a component that sits between the client application and the database server.

Such components are therefore referred to as *middle-tier components*. Middle-tier components accept requests from client applications, responding by making requests and issuing command to the database server.

Because the phrase "component" describes what's on the middle tier, you may have already surmised that in the Visual Basic universe, the middle-tier is an ActiveX component. Middle-tier ActiveX components work the same way as other types of ActiveX components you've already discussed, in the sense that they chew up data and spit out objects. Middle-tier components are specifically geared toward client-server database access.

Note: The techniques discussed in this section are only available in the Enterprise Edition of Visual Basic. These features became available in Visual Basic 4.0, but were altered slightly in VB5.

In addition to providing an object-oriented interface into databases, ActiveX components can be accessed remotely over a network. This is possible through a technology known as Distributed Component Object Model (DCOM). With DCOM, a client application has the capability to instantiate objects from an ActiveX server, whether or not the server resides on the same computer as that client application. (In object-geek-speak, this is referred to as *instantiation across machine boundaries*.)

As with many aspects of programming in Visual Basic, there's very little having to do with the internals of DCOM that you can access directly. It's like trying to shift the gears of a car with automatic transmission. For the remainder of this section, you walk through the practical steps involved in setting up an ActiveX server for remote access by client computers.

Note: If you're interested in knowing more about how COM and DCOM do their magic, check out Daniel Appleman's *Developing ActiveX Components with Visual Basic 5.0* (Ziff-Davis Press, 1997). It's not vital for you to have an under-the-hood understanding of this in order to deploy applications, though, because as I said previously, there's very little about DCOM that you can get access to from within VB. But it is interesting to know what's going on behind the scenes, and Dan does a great job explaining it.

Setting Up a Hardware Architecture for DCOM

There are potentially endless combinations of client and server computers you can put together in order to implement a client-server hardware architecture. This chapter's goal is to keep things as simple as possible in order to provide a solution that works for you in the most common situations you encounter. Bear in mind, though, that the technologies used to make database access happen in Windows are flexible, so that even if some aspect of the scenarios described in this chapter don't apply to you, you can use three-tier client-server.

This chapter assumes that you have two computers and that the first is a Windows NT Server running Microsoft SQL Server. This computer is referred to as the server from here on out. The client machine is a Windows 95 computer.

> **Note:** Don't sweat it if you don't have immediate access to all the software and hardware described in this section. If you don't have two computers connected over a network, the demonstrations should work fine on a single computer. If you don't have a Windows NT machine, you should be able to fake it by using a Microsoft Jet database. The examples in this chapter are all written in DAO rather than RDO in order to accommodate this.
>
> Although this chapter was written with a Windows NT server in mind, you can set up DCOM on Windows 95 as well. The files that let you do DCOM on Windows 95 are on the VB5 CD-ROM, in the \TOOLS\DCOM95 directory. For more information and access to the downloadable DCOM files, check out the DCOM for Windows 95 Web page at **http://www.microsoft.com/com/ dcom95/download-f.htm**.

The premise of the demonstrations in this chapter is that users on the network need to get access to customer data. The architecture of the customer database has been established already; in the interest of consistency, code reuse and ease of programming and maintenance, it's to your advantage to channel access to the database through ActiveX server components based on classes (introduced in Chapter 6). These components (specifically, ActiveX EXEs) are compiled and set up on the network so that client applications can access it remotely.

Expressed graphically, a typical three-tier client-server architecture is illustrated in Figure 7.1.

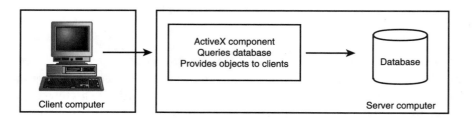

Figure 7.1: A generic three-tier architecture. This diagram merges the physical architecture (composing two computers) with the logical architecture (comprising tiers that provide different types of functionality).

Figure 7.1 gives you an idea of how you'd split the logic of your application across two computers. There's no reason why you have to stop there—you can split middle-tier components across any number of computers. For this reason, three-tier client-server architecture is increasingly being referred to as an *n-tier architecture*, as illustrated in Figure 7.2.

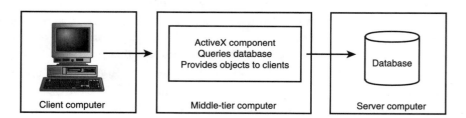

Figure 7.2: An n-tier client-server architecture, showing the middle tier deployed to a machine of its own.

You deploy middle-tier components on a computer of its own in situations in which:

▶ The database server runs an operating system that does not support ActiveX.

▶ You want to conserve processing power on the database server.

▶ You want to enhance your application's scalability by deploying multiple copies of the same ActiveX server to more than one computer.

The disadvantage of giving your ActiveX component a computer of its own is that such a setup requires an additional network hop to get from client to database and back again. This can degrade performance and cause increased network traffic. Whether this situation is acceptable to you is a function of your specific network configuration and the prototyping you do during the design phase of your project.

Even if you don't have control of the operating system on which your database runs, you can still use an ActiveX middle tier—if you deploy it to a computer of its own. The database tier is a UNIX box, or a corporate mainframe. This is no big deal to DCOM or to your client applications for two reasons. First, your client applications never get access to the database server; instead, they access data through the ActiveX component. More importantly, DCOM shields the application from the specific implementation of network protocol, platform, and machine boundary.

In some respects, deploying a client-server system in which the database server is on a non-Windows platform is easier in the world of three-tier, because you don't have to configure the *middleware* (the collection of drivers that handles cross-platform communication and network protocols) on every client computer. In three-tier, you only have to configure this software once—in the section of the architecture between the middle tier and the database server. This can save you quite a bit of time and trouble when you're configuring and deploying your application to many clients.

Using DCOM on Other Platforms

By the time you read this, DCOM might be happening on platforms other than Windows. Don't hold your breath. Microsoft has been working toward making COM and DCOM multiplatform since 1996, but the release date keeps getting moved back.

At some point COM and DCOM will begin (or have begun) to appear on UNIX computers. The ActiveX Software Development Kit for Macintosh has been around since late 1996; it's possible that using ActiveX on a Macintosh computer will be a reality by the time you read this.

> **Note:** Microsoft's Web site is the best source of information on what's happening with the portability of ActiveX components. The pages you want to keep your eyeballs on are **http://www.microsoft.com/cominfo/** and **http://www.microsoft.com/oledev/**.

Creating Your First DCOM Application

Now that you have a sense of why DCOM is useful and wonderful, it's time to get started using the technology to provide a real-world business software solution. To keep this example as simple as possible, do it using the CustomerServer project you created in Chapter 6. This simple ActiveX component has a grand total of one class, CdaoCustomer, designed to query the database and return a Customer object.

Compiling and Deploying the ActiveX Server

There are few differences between compiling an ActiveX component that's destined to be used remotely and compiling other types of ActiveX servers. For the ActiveX server, you must remember to mark the ActiveX project as a remotely deployable component, so the Setup Wizard builds it correctly.

> **Note:** You should only follow these steps if you want to create an ActiveX server that is deployed across a network and accessed by clients through DCOM. For general instructions on how to compile non-remote ActiveX components, see Chapter 6.

To compile and deploy the ActiveX CustomerServer, do the following:

1 Open the CustomerServer project in Visual Basic. (You have the option of building this server from scratch, or you can use the code in the Chapter07\ActiveXServer folder in the CD-ROM that accompanies this book.)

2 Select CustomerServer Properties from VB's Project menu. The Project Properties dialog appears.

3 Change the project type to ActiveX EXE in the General tab, if it isn't already set to ActiveX EXE.

4 Click the Component tab. Click the Remote Server Files check box.

When you indicate that a project should be compiled with Remote Server files, Visual Basic creates a data file with a .VBR extension at the time you compile your component. The Setup Wizard uses this file to deploy your component remotely.

5 Click OK to dismiss the Project Properties dialog.

6 Save the project.

7 Choose Make CustomerServer.exe from VB's File menu. Select a folder and a filename to save the executable file in, then click OK to compile.

8 Close Visual Basic.

Next you create an installable Setup application for the ActiveX server component. The Setup application can either be run on the same machine as the one you used to develop the component, or on any other machine on your network.

To create a Setup application for your ActiveX component:

1 From the Windows Start menu, select the Visual Basic 5.0 program group. From that program group, launch the Application Setup Wizard.

2 The Setup Wizard launches, displaying an introductory screen. Click Next.

3 The Setup Wizard's Setup Project and Options screen is displayed, as shown in Figure 7.3.

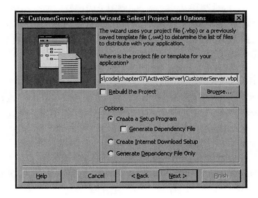

Figure 7.3: Specifying the name of the Visual Basic project in Setup Wizard.

This step gives you the ability to specify a Visual Basic project that will be packaged by the Setup Wizard. This step also gives you the option to rebuild the project (which means that you want to compile the components in the project). Rebuilding the project isn't necessary; you've already compiled your application, so leave the box unchecked.

4 Click the Browse button and locate the Visual Basic .VBP project file that contains your ActiveX component.

5 Click Next. The Setup Wizard asks you how you'd like to distribute your application. Presumably you're either on the server computer or you have access to it through the network, so it will make sense to choose the default, which is Single Directory.

6 Click Next. In this step, the Setup Wizard asks you to designate a directory into which your Setup package will be created. Select a directory and click Next.

Note: When you're selecting a directory to which to save the completed Setup application, you can type the name of a directory that doesn't exist if you want. If you do this, the Setup Wizard asks if you want to create the directory. I like doing it this way because you don't have to think ahead to make a place to store your setup application. (I like to store my setup applications into a directory called Setup under the source code directory.)

7 The Setup Wizard's Data Access screen appears. Because this ActiveX server doesn't use any ISAM data sources, you don't have to do anything here. (Make sure that dbUseJet is checked, however, because the ActiveX server does use the Jet database engine.)

8 Click Next. The ActiveX Server Components screen appears, asking you to add references to any ActiveX servers required by your component. Here's the tricky part—although the component you're packaging is a remote ActiveX server, it doesn't use a remote ActiveX server. You can skip this step. Click Next.

9 The Confirm Dependencies screen appears. In this step, the Setup Wizard detects that your installation will require Data Access Objects. Make sure that the Data Access Objects file DAO350.DLL is checked, then click Next.

10 The Shared ActiveX Application screen appears. In this screen, you inform the Setup Wizard that this component should be packaged for remote execution. To do this, make sure the option Install as a Shared Component is selected. In the second option, select No to indicate that although this component will be accessed remotely, it will not be accessed through Remote Automation. The screen should look like Figure 7.4.

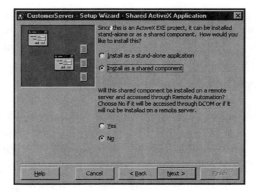

Figure 7.4: The Setup Wizard's Shared ActiveX Application dialog, enabling you to deploy a component for remote access.

Note: Remote Automation is an older technology for providing access to objects over a network. It's provided as an option in Visual Basic 5.0 for backward compatibility with existing Visual Basic 4.0 applications and for use with 16-bit Windows clients (because DCOM doesn't support 16-bit). For new 32-bit applications you build in VB5, you should use DCOM rather than Remote Automation because DCOM is more efficient.

11 Click Next. After a moment, the File Summary screen appears, displaying a list of the many files that will be incorporated into the component's Setup application.

If at this point you were interested in including additional files in the installation (such as an online help file, a README file, or a copy of the database novelty.mdb), you could add it at this point by clicking the Add button. For this example, just click Next.

Note: Because the CdaoCustomerServer class wants to refer to a copy of novelty.mdb that is its own directory, you'll want to either include a copy of the database novelty.mdb along with the Setup application or change the code in the CustomerServer to give the server better information about where the database is actually located.

12 The Finished! step appears. You now have the option of saving a template of your installation. This saves the steps you went through in the Setup Wizard to get to this point and makes subsequent builds of your Setup application go more quickly.

13 Click Finish. The Setup application is created.

14 Run the Setup application by locating the Setup.exe file (located in the directory you chose in the Setup Wizard) and executing it. This places a copy of your ActiveX server application into your computer's Windows system directory.

At this point, you must configure the component using the DCOM configuration utility dcomcnfg.exe in order to enable remote systems to get access to your component using DCOM:

1 From the Windows Start menu, choose Run.

2 Enter dcomcnfg.exe in the Run dialog box.

3 The Distributed COM Properties dialog appears.

4 Double-click on the class you want to configure. The properties dialog appears.

5 Click the Security tab. This tab gives you the ability to set security permissions for remote execution of the server.

6 Select Use Custom Access Permissions, then click Edit. The Registry Value Permissions dialog appears. Click Add.

7 The Add Users and Groups dialog appears. Select the user group Everyone, then click Add.

8 Click OK. Everyone is added to the Registry Value Permissions dialog. Click OK.

9 You're back in the object server Properties dialog. Select Use Custom Launch Permissions and add the group Everyone the same way you did in the previous steps.

10 Click OK. A message box indicating that the operation completed successfully appears.

The server is now successfully deployed and should be able to accept remote requests for objects over your network.

Unregistering an ActiveX EXE

All ActiveX components must be registered on a computer before they can be used by client applications. This is the case for remote components as well as conventional components.

Registering a component is straightforward. On a development computer, your component is registered when you compile it. When you deploy your component to a remote machine, it's registered by the Setup application. You can also register and unregister an ActiveX control or ActiveX DLL manually.

But ActiveX EXEs also have a capability that ActiveX DLLs and ActiveX controls don't have—the capability to register and unregister themselves. In fact, the regsvr32 utility doesn't work on ActiveX EXEs. In order to unregister an ActiveX EXE, you simply run it with the /UNREGSERVER switch.

For example, if you want to unregister an ActiveX EXE called MYSERVER.EXE located in the SERVER directory, you run the command line:

```
C:\SERVER\MYSERVER.EXE  /UNREGSERVER
```

You can run this command line by selecting Run from the Windows Start menu. When you execute it, the ActiveX EXE will run, unregister itself, and terminate.

Creating a Client Application that Uses a Remote ActiveX Server

For a client application that depends on a remotely-deployed ActiveX server, you must indicate that the server is to access a remote component. This is done at the time you build the client application's Setup package.

In this example you create a simple application that uses the remote ActiveX server. You first test this application locally, then deploy it remotely:

1 Start Visual Basic and create a new Standard EXE project.

2 Add a command button to the project's form.

3 Using the Project References dialog, make a reference to the CustomerServer ActiveX EXE you created and deployed in the previous example.

4 In the form, enter the code shown in Listing 7.1.

Listing 7.1: Client-Side Code to Instantiate an Object from the ActiveX CustomerServer

```
Option Explicit

Private Cust As CustomerServer.CdaoCustomer
```

continues

Listing 7.1: Client-Side Code to Instantiate an Object from the ActiveX CustomerServer (Continued)

```
Private Sub Form_Load()

    Set Cust = New CustomerServer.CdaoCustomer

End Sub


Private Sub Command1_Click()

    Cust.CustomerID = 3
    Cust.GetData

    MsgBox Cust.FirstName & " " & _
           Cust.LastName & " " & _
           Cust.Address & " " & _
           Cust.City & ", " & _
           Cust.State
End Sub
```

5 Run the program and click the command button. Information from the CustomerServer should appear in the message box.

Deploying the Client Application

Creating a Setup application for the client application is the next step in the process of creating a client application that calls a remote server. You do this by compiling the application, then using the Setup Wizard to create an installable Setup application.

Build a Setup application for an ActiveX client application as you normally would. The only thing that changes is the location of the ActiveX server—rather than referring to it and distributing it locally, you must tell the Setup Wizard that the application will access the server remotely.

To create a Setup package for the client application:

1 Launch the Application Setup Wizard from the Windows Start menu.

2 In the Select Project step, locate the client application's .VBP file and check the option to rebuild the project (if you haven't compiled it to an EXE file already). If you didn't build this project yourself, you can use the version in the Chapter07 folder on the CD-ROM that accompanies this book; the name of the client project is CustClient.vbp.

3 Continue through the steps of the Setup Wizard as you normally would, until you come to the ActiveX Server Components step.

4 If the Setup Wizard displays the CustomerServer EXE in the list of ActiveX server components, uncheck it. You want to designate this ActiveX server as a remote component. Do this by clicking the Add Remote button.

5 The Add ActiveX Server Components dialog appears. Locate and select the ActiveX DLL's .VBR file (created at the time your ActiveX server was created, in the previous demonstration). Click Open.

6 The Remote Connection Details dialog appears.

7 The component needs to know the name of the computer that acts as the server for this application. Enter the name in the Network Address dialog, then click OK.

8 You're back in the ActiveX Server Components dialog. Click Next.

9 Finish creating the Setup application as you normally would. The Setup Wizard assembles and compresses the files required to be distributed.

When the Setup application is run on a machine connected to the remote server, it should find the remote server and instantiate objects from it.

Using Registration Utilities to Work with ActiveX Components

If you've deployed Visual Basic applications in the OLE epoch (that is, since Visual Basic 4.0 came out), you know that you can't just copy EXE, DLL and OCX files onto a user's machine anymore. You must register any ActiveX components and other dependent libraries (such as Data Access Objects) that are required for use by your appplication.

If you're using the Setup Wizard, this is all done for you behind the scenes. There are situations—particularly in development environments—in which you want to have more control over how components are registered and unregistered.

You use the utility regsvr32.exe to register (and unregister) an ActiveX component on your computer.

A different utility, clireg32, is used to register or uninstall ActiveX component registration files (.VBR files) installed on your computer. Like regsvr32, clireg32 is a command-line utility, which means that you must execute it with the Windows Start menu's Run command.

Both regsvr32 and clireg32 are on the VB5 CD-ROM; regsvr32 is copied to your Windows system directory when you install VB. Bear in mind that most of the work performed by these utilities is done for you behind the scenes by the

Setup applications you build for your applications and components. At the same time, it's nice to be able to run these utilities manually when you want to register or unregister ActiveX DLLs or OCXes.

USING ACTIVEX COMPONENTS TO FACILITATE DATABASE ACCESS

In Chapter 6 you learned how to access databases using classes and objects. This technique gives you the ability to encapsulate the logic of your programs into easily reusable class modules. The ability to independently compile class modules you write in the form of ActiveX DLLs and EXEs makes your classes even easier to reuse, giving you the ability to create extremely flexible and powerful database access applications.

In addition to permitting you to deploy and distribute program logic over a network, putting an ActiveX component between your database client application and your database server opens the doors to other database access techniques. For example, using ActiveX components, you can write an application that does not make a reference to any database access library, yet has the capability to read from and write to a database.

One advantage of writing such an application is performance: If your client application doesn't have to load the DAO/Jet library, for example, each client conserves over a megabyte of RAM. (You also avoid having to distribute the Jet DLLs to your users along with each database access application you create.)

The following section describes how to use database access with remotely deployed ActiveX components to implement this technique.

Using GetRows to Return Data in an Array

You can use the GetRows method of the Recordset object to return data from an ActiveX server to a client application in the form of a two-dimensional array of Variants. This technique is desirable because it keeps you from having to deploy any database engine libraries or perform any client-side database configuration. The client only knows about the arrays provided by the ActiveX server, which is remotely deployed over a network.

You typically follow these steps when using the GetRows method:
▶ Create a Recordset object (typically as the result of a client request to a remotely-deployed ActiveX component).

▶ Determine the number of rows in the Recordset object.

▶ Declare a Variant array.

▶ Execute the GetRows method of the Recordset object to assign the data in the Recordset to the Variant array.

▶ Execute code to convert the data in the resulting Variant array to something your application can use.

You use this technique when you need to squeeze every ounce of performance out of your client-side applications. This performance stems from the fact that your client applications don't have to load a database engine (either Jet or RDO) when they are started. This saves a significant amount of memory and makes the application start much more quickly.

Another benefit of this technique is the fact that your application's distributable footprint becomes much smaller, because you don't have to load the lumbering Jet database engine DLLs onto every client computer.

If your client application is part of a client/server solution, you gain a number of benefits. You don't have to distribute and configure ODBC data sources and client/server middleware on client computers, which can be a source of mind-numbing grief for client/server developers and system administrators alike.

Listing 7.2 shows an example of a class module that returns a Variant array after making a database call. The call is made after passing the record's primary key (in this case, set in the form of the EmployeeID property) to the database. The Variant array is returned in the form of the ArrayData property.

Listing 7.2: Retrieving a Record from a Database and Providing It in the Form of a Variant Array

```
Option Explicit


' References DAO 3.5

' Properties
Private mvarArrayData As Variant
Private mlngEmployeeID As Long

' Private variables
Private db As Database
Private rs As Recordset
'


Public Property Get EmployeeID() As Long
```

continues

Listing 7.2: Retrieving a Record from a Database and Providing It in the Form of a Variant Array (Continued)

```
    EmployeeID = mlngEmployeeID
End Property

Public Property Let EmployeeID(ByVal lngNew As Long)
    mlngEmployeeID = lngNew
End Property

Public Property Get ArrayData(col As Long, row As Long) _
    As Variant
' This property is read-only. It is set
' by the GetData method.
    ArrayData = mvarArrayData(col, row)
End Property

Public Sub GetData()
' Retrieves a single employee and
' places it into a variant array
' using GetRows.

    Set db = OpenDatabase(App.Path & "\novelty.mdb")

    ' Retrieve a single employee
    Set rs = db.OpenRecordset("SELECT [FirstName], " & _
        "[LastName], " & "[Department], " & _
        "[PhoneNumber] " & "FROM tblEmployee " & _
        "WHERE [ID] = " & EmployeeID)

    mvarArrayData = rs.GetRows(1)

End Sub
```

Assuming you've put this code in a class module and set the class module's Name property to CEmployeeServer, you can use this code by first instantiating an object from it as you normally would.

```
Private MyEmpSrv As CEmployeeServer
Set MyEmpSrv = New CEmployeeServer
```

To retrieve data from the database, you must provide an Employee ID to look up, then execute the CEmployeeServer object's GetData method.

```
MyEmpSrv.EmployeeID = 1
MyEmpSrv.GetData
```

At this point, inside the class, the database is accessed, the record for Employee ID number 1 is retrieved, and the results are stored in a Variant array. You can now retrieve individual pieces of data from the ArrayData property (which stores an array of the row retrieved from the database). For example, the code

```
MsgBox MyEmpSrv.ArrayData(0,0)
```

displays the value Steve, which is the zeroth value of the zeroth member of the array. (Don't forget that in Visual Basic, members of arrays are numbered beginning at zero by default.)

Note that the conversion of a Recordset object to a Variant array is totally meaningless, unless CEmployeeServer is compiled in the form of an ActiveX component and deployed over a network. However, if you deploy the EmployeeServer over a network, you gain the freedom from having to deploy client-side database libraries and ODBC drivers, as well as not having to configure each client for database access. This can make your client-side applications more efficient as well as easier to administer.

The disadvantage is that you have to write extra code to deal with the Variant array returned by the ActiveX component. One solution to that problem is to write another ActiveX component to decode the array.

Creating a Class to Decode Variant Arrays

When you make calls to an ActiveX server that returns data in the form of Variant arrays, you have a problem. How do you determine which column of the array maps to which field in the database? More importantly, how do you use your new best pal, object-oriented programming, to make your life simpler and make your code more reusable in conjunction with this technique?

One solution is to deploy a second ActiveX component, this time on the client side, to decode the Variant array served up by the middle tier. This component knows how to do only two things: place calls to CEmployeeServer and return an Employee object constructed from the data in the Variant array passed back from the middle tier.

This class, CEmployee, is implemented as part of the client application. It contains no reference to any database library and exists solely for the purpose of retrieving Variant arrays from CEmployeeServer and mapping them to properties of an Employee object.

The beauty of this technique is that the client application deals exclusively with the Employee object. No direct database access takes place on the client computer; the client-side programmer doesn't even need to know what kind of database exists on the back end. He or she only needs to know how to code against CEmployee. The code for the CEmployee class is shown in Listing 7.3.

Listing 7.3: The CEmployee Class

```
Option Explicit

' Note that this class doen't require
' a reference to any database engine.
' It only needs to reference the GetRowsExample
' ActiveX server component.

' Contained CEmployeeServer object
Private mEmployeeServer As CEmployeeServer

' Private member variables for properties
Private mstrFirstName As String
Private mstrLastName As String
Private mstrDepartment As String
Private mstrPhoneNumber As String

Private Enum EmployeeArrayColumn
    acFirstName = 0
    acLastName = 1
    acDepartment = 2
    acPhoneNumber = 3
End Enum
'

Private Sub Class_Initialize()

    Set mEmployeeServer = New CEmployeeServer

End Sub

Public Property Get ID() As Long
    ID = mEmployeeServer.EmployeeID
End Property

Public Property Let ID(ByVal lngNew As Long)
' Setting the ID property causes the Employee
' Server to query the database and retrieve
' a variant array, which is then decoded and
' exposed as properties of the Employee object.

    mEmployeeServer.EmployeeID = lngNew
    mEmployeeServer.GetData

    FirstName = mEmployeeServer.ArrayData(acFirstName, 0)
```

Listing 7.3: The CEmployee Class (Continued)

```
    LastName = mEmployeeServer.ArrayData(acLastName, 0)
    Department = mEmployeeServer.ArrayData_
        (acDepartment, 0)
    PhoneNumber = mEmployeeServer.ArrayData_
        (acPhoneNumber, 0)

End Property

Public Property Get Department() As String
    Department = mstrDepartment
End Property

Public Property Let Department(ByVal strNew As String)
    mstrDepartment = strNew
End Property

Public Property Get FirstName() As String
    FirstName = mstrFirstName
End Property

Public Property Let FirstName(ByVal strNew As String)
    mstrFirstName = strNew
End Property

Public Property Get LastName() As String
    LastName = mstrLastName
End Property

Public Property Let LastName(ByVal strNew As String)
    mstrLastName = strNew
End Property

Public Property Get PhoneNumber() As String
    PhoneNumber = mstrPhoneNumber
End Property

Public Property Let PhoneNumber(ByVal strNew As String)
    mstrPhoneNumber = strNew
End Property
```

The core of the CEmployee class is the ID property's Let procedure. Because an object based on a record has enough information to initialize itself as soon as you provide its primary key, the Employee object's properties can be retrieved in the ID property's Property Let procedure. That way, as soon as the object's ID property is called, CEmployeeServer retrieves all other properties pertaining to the object from the database and passes them back to the client application in the form of a Variant array.

After you have the CEmployeeServer class performing database access and the CEmployee class converting its arrays into Employee objects, you can write code in a form to retrieve employees and work with them. Listing 7.4 is an example of code in a form that uses the CEmployee class to retrieve an Employee object.

Listing 7.4: Client-Side Code to Retrieve Data by Using the CEmployee Class

```
Option Explicit

Dim mEmployee As CEmployee

Private Sub cmdLookup_Click()

    Set mEmployee = New CEmployee
    mEmployee.ID = txtEmployeeID.Text

    MsgBox mEmployee.FirstName & " " & _
           mEmployee.LastName & vbCrLf & mEmployee.Department & _
           vbCrLf & mEmployee.PhoneNumber, _
           vbInformation, "Data for Employee ID " & mEmployee.ID

End Sub
```

Notice how little code goes into the retrieval of data from the database using this class; all the complicated stuff is under the hood, safely out of your way—contained in the classes CEmployee and CEmployeeServer.

When you combine this technique with the ActiveX/DCOM technique described earlier in this chapter, you gain significant benefits. By compiling the CEmployeeServer class in an ActiveX EXE and deploying it over a network, you gain the benefit of centrally located business rules accessible from anywhere on your network. And because this component passes data to client applications over DCOM in the form of arrays, you don't need to deploy a database access engine (of any kind) onto individual client machines. This can make client-side software faster to execute and easier to configure and manage.

Conversely, bear in mind that if you don't deploy the database access component remotely, there isn't much point to this technique.

TRANSFERRING DATA WITH DATABASE REPLICATION

Centrally located databases can be both a blessing and a curse. Because all your business data is in one place, it's hypothetically possible to access it from anywhere on your corporate network. In order for that centralization to work, it means that the data must be rooted to the spot—it's difficult to move or modify your database it without breaking client applications, and it's tricky to permit users whose computers aren't on your corporate LAN to gain access to the data they might need.

For example, if your company has a field sales force, it's possible (even likely) that some of your salespeople will never set foot in your office. In a situation like this, your salespeople can't easily get access to the database by simply hooking up their laptops to your LAN.

To get around this problem, Microsoft Jet gives you the ability to replicate a database from one computer to another. Rather than duplicating all the components of a database (as you would if you simply copied the database file), replication applies a bit more logic. Jet has the capability to perform *synchronization* on databases—comparing them record by record to ensure that they contain the same data, then copying the changes from the *master* database to any one of a number of *replica* databases.

> **Note:** The master database is also referred to as the *design master*, because it stores the design of the database as well as serves as a central repository for shared data. In a replication system, design changes to the database—such as adding or deleting fields, tables, and query definitions—can be done only in the design master. However, when you make a change to a database object that resides in a design master, those changes can be distributed to replicas at the time the databases are synchronized. This is the only way to make a change to a replica database.

For example, say you're a user of a corporate database application. You want to take work home, but the database application resides on a server in your office. Replication gives you the ability to "check out" a copy of the master database—by loading it on your laptop, for example—so you can work on it at home. The copy of the database you load onto your laptop is referred to as a *replica*.

When you return to the office, you check the database back in. At that time, Jet replication compares the records in your replica with the records in the master database. If you added any records, they are copied to the main system; if you made any changes to records, these changes are also made in the main system. Likewise, if any new data appeared in the master, it is copied to your replica at this time.

Now consider this scenario: What happens when your database grows to be 200MB in size? Backing up the database would be a colossal pain; it would require quite a bit of downtime to simply copy the file across the network, during which time other users would be denied access to the database to avoid the database being made inconsistent.

Replication solves this problem as well by enabling copying of only those records that have changed since the last backup. Because it only copies new and changed files, you don't have to back up the entire database each time you want to back up.

Finally, you can also use replication to perform updates to your database applications. This might be appropriate in situations where some of your application's logic is embedded in the database in the form of query definitions. If the query definition needs to change to reflect a change in the application or a change in your business practices, replication can automatically push the change out to all the clients who require it.

Designing a Database with Replication in Mind

As with any multiuser database, you must take several things into consideration when you're designing a database that will be replicated. This doesn't mean that you can't convert your existing single-computer databases into replicable databases, but planning ahead from the start will make the transition go more smoothly.

One of the most important issues to consider is your tables's primary key. This is particularly the case when a table's primary key is based on an AutoNumber field.

For example, consider a new database with tables whose primary keys are all based on AutoNumber fields. Default AutoNumber fields begin numbering at 1 and increment themselves, one number per record. If several users enter records in database replicas and then synchronize their data back to the master database, it's very likely that two or more users will have entered a record with the ID of 1. To avoid this, you should design your databases's primary key fields using one of the following techniques:

▶ Set the AutoNumber field's New Values property to Random.

▶ Set the AutoNumber field's Field Size property to Replication ID.

Setting the primary key field to Random ensures that each new record gets a primary key in the range of a long integer. A Replication ID, on the other hand, is a 128-bit number which, because of its size, is much more likely to be unique from one replica to the next.

Although a Replication ID takes more storage space than a random long integer AutoNumber, it's a good idea to use this data type when you're designing new tables slated for replication; it minimizes the chance for collision of records during synchronization. However, because it's expressed as a long hexadecimal number, a Replication ID can be difficult to refer to conveniently. If you want a primary key to serve double-duty in the real world (as an invoice number or employee ID, for example), you might want to consider using a random long integer AutoNumber instead.

Note: Because of the changes a database goes through when it's converted into a design master, it should go without saying that you should back up a database before converting it. Fortunately, when you convert a database into a design master in Microsoft Access, Access performs a backup for you automatically.

Replicated databases are handled differently than single-user databases. When you designate a database as a design master, Jet makes a number of changes to your database under the hood. For example, Jet must create a number of new hidden system tables to your database to support such things as conflicts between multiple users who attempt to update the same record and then check their data back into the system. Replication can also add fields to each table in your system, which can cause problems if you've written code (or developed a user interface) that expects a set number of fields. The basic moral to the story is that you should make your database replicable as early in the development cycle as possible, to make it easier to work around these kinds of problems.

As an example of how much larger a database gets when you convert it into a design master, you may want to examine the experiment1.mdb database in the code directory on the CD-ROM that accompanies this book. That database, which contained a single table with no data at the time it was replicated, swelled from 92K in size to a whopping 248K after it was converted to a design master. However, that size increases for larger databases are not necessarily proportional.

Doing Replication in Microsoft Access

In order to begin with a replicable database system, you must first determine how the databases will be synchronized and where the master database will reside. The particulars involve determining how remote users can connect to the design master (over a wide area network, for example, or through dial-up networking—potentially even over the Internet, as described later in this section). The important part here is to plan ahead in an effort to maintain accessibility to reasonably recent versions of data for most (if not all) of your users.

After you've planned the structure of your replicable database system, you're ready to set it up. When you're setting up replication, you go through the following general steps:

1 Create a database (or use an existing database).

2 Designate a database as the design master.

3 Create one or more replicas from that design master.

You can perform the steps to set up replication using either Microsoft Access, or in code, using Data Access Objects. Both techniques are described in the following sections.

Creating a Design Master and Replica in Microsoft Access

Microsoft Access is the easiest way to get started with database replication. This is because Access has menu commands that govern the creation of design masters and database replicas automatically.

To create a design master using Microsoft Access, you must have a feature called briefcase replication installed. You're given the option to install briefcase replication when you first install Access; if you don't have it installed, Access will let you know what you need to do when you attempt to create a design master.

To create a design master and a database replica in Access, do the following:

1 Back up your database. If you're working with the Jones Novelties database novelty.mdb, you might want to give it a name like master-novelty.mdb.

2 Open the database in Microsoft Access.

3 Choose the Tools, Replication menu. Select Create Replica from the submenu.

4 Access issues a warning that the database must be closed before you can create a replica from it. It asks if you want to close this database and convert it into a design master. Choose Yes.

5 The database closes. Access next warns you to create a backup of the database and asks if you want to do so before proceeding. Click Yes.

Note: For more information on how converting a database to a design master changes the database's structure, see "How Replication Changes a Database" earlier in this chapter.

6 Access converts the database into a design master and creates a replica from it, asking you to name the replicated database. If you're using the Jones Novelties database, you might want to give it a name like replica1-novelty.mdb.

7 When the replication procedure is done, Access displays a dialog explaining what it did, as shown in Figure 7.5.

Figure 7.5: The extremely verbose message box provided by Access after a successful initial replication.

To be precise, the replication process in Access actually creates two new files—the replica and the backup of the original database. When this process is complete, you can create additional replicas, enter data into either database, and perform synchronization between them, copying new or altered records back to the design master.

Adding Replicable Objects to a Database in Microsoft Access

When you initially add a new object (such as a table or query definition) to a design master database, it's not replicated by default. In Microsoft Access, this is obvious because the different types of database objects (replicable and unreplicable) have different icons in Access's Database window, as shown in Figure 7.6.

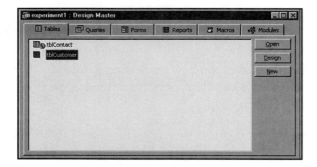

Figure 7.6: Microsoft Access's Database window, displaying a replicable table (tblContact) and a unreplicable table (tblCustomer).

It's simple to make a new database object replicable in Access:

1 In the Database window, right-click on the database object whose replication status you want to change.

2 From the pop-up menu, select Properties.

3 The Database Object Properties dialog appears, as shown in Figure 7.7.

Figure 7.7: Microsoft Access's Database Object Properties dialog, permitting you to change the replication status of a database object.

4 Click the Replicable check box, then click OK.

The database object's icon changes to reflect its new status as a replicable object. The next time you perform a database synchronization, the new database object is copied into the replica database.

You can change the replication status of any database object at any time using this technique. In order to make a database object nonreplicable, you simply uncheck the replicable box in the database object's properties dialog. Note, however, that when you make a particular database object nonreplicable, any objects previously copied into a database replica are deleted when the next synchronization takes place.

Note: You can also create new database objects and mark them as replicable using Data Access Objects programming. This approach is used in situations in which you do not want to use Microsoft Access to manage replication. For more information on this technique, see the section "Setting Up Replication in Data Access Objects" later in this chapter.

Performing Synchronization in Microsoft Access

After you've created your first replicable database in Microsoft Access, you may want to test it. The simplest way to do this is to enter a single record in the design master, then run a syncronization to cause the new record to be copied to the replica:

1 Open the design master database and enter a record into one of its tables. If you used Replication ID as the data type of its primary key, you should notice that the ID is generated as you enter the record. This is shown in Figure 7.8.

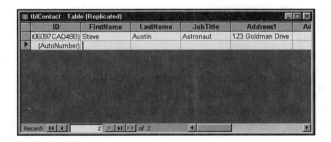

Figure 7.8: Addition of an automatically generated Replication ID in data entry in Microsoft Access.

2 Close the table. The database objects must be closed in order to perform synchronization.

3 Select Replication from Microsoft Access's Tools menu. Select Synchronize Now from the submenu.

4 The Synchronize Database dialog appears, as shown in Figure 7.9.

Figure 7.9: The Synchronize Database dialog, which lets you select a replica to synchronize with the master.

5 Note that the Synchronize Database lets you select an existing replica or choose from a list of replicas (using the combo box's drop-down list). Because presumably you haven't created more than one replica so far, you can accept the proposed filename and click OK.

6 After a short delay, Access reports that the synchronization was completed successfully. It also asks if you want to close and reopen the current database in order to ensure that all the synchronized data appears. It's not necessary in this case because you know that no new data was copied from the replica to the design master.

7 To confirm that the new record was transmitted from the design master to the replica, close the design master database and open the replica. You should be able to see that the data you entered in the design master has been copied to the replica.

At this point you can try reversing the process, adding a record, or making a change in the record that resides in the replica and resynchronizing the replica with the design master. This reveals an important point about synchronization—you can initiate synchronization from either the replica (in which case records are "pulled" into the replica from the design master), or you can synchronize from the design master (in which case data is "pushed" into the replica from the design master). As long as there is database connectivity between the replica and the design master, and no open database objects, replication will succeed.

Doing Replication in Data Access Objects

In Visual Basic, you can control how databases are replicated using Data Access Objects. DAO, introduced in Chapter 3, "Data Access Objects," is an object-oriented technique for accessing databases. When you use DAO to control replication, you gain the ability to control how replicable database are set up, configured, and synchronized in code. The DAO objects that contain properties relevant to replication are listed in Table 7.1.

Table 7.1: DAO Objects and Their Features Pertaining to Replication

Replica Functionality	Object	Description
KeepLocal property	TableDef, QueryDef (as well as other Microsoft Access objects such as Forms and Reports)	Determines whether the object can be made replicable
Replicable property	Database, database object (TableDef, QueryDef, as well as other Access database objects such as Reports and Code Modules)	Determines whether the object (and for TableDefs, the data it stores) is replicated at synchronization time
MakeReplica method	Database	Makes a replica from a Design Master
Synchronize method	Database	Synchronizes a replica database with its design master
ReplicaFilter property	TableDef	Enables you to supply a SQL WHERE clause that governs which records from the table are replicated (this property supports partial replicas—for more information, see the section "Partial Replicas" later in this chapter)
PartialReplica property	Relation	In a partial replica, enables you to determine which relationship governs the replication of records
ReplicableBool	Database	Equivalent to the Replicable property, but easier to set

Note: You want to make sure you back up your database before fiddling with its replication properties in DAO. This is because there are a few seemingly innocent things you can do with replication that can mess up your database permanently.

Setting Up Replication in DAO

To begin using replication with DAO code, you must make your database replicable. To do this, add a custom property to the Database object that represents the database. The idea of custom properties is crucial to understanding how to do replication in DAO; custom properties permit extensibility of the DAO object model.

Note: Because the Replicable property is a custom property of a Jet database, in order to use it, the property must first be appended to the Properties collection of the database object in question. Every Jet database object, including the database itself, has its own Properties collection.

Jet database's custom properties were introduced in Chapter 3's "Creating and Using Custom Properties of Database Objects" section. Using DAO, you can write code to determine which properties a particular database object has. As a refresher of how this code works, Listing 7.5 shows how to list all the properties for a particular table in a design master.

Listing 7.5: Listing all the Custom Properties for a Particular Database Object

```
Option Explicit

' References DAO 3.5

Dim db As Database
Dim td As TableDef
Dim pr As Property

Public Sub ListProps()

    Set db = OpenDatabase(App.Path & "\experiment1.mdb")
    Set td = db.TableDefs("tblCustomer")

    For Each pr In td.Properties
```

Listing 7.5: Listing all the Custom Properties for a Particular Database Object (Continued)

```
        Debug.Print pr.Name
    Next

End Sub
```

You make a database replicable by creating a Replicable property, then setting that property to the string value T. Making the database replicable converts it into a design462 master; this is different than making individual objects within the database replicable (as described in subsequent sections). It's different in DAO than it is in Access because, as with most things, Access does a bunch of the replication for you behind the scenes; when you ask it to make a replica, it makes the database replicable in addition to the database objects you select.

Use code similar to that in Listing 7.6 to make your database replicable in DAO.

Listing 7.6: Making a Database Replicable by Adding a Custom Replicable Property

```
Option Explicit

' References DAO 3.5.

Dim db As Database
Dim pr As Property

Private Sub Command1_Click()

    DBReplicable

End Sub

Sub DBReplicable()

On Error GoTo ErrHandler

    ' The "True" parameter in the OpenDatabase method
    ' tells Jet to open the database for exclusive
    ' access, which is required for creating properties.

    Set db = OpenDatabase(App.Path & "\experiment2.mdb", True)

    With db
```

continues

Listing 7.6: Making a Database Replicable by Adding a Custom Replicable Property (Continued)

```
        Set pr = .CreateProperty("Replicable", dbText, "T")
        .Properties.Append pr
        .Properties("Replicable") = "T"

    End With


    MsgBox "The Replicable property is " & db.Properties("Replicable").Value

    db.Close
    Set db = Nothing       ' Release exclusive lock on db.

Exit Sub
ErrHandler:
    Select Case Err.Number
        Case 3367       ' Replicable property already exists
        Exit Sub        ' So ignore the error and exit

        Case Else       ' Something unforeseen happened
        MsgBox "Error: " & Err & " - " & Error

    End Select

End Sub
```

Note that this code works whether the current database has a Replicable property or not; if the current database has a Replicable property, the code does not attempt to create it.

However, there's something tricky about creating a Replicable property for a database—when you create it, you can't get rid of it. You might think you could kill it using code like this:

```
db.Properties.Delete "Replicable"
```

You can't. That code generates runtime error 3607: "The replication property you are attempting to delete is read-only and cannot be removed." This is the reason why you were instructed to make backups of your database before fooling around with replication. Aren't you glad?

Making a Database Object Replicable with the Replicable Property in DAO
After you've made the database replicable, you must make individual objects within the database replicable by creating Replicable properties for them, the same way you did for the database itself. The Replicable property governs

whether a particular database object is replicated at synchronization time; those database objects whose Replicable property is set to T are replicated at synchronization time.

To do this, you use code like that shown in Listing 7.7. This code assumes that the database itself has already been made replicable; it takes an existing table in a database and makes it replicable.

Listing 7.7: Making a Single Table Replicable

```
Option Explicit

' References DAO 3.5.

Dim db As Database
Dim pr As Property
Dim td As TableDef

Private Sub Command2_Click()

    TableReplicable

End Sub

Sub TableReplicable()

On Error GoTo ErrHandler

    Set db = OpenDatabase(App.Path & "\experiment2.mdb", True)
    Set td = db.TableDefs("tblContact")
    td.Properties("Replicable") = "T"

    On Error GoTo 0

    db.Close
    Set db = Nothing     ' Release exclusive lock on DB

Exit Sub

    ErrHandler:

    If Err.Number = 3270 Then
        Set pr = td.CreateProperty("Replicable", dbText, "T")
        td.Properties.Append pr
    Else
        MsgBox "Error " & Err & " - " & Error
    End If

End Sub
```

This code is fairly similar to the code that set up the initial Replicable property for the database. In this case, the error trapping takes care of the situation where the Replicable property has not been created for the object. The code uses error trapping to determine whether the Replicable property for a database object exists; if it doesn't exist, it creates it and sets the custom property to the string value T. Setting a database object's Replicable property to T causes the object (and any data it contains) to be copied to replica databases at synchronization time.

Setting a database object's Replicable property to T causes its KeepLocal property to be set to F.

Making an Object Replicable Using the ReplicableBool Property

You might have noticed that the custom properties used so far in this chapter all take text arguments—the letters T or F instead of the actual Boolean values True or False. That's because when they were introduced to Jet, custom database properties could only store text values. In Jet 3.5, custom properties can store a richer set of data types. This may make it easier for you to create properties pertaining to replication in DAO if you prefer to work with Trues and Falses instead of Ts and Fs.

If you want to set the Replicable property of a database object using Boolean values, you can create and set the ReplicableBool property rather than the Replicable property. ReplicableBool takes a Boolean value rather than a string. The code to make a database object replicable using the ReplicableBool property is shown in Listing 7.8; note that the code is startlingly similar to the code that uses the Replicable property.

Listing 7.8: Making a Particular Database Object Replicable Using the ReplicableBool Property

```
Option Explicit

' References DAO 3.5.

Dim db As Database
Dim pr As Property
Dim td As TableDef
```

Listing 7.8: Making a Particular Database Object Replicable Using the ReplicableBool Property (Continued)

```
Private Sub Command3_Click()

    TableRepBool

End Sub

Private Sub TableRepBool()

On Error GoTo ErrHandler

    Set db = OpenDatabase(App.Path & "\experiment2.mdb", True)
    Set td = db.TableDefs("tblClient")
    td.Properties("ReplicableBool") = True

    On Error GoTo 0

    db.Close
    Set db = Nothing     ' Release exclusive lock on DB

Exit Sub

    ErrHandler:

    If Err.Number = 3270 Then
        Set pr = td.CreateProperty("ReplicableBool", dbBoolean, True)
        td.Properties.Append pr
    Else
        MsgBox "Error " & Err & " - " & Error
    End If

End Sub
```

When you create and set the ReplicableBool property, the Replicable property also becomes available, and the two properties return the same value. That is, when you set ReplicableBool to True and then read the Replicable property, it returns the value T.

Making a Replica in DAO

You make a replica database from a design master by executing the MakeReplica method of the Database object. The MakeReplica method has the following syntax:

```
db.MakeReplica filename, [description], [options]
```

filename is the new database replica file you want to create. *description* is a textual description for the new replica. This argument is optional.

options can be one of two values. The first option, dbRepMakePartial, creates a partial replica, which means you can control which records are copied from the design master to the replica. The other option, dbRepMakeReadOnly, permits you to make the replica read-only to replica users (you can still send data and new data objects to the replica through synchronization, however).

> **Note:** You can make a replica both a partial replica and a read-only replica by adding the values dbRepMakePartial and dbRepMakeReadOnly together in the options argument.
>
> Also, I tried my darnedest, but I couldn't figure out what that *Description* argument is used for. You'd think that it would become a custom property of the replicated database, but it doesn't. I'm sure it's useful for something, but I wasn't able to figure out what, and none of the documentation I have access to is any help. (Naturally, if you're interested in adding custom name properties to your replicated databases, there's nothing to keep you from doing that yourself; that's what custom properties are for.)

In order to replicate an existing design master, you use code like that shown in Listing 7.9.

Listing 7.9: Creating a Replica Database Using Data Access Objects Code

```
Private Sub Command4_Click()

    Dim db As Database
    Set db = OpenDatabase(App.Path & "\experiment2.mdb", True)

    db.MakeReplica App.Path & "\exp2rep1.mdb", "MyRepDescription"

    db.Close
    Set db = Nothing

End Sub
```

Performing Synchronization in DAO

In order to synchronize a replica and a design master using DAO code, follow these steps:

1 In code, create a Database object variable that represents the *replica* database.

2 Execute the Database object's Synchronize method in order to synchronize the replica to its design master. The Synchronize method takes the filename of a design master database as an argument.

Listing 7.10 gives an example of code that synchronizes two databases. In the example, exp2rep1.mdb is the replica, while experiment2.mdb is the design master.

Listing 7.10: Synchronizing a Replica and a Design Master Database

```
Option Explicit

' References DAO 3.5.

Dim db As Database

Private Sub Command5_Click()

    Dim db As Database
    Set db = OpenDatabase(App.Path & "\exp2rep1.mdb")

    Screen.MousePointer = vbHourglass
    db.Synchronize App.Path & "\experiment2.mdb"
    Screen.MousePointer = vbNormal

    db.Close
    Set db = Nothing

End Sub
```

User-interface code (using the Screen object's Mousepointer property) is used to tell the user that the replication is in progress.

Using Partial Replication

Often you don't want to transmit a complete set of data from the design master to the replica. This happens in situations where it's inappropriate and impractical to send the entire contents of the master database to remote users.

Examples of information that shouldn't be transmitted include confidential business information such as salaries, as well as any security-oriented information pertaining to your database such as user IDs and passwords. Your database may also simply be set up such that only data pertaining to an individual user is replicated to that user's computer. This kind of replication is more efficient than full replication because it only copies the data that a particular user is likely to use.

A *partial replica* is a database that doesn't replicate all the data in the design master. In order to create a partial replica, you follow these general steps:

1 Create a partial replica using the MakeReplica method of the Database object, specifying the dbRepMakePartial option.

2 Set the TableDef object's ReplicaFilter property to restrict the records copied to the partial replica. ReplicaFilter lets you set a criterion SQL WHERE clause to limit the number of records that are copied into the partial replica from the source database.

3 Optionally, set the Relation object's PartialReplica property to restrict records copied to the replica based on joins between tables.

4 Execute the Database object's PopulatePartial method to copy data from the design master to the partial replica.

In partial replication, you can filter out records, but you can't filter out fields. In order to restrict the columns visible to the user, you may want to consider using database security to restrict users' access to database objects. For more information on this, see Chapter 8, "Multiuser Issues."

Creating a Partial Replica Using the MakeReplica Method

In Data Access Objects, you use the Database object's MakeReplica method to create a partial replica database from either a design master or another full replica (you can't create a partial replica from another partial replica).

Use code like that in Listing 7.11 to create a partial replica.

Listing 7.11: Creating a Partial Replica Database from a Design Master Database

```
Option Explicit

' References DAO 3.5

Private db As Database

Private Sub Command1_Click()

    Set db = OpenDatabase(App.Path & "\experiment2.mdb")
    db.MakeReplica App.Path & "\exp2rep2.mdb", _
                   "Partial", dbRepMakePartial

End Sub
```

When you create a partial replica using the code in the previous listing, the partial replica initially contains the structure of the replicated database, but no data.

When you've created a partial replica, you can't convert it into a full replica. However, it is possible to replicate all the data in a design master into a replica by setting the ReplicaFilter property to True (as described in the next section).

Performing a Partial Replication

After you've created a partial replica, you can copy records from another full replica or design master by following these general steps:

1 In Data Access Objects code, declare and set a Database variable for the partial replica database.

2 Declare TableDef variables for the tables in the partial replica that will store replicated data.

3 Set the ReplicaFilter property of each TableDef object to a valid SQL WHERE criterion. This determines which records are copied into the partial replica.

4 Execute the PopulatePartial method of the Database object, specifying the path and filename of the design master or full replica database from which you want to copy records.

You use the ReplicaFilter property of the TableDef object to replicate a partial set of records from a database to a partial replica database. The ReplicaFilter property can be set to one of three values:

▶ If ReplicaFilter is set to True, all the records in the source database are copied to the partial replica database.

▶ If ReplicaFilter is set to False, no records in the source database are copied to the partial replica.

▶ If ReplicaFilter is set to a string, the database engine assumes that the string is a SQL WHERE clause.

To assign a replica filter and copy records from a design master or full replica into a partial replica, use code similar to that in Listing 7.12.

Listing 7.12: Copying Records that Meet a Specific Criterion into a Partial Replica

```
Option Explicit

' References DAO 3.5
```

continues

Listing 7.12: Copying Records that Meet a Specific Criterion into a Partial Replica (Continued)

```
Private db As Database
Private td As TableDef

Private Sub Command2_Click()

    ' Open partial replica in exclusive mode
    Set db = OpenDatabase(App.Path & "\exp2rep2.mdb", True)
    Set td = db.TableDefs("tblContact")

    td.ReplicaFilter = "JobTitle = 'Director'"

    ' Populate with data from design master
    db.PopulatePartial App.Path & "\experiment2.mdb"

    ' Release exclusive lock on database
    Set db = Nothing

End Sub
```

This code assumes that the file exp2rep2.mdb is a partial replica of experiment2.mdb. After you run this code, only the contacts with the job title Director are copied to the partial replica, as shown in Figure 7.10.

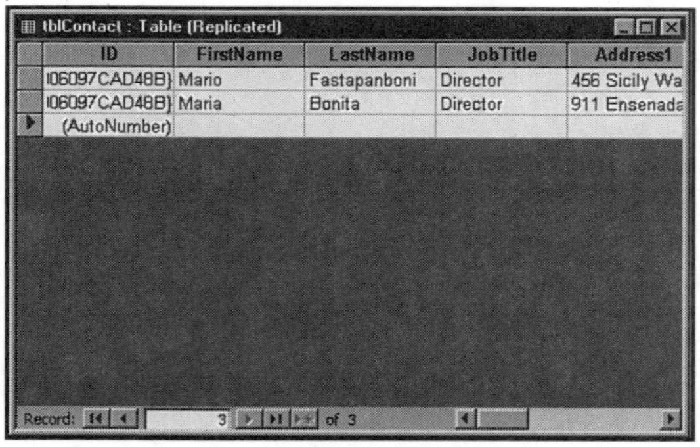

Figure 7.10: A subset of data after it has been copied to a partial replica.

Performing Database Replication Over the Internet

Microsoft Jet Replication gives you the ability to synchronize data with a design master located on a Web server on the Internet. In order to set up a system like this, follow these general steps:

1 Create a design master and one or more replicas as you normally would.

2 Place the design master on a Web server using whatever technique you normally use to place a file on a Web server. This can involve a simple file copy to a public directory (if the Web server machine is located on a machine accessible to your machine over a LAN) or an FTP upload (if the Web server machine isn't directly accessible).

3 When it's time to synchronize data, use the dbRepSyncInternet argument with the Synchronize method of the Database object. This argument lets you pass a uniform resource locator (URL) to the Synchronize method, causing the database to be replicated over the Internet.

The advantage of this technique is that anyone can get access to this data from anywhere on earth at any time. This can be a disadvantage as well, but presumably you'll take care to secure your replicated database in such a way that your valuable data doesn't fall into the hands of your enemies.

Note, however, that you can only use this technique if you have a utility called the Replication Manager, a utility that comes with the Developer Edition of Microsoft Office 97.

Summary

This chapter covered two major topics having to do with distributing data over a network to multiple users. In the first section, you learned how to use ActiveX components to gain object-oriented access to data. This included a discussion of DCOM deployment of ActiveX components, permitting you to deploy business objects across a LAN.

In the second section, you learned how to replicate Jet databases across a network in order to distribute data across two or more database files.

Although the discussion of ActiveX middle-tier components and replication represent separate major sections of this chapter, they're by no means mutually exclusive. In a production application, you could take advantage of both techniques in concert to distribute your data far and wide. Which technique you use depends on your application's architecture, the number of users you need to support, and the degree of consistency your data requires.

In the next chapter, you continue reading a discussion of multiuser database, which extends to such topics as record-locking and security.

QUESTIONS AND ANSWERS

Q. I have a whole carload of database-accessing ActiveX DLLs I've created. Do I need to recompile them as ActiveX EXEs in order to access them remotely over a network?

A. Heavens, no. If you use Microsoft Transaction Server, you can package those pesky little ActiveX DLLs right up and access them remotely. MTS acts as a proxy for ActiveX DLLs in situations where you want to deploy them remotely on a Windows NT machine.

Version 1.0 of MTS shipped with the Enterprise Edition of Visual Basic 5.0. As this chapter was being written, the current version of MTS was 2.0. It is officially licensed as a feature of Windows NT 4.0, so if you have that, you can use MTS (the latest version is downloadable from the Web). For more information on MTS, check out the Microsoft Web site at http://www.microsoft.com/transaction.

Q. When I'm doing database replication, my database system is essentially offline. How can I know how long it's going to take?

A. That's a tricky question to answer, because there are so many variables—the amount of data you have to convey, your network bandwidth, the speed of the computers crunching records. If you're running into performance problems with replication you may want to consider automating the process if you can (preferably by writing a VB application to synchronize data when the database isn't being used much—like in the middle of the night). You also might want to consider using partial replication in order to minimize the amount of data being copied hither and yon.

Q. Because partial replication gives you the ability to replicate none, some, or all records, given the fact that you can't convert back and forth between partial replicas and full replicas, why not make all replicas partial?

A. You can only do synchronization between design masters and full replicas, not between partial replicas and other replicas. This gives you more flexibility in situations where you want to synchronize multiple replicas to each other to offload the processing crunch from the computer that contains the design master.

Multiuser Issues

How can multiple users access the same database at the same time?

How can my database protect itself from multiple users attempting to access or change the same data at the same time?

How can I protect my database from access from unauthorized users?

How can I restrict access to parts of my database to those users I designate?

Chapter 8

When your database applications require access by multiple users at the same time, you need to make special accommodations. From the planning and design stage to the development and deployment of your database application, multiuser applications demand much more of the software developer—it's not just a matter of throwing a multiuser switch and copying client applications to all the computers in your organization.

Previous chapters scratched the surface of what goes into a multiuser database system. Previous chapters have covered the deployment of components that enable users to gain access to your program logic over a network using ActiveX and DCOM technology, as well as the database replication technology made available to you by the Microsoft Jet database engine.

This chapter covers two techniques that are crucial to making a multiuser database run smoothly—locking data and the security model provided with the Microsoft Jet database engine.

LOCKING DATA IN MICROSOFT JET

When two or more users have access to data in a database system, those users can cause problems for each other. For example, when one user opens a record in a table, then another user opens the same record and makes a change to it, the first user is working with an out-of-date record. And this is just one scenario; there are several others.

Your software must manage contention between users. To do this, your software, in conjunction with the database engine, has the capability to lock various parts of the database. An error occurs when a user attempts to gain access to a part of the locked database; how your application deals with that error is up to you.

In order to give you flexibility and control, the Microsoft Jet database permits you to lock the database on a number of levels. From the most restrictive to the least restrictive, the levels of locking available in Jet are:

▶ *Database-level locking.* Also known as exclusive mode. This involves opening the database in such a way that no other user can edit records in any table in the database.

▶ *Table-level locking.* A single user has exclusive access to a table in a database. All the records in the table are locked, preventing other users from editing records.

▶ *Pessimistic page-level locking.* A lock is placed on data at the time the user begins to edit it. The lock is released when the edit is committed to the database or when the user aborts the edit.

▶ *Optimistic page-level locking.* The record is locked the instant it is committed to the database, and released when the update is complete.

The following sections in this chapter discuss each locking option in detail, giving you code examples so you can use the locking techniques in your applications.

Before you proceed, note that none of these techniques permit you to lock an individual record. This is because the Jet engine locks pages of records, rather than individual records. A page is 2048 bytes of memory. If a particular record comprises less that 2048 bytes worth of data, the record, and potentially one or more records adjacent to it, will be locked as well.

Jet database locks are implemented through the use of a *locking file.* This file is given the same name as the database, but an .LDB extension. In Jet 3.x, unlike previous versions of Jet, the locking file is automatically deleted by the database engine when all users have closed the database.

Locking the Entire Database Using Data Access Objects

You have the ability to lock the entire database using Data Access Objects code. You do this in situations where you need to perform maintenance on the database, when you're performing design changes on the database, or when it's simply not appropriate for other users to have access to the database for a period of time.

To restrict access to the entire database in Data Access Objects, supply a parameter to the OpenDatabase method, as shown in Listing 8.1.

Listing 8.1: Placing a Lock on the Entire Database Using Data Access Objects Code

```
Option Explicit

' References Microsoft DAO 3.5
'
Private db As Database

Private Sub cmdExclusive_Click()

On Error GoTo ErrHandler

Dim rs As Recordset

    Set db = OpenDatabase(App.Path & "\locking.mdb", True)

Exit Sub
ErrHandler:
    MsgBox Err & " - " & Error
End Sub
```

The Database object is declared in the Declarations section of the form, not in the Click event procedure. While you wouldn't normally declare a Database variable in a procedure, in this test application it's particularly important that the Database variable have module-level scope. That's because the database lock only persists as long as the database variable is in scope. If you write the code in Listing 8.1 to look like the following, the object variable db would go out of scope as soon as the procedure finished executing:

```
Private Sub cmdExclusive_Click()

Dim db As Database
Dim rs As Recordset

    Set db = OpenDatabase(App.Path & "\locking.mdb", True)

End Sub
```

The database lock would also be removed when the procedure was done. That isn't to say that you would never want to have a procedure-level declaration for a Database variable; it just means that you need to carefully consider where and how you declare variables when performing actions with them in database access.

When your application attempts to open a database that is already opened exclusively by another user (or another application), an error occurs: number 3045, "Couldn't open X, file already in use." By trapping this error in your applications, you can ensure that your application won't inadvertently attempt to open a database that is exclusively locked by another user.

Using Recordset-Level Locking

You can use Data Access Objects to place a lock on an entire table (or multiple tables, in the case of a Recordset based on a join between more than one table). You might do this in a situation where you need to perform maintenance on the table or if you need to change the table's design, but you don't want to deny users access to the entire database.

Listing 8.2 gives an example of DAO code that locks a database table, returns its record count, and unlocks it by releasing its object variable.

Listing 8.2: Data Access Objects Code to Lock an Entire Database Table

```
Private Sub cmdTable_Click()

    Dim rs As Recordset

    ' Open in multiuser mode - no database lock
    Set db = OpenDatabase(App.Path & "\locking.mdb")

    Set rs = db.OpenRecordset("tblPerson", dbOpenTable, _
            dbDenyWrite + dbDenyRead)
    rs.MoveLast

    MsgBox "The table contains " & rs.RecordCount & " records."
    Stop

End Sub
```

One quick way to test this code is to run this code in Visual Basic, then attempt to open the table in Microsoft Access (the Stop statement in the procedure permits you to do this). If it worked properly, Access should refuse to open the table, instead generating an error message indicating that the table is exclusively locked.

Using Page-Level Locking

Page-level locking is the least restrictive level of locking available in the Jet database engine. With page-level locking, records that are being updated are locked for some period of time to ensure that other users's operations don't interfere with the update.

Remember that Jet locks pages (of 2048 bytes each) rather than records. This means that it's possible that when locking a page, more than one record will be locked. This has historically been a source of frustration for Jet programmers, but after you become accustomed to it, you may find that it isn't such a big deal.

> **Note:** Microsoft SQL Server 6.5 does not offer record locking as a feature; it too locks pages in 2048-byte increments.

You have two options to enforce page-level locking: *optimistic* and *pessimistic* locking. Optimistic locking is turned on at the instant a record is being committed to the database; pessimistic locking is activated as soon as you open a record for editing. Both techniques have advantages and disadvantages.

Using Optimistic Locking   You use optimistic locking when you need to minimize the number of locks on records in your database. It's particularly appropriate when a large number of users need access to all the records in your database at all times. Optimistic locking might also be appropriate for an application whose purpose is primarily inserting, rather than updating, information in a database.

To explicitly specify that you want to open a recordset with optimistic locking, supply the dbOptimistic flag to the options parameter of the OpenRecordset method.

```
db.OpenRecordset("tblPerson", dbOpenDynaset, False, dbOptimistic)
```

Optimistic locking requires error trapping associated with the process of updating a record; an Update method on an optimistically-locked recordset generates an error if another user makes a change to a record between the time you started editing and when you committed it back to the database.

Listing 8.3 shows an example of such a collision using optimistic locking.

Listing 8.3: Retrieving and Updating a Record from a Database Using Optimistic Locking

```
Option Explicit

' References Microsoft DAO 3.5
'
Private db As Database
Private rsOp As Recordset

Private Sub cmdOpOpen_Click()
    Set db = OpenDatabase(App.Path & "\locking.mdb")

    ' Optimistic lock by default
    Set rsOp = db.OpenRecordset("tblPerson", _
                          dbOpenDynaset, _
                          False, _
                          dbOptimistic)

    ' Even though we're doing an Edit here
    ' there's no lock on the data.
    rsOp.Edit

    ' Populate the user interface
    txtFirstName.Text = rsOp!FirstName
    txtLastName.Text = rsOp!LastName
    txtAddress.Text = rsOp!Address

End Sub

Private Sub cmdOpSave_Click()

    If rsOp Is Nothing Then
        Exit Sub
    End If

    rsOp!FirstName = txtFirstName.Text
    rsOp!LastName = txtLastName.Text
    rsOp!Address = txtAddress.Text

    ' If this is the 2nd copy of the app,
    ' this should cause an error
    rsOp.Update

End Sub
```

Follow these steps to demonstrate a collision between two applications attempting to edit the same record at the same time using optimistic locking:

1 Compile the pg-lock.exe application.

2 Launch two copies of the application by double-clicking on pg-lock.exe twice in Windows Explorer.

3 Click Optimistic Open in the first copy of the application. The data loads into the application.

4 Click Optimistic Open in the second copy of the application. The same record is loaded.

5 Make a change in the data in the application's first copy, then click Optimistic Save. The data is written to the database.

6 Make a change in the data in the application's second copy, then click Optimistic Save.

7 The second application generates an error, as illustrated in Figure 8.1.

Figure 8.1: Example of a collision between two applications accessing data using optimistic locking.

To avoid this situation, trap the error and report it back to the user. Optionally, you could also provide a service in the user interface to preserve the data entered by the user until it's entered at a later time, comparing the latest version of the record with the data entered by the user.

Using Pessimistic Locking   You use pessimistic locking when you want to make sure that no other user accesses data while you're working with that data. When pessimistic locking is activated, a lock is placed on the database page containing the record you're editing as soon as you execute the Edit method against the record. If other users attempt to retrieve a record that's on the locked page containing your record, their application generates an error.

Activate pessimistic locking by using the dbPessimistic flag when executing the OpenRecordset method. Listing 8.4 shows an example of a procedure that opens a recordset with pessimistic locking.

Listing 8.4: Opening a Recordset in Data Access Objects Using Pessimistic Locking

```
Option Explicit

' References Microsoft DAO 3.5
'
Private db As Database
Private rsPess As Recordset

Private Sub cmdPess_Click()

    Set db = OpenDatabase(App.Path & "\locking.mdb")

    Set rsPess = db.OpenRecordset("tblPerson", _
                 dbOpenDynaset, _
                 False, _
                 dbPessimistic)

    ' Get a lock on the data. If this
    ' is the 2nd copy of the app,
    ' this should cause an error
    rsPess.Edit

    ' Populate the user interface
    txtFirstName.Text = rsPess!FirstName
    txtLastName.Text = rsPess!LastName
    txtAddress.Text = rsPess!Address
```

Listing 8.4: Opening a Recordset in Data Access Objects Using Pessimistic Locking (Continued)

```
End Sub

Private Sub cmdSave_Click()

    If rsPess Is Nothing Then
        Exit Sub
    End If

    rsPess!FirstName = txtFirstName.Text
    rsPess!LastName = txtLastName.Text
    rsPess!Address = txtAddress.Text

    rsPess.Update

End Sub
```

A lock—either optimistic or pessimistic—is released after the successful execution of the Update method.

You can test pessimistic locking with this application by doing the following:

1 Compile the application.

2 Launch two copies of the application (by double-clicking on the file pglock.exe twice in Windows Explorer).

3 In the first copy of the application, click Pessimistic Open to load the first record in the recordset.

4 The data appears in the application's interface. Click Pessimistic Open in the second application's copy.

5 The second application generates an error, as illustrated in Figure 8.2.

The moral of this story is that although pessimistic locking keeps you from having to worry about data changing while you're working, you must include additional error handling to account for situations in which two users attempt to open the same record at the same time.

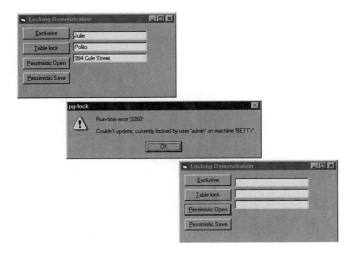

Figure 8.2: Two applications contending for the same record generate an error in pessimistic locking.

USING MICROSOFT JET DATABASE SECURITY

One compelling reason to use the Microsoft Jet database engine is the fact that it supports multiple concurrent users—but database locking is only one way in which Jet supports multiple users.

You can also use database security to identify individual users and groups of users so that you can permit or restrict access to various parts of your database. When you restrict access to a database, that database is described as *secure*—although the Jet security model allows for many different shades of meaning within the word secure. The level of security you choose to implement in your databases depends on your needs, the needs of your users, and the amount of effort you want to expend.

You have the ability to secure a database using the graphical user interface in Microsoft Access. This route has the advantage of being easier for you, but even with this tool you can't write applications that secure databases unless you have a handle on the internals of the Jet security model. Accordingly, this section focuses on how to manage the security of your database using DAO code.

One advantage of Data Access Objects 3.x is the fact that unlike previous versions of DAO, you can now access the Jet security model in Visual Basic code (either in Visual Basic, or in the version of Visual Basic for Applications found in Microsoft Access and other Microsoft Office applications). The ability to write code to access the database's security features gives you a great deal of flexibility to create and maintain a secure database system.

> **Note:** You can use Data Access Object programming to perform all but one task pertaining to managing database security—the creation of a workgroup information file. For this, you need a utility provided with Microsoft Access. More on this in "Creating a Workgroup Information File," later in this chapter.

Unfortunately, the Visual Basic documentation is extremely deficient in the area of documenting how Microsoft Jet security works. This section gives you a complete introduction into how security works, including examples of how to perform security operations using Data Access Objects.

Because security from the Microsoft Access perspective is fairly well documented, this section seeks to avoid a discussion of using Access as a security-enabling tool (with one exception: creating a workgroup information file, the single Jet security operation that requires a utility found only in Microsoft Access).

Understand, however, that Access provides an simple set of menus and dialog boxes to implement security. If you're interested in setting up security for an existing application on a one-time basis and you don't need programmatic access to Jet's security model, you may find it more efficient to take advantage of Access's interface into Jet database security.

Accessing a Secured Jet Database in Code

In order to gain access to a secured database, you must identify yourself with either a username, a password, or both (depending on how your database was secured). If your code accessed a secure database, the code generates an error unless it supplies this information to the database engine.

To specify a username and password in Data Access Objects code, use the connect parameter of the OpenDatabase method. As you've seen in previous chapters's discussions involving connecting to ODBC databases, the connect string permits you to supply additional information to the database engine about the user's identity and how they are to be connected to the database.

As introduced in Chapter 5, connect strings are composed of a series of settings separated by semicolons. This syntax, while unwieldy at times, permits the connect string to convey a potentially unlimited amount of information about how the user should be connected to the database.

Normally when you build a connect string in code, the first setting is ODBC. This indicates that you want to connect to a remote database using an ODBC driver.

However, when you want to connect to a Jet database, you supply a connect string solely for the purpose of indicating a username and a password. In this case, replace the ODBC setting with a blank.

The database name is the next connect string setting. The DATABASE setting provides the path and filename of a Jet database.

For example, a connect string to open the Jones Novelties database would look like this:

```
";DATABASE=c:\data\novelty.mdb"
```

Use the PWD value to provide a password in the connect string. This logs you into the database whether you use simple password protection or user-level security. For example, if the Jones Novelties database had a password of prince, you'd use the following connect string:

```
";DATABASE=c:\data\novelty.mdb;PWD=prince"
```

Remember that in Jet, passwords can be up to 20 characters in length, and are case-sensitive.

In a database that contains user-level security (described later in this chapter), all users must identify themselves to the system with a unique username (of up to 14 characters). You include this information in the connect string using the connect string's USR value. To extend the previous example, the connect string to get into the Jones Novelties database with a username of randy and a password of prince is:

```
";DATABASE=c:\data\novelty.mdb;USR=randy;PWD=prince"
```

The order in which the connect string values appear is unimportant, with the exception of the first value, which specifies which type of data source you're opening (ODBC or non-ODBC). The previous connect string could also have been expressed as:

```
";DATABASE=c:\data\novelty.mdb;PWD=prince;USR=randy"
```

Listing 8.5 demonstrates how to gain access to a password-protected database using a connect string passed as a parameter to the OpenDatabase method.

Listing 8.5: Logging In to a Secured Database Using a Connect String

```
Option Explicit

Private db As Database

' References DAO 3.5

Private Sub Command1_Click()
On Error Resume Next

Dim strConnect As String
strConnect = ";DATABASE=" & App.Path & "\secure.mdb" & _
             ";PWD=" & txtPassword.Text

    ' Open in non-exclusive mode and pass connect string
    Set db = OpenDatabase("", True, False, strConnect)

    If Err Then
        MsgBox "Error: " & Err.Description & _
               " [" & Err.Number & "]", vbExclamation
        Exit Sub
    Else
        MsgBox "Database successfully opened.", vbInformation
    End If

    db.Close
    Set db = Nothing

End Sub
```

There are two important differences between this code and the code you've used previously to open databases using DAO.

First, the DATABASE= value in the connect string replaces the filename parameter you typically supply to the OpenDatabase method. You pass the OpenDatabase method an empty string (as a placeholder) in place of the filename parameter.

Error handling is used to account for a situation where the database can't be opened. You should have an error handler active in any situation in which you perform a file access operation, but it's particularly important when you're accessing a secure database. This is because the user typically supplies login information, and it's quite common for the user to supply incorrect information (such as a misspelled username or an expired password). An error trap is the only way your application can gracefully recover from this situation.

Assigning a Password to a Database

Assigning a password to a Jet database is one of the easiest ways to restrict access to a database. When you password-protect a database, only authorized users can get access to the database.

However, merely assigning a password to a database does not represent airtight security. In fact, it's one of the least rigorous security measures you can apply to a Microsoft Access database. Simply assigning a password to a database is used primarily because it's easy to implement. For many systems, locking unauthorized users out of the database with a password check is all the security that is required. Note, however, that this technique does not permit you to require users to log in with a unique username; consequently, it does not permit you to restrict particular users's access to particular database objects (to do this, you must implement user-level security, as described later in this chapter).

In Data Access Objects programming, you assign a password to a database by using the Database object's NewPassword method. The NewPassword method's syntax is as follows:

```
db.NewPassword oldpassword, newpassword
```

oldpassword is the database's current password, and *newpassword* is the password you want to apply. If the database doesn't currently have a password (by default, it does not), you supply an empty string in place of oldpassword. (Similarly, if you're interested in removing a password from a previously password-protected database, supply an empty string to the newpassword argument.)

To assign a password to a database that currently doesn't have a password, use code similar to that in Listing 8.6.

Listing 8.6: Assigning a Password to a Database that Doesn't Currently Have a Password

```
Dim db As Database

On Error Resume Next     ' Activate inline error handling


    Set db = OpenDatabase(App.Path & "\mydata.mdb", True, False)

    db.NewPassword txtOld.Text, txtNew.Text

    If Not Err Then
        MsgBox "Database password changed.", vbInformation
```

Listing 8.6: Assigning a Password to a Database that Doesn't Currently Have a Password (Continued)

```
Else
    MsgBox "Error: " & Err.Description & _
            " [" & Err.Number & "]", vbExclamation
End If


db.Close
Set db = Nothing
```

Remember from the discussion of the Database object in Chapter 3 that the OpenDatabase method takes several arguments. In this context, the True and False arguments supplied to OpenDatabase indicate that the database should be opened in read-write, exclusive mode (the True argument means open the database in read-write mode, the False argument means open it in exclusive mode). You must open a database in read-write, exclusive mode before you can assign the database a password.

You should make judicious use of error-handling when your code manipulates a database's security information, or when you open a database that has been secured with a password. Just as with other data access and file operations, a number of things can go wrong when you access a database. In this case, the likeliest problems are:

▶ Another user already has the database open.

▶ The user attempted to change to an invalid password.

Remember once again that passwords are case-sensitive and must be 20 characters or less. After you've assigned a password to a database, remember it. If you forget it, you'll never be able to open the database again.

Note: The topics pertaining to security in the rest of this chapter cover user-level security, in which you create user accounts and groups that can have permissions to access objects in the database. In order to set up this type of security, you must go through a complicated series of steps, including creating a special type of external database that manages information pertaining to users, groups, and permissions. This database is called a *workgroup information file*, and it's covered later in this chapter. Bear in mind, though, that you don't need a workgroup information file if you only want to assign a password to the database. When you assign a password to the database using the technique described in this section, the password is stored in the database itself (in encrypted form, of course).

The concept of assigning a password to a database is new to Jet 3.x.

Business Case 8.1: Working with a Secured Database The Jones Novelties database system requires a password to protect the system's data from intruding outsiders. In addition, the developers are interested in developing a standard call to open the database, given the fact that a password is now required to open it.

The development team must use three techniques in order to do this:

▶ In the user interface, provide a means for the user to enter a password.

▶ Supply a connect string (in the form of the Database object's Connect property) to inform the database engine of the password required to open the database.

▶ Provide error handling for the line of code that opens the database (in case the password entered by the user is incorrect).

To do this, the database developers write a utility to change the database's password. This utility is composed of a single form with two text boxes and a command button, as pictured in Figure 8.3.

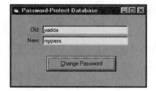

Figure 8.3: Changing the password of the Jones Novelties database.

To use this utility, the user types the existing password in the text box called txtOld, types the new password in the text box called txtNew, and clicks the command button. The password is changed. Listing 8.7 shows the code that implements this utility.

Listing 8.7: Code to Change a Password in a Jet Database

```
Option Explicit

Private db As Database

Private Sub Command1_Click()
On Error Resume Next
```

Listing 8.7: Code to Change a Password in a Jet Database (Continued)

```
Dim strConnect As String
strConnect = ";DATABASE=" & App.Path & "\novelty.mdb" & _
             ";PWD=" & txtOld.Text

    ' Open in exclusive mode with existing password, if any
    Set db = OpenDatabase("", True, False, strConnect)

    If Err Then
        MsgBox "Error: " & Err.Description & _
               " [" & Err.Number & "]", vbExclamation
        Exit Sub
    End If

    ' Change password
    db.NewPassword txtOld.Text, txtNew.Text
    db.Close

End Sub
```

This utility uses the code shown in the previous example of the NewPassword method, extending it for use in a general application. The resulting utility has the capability to change the password from any legal value to any other legal value, and it includes error traps that can handle situations in which the database can't be opened exclusively or the password supplied by the user isn't legal.

When you attempt to use Microsoft Access to open a password-protected database, Access displays a password dialog, as shown in Figure 8.4.

Figure 8.4: Logon dialog box displayed by Microsoft Access for databases secured at the share level.

Access displays a similar dialog for databases that have been secured with user-level security, as shown in Figure 8.5.

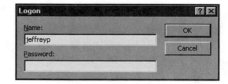

Figure 8.5: Logon dialog displayed by Microsoft Access for databases secured at the user level.

Identifying the Current User in Code

In a secure database, users must identify themselves to the database engine via a username and a password. This is the case regardless of whether you've explicitly done anything to secure your database; if the database is unsecured, the user is always identified with a username of Admin and no password. The reason you may have never come across this is because in an unsecured Jet database, the username Admin is assumed unless you specify otherwise.

You can see this for yourself by creating an application that inspects the username in the default Jet workspace, Workspaces(0). Remember that Workspaces(0) is created automatically when you run an application that contains a reference to the Jet database engine library. The code to return the name of the current user in Jet is shown in Listing 8.8.

Listing 8.8: Displaying the Current User in Microsoft Jet Security

```
Option Explicit
Private db As Database


' References DAO 3.5


Private Sub Form_Load()

    MsgBox Workspaces(0).UserName, vbInformation

End Sub
```

Again, note that even though this is DAO code, you don't have to declare or set any object variables for it to work, because Workspaces(0) is always available to you.

Logging In to the Database Using the Workspace Object   In an unsecured Jet database, you are implicitly logged on as the Admin user. When logging on to a secured database using DAO code, however, you must identify yourself as a database user. You typically do this by creating a new workspace, passing your username and password to the CreateWorkspace method of the DBEngine object. Listing 8.9 gives an example of how to do this.

Listing 8.9: Opening a Secured Database Using the CreateWorkspace Method of the OpenDatabase Object

```
Option Explicit

' References DAO 3.5

Private ws As Workspace
Private db As Database
Private rs As Recordset

Private Sub Form_Load()
    DBEngine.SystemDB = App.Path & "\mygroup.mdw"
    Set ws = DBEngine.CreateWorkspace("", "johnny", "johnny")

    Set db = ws.OpenDatabase(App.Path & "\secure.mdb")
    Set rs = db.OpenRecordset("tblCustomer")

    rs.MoveLast
    MsgBox "The table contains " & rs.RecordCount & " records.", vbInformation

End Sub
```

The CreateWorkspace method takes three arguments here: a blank string that represents the name of the workspace, a username, and a password. (In the secured example database, users's names and passwords are all the same.) When you open the database using this technique, you use the workspace object's OpenDatabase method, instead of the way you'd normally do it—using OpenDatabase by itself:

```
OpenDatabase(App.Path & "\secure.mdb")
```

When you use OpenDatabase this way, you're really excuting the DBEngine object's OpenDatabase method, which doesn't permit you to include security login information generated by the DAO workspace object. Remember when you're logging into a secured database to use the OpenDatabase method of the Workspace object, not the DBEngine's OpenDatabase method.

Note also that if the user johnny doesn't have permission to open the tblCustomer table, the application generates an error (number 3112, "Record(s) can't be read, no read permission on 'tblCustomer'.") Accordingly, make sure that this error is trapped and handled appropriately in your applications that use secured databases.

Creating a Workgroup Information File

A *workgroup information file* is a type of database that stores information about users and groups. This information is stored in a different file (as opposed to in your database) because it's possible you'd want to share security information across multiple databases.

The workgroup information file is typically named SYSTEM.MDW (although it doesn't have to be). You use the Workgroup Administrator utility, WRKGADM.EXE, to create a workgroup information file. Irritatingly, though, this utility does not come with Visual Basic; it only comes with Microsoft Access. (This is the only component of Jet security you can't manipulate using Visual Basic alone.)

To create a workgroup information file:

1 If you're running Microsoft Access, exit it.

2 Launch the Workgroup Administrator utility WRKGADM.EXE. This file is located in the Windows system folder.

3 The Workgroup Administrator launches, as shown in Figure 8.6.

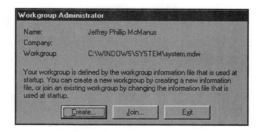

Figure 8.6: The Microsoft Access Workgroup Administrator, displaying the current default workgroup information file.

4 To create a new workgroup information database, click Create. The Workgroup Owner Information dialog appears, as shown in Figure 8.7.

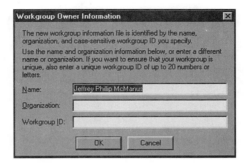

Figure 8.7: The Workgroup Owner Information dialog, which lets you supply information used to create a new workgroup information file.

5 Enter your name and company name in the appropriate text boxes. (If you entered these when you set up Microsoft Access, these are entered into the text boxes for you.) Additionally, in order to make your workgroup information file unique, enter a workgroup ID of up to 20 alphanumeric characters. When the Workgroup Owner Information dialog box is complete, it should look something like Figure 8.8.

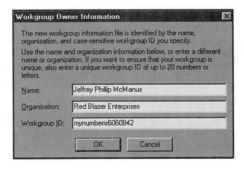

Figure 8.8: The Workgroup Owner Information dialog box, containing the owner's information and a workgroup ID.

6 Click OK. A dialog box appears, asking you for the folder into which you want to save your workgroup information file. Choose a folder, then click OK.

7 The Confirm Workgroup Information dialog box appears, as shown in Figure 8.9.

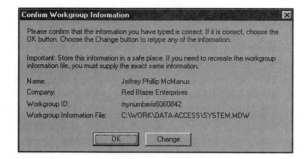

Figure 8.9: The Confirm Workgroup Information dialog box showing you the information you entered.

The Confirm Workgroup Information dialog box displays the information you entered; this information is used to create a unique workgroup information file. It's important to record this information, otherwise your workgroup information file can't be replaced if it becomes destroyed or deleted in the future. Because all the information you need is being displayed for you in the Confirm Workgroup Information dialog box, now is a good time to record the information and put it away for future reference.

Note: You might take a screen shot of this dialog and print it out so you have a permanent copy of your user information and workgroup ID. You can do this by pressing the Print Screen key on your keyboard. This places a copy of the screen on the Windows clipboard. You can then print out the screen shot by pasting the image into any application that accepts images. Microsoft Word and Windows Paint both work well for this purpose.

You should also keep your workgroup ID secret. If an unscrupulous person obtains your workgroup ID, he or she can re-create your workgroup information file and gain access to the database.

8 Click OK to create the new workgroup information file. You'll receive a confirmation message, then you're returned to the original Workgroup Administrator utility dialog box.

It's important to note that creating a new workgroup information file also makes the new file your default workgroup file. This can have implications for existing secured databases; if you're currently using security based on the default SYSTEM.MDW file located in your Windows system directory and you create a new workgroup information file, you may have to switch back to your original .MDW file (using the Workgroup Administrator utility) in order to access databases secured with the original workgroup information file.

Assigning a Workgroup Information File in DAO Code You can designate a specific workgroup information database for your Visual Basic application. Your applications should do this where possible to avoid inadvertently utilizing whatever default workgroup file a user may have set up on his or her computer.

You direct the database engine to use a particular workgroup information database by assigning the workgroup file's filename to the DBEngine object's SystemDB property.

```
DBEngine.SystemDB = App.Path & "\mygroup.mdw"
```

Remember that you don't have to instantiate the DBEngine object; it's one of those DAO objects that's always available to you. But if you're going to assign an alternate workgroup information database using this technique, ensure that it's the first DAO operation your application makes. You need to do this because the DBEngine object is initialized as soon as you create a DAO object. If you don't assign a workgroup database to the DBEngine first, it will use whatever is set up as the default on your computer (or, it will use no workgroup information database at all). If that happens, you have to restart your application to get the database engine to recognize the new workgroup database.

Creating and Deleting Users

After your application has a unique workgroup information database, you can create user accounts (usually referred to as *users*). A *user account* allows an individual to log into and use a database. An account also uniquely identifies a user, permitting the database administrator to permit and deny that user access to specific elements of the database.

User information is stored in the workgroup information database (as opposed to the database itself). This means that the same sets of users, groups, and permissions can be applied to many databases, as long as the databases share the same workgroup information database.

You can access the list of user accounts by iterating through the Workspace object's Users collection. Remember that you can always access a default Workspace object by using the expression Workspaces(0); this workspace is always available to you, and you don't have to instantiate it.

An example of DAO code that uses a list box to display all user accounts in the Users collection is shown in Listing 8.10.

Listing 8.10: Adding the Contents of the Users Collection to a List Box

```
Option Explicit

' References DAO 3.5

Private ThisUser As User

Private Sub Form_Load()
    DBEngine.SystemDB = App.Path & "\mygroup.mdw"
End Sub

Private Sub cmdUser_Click()
    List1.Clear

    For Each ThisUser In Workspaces(0).Users
        List1.AddItem ThisUser.Name
    Next

End Sub
```

To create a new user account, create a User object using the Workspace object's CreateUser method. You then assign its name, password, and a unique identifier called a personal identifier (PID). The PID is a string of between 4 and 20 characters that provides uniqueness to a user account; if your workgroup information file is lost, you can use the combination of username and personal identifier to re-create the user's account. (Users should keep their PIDs secret.)

Listing 8.11 shows an example of how to create a new user account in DAO code.

Listing 8.11: Creating a New User Account

```
Option Explicit

' References DAO 3.5

Private ThisUser As User
Private ThisGroup As Group

Private Sub cmdNewUser_Click()
Dim strName As String
Dim strPID As String
Dim strPassword As String
```

Listing 8.11: Creating a New User Account (Continued)

```
    strName = InputBox("Enter the new user's name.", "New User")
    strPassword = InputBox("Enter the new password.", "New User")
    strPID = InputBox("Enter a personal ID.", "New User")

    Set ThisUser = Workspaces(0).CreateUser(strName)
    ThisUser.PID = strPID
    ThisUser.Password = strPassword

    Workspaces(0).Users.Append ThisUser

    ' Extra step required in DAO but
    ' done automatically in Access
    Set ThisGroup = ThisUser.CreateGroup("Users")
    ThisUser.Groups.Append ThisGroup

    ' Refresh list of users
    cmdUser_Click

End Sub
```

The code that adds the user to the default Users group is described more fully in "Adding Users to Groups," later in this chapter. The process of adding a new user to the default Users group is done automatically when you use Microsoft Access to manage security. However, in DAO code, users aren't automatically added to any groups. You must write code to give the user access to the database.

To delete a user account, simply delete the User object from the Users collection, as shown in Listing 8.12.

Listing 8.12: Deleting a New User Account

```
Option Explicit

' References DAO 3.5

Private Sub cmdDeleteUser_Click()
Dim strUser As String

    strUser = InputBox("Enter the user to delete.", "Delete user")
    Workspaces(0).Users.Delete strUser

    ' Refresh list of users
    cmdUser_Click

End Sub
```

Note: Don't delete all the user accounts from the Admins group. If you do this, you won't be able to administer the database, which means that you won't be able to create new users, assign ownership of objects, or assign permissions to users and groups.

Adding a Password to a User   Normally you assign a password to a user account when you create the user's account, but occasionally you need to add a password to a user after the fact. You also may need to change a user's password or permit the user to change his or her own password.

Use the User object's NewPassword method to do this, as shown in Listing 8.13.

Listing 8.13: Changing a User's Password Using the NewPassword Method

```
Private Sub cmdChangePwd_Click()
On Error Resume Next

Dim strOld As String
Dim strNew As String

    strOld = InputBox("Enter this user's current password:", _
            "Password Change")
    strNew = InputBox("Enter this user's new password:", _
            "Password Change")

    Set ThisUser = Workspaces(0).Users(List1.Text)
    ThisUser.NewPassword strOld, strNew

    If Err = 0 Then
        MsgBox "Password changed.", vbInformation
    Else
        MsgBox Err.Description
    End If

End Sub
```

This code assumes that the application has populated a list box called List1 with the list of users in the workgroup information database. To change the password, select a user in List1, then click Change Password. The procedure asks for the existing password and the new password, then changes the password.

If you are logged on to the database as an administrative user, you can change a user's password whether or not you know their existing password. To do this, pass an empty string as the first parameter of the NewPassword method.

Default Accounts Created by the Jet Database Engine   In addition to the default Admin account discussed earlier in this chapter, Jet creates two additional accounts by default. These accounts are called Creator and Engine, and they're used to support internal operations by the database engine. You can't utilize these objects in your code.

Creating and Deleting Groups

You make the process of assigning permissions to users easier by assigning sets of users and permissions to groups. Although you can assign permissions to either individual users or groups, it's generally better to assign permissions to groups only. The process of assigning a large number of permissions to a large number of users can grow very burdensome very quickly. Assigning permissions to groups and then assigning users to groups makes the process of managing permissions exponentially simpler.

When you create a new user, for example, you need simply assign the user to whichever groups are appropriate for that user, as opposed to having to remember all nine million permissions appropriate for that type of user. The process of assigning permissions to both users and groups is discussed in the next section.

You can access the list of groups that exist in a database by iterating through a workspace object's Groups collection. Listing 8.14 shows an example.

Listing 8.14: Assigning the Groups in the Groups Collection to a List Box

```
Option Explicit

' References DAO 3.5

Private ThisGroup As Group

Private Sub cmdGroup_Click()
    List1.Clear

    For Each ThisGroup In Workspaces(0).Groups
        List1.AddItem ThisGroup.Name
    Next

End Sub
```

To create a group, create a Group object using the Workspace object's CreateGroup method, then append it to the Groups collection using code similar to that in Listing 8.15.

Listing 8.15: Creating a New Security Group Using Data Access Objects

```
Option Explicit

' References DAO 3.5

Private ThisGroup As Group

Private Sub cmdNewGroup_Click()
Dim strName As String

    strName = InputBox("Enter the name of the new group.", "New group")
    Set ThisGroup = Workspaces(0).CreateGroup(strName)
    ThisGroup.PID = InputBox("Enter a unique PID for this group.", "New group")
    Workspaces(0).Groups.Append ThisGroup

    cmdGroup_Click

End Sub
```

To delete a group, you delete it from the Groups collection, as shown in Listing 8.16.

Listing 8.16: Deleting a Group from the Groups Collection Using DAO Code

```
Option Explicit

' References DAO 3.5


Private Sub cmdDeleteGroup_Click()
Dim strGroup As String

    strGroup = InputBox("Enter the group to delete.", "Delete group")
    Workspaces(0).Groups.Delete strGroup

    ' Refresh list of groups
    cmdGroup_Click

End Sub
```

This is another one of those procedures that doesn't require you to declare any database object variables, because it uses the implicit Workspace object that's always available to you through the database engine.

Adding Users to Groups

You can add users to groups to give users access to the database. When you add a user to a group, that user inherits all the permissions assigned to the group.

To determine which groups a user belongs to, iterate through the User object's Groups collection. To add a user to a group, create a Group object using the CreateGroup method of the User object, then append the Group object to the User object's Groups collection. Listing 8.17 shows an example of how to display lists of groups and add a user to a group.

Listing 8.17: Adding a User to a Group Using the CreateGroup Method of the User Object

```
Option Explicit

' References DAO 3.5

Private ThisUser As User
Private ThisGroup As Group

Private Sub Form_Load()
    DBEngine.SystemDB = App.Path & "\mygroup.mdw"
End Sub

Private Sub cmdUser_Click()
    List1.Clear

    For Each ThisUser In Workspaces(0).Users
        List1.AddItem ThisUser.Name
    Next

    Label1.Caption = "Users"

End Sub

Private Sub cmdUserGroup_Click()
On Error Resume Next

Dim strGroupName As String

    If Label1.Caption <> "Users" Or List1.Text = "" Then
        Exit Sub
    End If
```

continues

Listing 8.17: Adding a User to a Group Using the CreateGroup Method of the User Object (Continued)

```
        strGroupName = InputBox("Enter the group to add " & _
                       List1.Text & " to.", _
                       "Add user to group")

        Set ThisUser = Workspaces(0).Users(List1.Text)
        Set ThisGroup = ThisUser.CreateGroup(strGroupName)
        ThisUser.Groups.Append ThisGroup

        If Err = 0 Then
            MsgBox "User added to group.", vbInformation
            ShowUserGroups
        End If

End Sub

Private Sub ShowUserGroups()

    ' List groups for this user
    Set ThisUser = Workspaces(0).Users(List1.Text)

    List2.Clear
    Label2.Caption = "Groups"

    For Each ThisGroup In ThisUser.Groups
        List2.AddItem ThisGroup.Name
    Next

End Sub
```

This code works by populating a list box with the contents of the Users collection. After the list box is populated, clicking on a user in the list displays the groups to which that user belongs, as shown in Figure 8.10.

After the application displays a list of users, you can click on a user to select that user. Clicking cmdUserGroup adds the selected user to a group you specify.

Default Groups Created by the Jet Database Engine The Microsoft Jet database engine creates two groups by default. These groups have special attributes you should keep in mind as you design your database application's security model.

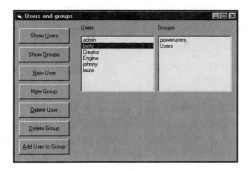

Figure 8.10: An application that displays the list of groups associated with a user.

Members of the Admins group have the ability to create and delete users and groups, and to assign permissions to database objects. They also have the ability to change users' passwords, thereby denying users access to the database and restoring access to the database when a user forgets a password.

The Users group is the default group to which all new users are added when they are created. Members of the Users group have full permissions for any new database objects you create. The Jet database engine does this to support the idea of maintaining easy database access, even in light of the fact that database security is always turned on—if it weren't for the fact that all new users were added to this default group, you'd have to assign permissions to new users (or assign them to a group you created) in all your Jet databases, even if you weren't really taking advantage of Jet security features.

Assigning and Removing Ownership of Database Objects

Every object in the database has an owner. By default, the owner of a database object is the user who created it; in an unsecured database the owner of every object is the Admin user (however, ownership in an unsecure database doesn't mean much, because every user has full access to every database object).

Owners of objects can always assign permissions to the objects they own. This power can't be revoked, even by database administrators. Accordingly, if you must maintain control over objects in the database, you need to do one of two things:

▶ If you're creating a new database, create the database using your own administrative user account. This ensures that you own the database, as well as all the objects in the database.

▶ If you're securing an existing database, transfer ownership of all the objects in the database to an administrative account under your control. You can do this by creating a new database using your administrative account, then importing all the objects from the existing database into the new database.

Note: Microsoft Access is an extremely handy tool in situations where you want to take ownership of a database. This is the case because Access provides a utility called the User-Level Security Wizard, which automates the task of taking ownership of all the objects in a database.

You can manage ownership of an object in a Jet database through the Document and Container objects associated with each database object. The Document and Container objects, which were introduced in Chapter 3, are accessible through the Containers and Documents collections. These containers exist to provide database extensibility, so your database can conceivably have an unlimited number of types of containers and documents. A Jet database created in Microsoft Access has the containers listed in Table 8.1.

Table 8.1: Containers that Exist in a Jet Database Created Using Microsoft Access

Container Name	Description
Databases	Contains the Database document
Forms	Contains a collection of Microsoft Access form documents (not accessible though DAO)
Modules	Contains a collection of Microsoft Access code module documents (not accessible though DAO)
Relationships	Contains a collection of relationship documents
Reports	Contains a collection of Microsoft Access report documents. Access reports aren't accessible through DAO, but they are accessible through Automation; see Chapter 4 for more information
Scripts	Contains a collection of Microsoft Access macro documents (not accessible though DAO)

Container Name	Description
SysRel	Used internally by Jet; undocumented
Tables	Contains a collection of table documents

Remember that because containers and documents exist to provide application extensibility to a Jet database, the only way to know which containers exist in a particular Jet database is to inspect the Containers collection using code like that shown in Listing 8.18.

Listing 8.18: Iterating Through the Containers Collection, Displaying the Names of Containers in a Database

```
Dim Thiscon As Container
Dim db As Database

Set db = OpenDatabase(App.Path & "\novelty.mdb")

For Each Thiscon In db.Containers
    Debug.Print Thiscon.Name
Next
```

You can inspect the Document object's Owner property to determine the owner of a database document. To change the owner, you simply change the Owner property. Listing 8.19 is an example of how to change the owner of a table using DAO code.

Listing 8.19: Changing a Database's Owner Property

```
On Error Resume Next

    With db.Containers("Tables").Documents("tblCustomer")
        .Owner = InputBox("Enter the new owner.", "New Owner")
        If Not Err Then
            MsgBox "The database owner was changed to " & .Owner
        End If
    End With
```

Again, this code assumes you've already created a valid Database object and opened it in code.

Assigning Permissions to Users and Groups

Permissions enable a user to gain access to database objects and data. By assigning and revoking permissions to users and groups, you can take control of who has access to what in the database.

In an unsecured database, all users are logged in as the Admin user, with no password. Because the Admin user is a member of the Users and Admins group, that user has full access to all the objects in the database by virtue of the permissions granted to those groups.

When you secure a database, you gain the ability to identify each user and add users to groups. Users inherit permissions from groups; although it's possible to assign permissions directly to users, it's easier to manage a set of permissions when all users's permissions are inherited through a group. If you need to revoke a particular set of permissions for a particular user within a group, you simply remove the user from the group. This prevents you from having to keep track of information pertaining to which users have which permissions on which database objects. This technique is also better from a security standpoint, because you're less likely to inadvertently assign permissions to groups than to users.

Table 8.2 provides a summary of the permissions available for Jet database objects.

Table 8.2: Permissions for Objects in Microsoft Jet

Permission	Description	Applies To
dbSecNoAccess	No access	All database objects
dbSecFullAccess	Full access	All database objects
dbSecDelete	Can delete	All database objects
dbSecReadSec	Can read object's security information	All database objects
dbSecWriteSec	Can read object's security information	All database objects
dbSecWriteOwner	Can change Owner property	All database objects

Permission	Description	Applies To
dbSecCreate	Can create new documents	Container object
dbSecReadDef	Can read object's definition	Tables Container objects or Document objects
dbSecWriteDef	Can modify or delete object definition	Tables Container object; Document objects
dbSecRetrieveData	Can query records	Tables Container object; Document objects
dbSecInsertData	Can add records	Tables Container object; Document objects
dbSecReplaceData	Can modify records	Tables Container object; Document objects
dbSecDeleteData	Can delete records	Tables Container object; Document objects
dbSecDBCreate	Can create databases	Databases Container object; Document objects
dbSecDBExclusive	Can open database in exclusive mode	Databases Container object; Document objects
dbSecDBOpen	Can open database	Databases Container object; Document objects
dbSecDBAdmin	Can change database's password or make database replicable	Databases Container object; Document objects

To change a permission associated with a user account, you first log in to the database with a username that has administrative privileges. That user then sets the appropriate Document object's UserName property to the name of the user for whom you want to set the permission.

After you've set the UserName property, you can either add or revoke a permission for the database object in question. To add a permission, you perform a logical or operation on the Permissions property. Perform a logical and not operation on the Permissions property to revoke a property. Listing 8.20 gives an example.

Listing 8.20: Using the Permissions Property of a Document Object to Grant a User Access to a Database Object in DAO

```
Option Explicit

' References DAO 3.5

Private ws As Workspace
Private db As Database
Private rs As Recordset

Private Sub Form_Load()
    DBEngine.SystemDB = App.Path & "\mygroup.mdw"

    ' To log in as admin, uncomment this line
    Set ws = DBEngine.CreateWorkspace("", "johnny", "johnny")

    ' To log in as johnny, uncomment this line
    'Set ws = DBEngine.CreateWorkspace("", "admin", "")

    Set db = ws.OpenDatabase(App.Path & "\secure.mdb")

    lblUser.Caption = "Logged in as " & Workspaces(0).UserName

End Sub

Private Sub cmdGrant_Click()
On Error Resume Next

    With db.Containers("Tables").Documents("tblCustomer")
        .UserName = "johnny"
        .Permissions = .Permissions Or dbSecRetrieveData
        If Err = 0 Then
            MsgBox "Permission granted to user johnny."
```

Listing 8.20: Using the Permissions Property of a Document Object to Grant a User Access to a Database Object in DAO (Continued)

```
            Else
                MsgBox "Permission not granted (" & Err.Description & ")."
            End If
        End With

End Sub

Private Sub cmdRevoke_Click()

    With db.Containers("Tables").Documents("tblCustomer")
        .UserName = "johnny"
        .Permissions = .Permissions And Not dbSecRetrieveData
        If Err = 0 Then
            MsgBox "Permission revoked from user johnny."
        Else
            MsgBox "Permission not revoked (" & Err.Description & ")."
        End If
    End With

End Sub

Private Sub cmdShow_Click()

' This fails if the user doesn't have

' Retrieve permissions on this table

    Set rs = db.OpenRecordset("tblCustomer")

    rs.MoveLast
    MsgBox "The table contains " & rs.RecordCount & _
            " records.", vbInformation

End Sub
```

Remember that you must log on as a user with administrative privileges (that is, a member of the Admins group) in order to add or revoke permissions from another user.

You assign permissions with groups the same way you assign permissions to users; the only exception is replacing the name of the user with the name of the group. Listing 8.21 shows a modified version of the procedure that grants a permission on the table to the powerusers group.

Listing 8.21: Granting a Permission to a Group, Rather than to an Individual User

```
Private Sub cmdGrant_Click()
On Error Resume Next

With db.Containers("Tables").Documents("tblCustomer")

    ' Grant permission to all users in PowerUsers group
    .UserName = "powerusers"
    .Permissions = .Permissions Or dbSecRetrieveData
    If Err = 0 Then
        MsgBox "Permission granted to " & .UserName & "."
    Else
        MsgBox "Permission not granted (" & Err.Description & ")."
    End If
End With

End Sub
```

This example assumes that you've declared, set, and opened a Database object variable earlier in your code.

Determining a Document's Permissions for a User You can determine which permissions a user has for a particular database object by using the AllPermissions property of that object's underlying Document object. A document's AllPermissions property is a function of a particular username; you can set or retrieve the username associated with a document through a document's UserName property.

Note: Document objects have a Permissions property in addition to an AllPermissions property. The Permissions property returns the user's permissions for the database document; the AllPermissions property returns the permissions granted to the user, in addition to the permissions the user inherited by virtue of his or her membership in groups that have permissions on the database document in question. In other words, if you're looking to figure out what permissions a user really has for a particular database document, use AllPermissions, not Permissions.

The AllPermissions property is new in Jet 3.x.

You determine if a user has a particular permission on a database object by performing a logical and comparison on the database document's AllPermissions property and the particular permission you want to know about (using the permission constants listed in Table 8.2). If the value of the and comparison is not 0, then the user has the permission in question.

For example, use the code in Listing 8.22 to determine if the currently-logged-in user has permission to delete the database table tblCustomer.

Listing 8.22: Code to Determine whether a User Has Permission to Delete a Database Object

```
With db.Containers("Tables").Documents("tblCustomer")
    If .Permissions And dbSecFullAccess Then
        MsgBox "This user can delete the object."
    Else
        MsgBox "The user can't delete the object."
    End If
End With
```

This code assumes you've already defined and created a Database object and used the Database object to open the database successfully. If the username does not exist in the current workgroup information file, this code generates an error.

Preventing Users from Opening the Database in Exclusive Mode   Only administrative users should have the ability to open a database in exclusive (single-user) mode. To enforce this restriction in a multiuser environment, you can withhold permission to open the database in exclusive mode to members of the Users group. Listing 8.23 shows an example.

Listing 8.23: Removing Permission from Opening the Database in Exclusive Mode to Members of the Users Group

```
Private Sub cmdExclusive_Click()
' Keeps members of the Users group from
' opening the database in exclusive mode.


    With db.Containers("Databases").Documents("MSysDB")
        .UserName = "Users"
        .Permissions = .Permissions And Not dbSecDBExclusive
        If Err = 0 Then
            MsgBox "Permission revoked from user " & .UserName & "."
        Else
            MsgBox "Permission not revoked (" & Err.Description & ")."
        End If

    End With

End Sub
```

> **Note:** The constant dbSecDBExclusive is referred to in the *Jet Database Engine Programmer's Guide* as dbSecDBOpenExclusive. This is a documentation error; it should be dbSecDBExclusive.

This code works the way it does because there is a special Document object, MSysDB, that represents the database itself. You can assign or remove the dbSecDBOpen and dbSecDBAdmin permissions from MSysDB as well. For more information on these permissions, refer back to Table 8.2.

Disabling the Admin User   It's important to disable the Admin account when you're securing a database. This is because the Admin user is the same in every workgroup information database created by Microsoft Access. As a result, if you don't disable the Admin account, anyone could replace your workgroup information file with their own and then, using the Admin account, take ownership of the database and proceed to wreak havoc on your database.

To disable the Admin account, simply remove it from the Admins group.

In addition to removing the Admin user from the Admins group, you also must add a password to the Admin user. Although it may seem less than meaningful to add a password to a user that has no permissions, it's important in Access. That's because Admin is the default user—if the Admin user has no password, then Access users won't see a login dialog, and are automatically logged in as Admin when they open the database (which means that they will have a hard time doing anything, because at this point the Admin user has no permissions).

> **Note:** This seems like an awful design, but it's done this way to support two concepts: a security system that is always on, whether you want it or not, and the ability to log in to the database using a default identity (that of the Admin user) with no password, in situations where security isn't important.

You supply a password to a user account using the User object's NewPassword method, as described in "Adding a Password to a User," earlier in this chapter.

Encrypting a Microsoft Jet Database

Encrypting a database is an important final step in securing a database. Although your database may be password-protected, the database can be opened and viewed with any application that has the capability to open large data files. Though the database can't be used, chunks of its data can still be discerned by pesky intruders.

To resolve the problem, you can encrypt your database. To do this using DAO code, use something such as that shown in Listing 8.24. This codetakes an existing database, before.mdb, and creates an encrypted copy called after.mdb.

Listing 8.24: Encrypting a Database Using the CompactDatabase Method of the DBEngine Object

```
Option Explicit

' References DAO 3.5

Private Sub cmdGo_Click()
On Error Resume Next

Dim strTarget As String

    strTarget = App.Path & "\after.mdb"

    DBEngine.CompactDatabase App.Path & "\before.mdb", _
                             strTarget, "", _
                             dbEncrypt
    If Err Then
        MsgBox "Encryption failed. (" & _
               Err.Description & ")", vbExclamation
    Else
        MsgBox "Database encrypted as " & strTarget, vbInformation
    End If

End Sub
```

The original database is not altered in this operation. The blank string passed to the CompactDatabase method also indicates the database's international locale; this is important for sorting purposes. Passing a blank string as the locale parameter means that you want the new, encrypted database to have the same international locale settings as the original database.

Given the benefits of encryption, why wouldn't you always encrypt the database? The answer is performance—an encrypted database runs 10 to 15 percent slower than an unencrypted database. Encryption is an important aspect of a secured database, however, so take advantage of it in order to make it harder for unauthorized users to gain access to your information.

Checklist for Implementing Jet Database Security

Many developers who use secure Jet databases find it useful to have a checklist to follow when securing the database. Accordingly, this section introduces a step-by-step list of instructions for securing a Jet database.

It's important to follow these instructions in order. For example, if you remove the default Admin user from the Admins group before creating an administrative account for your own use, you'll be locked out of the database. If you use Microsoft Access as a security tool, you get a warning message when you try to remove the last user from the Admins group; if you use DAO, the database engine happily locks you out of the database when you delete the last user from the Admins group. Be careful.

Table 8.3: Checklist for Securing a Microsoft Jet Database

Operation	Completed
Using the Workgroup Administrator utility, create a new workgroup information database with a unique and secret workgroup ID. Record the workgroup ID for future use in case you need to re-create it.	✓
Assign a password to the Admin user.	✓
Create a new user account for your administrative use. Add this user to the Admins and Users groups.	✓
Remove the Admin user from the Admins group.	✓
If the database contains database objects such as tables and query definitions, take ownership of all the objects in the database by creating a new database and importing all the database objects from the original database.	✓
Create groups.	✓
Assign permissions to groups.	✓
Create users.	✓
Assign users to groups.	✓
Encrypt the database.	✓

The details on how to implement each of these steps appear earlier in this chapter. Note that "Assign a password to the database" does not appear in this checklist. That's because this is a checklist for user-based security, and in user-based security, assigning a password to the database is irrelevant.

SUMMARY

In this chapter, you learned how to implement two important components of a multiuser Jet database: record-locking and security. With these important topics under your belt, you now have the ability to create database applications on Jet that permit more than one user to have access to your database at the same time.

While the theoretical limit on the number of users that can work with a Jet database seems large—Microsoft says that a maximum of 255 users can be hooked up at the same time—in a practical sense, you're asking for trouble whenever your Jet database needs to support more than about a dozen users inserting and updating records simultaneously. That's because Jet isn't a true client/server database management system. There's no centralized intelligence to handle contention between users. In a situation where you need to support more users simultaneously updating and inserting records, or when you need to implement a stronger security model, consider migrating your database to a true client/server architecture such as Microsoft SQL Server or Oracle.

QUESTIONS AND ANSWERS

Q. My boyfriend keeps questionable, immoral, and possibly illegal material in a Jet database. Accordingly, he's become something of an encryption and security nut. How strong is the encryption provided by the Microsoft Jet engine?

A. When you encrypt a Jet database, it encrypts the database one page at a time. Each database page has a 32-bit encryption key (remember that a page of data in a Jet database is 2,048 bytes of data). Microsoft Jet uses an RSA encryption algorithm to work its magic. Whether that makes an Access database an adequate place to store his encrypted data is up to him.

Q. I have an application that uses optimistic locking. What would you suggest I do in a situation where my users are running into an unacceptable number of collisions while updating records?

A. I'd suggest that you not use optimistic locking. Redesign your application to use pessimistic locking.

Q. **If I go with pessimistic locking, how do I deal with the situation where some users need to update while other users are reporting?**

A. What are your reporting users doing with read-write access to the database anyway? Reports should be run against read-only, forward-scrolling snapshots, unless you have a good reason to do otherwise. Not only is locking not an issue in a read-only recordset, but you may notice increased performance—both for your report-running users and your record-updating users.

Q. **Why would I want to perform security work in a VB application instead of using Access?**

A. Use Access in situations where you need to set up your application's security system once and never touch it again. Use Visual Basic when your application needs programmatic access to the Jet security model.

Internet Database Applications and ADOs

How can I access client/server data over the Internet?

Is there a way to gain access to both relational and nonrelational data sources using a common object model and set of technologies?

How can I gain access to client/server databases using an object model that is easier to understand and program than Remote Data Objects?

How can I ensure that my brain is clouded with the maximum number of sound-alike acronyms for Data Access Object models in Visual Basic?

A ctiveX Data Objects (ADO) is the cornerstone of Internet database access if you're living on Planet Microsoft. And as you'll see from the demonstrations in this chapter, you can use ADO for more than just getting access to your database through a Web page—you can use it to get to your data from a Visual Basic application as well.

In addition to being yet another object model for database access, ADO is an object-based interface to an emerging data technology called OLE DB.

OLE DB is designed to supplant ODBC as a method of accessing data. ODBC is currently a pervasive Windows client-side standard for accessing relational data, because it makes relational database servers as generic as possible to the client application. OLE DB attempts to take that a step further, by making all data sources generic to client applications.

Unfortunately, this book can't demonstrate that promise, because the idea of getting to any data from ADO and OLE DB just isn't soup yet. This chapter instead gives you a working knowledge of what you can do with ActiveX Data Objects today, in preparation for ADO taking over the database access world in the future. Bear in mind that even though ADO's functionality does not yet rival that of Remote Data Objects, there are still some compelling reasons to use it.

BUILDING VISUAL BASIC APPLICATIONS WITH ACTIVEX DATA OBJECTS

Microsoft ActiveX Data Objects (ADO) is an object-oriented database access technology similar to Data Access Objects and Remote Data Objects (both of which are described in chapters of their own earlier in this book). It is part of Microsoft's Universal Data Access initiative, which seeks to make all data sources generic in the way that, currently, all relational data sources are generic—by virtue of ODBC.

> **Tip:** To get the latest information on Microsoft's Universal Data Access initiatives, including a link to the download page for the files that comprise ActiveX Data Objects 1.5, check out the Data Access Components Web page at **http://www.microsoft.com/data/**. For more specific information on Active Data Objects, check out **http://www.microsoft.com/data/ado/**.

ADO is currently being positioned by Microsoft as a technique for accessing databases from a Web server. Because ADO is provided in the form of an ActiveX server library (just like DAO and RDO are), you can use ADO in your Visual Basic application with no problem. In fact, in many ways, you'll find that it's easier to get to a client/server database using ADO than the other alternatives discussed earlier in this book. Even though ADO is one of the newest technologies for database access, you'll find that in almost every case its performance rivals that of Remote Data Objects.

The first part of this chapter focuses on building conventional Visual Basic applications with ADO, including a discussion of the ADO object model. In the last part of the chapter, I'll show you how to build a simple Web application based on Active Server Pages accessing an ADO database.

> **Tip:** The online help files for ADO 1.5 are installed along with the data access libraries. On my computer, they got dumped into C:\Program Files\Common Files\System\Ado\Docs. Use Microsoft Internet Explorer to view them.
>
> As of this writing, the ADO 1.0 documentation was available on the Microsoft Web site; you don't want to mess with that—it's out of date.

Understanding the OLE DB/ADO Architecture

Most Visual Basic Developers never interact with OLE DB directly. Instead, they program against ActiveX Data Objects, the object model that provides interfaces into OLE DB. This architecture is illustrated in Figure 9.1.

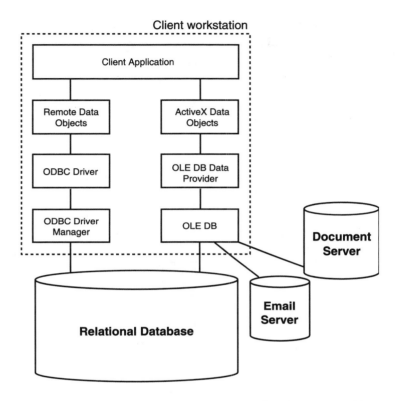

Figure 9.1: Gaining access to information in a database using ADO and OLE DB

Note: If you're having trouble getting your head around the idea of data "providers," you might find it helpful to think of them simply as "drivers." The two are conceptually analogous in their roles when you put the ODBC and OLE DB architectures side by side.

The problem with this architecture is that, in all likelihood, you can't use ADO and OLE DB to get your database server of choice today—at least not directly. This is because there are currently very few database-specific OLE DB providers.

However, it's very likely that you can get to a relational data source using ADO and OLE DB indirectly because there is a generic OLE DB provider for ODBC relational databases. This provider, also known by its development name Kagera, lets you get to ODBC databases from OLE DB and ADO today. The (rather convoluted-looking) architecture for this is illustrated in Figure 9.2.

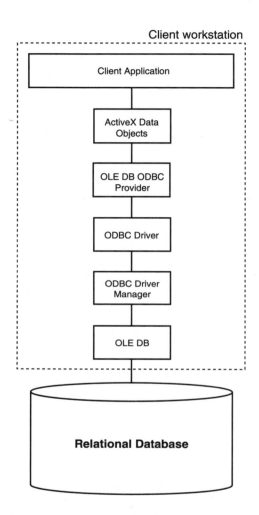

Figure 9.2: Architecture for accessing an ODBC database using the ODBC OLE DB provider.

Microsoft has stated that ADO is tuned for Internet use, with the capability to serve a large number of users simultaneously from a server that is rebooted infrequently. The easiest way to use ADO from a Web application is in the form of Active Server Pages.

Because you can also access ADO from an application or component built in Visual Basic, you can create a single source for access to your data and business logic that is accessible from Visual Basic as well as from Web applications. Figure 9.3 gives an illustration of this architecture.

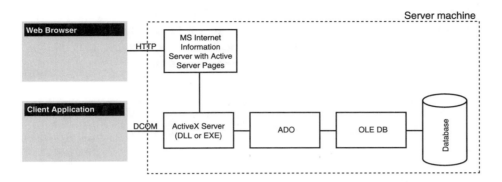

Figure 9.3: Architecture that permits you to use a common ActiveX code component with both Web browser and Visual Basic client applications.

In this scenario, all the logic pertaining to your business is placed in class modules and compiled in the form of an ActiveX component (typically an ActiveX EXE). That way, the amount of code that needs to exist on the client side is minimal. You should only need user-interface code on the client side. Because data access for both the Web browser and the VB application is channeled through the ActiveX server, you can be sure that your program logic is always applied consistently, no matter what kind of application is used.

This chapter gives an introduction to creating applications using ADO in both Visual Basic and Active Server Pages. For more information on how to build and deploy ActiveX code components to gain access to databases, see Chapter 7, "Remote Database Access."

Installing and Creating a Reference to ADO in Your Visual Basic Application

Before you can begin working with ADO in your Visual Basic application, you must install it on your computer. The tricky part is the fact that ADO doesn't come with Visual Basic 5.0; you must install it separately. You can get ADO by installing any other product, including Visual InterDev and Microsoft Internet Information Server 3.0.

> **Note:** Microsoft has strongly hinted that it's going to include ADO in future releases of Visual Basic.

It's also possible to install ADO by itself, which makes the most sense if you simply want to create a Visual Basic application with the ADO object library. (Installing ADO on its own also makes sense because you know exactly which version of ADO you're getting.)

Note: ActiveX Data Objects is available as a free download from the Microsoft Web site at **http://www.microsoft.com/ado.** ADO functions with any development environment that can deal with COM objects, including Visual Basic, Visual C++, and the Microsoft Office suite.

After you've downloaded and installed ADO on your computer, you can begin using it; make a reference to the ADO library in your VB application, the same way you make references to the DAO or RDO libraries:

1 In your Visual Basic project, choose Project, References.

2 The References dialog box appears, as shown in Figure 9.4.

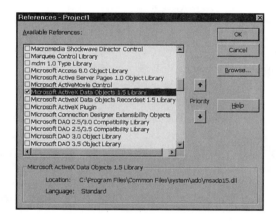

Figure 9.4: Visual Basic References dialog box with Microsoft ActiveX Data Objects 1.5 Library displayed.

3 Check the box for Microsoft ActiveX Data Objects 1.5 Library, then click OK.

You can now make references to ADO objects in your code.

Using ADO with Other Data Access Object Libraries If you're creating an application designed to use ADO in conjunction with another data access object library such as DAO, you need to be careful to differentiate between, for example, the DAO Recordset object and the ADO Recordset object. They aren't interchangeable.

If you have references to both DAO and ADO in your project and you create a Recordset variable, how do you know whether you have a DAO or ADO-style

Recordset? The answer has to do with the order in which you added the reference to your project. If you add a reference to the DAO library first, creating a Recordset object gives you a DAO-style recordset; you need to use the class name ADODB.Recordset to explicitly create an ADO-style recordset.

If you don't want to make a direct reference to the object library in your code, you have an alternative. You can control which object library is accessed by default by using the priority control in the References dialog box. For example, to give the DAO Object Library priority over the ADO object library, do the following:

1 In your VB project, choose Project, References.

2 References to both the Microsoft DAO 3.5 Object Library and Microsoft ActiveX Data Objects 1.5 Library should appear in the list of references (assuming it's installed on your computer).

3 Click on (but don't uncheck) the reference to the DAO object library.

4 Click the upward-pointing arrow labeled Priority. The reference to the DAO object library moves up in the list. This means that DAO will be used when you create an object (such as the Recordset object) that has the same name as an object in the ADO library.

Having control over the priority of the object models ensures that whenever you create a Recordset object variable in your code, it's a DAO Recordset, not an ADO Recordset. (In this scenario, to create an ADO Recordset, you have to explicitly specify in code that you want an ADODB.Recordset—see Listing 9.1 for an example.)

While assigning priorities to object libraries gives you the ability to manage name space collisions between libraries, an even better technique is to explicitly denote which object library you're using when you create the object variable. Listing 9.1 shows an example of a procedure that creates two Recordset object variables—one from the ADO library, the other from the DAO library.

Listing 9.1: Creating Both DAO and ADO Recordset Objects in Visual Basic Code Using Extended Syntax

```
Option Explicit

' References DAO 3.5
' References ADO 1.5
```

continues

Listing 9.1: Creating Both DAO and ADO Recordset Objects in Visual Basic Code Using Extended Syntax (Continued)

```
Private adoRS As ADODB.Recordset
Private daoRS As DAO.Recordset
Private cn As Connection

Private rs As Recordset
Private cm As Command
Private pr As Parameter

Private Sub Form_Load()

Dim db As Database
Dim strSQL As String

    strSQL = "SELECT * FROM tblCustomer"

    ' ******** DAO vs. ADO demonstration
    ' Create DAO recordset
    Set db = OpenDatabase(App.Path & "\novelty.mdb")
    Set daoRS = db.OpenRecordset(strSQL)
    MsgBox "DAO data is " & daoRS!FirstName

    ' Create ADO recordset
    Set cn = New ADODB.Connection
    cn.ConnectionString = "DRIVER={Microsoft Access Driver (*.mdb)};" & _
                          "DBQ=" & App.Path & "\novelty.mdb;"

    cn.Open
    Set adoRS = cn.Execute(strSQL)

    MsgBox "ADO data is " & adoRS!FirstName

End Sub
```

Note: Some development environments, such as Active Server Pages and older versions of Microsoft Office applications, don't support early binding, so they can't make references to object libraries the way you can with the References dialog in Visual Basic. For environments like these, you always have to use the library.object syntax to create objects from the ADO library. You can see examples of this in the section "Writing Scripts with Active Server Pages" later in this chapter.

Using the ADO Connection Object to Connect to a Data Source

In ActiveX Data Objects, you use the Connection object to establish a connection to a data source. At the same time, as code examples later in this section demonstrate, you don't need to use a Connection object to perform useful work with ADO—this aspect of ADO is one of its advantages over Remote Data Objects, which is far more dependent on the concept of a connection object.

The position of the ADO Connection object in the ADO object model, as well as its properties and methods, is shown in Figure 9.5.

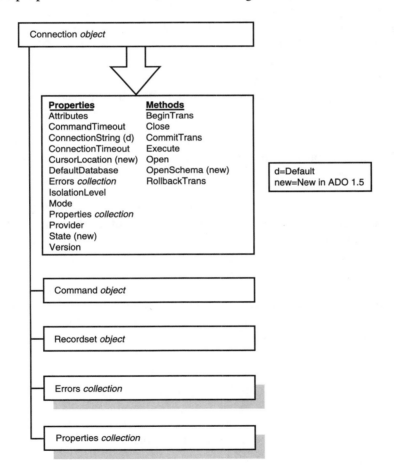

Figure 9.5: Properties and Methods of the ADO Connection object.

You use the ADO Connection object's Open method to establish the connection with the data source. In order to tell ADO how to get to the data source, you must provide information in the form of a connect string identical to the ODBC connect string. You use the Connection object's ConnectionString property to do this. In the future, when more OLE DB data providers become available, you will have the option of choosing which provider you want to use by setting the Connection object's Provider property. The next few sections in this chapter give code examples that demonstrate how to do this.

Specifing an OLE DB Provider   You specify an OLE DB provider using the Provider property of the ADO Connection object. This property tells ADO which OLE DB provider to use in order to execute commands against the server.

The Connection object's Provider property is a text string that tells the connection which OLE DB provider to use. (Remember that you don't have a lot of choices for OLE DB providers at this point, although it's possible—even likely—that new providers will appear by the time you read this book.)

```
Cn.Provider = "MDDSAQL"
```

This code example tells the Connection object to use the ODBC OLE DB provider.

> **Note:** If you don't designate an OLE DB provider, ADO assumes you want to use the ODBC provider. Consequently, you may not use the information in this section until more OLE DB providers become available and your applications need to make a differentiation between them.

Assigning a Connection String   You use a *connection string* in ADO to provide information about how to connect to the database server. When you're using the ODBC provider for OLE DB, the connection string is the same as an ODBC connect string. This means that the exact information expected by the ODBC driver can vary from implementation to implementation. For information on what an ODBC connect string is and how to create one, see Chapter 5.

You assign a connect string to the ADO Connection object's ConnectString object. Because this string tells ADO how to connect to the database, you want to set this property before opening the connection.

```
Private cn as Connection

Set cn = New Connection
cn.ConnectionString = "DRIVER={Microsoft Access Driver (*.mdb)};" & _
                      "DBQ=" & App.Path & "\novelty.mdb;"
```

You can also assign a connect string to a parameter of the Recordset object's Open method, as described in the section "Using the ADO Recordset Object to Manipulate Data" later in this chapter.

Working with Cursors   Just as with RDO and DAO with ODBCDirect, ADO provides support for a number of types of cursors. In addition for providing support for navigating through the recordset one record at a time, different types of cursors permit you to determine how the management of a recordset takes place.

You set the location of the cursor by assigning a value to the CursorLocation property of the Recordset object. Table 9.1 lists the types of cursors available with the ADO Connection object.

Table 9.1: Cursor Locations Available in ActiveX Data Objects

Cursor Type	Constant	Description
Client-side	adUseClient	Creates the cursor on the client side
Server-side	adUseServer	Creates the cursor on the server

In ADO, the CursorLocation property is applicable to both the Recordset and Connection objects. If you assign the CursorLocation property of a Connection object, all Recordsets you create from that connection have the same cursor location as its associated Connection object.

In addition to specifying the cursor's location, you have the ability to create four different types of cursors in ADO. Your choice of cursor is generally governed by a balance between functionality and performance.

You specify a cursor type by assigning the CursorType property of the Recordset object. Table 9.2 lists the types of cursors you can create in ADO.

Table 9.2: Cursor types Available Using the ADO Recordset Object

Cursor Type	Constant	Description
Forward-only	adOpenForwardOnly	No cursor at all—you can only move forward in the recordset; the MovePrevious and MoveFirst methods generate an error.

continues

Table 9.2: Cursor types Available Using the ADO Recordset Object (Continued)

Cursor Type	Constant	Description
Keyset (known in DAO as a Dynaset)	adOpenKeyset	You can't see records that have been to the recordset by other users, but updates and deletes performed by other users do affect your recordset; can be the most efficient kind of cursor, particularly when the recordset is large.
Dynamic	adOpenDynamic	You can see all changes to the data performed by other users while your recordset is open; this is usually the least efficient, but most powerful, type of cursor.
Static (known in DAO as a Snapshot)	adOpenStatic	A copy of all the data for a recordset; particularly useful when you're looking up data or running reports; can be very efficient when your recordset is small.

Listing 9.2 gives an example of creating several cursor types.

Listing 9.2: Creating Different Types of Cursors in ActiveX Data Objects

```
Option Explicit

' References ADO 1.5

Private cn As Connection
Private rs As Recordset
```

Listing 9.2: Creating Different Types of Cursors in ActiveX Data Objects (Continued)

```
Private Sub Form_Load()

    Set cn = New Connection
    Set rs = New Recordset

    cn.CursorLocation = adUseClient
    cn.ConnectionString = "DRIVER={Microsoft Access Driver (*.mdb)};" & _
                          "DBQ=" & App.Path & "\novelty.mdb;"
    cn.Open


    Set rs.ActiveConnection = cn
    rs.CursorType = adOpenForwardOnly
    rs.Open "SELECT LastName FROM tblCustomer"

    Do Until rs.EOF
        Debug.Print rs.Fields("LastName")
        rs.MoveNext
    Loop

Exit Sub
```

Of course, the reason you'd choose a forward-only cursor rather than a keyset or dynamic cursor is performance—if you're simply populating a list box or printing a list of items stored in the database, a forward-only cursor makes more sense and will give you better performance.

Note that if the data provider can't create the specific type of cursor you ask for, it will create whatever type of cursor it can—it will not, generally, generate an error. The types of cursors that can be created by a particular data provider are discussed in the next section.

Determining the Cursors and Other Features a Provider Supports Because OLE DB and ADO are designed to give you access to a broad spectrum of data sources, your application may need to determine which features a particular provider supports. It's possible that while an enterprise relational database management system might let you create a server-side, forward-only cursor, a desktop or file-based database might not.

The Supports method of the ADO Recordset object determines which cursors a data provider supports. Table 9.3 is a list of values you can pass to the Supports method to determine which features a particular Recordset object supports.

Table 9.3: Constants Used by the Supports Method

Constant	Description
adAddNew	New records can be added to the recordset.
adApproxPosition	The AbsolutePage and AbsolutePosition properties are available; they are used in conjunction with the PageSize and PageCount properties of the Recordset object to permit you to determine on which page the current record is located.
adBookmark	You can set bookmarks in the recordset.
adDelete	Records can be deleted from the recordset.
adHoldRecords	Records can be retrieved from the database without committing existing changes.
adMovePrevious	The recordset can be scrolled backward as well as forward.
adResync	The Resync method is available.
adUpdate	The recordset is updatable.
adUpdateBatch	The recordset is batch-updatable using the UpdateBatch method. With batch updates, you can commit changes to many records in a single operation, improving client/server efficiency.

For example, to determine whether a data provider has the capability to provide a scrolling cursor, you use this expression:

```
rs.Supports(adMovePrevious)
```

where rs is a Recordset object. If the expression evaluates to True, the data provider supports a scrolling cursor.

Using VB's Intellisense Features with ADO   An advantage ADO has over other database access object models is the fact that its constants are publicly enumerated. For the VB 5.0 developer, this means you get a drop-down list of constants in the integrated development environment while you're writing code.

An example is shown in Figure 9.6. As you can see, when you're typing code in ADO, there's no need to hit F1 every time you want to use a method of an object or determine which constant is appropriate.

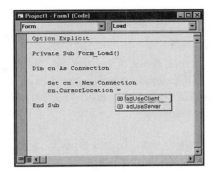

Figure 9.6: Example of the extremely helpful list of constants provided by ActiveX Data Objects.

Considering the popularity of this Visual Basic 5.0 feature, for some developers, the presence of these drop-down lists can be a powerful argument in favor of migrating to ActiveX Data Objects.

Record Locking in ADO   As with other database access object models, ADO permits you to set different types of record-locking modes. You do this in situations where you need control over how records are updated by multiple users in the database. For more information on the appropriateness of the different record-locking modes, see Chapter 8. Table 9.4 lists the four types of record-locking available in an ADO Recordset object.

Table 9.4: Record-Locking Modes Available Through the ADO LockType Property

Constant	Description
adLockReadOnly	No updates to the recordset are permitted.
adLockPessimistic	Pessimistic locking. Records in the recordset are locked when editing begins, and remain locked until you execute the Update method or move onto another record.
adLockOptimistic	Optimistic locking. Records are locked only at the instant you execute the Update method or move to another record.
adLockBatchOptimistic	Optimistic batch locking. Provides support for updating multiple records at once.

It is extremely important to understand that the default lock method is read-only in ADO. This is one of the most significant differences between the way

ADO generates recordsets and the way DAO and RDO do the same thing. This means that if you don't explicitly set the LockType property to something, your recordsets will always be read-only.

The availability of different types of locking is dependent on what the data provider supports. You can determine whether a provider supports a particular type of locking by using the Supports method of the Recordset object (described earlier in this chapter).

Opening and Closing a Connection to the Data Source In order to issue commands to a data source using ADO, you open a connection to that data source. You typically do this using the ADO Connection object's Open method. When you're done with the data source, you close it using the Connection object's Close method. The ADO Connection object's Open method syntax follows:

```
cn.Open connect, userid, password
```

All the arguments to the Open method are optional. The connect argument is a connect string, the contents of which are technically set by the data provider, but in practical terms is equivalent to an ODBC connect string. The userid and password arguments are self-explanatory. Listing 9.3 gives an example of opening a connection to an ODBC database using an ADO Connection object.

Listing 9.3: Opening a Connection to a Data Source Using the ADO Connection Object

```
Option Explicit

' References ADO 1.5

Private cn As Connection

Private Sub Form_Load()
    Set cn = New Connection
    cn.Open "DSN=novelty;", "admin"

End Sub
```

This code assumes you have an ODBC data source name (DSN) called novelty set up on your computer (Chapter 5 discusses how to do this). If you don't have this DSN set up, or you don't care to create it on the client computer, you can instead supply all the connection information at once, creating what is known as a "DSN-less" connection. For a Jet database, the code looks like that in Listing 9.4.

Listing 9.4: Creating a DSN-less Connection to a Jet Database Using ADO

```
Option Explicit

' References ADO 1.5

Private cn As Connection

Private Sub Form_Load()

    Set cn = New Connection
    cn.Open "DRIVER={Microsoft Access Driver (*.mdb)};" & _
            "DBQ=g:\work\data-access\code\chapter09\novelty.mdb;", _
            "admin"

End Sub
```

Of course, if your back-end data source is SQL Server, Oracle, or something else entirely, you must supply the name of the ODBC driver that's appropriate for your data source in the DSN-less connection string. (Yes, the official name of the ODBC driver for Jet is "Microsoft Access Driver (*.mdb)." It's lame, but this kind of lameness is what data source names were supposed to shield you from in the first place.)

When you're finished with an ADO Connection object, you should always close it using its Close method.

```
cn.Close
```

Explicitly closing the connection to the data source ensures that any resources (either on the client, the server, or both) associated with the connection are released.

Using the ADO Recordset Object to Manipulate Data

The ADO Recordset object, like DAO's Recordset and RDO's rdoResultset object, is the way to access information retrieved from the data provider. The ADO Recordset has many of the same properties and methods as the other object models' recordset objects, so you can work with it the same way.

The position of the ADO Recordset object in the ADO object model, as well as its properties and methods, is shown in Figure 9.7.

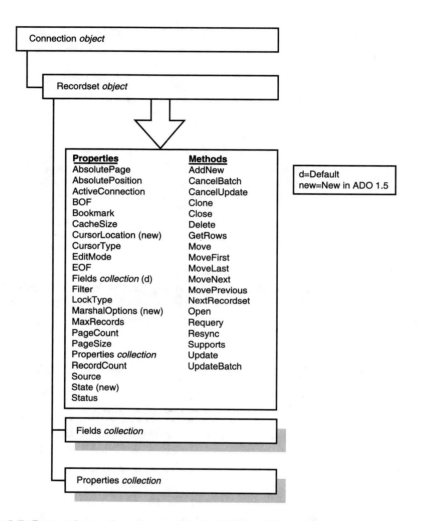

Figure 9.7: Properties and methods of ActiveX Data Objects Recordset object.

The procedure for creating an ADO Recordset object is similar to creating an rdoResultset object in Remote Data Objects. However, ADO adds an interesting twist: the ability to create a Recordset object that does not require an implicit Connection object.

As an example, Listing 9.5 shows how to create an ADO Recordset object in a traditional manner. This technique will be familiar to RDO programmers—first create a Connection object, then run a query against the connection by passing a SQL query to the Connection object's Execute method.

> **Note:** A command string that creates an ADO Recordset can be a table name, the name of a stored query, or a SQL statement—it works the same way as the OpenRecordset method in Data Access Objects.

Listing 9.5: Creating an ADO Recordset Object by Executing the Connection Object's OpenRecordset Method

```
Option Explicit

' References ADO 1.5

Private cn As Connection
Private rs As Recordset

Private Sub Form_Load()

Dim strConnect As String

    Set cn = New Connection
    Set rs = New Recordset

    strConnect = "DRIVER={Microsoft Access Driver (*.mdb)};" & _
                 "DBQ=g:\work\data-access\code\chapter09\novelty.mdb;"

    cn.Open strConnect, "admin"

    Set rs = cn.Execute("select * from tblCustomer")

    MsgBox rs!FirstName

End Sub
```

The alternative to this technique offered by ADO lets you create the Recordset without creating a Connection object first. You do this by passing a connect string to the Open method of the Recordset object, as shown in Listing 9.6.

Listing 9.6: Creating an ADO Recordset Object without First Creating an ADO Connection Object Using a DSN-less Connection

```
Private rs As Recordset

    Dim strConnect As String
    strConnect = "DRIVER={Microsoft Access Driver (*.mdb)};" & _
                 "DBQ=g:\work\data-access\code\chapter09\novelty.mdb;"

    Set rs = New Recordset
    rs.Open "select * from tblCustomer", strConnect
    MsgBox rs!FirstName
```

This example uses a DSN-less connection, but you don't have to. The code gets much simpler if you have a DSN called novelty, as Listing 9.7 demonstrates.

Listing 9.7: Creating an ADO Recordset Object without First Creating an ADO Connection Object

```
Private rs As Recordset

    Set rs = New Recordset
    rs.Open "select * from tblCustomer", "DSN=novelty"
    MsgBox rs!FirstName
```

Of all this book's techniques for getting information from a database, this is the simplest in terms of how many lines of code it requires—a mere four lines. This code works, unmodified, on any type of relational data source for which there are ODBC drivers. In the future, as new data providers emerge, the code will work against those, as well.

This technique is best used in situations where you don't need a persistent connection to the database—you're simply interested in getting in, getting the data, and getting out with a minimum of fuss. If your application needs to maintain a persistent connection to the database, on the other hand, you may want to consider opening and maintaining a Connection object. It's often better to hold open a connection to the database rather than open and close it repeatedly.

Note: The ADO Recordset doesn't work with the Visual Basic Data control the way the DAO Recordset does. That means you can't use the ADO Recordset to directly bind to a Data control. This isn't a major tragedy, just something to be aware of. Chapter 10, "User-Interface Controls," provides a number of techniques to display information from database in a GUI, most of which don't require use of the data control. These techniques are equally applicable to DAO, RDO, and ADO.

Updating and Inserting Records Using the Recordset Object

Performing inserts and updates of records in ADO is almost precisely the same as in DAO. To insert a record:

▶ Open a recordset.

▶ Execute the AddNew method of the Recordset object.

▶ Assign values to the fields in the Recordset object.

▶ Save the record by executing the Update method of the Recordset object.

To update a record using the ADO Recordset object:

▶ Open a recordset.

▶ Execute the Edit method of the Recordset object.

▶ Assign values to the fields in the Recordset object.

▶ Save the record by executing the Update method of the Recordset object.

Listing 9.8 gives an example of creating and updating a record in ADO.

Listing 9.8: Editing and Updating Records in ActiveX Data Objects

```
Option Explicit

' References ADO 1.5

Private cn As Connection
Private rs As Recordset

Private Sub Form_Load()

    Set cn = New Connection
    Set rs = New Recordset

    strSQL = "SELECT * FROM tblCustomer"

    cn.ConnectionString = "DRIVER={Microsoft Access Driver (*.mdb)};" & _
                          "DBQ=" & App.Path & "\novelty.mdb;"
    cn.Open

    ' Insert record
    Set rs.ActiveConnection = cn
    rs.LockType = adLockOptimistic     ' required for read/write
    rs.CursorType = adOpenKeyset
    rs.Open "SELECT * FROM tblCustomer"
```

continues

Listing 9.8: Editing and Updating Records in ActiveX Data Objects (Continued)

```
rs.AddNew
    rs.Fields("FirstName") = "John"
    rs.Fields("LastName") = "Smith"
rs.Update

' Update the record you just entered
rs.Fields("FirstName") = "Betty"
rs.Update

End Sub
```

This code creates an ADO Recordset object and adds a new record to it, then alters the record it just created by changing the contents of its FirstName field.

Remember that in ADO, the default locking mode is read-only (as discussed in the locking section earlier in this chapter), so you must set the LockMode property of the Recordset object to an editable mode before you can perform updates or inserts on it.

Other than that, the only significant difference between this code and the equivalent code in Data Access Objects is the fact that ADO doesn't have (or need) an Edit method. If the Recordset is editable, you need only change the contents of a field, then execute the Update method to write the information back to the database.

Executing a Query Using the ADO Command Object

After you've successfully achieved a connection to your data source using the Connection object, you can begin issuing commands against the data source. You do this by using the ADO Command object.

The position of the ADO Command object in the ADO object model, as well as its properties and methods, is shown in Figure 9.8.

Bear in mind that you don't have to use a Command object to issue commands against a data source (the previous few code examples that use the Connection and Recordset objects demonstrate this). You generally use Command objects in situations where you want to issue the same command repeatedly, or when you need to issue a parameterized query. Listing 9.9 shows an example of a Command object that returns a Recordset when it is executed.

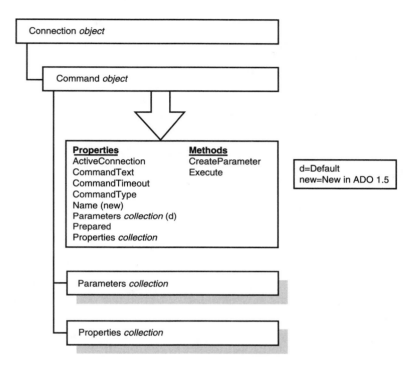

Figure 9.8: Properties and methods of ActiveX Data Objects Command object.

Listing 9.9: Returning a Recordset Using the Command Object

```
Option Explicit

' References ADO 1.5

Private cn As Connection
Private rs As Recordset
Private cm As Command


Private Sub Form_Load()

Dim strConnect As String
```
continues

Listing 9.9: Returning a Recordset Using the Command Object (Continued)

```
    Set cn = New Connection
    Set cm = New Command
    Set rs = New Recordset

    strConnect = "DRIVER={Microsoft Access Driver (*.mdb)};" & _
                 "DBQ=g:\work\data-access\code\chapter09\novelty.mdb;"

    cn.Open strConnect, "admin"

    Set cm.ActiveConnection = cn
    cm.CommandText = "select * from tblCustomer"
    Set rs = cm.Execute

    MsgBox rs!FirstName

End Sub
```

The result of this code is functionally identical to some previous code examples: Open the data source using a DSN-less connection, run a query against that data source, and return a piece of information from the first record returned. The next section demonstrates the use of the Command object with a Parameter object, permitting you to execute a parameterized query.

Note: One promise of the OLE DB and ADO technology is that other data providers will, in the future, provide other types of commands. For example, a spreadsheet might provide a recalculate command, or an email store might provide some type of send command. The abilities of future OLE DB providers is aggressively hypothetical at this point, because very few providers exist today. The point, though, is that ADO doesn't have to be wound up in relational database technology and structured query language the way DAO and RDO are.

The flip side of this is the fact that the ADO Command object is optional. Although the few ADO data providers that exist today all support the Command object this does not mean that all data providers will in the future.

Running Parameterized Queries Using the ADO Parameter Object

You can use the ADO Command object in conjunction with one or more Parameter objects to run a query or stored procedure that contains parameters.

As discussed in the introduction to queries in Chapter 3, queries stored in the database are generally superior to queries generated in your Visual Basic code. This is the case for many reasons, most of which have to do with efficiency—the database engine can optimize the query in advance of its execution.

This is the case when you're using both Microsoft Jet as well as a client-server database system, although ADO doesn't seem to support parameterized queries in Microsoft Access/Jet databases yet. You can expect documentation and support for specific database implementations in ADO and OLE DB to be spotty until each back-end data source gets its own provider.

Parameterized queries give you the ability to have the best of both worlds—the flexibility of a query that your application can alter at runtime, along with the efficiency of a precompiled query.

The position of the ADO Parameter object in the ADO object model, as well as its properties and methods, is shown in Figure 9.9.

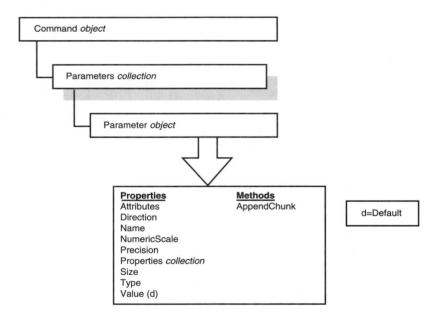

Figure 9.9: Properties and methods of ActiveX Data Objects Parameter object.

The code example for the ADO Parameter object retrieves information from a parameterized stored procedure in a SQL Server database. This is done for two reasons: to give an example of how to retrieve data from a SQL Server database using ADO, and because ADO doesn't seem to understand Jet parameterized queries.

Accessing Recordset Data Using the ADO Field Object

Use the Field object and the Fields collection when you have an ADO Recordset object and you're interested in reading or setting a field's value in the current record. This technique is nearly identical to the similarly named collections of fields in Data Access Objects and Remote Data Objects.

The position of the ADO Field object in the ADO object model, as well as its properties and methods, is shown in Figure 9.10.

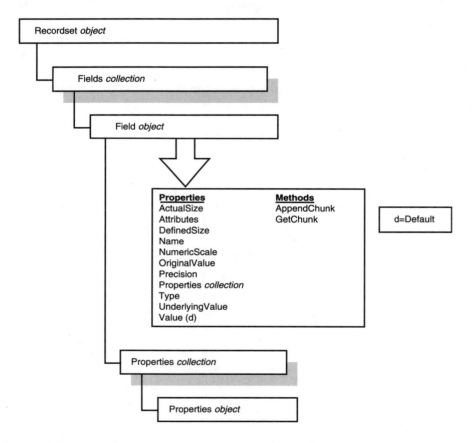

Figure 9.10: Properties and methods of ActiveX Data Objects Field object.

The later sections in this chapter on editing and updating records in a Recordset object give examples on how to use the Field object in code. In short, if you're accustomed to accessing values of fields in DAO Recordset objects, nothing changes in ADO.

Handling Errors Using the ADO Errors Collection

In ActiveX Data Objects, as in the other database access object models, a variety of errors can take place. They can occur particularly in client-server applications, in which a number of software layers must cooperate in order to shuttle data between the client and the server—a single fault can generate a number of error messages. As a result, ADO provides an Errors collection, which makes each error available to you when something goes wrong.

The position of the ADO Error object in the ADO object model, as well as its properties and methods, is shown in Figure 9.11.

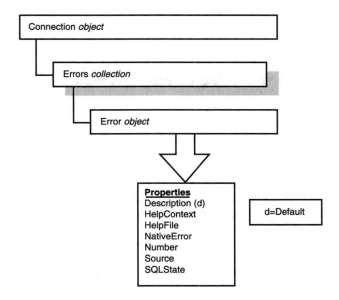

Figure 9.11: Properties and methods of ActiveX Data Objects Error object.

In Visual Basic, a trappable error is raised when ADO encounters an error. As with DAO and RDO, you can iterate through the Errors collection to display or act on all the error messages that were generated between the client and the server.

Inspecting Provider-Specific Attributes Using the ADO Properties Collection

In addition to the conventional objects and properties, Data Access Objects provides for an extensible Properties collection that can be assigned to each object in its object model. ActiveX Data Objects provides for similar collections of properties, but with one important difference—ADO Property objects can't be created and modified by your applications. Instead, they're under the control of the data provider.

The position of the ADO Property object in the ADO object model, as well as its properties and methods, is shown in Figure 9.12.

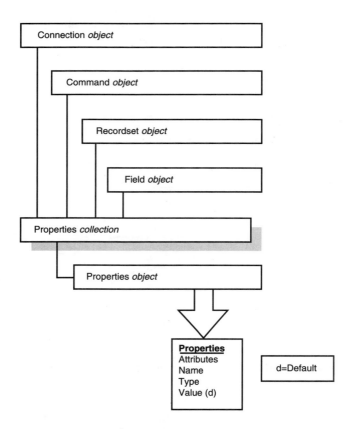

Figure 9.12: Properties and methods of ActiveX Data Objects Property object.

Listing 9.10 gives an example of code that dumps the contents of a Connection object's Properties collection to the Immediate window.

Listing 9.10: Outputting the Contents of a Connection Object's Properties Collection to the Immediate Window

```
Option Explicit

' References ADO 1.5

Private cn As Connection

Private Sub Form_Load()

    Set cn = New Connection

    cn.ConnectionString = "DRIVER={Microsoft Access Driver (*.mdb)};" & _
                          "DBQ=" & App.Path & "\novelty.mdb;"
    cn.Open

End Sub


Private Sub cmdProp_Click()
Dim pr As Adodb.Property

    For Each pr In cn.Properties
        Debug.Print pr.Name & " = " & pr.Value
    Next

End Sub
```

This code's output is shown in Listing 9.11.

Listing 9.11: Code Output that Iterates Through the Properties Collection of an ADO Connection Object

```
Password =
Persist Security Info =
User ID =
Data Source =
Window Handle =
Locale Identifier = 1033
Location =
Mode =
Prompt = 4
```

continues

Listing 9.11: Code Output that Iterates Through the Properties Collection of an ADO Connection Object (Continued)

```
Extended Properties = DBQ=G:\Work\data-access\code\chapter09\novelty.mdb;
    Driver={Microsoft Access Driver (*.mdb)};DriverId=25;FIL=MS
    Access;MaxBufferSize=512;PageTimeout=5;
Connect Timeout = 15
Active Sessions = 64
Asynchable Abort = False
Asynchable Commit = False
Pass By Ref Accessors = True
Catalog Location = 1
Catalog Term = DATABASE
Catalog Usage = 13
Column Definition = 0
NULL Concatenation Behavior = 1
Data Source Name =
Read-Only Data Source = False
DBMS Name = ACCESS
DBMS Version = 3.5 Jet
Data Source Object Threading Model = 2
GROUP BY Support = 2
Heterogenous Table Support = 0
Identifier Case Sensitivity = 4
Maximum Index Size = 255
Maximum Row Size = 2096
Maximum Row Size Includes BLOB = False
Maximum Tables in SELECT = 16
Multiple Parameter Sets = False
Multiple Results = 1
Multiple Storage Objects = False
Multi-Table Update = False
NULL Collation Order = 1
OLE Object Support = 1
ORDER BY Columns in Select List = False
Output Parameter Availability = 4
Persistent ID Type = 4
Prepare Abort Behavior = 2
Prepare Commit Behavior = 2
Procedure Term = QUERY
Provider Name = MSDASQL.DLL
OLE DB Version = 01.50
Provider Version = 1.50.3401.00
Quoted Identifier Sensitivity = 8
Rowset Conversions on Command = True
Schema Term =
```

Listing 9.11: Code Output that Iterates Through the Properties Collection of an ADO Connection Object (Continued)

```
Schema Usage = 0
SQL Support = 257
Structured Storage = 1
Subquery Support = 31
Transaction DDL = 8
Isolation Levels = 4096
Isolation Retention = 0
Table Term = TABLE
User Name = admin
Current Catalog = G:\Work\data-access\code\chapter09\novelty
Accessible Procedures = True
Accessible Tables = True
Driver Name = odbcjt32.dll
Driver Version = 03.50.3907.00
Driver ODBC Version = 02.50
File Usage = 2
Like Escape Clause = N
Max Columns in Group By = 10
Max Columns in Index = 10
Max Columns in Order By = 10
Max Columns in Select = 255
Max Columns in Table = 255
Numeric Functions = 1245033
Integrity Enhancement Facility = False
SQL Grammar Support = 0
Outer Join Capabilities = 83
Outer Joins = Y
Stored Procedures = True
Special Characters = ~@#$%^&*_-+=\}{"';:?/><,
String Functions = 360061
System Functions = 0
Time/Date Functions = 8127
Active Statements = 0
```

With the ODBC provider for OLE DB, the number of provider properties is quite extensive. Remember that the type and value of these properties changes from provider to provider.

BUILDING WEB APPLICATIONS WITH ACTIVEX DATA OBJECTS

Although ActiveX Data Objects promises universal access to any kind of data through OLE DB, the main application for ADO today is database access over the World Wide Web. This is the case because ADO provides an object model similar to RDO in terms of efficiency, but optimized for a large number of users connecting to a database that is rebooted infrequently.

In addition to providing a common database access object model, ADO integrates with another Microsoft database technology known as the Remote Database Connector (formerly known as the Active Database Connector). This tool extends ADO's capabilities, permitting you to create Web-based applications that unload more data onto the client browser.

> **Tip:** Because it's designed for Web-only use, the Remote Database Connector is beyond the scope of this book. The Microsoft Web site for the Remote Database connector is **http://www.microsoft.com/data/rds/**. *Teach Yourself Web Database Programming in 21 Days* (Sams.net, 1997) is a good book that discusses how to use the RDC in particular as well as Web database programming in general.

The remainder of this chapter gives you a taste of how to build a Web-based application that has the capability to display and insert records into a database in response to user requests issued through the Web browser.

Setting Up and Configuring Microsoft Internet Information Server for Active Server Pages

You must be running a Microsoft Web server in order to use Active Server Pages. Microsoft Internet Information Server (MS IIS) version 2.0 comes with Windows NT 4.0; IIS version 3.0 is the version that knows Active Server Pages. You can download IIS from **http://backoffice.microsoft.com/downtrial/moreinfo/iis3.asp**.

> **Note:** If you've installed IIS 2.0 along with Windows NT 4.0, it is upgraded to IIS 3.0 when you install Windows NT 4.0 Service Pack 2 or later. If you have Visual InterDev, you can also upgrade to IIS 3.0. From the Visual InterDev setup screen, choose "Active Server Pages."

Because Active Server Pages are executable scripts instead of normal HTML Web pages, they must be placed in a directory on the Web server that is marked as executable. You mark a directory as executable using the Internet Service Manager utility found in your Internet Information Server program group.

By default, the \scripts directory under your IIS directory is marked as executable, but you may not want to use the default directory. Follow these steps to create a different script directory:

1 Launch Internet Service Manager.

2 Double-click on the WWW service. The WWW Service Properties dialog box appears, as shown in Figure 9.13.

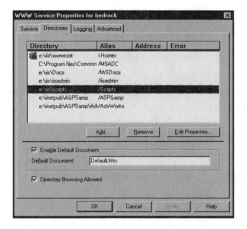

Figure 9.13: Internet Information Server's WWW Service Properties dialog box.

3 Click on the Directories tab. The list of directories available to the Web server appears.

4 Click on the Add button. The Directory Properties dialog box appears, as shown in Figure 9.14.

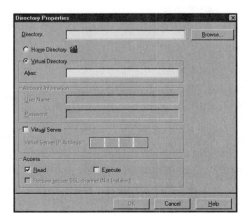

Figure 9.14: Internet Information Server's Directory Properties dialog box.

5 In the directory box, type (or browse for) the directory where you want to store scripts.

6 In the Access panel, check the Execute box. It's very important that you check this box; otherwise, the server won't interpret the Active Server Page (ASP). Instead, it simply disgorges the contents of the ASP at the client, which will be unsatisfactory to say the least.

7 Enter an alias for the directory. This is the directory name that browsers use when accessing the script. For example, if you assign the alias /myscript to an executable directory on the server betty, users can execute the script runme.asp by navigating to http://betty/myscript/runme.asp. This is the case even if the script is actually stored in a directory called g:\work\myscript.

8 Click on OK. You should be able to see that your new script directory has been created, as shown in Figure 9.15.

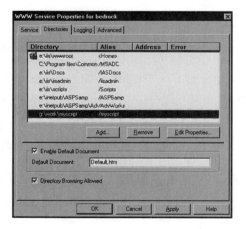

Figure 9.15: Internet Information Server's WWW Service dialog box containing a new script directory.

You must go through this process only if you're interested in creating a new script directory. If you're happy putting all your Active Server Pages in the default \scripts directory, that's fine.

Writing Scripts with Active Server Pages (ASP)

When you're writing an Active Server Page, the script's execution takes place on the server; none of the code is sent to the client application unless you indicate you want it to be sent.

In order to make a differentiation between client- and server-side code, enclose the code, in special brackets, that is to be executed on the server. The brackets look like this:

```
<html>

This text gets sent to the client.

<% 'This code gets executed on the server. %>

</html>
```

> **Note:** In the previous example, the expression that is marked as executed on the server is in the VBScript language, a subset of Visual Basic. (The actual code begins with an apostrophe to indicate that it should be treated as a comment.) For more information on VBScript, including online documentation, see the Microsoft VBScript Web site at **http://www.microsoft.com/vbscript**.

Running an ADO Query in ASP

The simplest application of ActiveX Data Objects and Active Server Pages is to run a simple query against a data source. With the exception of the fact that your code is embedded in an HTML page, there's not much difference between database access in ASP and in Visual Basic.

One important difference, though, is in the area of binding. In Visual Basic, you can make a reference to an object library (using the Tools References menu) to gain access to that library's objects.

This isn't the case in Active Server Pages. In ASP, you must instead use the CreateObject method of the Server object to create instances of objects. For example, to create an ASP Recordset object using CreateObject, you use the following code:

```
set rs = Server.CreateObject("ADODB.Recordset")
```

The end result is the same, in the sense that an ADO Recordset object is created—the syntax is just different.

Now that you have the ability to create ActiveX Data Objects in code, it's time to do something useful with them. Listing 9.12 gives an example of an Active Server Page that uses ADO to display a list of names from a database.

Listing 9.12: Using Active Server Pages to Query and Display Data in a Web Browser

```
<html>
<head>
<title>
ADO Query Demonstration
</title>
</head>

<body bgcolor=#ffffff>

<%

set rs = Server.CreateObject("ADODB.Recordset")

strConnect = "DRIVER={Microsoft Access Driver (*.mdb)};" & _
              "DBQ=g:\work\data-access\code\chapter09\novelty.mdb;"

rs.Open "select * from tblCustomer", strConnect

Do Until rs.EOF
    Response.Write(rs.Fields("FirstName") & " " & rs.Fields("LastName") & "<br>")
    rs.MoveNext
Loop

%>

</body>
</html>
```

The server-side script is enclosed in ASP brackets (the angle bracket and percent sign thingamajiggers). Notice also that when referring to fields in the Recordset object, you need to use the full syntax.

```
rs.Fields("FirstName")
```

You would not use the Visual Basic shortcut:

```
rs!FirstName
```

This is another minor difference between the programmability features of Active Server Pages versus Visual Basic.

If you find the idea of dumping the data to a textual HTML list unsatifying, you have a number of formatting options. One of the most popular (and easiest to implement) is the HTML table. By inserting HTML table tags into the data generated by the database call initiated by the ASP script, you can make the data much easier to read. Listing 9.13 gives an example.

Listing 9.13: Modified Version of ASP Script to Output a Query in an HTML Table

```
<table border>

<!-- Header -->

<tr bgcolor=#CCCCCC>
<td>
<b>First</b>
</td>
<td>
<b>Last</b>
</td>
</tr>

<%

set rs = Server.CreateObject("ADODB.Recordset")

strSQL = "select FirstName, LastName " & _
         "from tblCustomer " & _
         "order by LastName, FirstName"

strConnect = "DRIVER={Microsoft Access Driver (*.mdb)};" & _
             "DBQ=g:\work\data-access\code\chapter09\novelty.mdb;"

rs.Open strSQL, strConnect

Do Until rs.EOF
   Response.Write("<tr>")
   Response.Write("<td>")
   Response.Write(rs.Fields("FirstName"))
   Response.Write("</td>")
   Response.Write("<td>")
   Response.Write(rs.Fields("LastName"))
   Response.Write("</td>")
   rs.MoveNext
   Response.Write("</tr>")
Loop

%>

</table>
```

This script's output is illustrated in Figure 9.16.

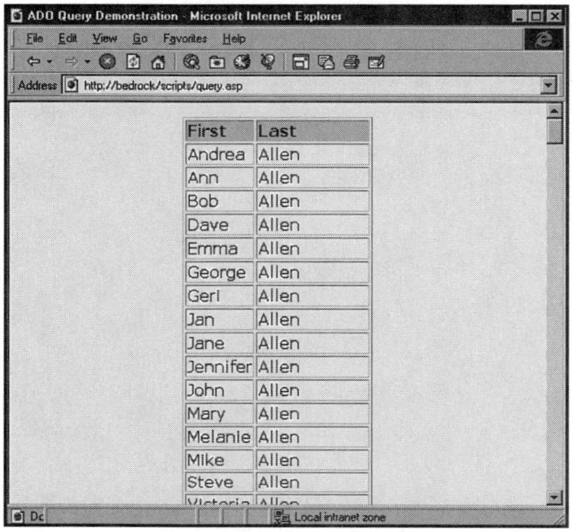

Figure 9.16: Output from the enhanced version of the Active Server script query.asp.

Note: The particulars of how to do HTML have been intentionally left out of this book. If you're interested in moving forward with HTML, there are a ton of great books out there. One of the best is Laura Lemay's *Teach Yourself Web Publishing With HTML 4.0 in 14 Days* (Sams.net, 1997).

Inserting Records Using ASP and HTML Forms

You can use a Web browser to insert records in a database. If you're using ADO, a database insert involves creating several things:

▶ A Web page that provides a user interface into which users can enter data

▶ An HTML form—a collection of HTML tags embedded in a Web page that submits information from the browser to the Web server

▶ An Active Server Page that takes information from the HTML form and inserts it into the database using ActiveX Data Objects

The following sections demonstrate how to build a minimal Web application, starting with a Web form as well as creating the Active Server Pages you need in order to perform the actual database update.

Creating an HTML Form To submit information to the database server, begin by creating an HTML form. An *HTML form* is a group of HTML code inserted into an HTML Web page, contained within the <FORM> tag.

```
<html>

<form method=post action="myscript.asp">
<input type=submit value="Run Me!">
</form>

</html>
```

As you can see in the example, this tag contains two parameters, METHOD and ACTION. You always set the METHOD parameter to post, which indicates that the form is to send information to the server.

The ACTION parameter gives the server the name of a script to execute in response to the form submission. If you're using Active Server Pages, this is the name of an Active Server Page stored in an executable directory on the server.

> **Note:** Active Server Pages are not the only type of scripting available to you; many other Web servers use other technologies, such as Common Gateway Interface (CGI) scripts or scripts written in the Perl language. However, if the Web server is Microsoft Internet Information Server 3.0, Active Server Pages is the scripting technology of choice. Conversely, it's worth noting that other types of Web servers don't support Active Server Pages, so if you commit to using ASP as the basis of your Web database solution, you're committing to Microsoft.

Listing 9.14 gives an example of an HTML page that includes an input form.

Listing 9.14: HTML Code that Generates a Data Input Form for display in a Web Browser

```
<html>
<head>
<title>
ASP/ADO Data Entry Form
</title>

</head>
```

continues

Listing 9.14: HTML Code that Generates a Data Input Form for display in a Web Browser (Continued)

```html
<body bgcolor=#ffffff>
<font face="Verdana, Arial, Helvetica">
<p>Instructions: Enter the new employee's first and last name in the fields
   provided, then click on Save.

<form method=post action="/scripts/save.asp">

<!- The table is here for formatting purposes -->

<table>
<tr>
<td>
First Name:
</td>

<td>
<input type=text name=txtFirstName>
</td>

</tr>

<tr>
<td>
Last Name:
</td>

<td>
<input type=text name=txtLastName>
</td>
</tr>

<tr>
<td>
Address:
</td>

<td>
<input type=text name=txtAddress>
</td>
</tr>

<tr>
<td>
```

Listing 9.14: HTML Code that Generates a Data Input Form for display in a Web Browser (Continued)

```
City:
</td>

<td>
<input type=text name=txtCity>
</td>
</tr>

<tr>
<td>
State:
</td>

<td>
<input type=text name=txtState>
</td>
</tr>

<tr>
<td>
 
</td>

<td align=right>
<input type=submit name=cmdSave value="Save">
</td>
</tr>

</table>
</form>

</font>
</body>
</html>
```

Note: This is a standard HTML page that works in any Web browser, including Netscape and Internet Explorer. Because the scripting takes place on the server, there's less chance that a user with an odd browser won't be able to use your Web application. The only thing that's required to deploy this solution is a Microsoft Web server—the browser can be virtually anything.

Figure 9.17 shows what this page looks like when loaded in Microsoft Internet Explorer.

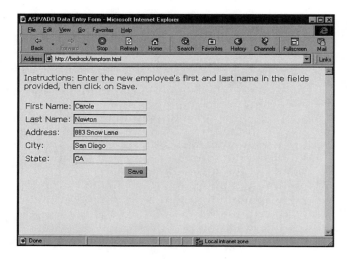

Figure 9.17: The Web page that permits a user to perform data entry and submit the data to the server.

Submitting Data to the Server and Updating the Database   After the user has navigated to a Web page that contains a data entry form, he or she then clicks on the command button (referred to in HTML as a SUBMIT control) to submit the form data to the Web server.

Building on the example form in the previous section, when the Web server receives the form data, the form tag's action parameter tells the server to run the save.asp ASP in response to a form submission. This ASP takes the data passed to it by the form, saves it to the database using ADO, and generates an output page indicating to the user what took place.

Before you get started writing the script file save.asp, you need to have a reference to ADO constants. Unlike Visual Basic, ASP can't make references to object libraries in advance of script execution.

Fortunately, it's easy to include references to other files in Active Server Pages. Use the #Include directive enclosed in an HTML comment. In order to write an Active Server Page that uses ActiveX Data Objects' predefined constants, you must reference a file, adovbs.inc, that is installed along with ADO. In a Web page, this reference looks like this:

```
<!-- #Include file="adovbs.inc" -->
```

This line should appear near the top of the Active Server Page that requires it (as shown in the next code example). In addition, the actual adovbs.inc file needs to be copied into a directory on your Web server, where it can be accessed by scripts that need it (an #Include directive can only refer to a file that is in the same directory as the page).

You didn't have to include this file when you were simply querying the database (in the example earlier in this chapter) because that code didn't require any ADO constants.

Now that you've set up the constants file, you can write the Active Server Page that actually processes the data. The remaining code for the script save.asp is shown in Listing 9.15.

Listing 9.15: Saving Data from a Form into a Database Using ActiveX Data Objects

```
<html>
<head>
<title>
ADO Insert Demonstration
</title>
</head>

<body>

<%
' *** Set up ADO data access

Set cn = Server.CreateObject("ADODB.Connection")
Set rs = Server.CreateObject("ADODB.Recordset")

' *** Create DSN-less connection (this could
' *** just as well have been a SQL Server
' *** database or a DSN name)

strConnect = "DRIVER={Microsoft Access Driver (*.mdb)};" & _
             "DBQ=g:\work\data-access\code\chapter09\novelty.mdb;"
cn.Open strConnect

Set rs.ActiveConnection = cn
rs.CursorType = adOpenKeyset
rs.LockType = adLockOptimistic
rs.Source = "tblCustomer"
rs.Open

' *** Create a record, assign values, and update
```

continues

Listing 9.15: Saving Data from a Form into a Database Using ActiveX Data Objects (Continued)

```
rs.AddNew
  rs.Fields("FirstName") = Request.Form("txtFirstName")
  rs.Fields("LastName") = Request.Form("txtLastName")
  rs.Fields("Address") = Request.Form("txtAddress")
  rs.Fields("City") = Request.Form("txtCity")
  rs.Fields("State") = Request.Form("txtState")
rs.Update

' *** Generate output indicating what you did

Response.Write(Request.Form("txtFirstName") & " ")
Response.Write(Request.Form("txtLastName") & "<br>")
Response.Write(Request.Form("txtAddress") & "<br>")
Response.Write(Request.Form("txtCity") & ", ")
Response.Write(Request.Form("txtState") & "<br>")
Response.Write("<p>Response written to database!")

%>

</body>
</html>
```

After the data has been written to the database, the page displays the data it entered, as shown in Figure 9.18.

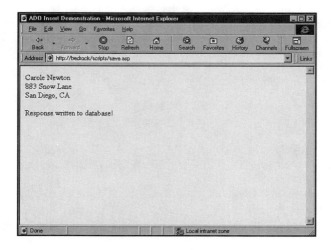

Figure 9.18: Result of the Active Server Page save.asp execution in the Web Browser.

This particular Active Server Page performs no validation or error-handling. It would be trivial to modify it to do so, however. As an alternative, you could write a client-side script to validate the data. Validation based on client-side scripting has the advantage of keeping bad data off the server; it's particularly appropriate in situations where the user is very likely to make data entry mistakes and you need to keep as much bad data off the server as possible. It has the disadvantage of requiring a Web browser that understands scripting, which means that your potential audience is a bit smaller.

SUMMARY

You learned how to take advantage of the newest database access object model, ActiveX Data Objects (ADO). This chapter also gives you a crash course in creating dynamic Web sites using Active Server Pages, in conjunction with ADO, to permit Internet users to access your database.

In this chapter, you also learned how to use ADO within a Visual Basic application. If you develop software targeted for the corporate LAN and the Web, this sets up a situation where you can share similar database access code between your VB applications and your Active Server Pages.

The remaining chapters in this book explore the challenges of creating database-enabled user interfaces with Visual Basic. In Chapter 10, you're shown how to use the basic user interface controls that ship with Visual Basic in your database client application. The final few chapters show you how to use Visual Basic's Professional and Enterprise Edition controls—as well as their commercial counterparts—to create the zippiest user interfaces imaginable.

QUESTIONS AND ANSWERS

Q. What's in store for the next version of ActiveX Data Objects?

A. Microsoft has stated that while the functionality of ADO is currently a subset of Remote Data Objects (discussed in Chapter 7), in the future ADO will surpass RDO in terms of functionality. This presumably means that ADO will gain support for asynchronous operations and events in its object model.

However, much of the work that needs to be done in this area is actually at a lower level: Development of new OLE DB data providers. As of this writing, the two main data providers for ADO were the ODBC provider (also known by its development name, Kagera) and a provider specially designed to provide online analytical processing (OLAP) services. In the future, Microsoft (or third parties) will create drivers that expose other data sources (such as, for example, Microsoft SQL Server, Jet, Oracle, or other nonrelational data source such as electronic mail) through ADO. After all, access to all kinds of data from one object model is the reason OLE DB and ADO were created in the first place.

Q. I like the idea of using ActiveX Data Objects, but using Notepad to create and manage my database-enabled Web site is driving me buggy. Is there an alternative?

A. Microsoft Visual InterDev may be what you're looking for. This development environment gives you the ability to create and manage complex Web sites that contain both server- and client-side scripting. The scripts themselves can be written in either VBScript or JScript, Microsoft's flavor of JavaScript. One of Visual InterDev's big features is its capability to create basic data-enabled Web sites through the use of wizards. Visual InterDev is beyond the scope of this book, but it's definitely worth looking into if you're planning a large Web database development project. For more information on Visual InterDev, see the Microsoft Web site at **http://www.microsoft.com/vinterdev/**.

User-Interface Controls

How can I build a user interface that permits me to display information from a database?

How can I list records in the user interface without downloading and storing the entire contents of a recordset to the client computer?

How can I use non-database-aware user-interface controls to display data from a database?

T he construction of a database-aware user interface isn't one of the most technically challenging tasks a database developer can take on. Visual Basic gives you so many options—not all of which are straightforward or intuitive—that it's helpful to have a guide to what's out there.

This chapter provides an overview of the user-interface components you typically use in your Visual Basic applications. The chapter's divided into two sections: *intrinsic controls*, which work with all versions and editions of Visual Basic, and *ActiveX controls* XE ActiveX controls, which are add-on components available with the Professional and Enterprise editions of VB.

> **Note:** A few of the user-interface controls that come with the Professional and Enterprise editions of VB are so chock full of features, they have their own chapters. Chapter 11, "Using the DBGrid and Apex True DBGrid Controls," covers the DBGrid control, while Chapter 12, "The MSFlexGrid and VideoSoft VSFLEX Controls," covers the MSFlex control.

USING INTRINSIC DATA-AWARE CONTROLS

Visual Basic comes with a number of user-interface controls out of the box. These controls are the most basic, yet most commonly used, controls in Windows applications. They are easy to use and don't require much effort to deploy—and most of them can connect to a field in a database directly through the Visual Basic Data control.

This section takes you a step further than Chapter 1's introduction to the VB Data control; this chapter introduces all the controls you can connect to the Data control and gives you some ideas about how to use controls that aren't intrinsically database-aware.

Entering Data with the TextBox Control

The TextBox control is most commonly used to display and permit users to edit textual and numeric data from a database. Because it is an intrinsic Windows control, the TextBox is available with every edition of Visual Basic. It does not require that an additional file be distributed to users when you deploy your application.

Chapter 1 shows an example of how to hook up a TextBox control to a field in a database through the Data control; this section demonstrates a few additional properties of the TextBox control related to database access.

The TextBox control can store a limited amount of data. If you're interested in permitting users manipulation of a large amount of data, use the RichTextBox control or a third-party data-aware textbox control. The RichTextBox control comes with the Professional and Enterprise editions of Visual Basic; it is introduced in the section "Displaying Formatted Data with the RichTextBox Control," later in this chapter.

Detecting a Change in Bound Data with the DataChanged Property You can determine whether data has been changed in a bound control by inspecting the value of the control's DataChanged property. This is useful if your application needs to do some processing based on a user making a change to the data at runtime.

Although this section's DataChanged example shows how to use the property with a bound TextBox control, the property exists for most data-aware controls.

Listing 10.1 gives an example of how to use the DataChanged property. In this example, the property indicates whether a user altered data in a database browser application using the Data control. This code inspects the value of the DataChanged property of each TextBox control in the form's Controls collection, setting the dirty flag bChanged to True if it detects a text box whose data has been changed. In the command button's Click event, the application notifies the user that the data has been changed.

Listing 10.1: Using the DataChanged Property to Detect Changes in Bound Text Boxes

```
Option Explicit

' References DAO 3.5

Private Sub Form_Load()
    Data1.DatabaseName = App.Path & "\novelty.mdb"
End Sub

Private Sub cmdChanged_Click()
Dim t As Control
Dim bChanged As Boolean

    bChanged = False

    For Each t In frmTextBox.Controls
        If TypeName(t) = "TextBox" Then
            If t.DataChanged Then
                bChanged = True
            End If
        End If
    Next

    If bChanged = True Then
        MsgBox "The data has been changed. " & _
               "Be sure to save this record!", vbExclamation
    End If

End Sub
```

Accessing Boolean Values with the CheckBox Control

You can use the CheckBox control to display a true or false value from a field in a database.

Because it is an intrinsic Windows control, the CheckBox is available with every edition of Visual Basic. It does not require an additional file to be distributed to users when you deploy your application.

Note: In Microsoft Access, a Boolean field is also referred to as a Yes/No field.

Figure 10.1 shows an example of a data entry interface that includes a CheckBox control.

Figure 10.1: Data-entry interface that uses a CheckBox control to represent the Preferred field.

In this version of the Jones Novelties database, each customer has a Boolean field that designates whether that customer is a preferred customer. The field is represented by a Checkbox control.

In addition to representing a Boolean field with a check box, you can use the CheckBox control to display images pertaining to the state of the field. You do this by using the Style and Picture properties of the CheckBox control.

With the Style and Picture properties of the CheckBox control, you can make the control take on the the appearance of any graphic you want. Figure 10.2 shows an example of a graphical CheckBox control with a custom image that makes it look like a command button.

Figure 10.2: A CheckBox control that has been altered to display custom graphics.

To convert a database-aware CheckBox control to display custom graphics, do the following:

1 Create a database-aware user interface with a CheckBox control bound to a Boolean field.

2 At design time, use the Properties window to set the CheckBox control's Style property to 1 - Graphical. The CheckBox becomes button-like in appearance.

3 Set the CheckBox control's DownPicture property to the filename of the bitmap you want displayed when the value of the field is True (that is, when the current record is for a preferred customer). You can use the bitmap file pref.bmp for this property; the file is in the Chapter 10 directory of the CD-ROM that accompanies this book.

4 Set the control's Picture property to the bitmap you want displayed when the value of the field is False. You can use the bitmap file norm.bmp for this property; the file is in the Chapter 10 directory of the CD-ROM that accompanies this book.

5 Optionally, you may want to set the control's Caption property XE Caption property to an empty string, particularly if the custom graphics contain text of their own. If you don't set the Caption property to nothing, it's possible that the graphic and the CheckBox's caption will interfere with each other.

In order to change the value of the graphical CheckBox control, the user simply clicks on it, as he or she would with a normal CheckBox control.

Using the ListBox Control to Display Data

You can use the ListBox control to display items in a user's choice list. You must be careful when using the ListBox control to display data from a database, because although the control is database-aware, there are limits to how much data it can store and display.

> **Note:** The ListBox control has the capability to *bind* to a field in the database, which means it can store a value that reflects the value of a field in the database. However, it doesn't have the capability to use a recordset as the basis of the list of choices it displays. This limitation will come as a disappointment to Microsoft Access developers, since Access' combo and list box controls do have this capability. However, there are third-party ActiveX controls that provide this functionality. Chapter 13, "Creating User Interfaces," discusses a few of these controls.

The ListBox control is available in every edition of Visual Basic. It does not require an additional file to be distributed to users when you deploy your application.

Adding Items to the ListBox Control   To add items to the ListBox control, use its AddItem method. The syntax of the AddItem method follows:

```
List1.AddItem data, [index]
```

The *data* argument represents the information you want added to the ListBox control.

The *index* argument indicates where in the list you want to insert the new item. This argument is optional; if you omit it, the item is added to the end of the list—unless the list is sorted XE - Sorted list, in which case the item is always added in the correct sorted order in the list. (To sort the items in a ListBox control, set its Sorted property to True.)

As an example of populating a conventional list box: to populate a list box named lstStockItem with the items Squirting Boutonniere, Plastic Vomit, and Fake Ants, you'd use the following code:

```
lstFruit.AddItem "Squirting Boutonniere"
lstFruit.AddItem "Plastic Vomit"
lstFruit.AddItem "Fake Ants"
```

Use this code to add an item to the top of the list:

```
lstStockItem.AddItem "Windup Dinosaur", 0
```

In order to display a database-generated list of information in a ListBox control, loop through the records in a Recordset object, adding information from each record to the ListBox control using the AddItem method.

Using the ListBox's ListIndex Property   Items in a ListBox control are numbered starting at 0; this number is referred to as the item's *index*. If no item is currently selected, the value of the ListBox's ListIndex property is -1.

Setting the ListIndex property to a value causes an item in the ListBox control to be selected; this is helpful in a database access application if you want to set a default value for the control. For example, in the list of stock items you populated earlier, if you wanted "Squirting Boutonniere" to be the default, you use the following code to populate the list box:

```
lstStockItem.AddItem "Squirting Boutonniere"
lstStockItem.AddItem "Plastic Vomit"
lstStockItem.AddItem "Fake Ants"

lstStockItem.ListIndex = 0
```

You can retrieve the value of the current item in the ListBox control by setting its ListIndex property, then inspecting its Text property. For example, to determine the textual value of the initial item in a ListBox control, use the following code:

```
lstStockItem.ListIndex = 0
strValue = lstStockItem.Text
```

This code would have the potentially undesirable side effect of altering the currently selected item in the list box. You can avoid this by using the List property. The List property returns the contents of a ListBox control in the form of an array. For example, use the following code to retrieve the initial value of a ListBox control using the List property:

```
strValue = lstStockItem.List(0).Text
```

Remember that the first item in a ListBox control is numbered 0.

Using a ListBox to Provide a Static List of Choices   You can use a ListBox control to provide the user with a list of choices from which to choose. Do this by binding the ListBox control to a field in the database, then populating the control using its AddItem method.

Figure 10.3 shows an example of such an application.

Figure 10.3: Data entry application with a ListBox control providing a static list of choices.

You create a data entry application with a list box by following these general steps:

▶ Create a bound database access application the way you normally would (with a Data control and bound controls linked to fields).

▶ For the field you want to link to a ListBox, create a ListBox control set its DataSource and DataField properties as you would for a text box.

▶ In code, populate the ListBox with a list of choices that are appropriate for the field.

Listing 10.2 shows a sample application that populates a ListBox control used for data entry.

Listing 10.2: Populating a ListBox Control in a Data Entry Application

```
Option Explicit

' References DAO 3.5

Private Sub Form_Load()

    Data1.DatabaseName = App.Path & "\novelty.mdb"

    lstZip.AddItem "80448"
    lstZip.AddItem "81735"
    lstZip.AddItem "84493"
    lstZip.AddItem "88475"
    lstZip.AddItem "88944"
    lstZip.AddItem "94117"
    lstZip.AddItem "94483"
    lstZip.AddItem "99485"

End Sub
```

To finish this application, assign the DataSource property of the ListBox to the Data control. You then assign the ListBox's control's DataField property to Zip, the name of the field that contains the customer's Zip code.

Using the ListBox control this way also has the side effect of performing airtight validation on the data-entry user—it's impossible to enter bad data if the bad data doesn't appear in the list of choices.

Of course, hard-coding a list of choices is unsatisfying; ideally, you'd provide some way for the list to be dynamically populated at runtime from a source other than your Visual Basic code. One of the most logical places for the list to reside is in the database itself. The following section gives an example of how to populate a ListBox with data from a database.

Creating a Recordset to Populate a ListBox When you're using a control that displays a list of records, you generally present a list of choices to the user. However, if those choices are hard-coded in your Visual Basic code, it becomes very difficult to alter the list over time. It's better for this reason to store the list of choices in the database, then populate the list box controls at runtime.

Unfortunately, while connecting a database-aware control to a database requires no code, populating a ListBox control with the contents of a Recordset requires code. Fortunately, the code required to perform this operation is not difficult to implement.

When you're creating a Recordset object for the purpose of populating a user-interface control—whether it's the list portion of a ListBox control or another type of list control—you generally use a forward-scrolling, read-only recordset for best performance. In Data Access Objects, the OpenRecordset method of the Database object permits you to specify that the recordset you're opening should be read-only and forward-scrolling. The code that creates such a recordset requires you to supply constants to the two optional parameters of the OpenRecordset method, like this:

```
Set rs = db.OpenRecordset("tblCustomer", dbOpenForwardOnly, dbReadOnly)
```

Listing 10.3 gives an example of an application that populates a ListBox control with the contents of a DAO Recordset object.

Listing 10.3: Populating a ListBox Control with the Contents of a Table

```
Option Explicit

' References DAO 3.5

Private db As Database
Private rs As Recordset

Private Sub Form_Load()
    Set db = OpenDatabase(App.Path & "\novelty.mdb")
    Set rs = db.OpenRecordset("tblCustomer", dbOpenForwardOnly, dbReadOnly)

    Do Until rs.EOF
        List1.AddItem rs!LastName & ", " & rs!FirstName
        rs.MoveNext
    Loop
End Sub
```

This code adds the contents of the tblCustomer table to the ListBox control, as shown in Figure 10.4.

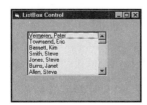

Figure 10.4: A ListBox control that has been populated with data from a database.

If you add the results of a very large query to the ListBox control, you experience the misery of a system crash after the ListBox control attempts to blindly suck in all the data you give it. (Ultimately, the rationale for using a data-aware control instead of a conventional control like the ListBox isn't its data storage capacity, but the fact that ListBox controls can take a really long time to populate.) If you're interested in a control that stores or displays a large number of items—say, hundreds or thousands of items—consider using the DBList control, discussed in the section "Displaying Data in Lists with the DBCombo and DBList Controls," later in this chapter.

Sorting Data Using the ListBox's Sorted Property   You can sort data in a ListBox control by setting its Sorted property to True. This can be set at either design time or at runtime. When you set the ListBox's Sorted property to True, the data in the list is immediately sorted and all additional items added to the list are inserted in alphabetical order. This means that when you add a new item to the list, it will probably not appear at the end of the list, unless it happens to appear there alphabetically.

Bear in mind that it is computationally expensive to sort data using the ListBox control's sort feature. It's much faster to sort the data using the database engine (by supplying an ORDER BY clause to the SQL statement you use to query the database).

Storing a Hidden Key Column in a ListBox Control Using the ItemData Property   The ListBox control has the capability to invisibly store a long integer alongside any element in the list. This lets you easily refer to the primary key of a record without actually displaying that record's primary key.

You store and retrieve this long integer value through the ItemData property of the ListBox control. To set the ItemData property of an item in a ListBox control, you must know its ListIndex. This syntax of the ItemData property is as follows:

```
List1.ItemData(List1.ListIndex) = keyvalue
```

This code assigns the value *keyvalue* to the currently selected item in the ListBox control.

However, you typically set this property at the time you're populating it with data, when no items in the list are selected. This leaves you with the alternative of assigning the ItemData property to the last item you added to the list. However, there's a problem here. To assign an ItemData value, you need to know the index of the item in the ListBox control to which you're assigning a key. How do you know what index number was assigned to the most recently added item in the list? You'd think that the index number would be equal to the number of items in the list, but that's not always the case—if the ListBox control's Sorted property is set to True, the last item you added could have any index number. This is because the control sorts the new entry before it adds it to the list; a new entry for a customer named Aaron that would normally take the thirtieth position in the list might be assigned index number 1 because of the way it alphabetizes in the list.

Fortunately, the ListBox control gets you out of this conundrum by providing a special property, NewIndex. This property always returns the index number of the most-recently-added item in the list. So, to assign the ItemData property to the item that was last added to the ListBox, you use the expression:

```
lstCustomer.ItemData(lstCustomer.NewIndex) = keyvalue
```

Listing 10.4 gives an example of how to add and retrieve the primary key of a recordset to a ListBox control using the ItemData and NewIndex properties.

Listing 10.4: Adding a Table's Primary Key to a List Box Using the ItemData and NewIndex Properties

```
Option Explicit

' References DAO 3.5

Private db As Database
Private rs As Recordset

Private Sub Form_Load()
    Set db = OpenDatabase(App.Path & "\novelty.mdb")
    Set rs = db.OpenRecordset("tblCustomer", dbOpenForwardOnly, dbReadOnly)

    Do Until rs.EOF
        lstCustomer.AddItem rs!LastName & ", " & rs!FirstName
        lstCustomer.ItemData(lstCustomer.NewIndex) = rs!ID
        rs.MoveNext
    Loop

End Sub

Private Sub lstCustomer_Click()
    MsgBox "The primary key of this item is " & _
            lstCustomer.ItemData(lstCustomer.ListIndex), _
            vbInformation
End Sub
```

Figure 10.5 shows what happens when this code is run.

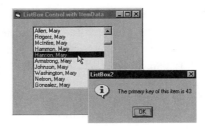

Figure 10.5: The application displays a message box showing each record's primary key as it's clicked.

You might use this technique in your application to open a form, permitting the user to edit the detail of each record when they click on an item in the list. In this case, the primary key stored in the ItemData property permits you to easily query each individual record as the user clicks on it.

Using the Standard ComboBox Control

You can use Visual Basic's standard ComboBox control to display values in a manner nearly identical to the ListBox control. The main difference between the ListBox and the ComboBox control is the fact that the ComboBox control displays choices in a drop-down list.

The ComboBox control is available in every edition of Visual Basic. It does not require an additional file to be distributed to users when you deploy your application.

While the ComboBox control is fully data-aware, it makes more sense to use the DBCombo to display the contents of large lists. This is for performance reasons, as well as the fact that the ComboBox is limited in how much data it can store (these limitations also affect the ListBox control). Visual Basic's data-aware list controls are introduced in the section "Displaying Data in Lists with the DBCombo and DBList Controls," later in this chapter.

Displaying Read-Only Data with the Label Control

The Windows Label control is data-aware; however, it is inherently non-editable. As a result, it's ideal for displaying data in a situation where you don't want users to be able to alter data.

Because it is an intrinsic Windows control, the Label is available with every edition of Visual Basic. It does not require an additional file to be distributed to users when you deploy your application.

This example uses Data and Label controls to provide a pure, read-only database browser with a grand total of zero lines of code. To construct this application, do the following:

1 In Visual Basic, create a new Standard EXE project.

2 Using the Visual Basic toolbox, add a Data control to the project's form.

3 Set the Data control's DatabaseName property to the name of your database. This step is optional; if you don't want to hard-code the path and filename of your database at design time, you can instead set the name of the database in the form's Load event, like this:

```
Private Sub Form_Load()

    Data1.DatabaseName = App.Path & "\novelty.mdb"

End Sub
```

4 Set the Data control's RecordSource property to the table, stored query, or SQL statement you want to use as a data source.

5 Set the Data control's ReadOnly property to True.

6 On the form, create one Label to represent each field in the data source.

7 Set each Label control's DataSource property to the name of the Data control.

8 Set each Label control's DataField property to the name of the field in the data source you want the label to display.

9 Run the application. Your data is displayed in soothing shades of non-editable black and grey, as shown in Figure 10.6.

Figure 10.6: A simple database browser application that keeps users from mucking around with your data.

Displaying Bitmap Images Using the PictureBox Control

The Visual Basic PictureBox control has the capability to store graphical data. It also has the DataField and DataSource properties common to data-aware controls. However, the PictureBox control can't bind to a Microsoft Access OLE Object field (the type of field in which you'd normally store images). This makes it essentially useless for creating database-aware interfaces based on the Data control.

When you bind a PictureBox control to an Access OLE Object field, things work fine until you hit a record that has data in the field; at that point, you get an Invalid Picture error. This is the case even though it's trivial to create a Microsoft Access form containing a picture field bound to an OLE Object field, as illustrated in Figure 10.7.

Figure 10.7: Microsoft Access form displaying a control bound to an OLE Object field.

Binding a PictureBox control to data stored in an OLE Object field has been a problem ever since controls became bindable to database fields in Visual Basic 3.0. As a workaround for this problem, you can instead bind the Visual Basic OLE control to the OLE Object field. This technique is introduced in the section "Displaying Binary Objects with the OLE Container Control," later in this chapter.

If you're brave, it's possible to write code to extract the data from the OLE Object field and assign it to the PictureBox control; Microsoft lists a code example showing how to do this on their Knowledge Base Web site at **http://premium.microsoft.com/support/kb/articles/q147/7/27.asp**. Bear in mind, though, that not only is this technique technically tricky, but also it's much slower than simply storing graphics in a directory on disk and storing references to their filename in textual fields in the database.

Note: The PictureBox and Image controls are significantly enhanced in Visual Basic 5.0; they now support GIF and JPEG graphics formats as well as the native Windows BMP graphic format.

There are also third-party picture controls (notably, the picture control that ships with the Crescent QuickPak suite) that can bind directly to a Jet OLE Object field that contains images.

Using the Image Control to Display Bitmaps   The Visual Basic Image control is designed to display graphics in a manner similar to the PictureBox control. Its main difference is that it's lighter and supports fewer features than the PictureBox control; it's faster in a number of ways. Frustratingly—but not surprisingly—it suffers from the same inability to bind to and display images from a Jet OLE Object field.

If you want to display images stored in a database without writing a bunch of complicated code, use the Visual Basic OLE Object control introduced in the next section.

Displaying Binary Objects with the OLE Container Control
In Windows, Object Linking and Embedding (OLE) is a technology that permits applications to exchange and display each others' data. Using OLE, you can take information from any application that knows about OLE and display and edit it in any other application that knows about OLE.

In Visual Basic, you display OLE data using the OLE Container control. This control permits you to display data created in another application on a Visual Basic form. This control is also database-aware, which means that it has the capability to bind to an OLE Object field in a Jet database.

You can use the OLE Container control to display graphical images stored in an OLE Object field.

1 Create a Visual Basic user interface based on the Data control. Connect the data control to a table or query that contains an OLE Object field.

Note: The version of the database novelty.mdb in this book's accompanying CD-ROM (Chapter 10 directory) contains a table, tblCustomer, that contains an OLE Object field. Picture is the name of the OLE Object field.

2 Create an OLE Container control on the form. When you create an OLE Container control, the Insert Object dialog box appears, as shown in Figure 10.8.

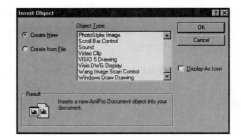

Figure 10.8: The Insert Object dialog box that appears when you create an OLE Container control.

3 Dismiss this dialog box by clicking on the Cancel button. You don't need to assign an object to this container at this time; instead, the container gets its data from the OLE Object field in the database.

4 Assign the DataSource property of the OLE Container control to the name of the Data control. Assign the DataField property of the container to the name of the OLE Object field in the database.

5 Run the application. For fields that contain data in the OLE Object field, you should see a picture displayed in the OLE Container control like that shown in Figure 10.9.

Figure 10.9: An application displaying graphical data using an OLE Container control.

This technique gives you the ability to display information from an OLE Object field in the OLE Container control. Although you can display data using the OLE Container control without writing code, you must write code to permit the user to insert and edit data in the control. The next few sections describe how to do this.

Inserting Information into an OLE Container Control Although the OLE Container control works great for displaying graphical data stored in an OLE Object field, you must write code to insert data into the field represented by the control.

> **Note:** This technique represents another difference between the ways Microsoft Access and Visual Basic let you handle OLE Object data; in Access, you simply create an OLE Object field and it works correctly with no code.

Applications that permit you to embed information using OLE typically enable you to embed the information using the Windows Clipboard. Listing 10.5 gives an example of the code your application must execute to permit a user to insert information from the Clipboard into an OLE Object field.

Listing 10.5: An Application that Displays Graphical Data Using the OLE Container Control

```
Option Explicit
'
' References DAO 3.5

Private Sub Form_Load()
    Data1.DatabaseName = App.Path & "\novelty.mdb"
End Sub

Private Sub cmdPaste_Click()
    ' Pastes data from clipboard into
    ' Picture field represented by
    ' OLE Container control olePicture.

    ' Allow only embedded (not linked) data.
    olePicture.OLETypeAllowed = vbOLEEmbedded

    If olePicture.PasteOK = True Then
        olePicture.Paste
    Else
        MsgBox "The information on the clipboard can't be pasted.",_
                vbExclamation
    End If

End Sub
```

Follow these steps to insert an image using this application:

1 Create an image using any application that permits you to create or handle images. You can use the Paintbrush application that comes with Windows if you want to create your own image; otherwise, you can use another application such as Internet Explorer to find a prefabricated image.

2 Use the application's technique for copying an image to the Clipboard. For most image-handling applications, this entails selecting the image, then choosing the menu command Edit, Copy. For Internet Explorer, you can right-click the image, then select Copy from the pop-up menu.

3 Run your VB application and click on the Paste Picture button. The image you copied should be pasted into the OLE Container control, as shown in Figure 10.10.

Figure 10.10: Graphical information acquired from an image-editing program and pasted into the database using the OLE Container control.

When you move off the current record using the Data control, the data you pasted in the control is saved in the database.

Editing Data in an OLE Container Control   Use the OLE Container control's DoVerb method to edit the information contained in an OLE Container control. Executing the DoVerb method causes the server application responsible for the data to launch, providing an editing interface for the data. This is particularly handy, because your application doesn't have to take responsibility for providing an interface for every new type of data that comes along. It only needs a place to store OLE Objects.

There are a few ways to open an OLE Object using the DoVerb method. Listing 10.6 gives an example of a command button that launches the server application in its own window—one of the simplest ways of providing an OLE editing interface.

Listing 10.6: Launching the Server Application of an OLE Container Object for Editing

```
Private Sub cmdEdit_Click()
    ' Open the data in its own window
    olePicture.DoVerb vbOLEOpen
End Sub
```

The constant vbOLEOpen constant instructs the OLE Container to open the server application in its own window. There are other alternatives to this, most notably the option of *in-place activation*, in which your application's interface automatically trades places with the interface of the OLE server, but that's more complicated to implement.

To demonstrate how this code works, do the following:

1 Run your VB application.

2 Move to a record that contains something in its Picture field.

3 Click on the Edit Picture button.

4 The Paintbrush application launches, as shown in Figure 10.11.

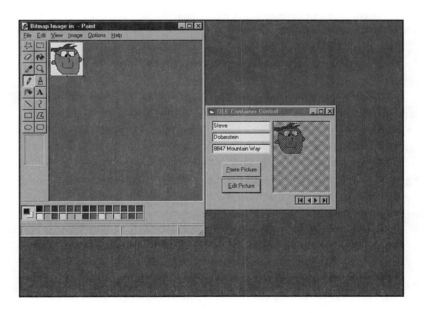

Figure 10.11: Editing an OLE object embedded in a OLE Container control.

5 Using the Paintbrush application's tools, alter the picture in some way. You may notice that the representation of the data in your application changes as you alter the data in Paintbrush.

6 When you're done editing, select File, Exit, and Return. The data in your VB application is updated, as shown in Figure 10.12.

Figure 10.12: The data in the OLE Container control after being updated in its server application.

If you hit the Edit Picture object for a record that has no picture, an error is generated (31004 - No object). Trap that error and have your application do something intelligent in response to this situation.

USING DATA-AWARE ACTIVEX CONTROLS

The controls discussed up to this point in this chapter are available to any Visual Basic developer. Most are basic controls that appear in any Windows application, and most are fairly unspectacular in appearance and behavior.

The controls in this section come with the Professional and Enterprise editions of Visual Basic 5.0. Unlike the user-interface controls introduced earlier in this chapter, the controls aren't provided by the operating system; instead, you must distribute additional controls to users' computers for your applications to use them. This isn't a big deal (most of this is handled transparently for you by the Setup Wizard), but in some cases it can be an issue—particularly when you're trying to keep your application's distributable footprint small, or if you're concerned about issues pertaining to component versioning.

Controlling Text Input with the MaskedEdit Control

In many situations when building a data entry interface, you need to give the user some visual cue. For example, if the field they're entering is a phone number, are they supposed to type an area code? How about the parentheses around the area code? If they're supposed to type the parentheses, why? If the parentheses are the same for every record, why doesn't the computer provide them instead of making the user type them?

The MaskedEdit control provides a solution to those and other problems. In addition to providing a visual cue for users entering data in a field, it provides validation at the user-interface level, preventing users from entering bad information in the control.

The MaskedEdit control comes with the Professional and Enterprise editions of Visual Basic. Its filename is MSMASK32.OCX. To use the Masked Edit Control in your Visual Basic project, do the following:

1 In Visual Basic, select Project Components.

2 The Components dialog box appears. In the list of components, scroll down until you see Microsoft Masked Edit Control 5.0.

Note: If you're running a service pack edition of Visual Basic, the name of the control in the Components dialog box may reflect the name of the service pack; for example, if you're running VB 5.0 Service Pack 2, the control is listed as Microsoft Masked Edit Control 5.0 (SP2).

3 Check the control in the list, then click on OK. The Masked Edit control is added to your Visual Basic toolbox, as shown in Figure 10.13.

Figure 10.13: The Microsoft Masked Edit control in the Visual Basic toolbox.

Setting the Input Mask Using the Mask Property When you're using the Masked Edit control, you have the ability to force the user to enter information according to a certain pattern. For example, in a Zip code field, you can force the user to enter five or more characters.

The rules that govern what a user can enter in a Masked Input control are called an *input mask*. You assign an input mask to a Masked Input control using the control's Mask property.

The Mask property is composed of a string of characters that indicate the pattern to be entered in the Masked Edit box. The characters you can use as part of this string are summarized in Table 10.1.

Table 10.1: Characters Used in the Mask Property of the Masked Edit Control

Character	Description
#	Digit
.	Decimal
,	Thousands separator
:	Hours and minutes separator
/	Day and date separator
\	Escape code to treat the next character in the string literally
&	Character placeholder
>	Convert characters to uppercase
<	Convert characters to lowercase
A	Required alphanumeric character
a	Optional alphanumeric character
9	Optional numeric character
C	Optional character or space
?	Letter
Anything else	Displayed as entered

As an example, if you wanted to force the user to enter a seven-digit phone number, you'd set the Mask property to the following:

```
#######
```

For information on how to display data differently than the way it's entered, see the discussion of the Format property in the following section.

If you want the user to enter a value such as an inventory number beginning with a letter and ending in five numbers, and you want to make sure that the first character is always displayed in uppercase, use a Mask property such as the following:

```
>?99999
```

> **Note:** If you set the Mask property to an empty string, the Masked Input control behaves like a normal TextBox control.

When a user violates the mask you've set, your application makes an audible beep and the bad character they entered is not accepted.

Changing the Display of Information Using the Format Property   In addition to using the Mask property to require the user to enter information in a certain pattern, you can also specify how the information in the control should be formatted on the screen. You do this using the Masked Edit control's Format property.

For example, if a field stores a telephone number that you want displayed with parentheses and dashes, you'd use a Format string such as the following:

```
(###) ###-####
```

This means that the user only needs to type the 10-digit telephone number, as shown in Figure 10.14. The extra formatting characters, such as the parentheses, show up automatically.

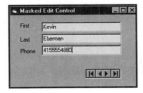

Figure 10.14: Data entry of a formatted field using the Masked Edit control.

After the focus moves off the Masked Edit control, the formatting kicks in and the data is displayed with the proper formatting, as Figure 10.15 shows.

Figure 10.15: Formatted information, as displayed by the Masked Edit control.

Displaying Formatted Data with the RichTextBox Control

The RichTextBox control looks like a conventional TextBox control, but has the capability to store much more text. In addition, it can store and display text formatting—all that, coupled with the control's capability to bind directly to a database field, makes the RichTextBox control a formidable bit of ActiveX juju indeed.

The RichTextBox control comes with the Professional and Enterprise editions of Visual Basic. Its filename is RICHTX32.OCX. To use the Rich Text Box Control in your Visual Basic project, do the following:

1 In Visual Basic, select Project Components.

2 The Components dialog box appears. In the list of components, scroll down until you see Microsoft Rich Textbox Control 5.0.

Note: If you're running a service pack edition of Visual Basic, the name of the control in the Components dialog box may reflect the name of the service pack; for example, if you're running VB 5.0 Service Pack 2, the control will be listed as Microsoft Rich Textbox Control 5.0 (SP2).

3 Check the control in the list, then click on OK. The Rich Textbox control is added to your Visual Basic toolbox, as shown in Figure 10.16.

One of the nice things about the RichTextBox control is that it works nearly identically to the conventional TextBox control; the two controls share many of the same properties. However, the RichTextBox control has a number of properties that control text formatting. You can see a few of them in the sample application shown in Figure 10.17.

Figure 10.16: The Microsoft RichTextBox control in the Visual Basic toolbox.

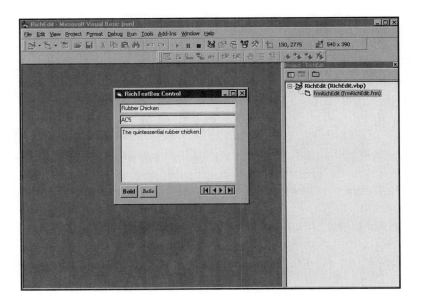

Figure 10.17: Interface of a data access application containing a RichTextBox control.

Because the RichTextBox control supports the same properties that the TextBox control supports, this application doesn't require any code changes at all; the RichTextBox is, for all intents and purposes, a standard TextBox control.

In order for this control to really sing, you need to write code that permits the user to apply formatting. Listing 10.7 shows an example of how to permit the user to apply boldfaced and italicized formatting to text they select in the field bound to the RichTextBox control.

Listing 10.7: Applying Boldfaced and Italicized Formatting to Text in a Field

```
Option Explicit

' References DAO 3.5

Private Sub Form_Load()
    Data1.DatabaseName = App.Path & "\novelty.mdb"
End Sub

Private Sub cmdBold_Click()
    rtfDescription.SelBold = Not rtfDescription.SelBold
End Sub

Private Sub cmdItalic_Click()
    rtfDescription.SelItalic = Not rtfDescription.SelItalic
End Sub
```

The bold and italic buttons use a Not expression to reverse the current state of bold or italic. This permits the controls to be used to either apply or remove formatting, depending on what's present.

None of this has a direct bearing on the application's database access features—even though formatted text is being saved to the database, the Data control handles it without any intervention from your code.

Displaying Data in Lists with the DBCombo and DBList Controls

The DBList control is designed to bind to a field in a table while it displays a list of data derived from elsewhere in the database. The DBCombo control is nearly identical to the DBList control, except it displays its list of choices in a drop-down.

A bug relating to the functionality of the Data List controls was fixed in Service Pack 3 of Microsoft Visual Studio. Specifically, you can't access Text or BoundText properties, and the control does not display data properly when the Locked property is set. You should consider applying the latest service pack in order to resolve all the problems fixed by each one. For more information, see **http://premium.microsoft.com/support/kb/articles/Q171/5/51.asp.**

Note: If you're running a service pack edition of Visual Basic, the name of the control in the Components dialog box might reflect the name of the service pack; for example, if you're running VB 5.0 Service Pack 2, the control is listed as Microsoft Data Bound List Control 5.0 (SP2).

As of this writing, the latest service pack was Service Pack 3. This service pack contains the fixes included in Service Packs 1 and 2. You can obtain Visual Studio Service Pack for free by downloading it from **http://www.microsoft.com/vstudio/sp/download.htm**.

The DBList and DBCombo controls come with the Professional and Enterprise editions of Visual Basic, in the file DBLIST32.OCX. Do the following to use the DBList or DBCombo controls in your Visual Basic project:

1 In Visual Basic, select Project Components.

2 The Components dialog box appears. In the list of components, scroll down until you see Microsoft Data Bound List Control 5.0.

3 Check the control in the list, then click on OK. The two list controls are added to your Visual Basic toolbox, as shown in Figure 10.18.

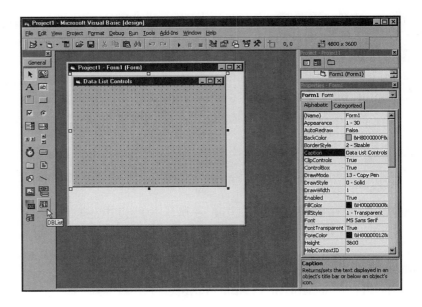

Figure 10.18: The Microsoft Data Bound List controls in the Visual Basic toolbox.

You bind the DBList control to a field in a recordset the same way you do with a conventional bound control—through its DataSource and DataField properties. Unlike the conventional ListBox control, you populate the list of choices using the RowSource and ListField properties.

Often when you're using a DBList control, you need at least two Data controls—one to provide the list of choices and one to connect to the main recordset.

For example, say you have two tables in the database, tblCustomer to store customers, and tblCustomerType to store a list of seven types of customers. There is a one-to-many relationship between customer types and customers; the CustomerID field in the customer table is a foreign key to the customer type table.

These tables and fields exist in the accompanying CD-ROM's Chapter 10 version of the Jones Novelties database, novelty.mdb. To express this relationship in a VB user interface using the DBList control, do the following:

1 Create a standard data-bound user interface based on the tblCustomer table using text boxes and a Data control. Include the FirstName and LastName fields. Name the Data control datCustomer and set its RecordSource property to tblCustomer.

2 Create a DBList control on the form. Name it dblCustomerType.

3 Set the DataSource properties of the two text boxes and the DBList control to the Data control datCustomer.

4 Set the DataField properties of the two TextBox controls to FirstName and LastName, respectively.

5 Set the DataField property of the DBList control to TypeID, the name of the field in tblCustomer that stores the customer type. This binds the DBList control to the field in tblCustomer.

6 Create a second Data control to display the list of customer types. Name this control datCustomerType.

7 Set datCustomerType's RecordSource property to tblCustomerType, and set its Visible property to False.

8 Go back to the DBList control dblCustomerType and set its RowSource property to datCustomerType.

9 Set the dblCustomerType's ListField property to Type.

10 Set the dblCustomerType's BoundColumn property to ID.

11 In the form's Load event, write the following code to initialize the two Data controls:

```
Option Explicit

' References DAO 3.5

Private Sub Form_Load()
    datCustomer.DatabaseName = App.Path & "\novelty.mdb"
    datCustomerType.DatabaseName = datCustomer.DatabaseName
End Sub
```

12 Run the application. The DBList control should be populated with the list of choices in tblCustomerType, as shown in Figure 10.19.

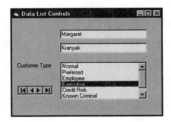

Figure 10.19: Database access application featuring a list of choices provided by the DBList control.

The trick to this is keeping straight what all the property names mean. There are five properties to keep track of:

▶ *DataSource* and *DataField*, which are the same for every bound control.

▶ *RowSource*, which indicates the name of the Data control that is to provide the list of choices.

▶ *ListField*, which indicates which field from the RowSource Data control is displayed in the list. This can be any field, as long as it's clear to the user what's being displayed. In the example, ListField is the name of tblCustomerType's Type field.

▶ *BoundColumn*, which indicates which field supplies the value that is inserted in the bound field. This has to be a piece of data that uniquely identifies the user's choice. In the example, BoundColumn is the name of tblCustomerType's primary key, ID.

Bear in mind as you're building applications using the DBList and DBCombo controls that their advantage lies not only in the fact that they let you create applications with very little code, but that much of the database access chores are handled transparently by the Data control.

Displaying Data in Rows and Columns with the DBGrid and MSFlexGrid Controls

The DBGrid control permits you to display a recordset in row and column form. The MSFlexGrid control is also a data-aware grid, but it permits users to perform ad hoc analysis of data using drag-and-drop techniques.

Chapter 11 discusses the DBGrid control, as well as its commercial cousin, Apex True DBGrid, in depth. Chapter 12 discusses the MSFlexGrid control as well as its commercial counterpart, VideoSoft VSFLEX.

THIRD-PARTY DATA-AWARE CONTROLS

In addition to the dozen or so database-aware controls that come with the Professional and Enterprise editions of Visual Basic, the third-party software market has provided a plethora of database-aware controls. In addition to improving on the standard existing database-aware controls, many vendors provide totally new controls: database-aware combo boxes that display a calendar for easy entry of date values, or outline controls that permit you to easily display one-to-many relationships in your database.

If you're looking for sources of third-party database-aware components, there are a number of vendors from which to choose. *Visual Basic Components Sourcebook* (Ziff-Davis Press, 1997) contains information on over 650 third-party controls; it contains an entire chapter on controls that are specifically designed for use with databases, and it highlights database-aware controls throughout the book with a special icon (which is perfect if you're a visual kind of person).

CREATING DATABASE-AWARE ACTIVEX CONTROLS

You have the ability to create your own data-aware ActiveX controls in Visual Basic 5.0. You typically do this in situations where you need to provide some additional functionality to an existing database-aware user-interface control.

You might create your own data-aware ActiveX control in situations where you need:

▶ A control that extends the functionality of an existing control—The TextBox control in particular is a common target of enhancement by ActiveX control developers.

▶ A control that combines the functionality of two controls into one— Visual Basic is particularly adept at creating these types of controls. This is because VB lets you create ActiveX controls graphically, based on one or more existing controls.

▶ A control that needs to graphically represent a unique aspect of your business—say you're dealing with racks of industrial material, and each rack is five units long by six units wide. Each cell in the rack has its own set of a few dozen properties that need stored in the database and manipulated graphically in the user interface. This is an ideal candidate for ActiveX control.

Tip: If you're looking to take this a step further, pick up *How to Program Visual Basic Control Creation Edition* (Ziff-Davis Press, 1997). This book gives you step-by-step information on creating ActiveX controls in any edition of VB5.

The Visual Basic Control Creation Edition, which is freely downloadable from Microsoft's Web site at **http://www.microsoft.com/vbasic/controls**, gives you the ability to create ActiveX controls, but does not include database access libraries; this means that if you use the Control Creation Edition, it's possible to create a database-aware control you can't test.

Summary

This chapter provides an introduction to the basic user-interface controls available in Visual Basic, as well as the additional ActiveX controls available in the Visual Basic Professional and Enterprise editions.

The next few chapters provide a more in-depth introduction into a number of third-party user-interface controls, including the MSFlexGrid and the DBGrid controls that ship with Visual Basic 5.0, as well as their enhanced commercial counterparts.

QUESTIONS AND ANSWERS

Q. I need a control that binds to a Date/Time field in a Jet database and permits the user to select a day of the month graphically, without entering any data.

A. There are a few dozen third-party database-aware calendar controls that I know about. One of the best is mh3dCalendar, part of the BeCubed Software's OLETools suite. This control does everything but sit up and beg—it even formats days and months in Esperanto. The OLETools package that contains the calendar control also contains more than fifty other controls, many of which are also database-aware. Check out more OLETools information at **http://www.becubed.com**.

By way of comparison, you might also want to check out Sheridan Calendar Widgets, which is slightly different than the calendar control in OLETools, but is also quite good. You can read about them on Sheridan's Web site at **http://www.shersoft.com/products/actvxlist.htm**, or download a demonstration from **http://www.shersoft.com/download/trials. htm**.

Q. Are there any other cool third-party, database-aware controls that weren't mentioned in this chapter?

A. Sure, a carload. DynamiCube is a data analysis tool simlar to VSFLEX (the topic of Chapter 12). It has the capability to summarize data in a few ways that VSFLEX can't, and it's also Web-friendly, so you can display data in a browser over your network or the Internet. Get more information on DynamiCube from the Data Dynamics Web page at **http://www. datadynamics.com**.

In addition, Formula One is one of the best spreadsheet-like data grids out there. If your application needs a grid interface and True DBGrid (the subject of the next chapter) doesn't do it for you, check this one out. You can get more information on Formula One from the Visual Components Web site at **http://visualcomp.com**.

Using the DBGrid and Apex True DBGrid Controls

How can I display database information in rows and columns?

How can I view two sections of a recordset at once without having to scroll back and forth through the recordset?

How can I visually highlight particular pieces of data in a recordset in order to display particular records?

The DBGrid control permits you to display information from a database in a row and column format. The effect is similar to the datasheet view provided in Microsoft Access—although applications built with Visual Basic and the DBGrid control generally have a much smaller distributable footprint and are, as a result, generally much peppier than Microsoft Access-based applications. Additionally, the DBGrid control has display properties, behaviors, and features not offered by Access, as this chapter demonstrates.

The DBGrid control is shipped with the Professional and Enterprise editions of Visual Basic 5.0. An earlier version of the DBGrid control also shipped with Visual Basic 4.0. The latest version of the grid control, True DBGrid 5.0, is available as an add-on to Visual Basic; both it and the DBGrid control are developed by Apex Software.

Note: Apex Software has a Web site at **http://www.apexsc.com/**. You can order the commercial True DBGrid control online from this book's Web site at **http://www.redblazer.com/software**.

In addition, the commercial version of the control, True DBGrid Pro, was formerly called TrueGrid Pro. True DBGrid Pro is an updated version of the TrueGrid and DBGrid controls.

This chapter introduces these two controls and demonstrates how you can use them to display and modify information in a database.

OVERVIEW OF DATABASE GRID CONTROLS

The DBGrid control ships with the Professional and Enterprise editions of Visual Basic 4.0 and 5.0. This chapter gives you an brief overview of how to use the DBGrid control in your applications, then gives a few examples of the extended capabilities of True DBGrid, the commercial version of the DBGrid control.

Note: In addition to the DBGrid and True DBGrid ActiveX Controls, Apex Software recently announced a new version of their grid aimed at Visual C++ developers. This product, True DBGrid Pro 5.0 VC++, is designed to integrate with Microsoft Foundation Class (MFC) libraries used by Visual C++ developers. For more information on this product, check out the Apex Web site at **http://www.apexsc.com/.**

Issues Relating to DBGrid Resolved in Visual Basic 5.0 Service Packs

A number of issues specifically relating to the functionality of the DBGrid control were fixed in Visual Studio service packs. Because Visual Basic is a part of Visual Studio, Visual Studio's service packs affect VB as well.

Specifically, the resolved issues are:

Bug	For More Information:
Control crashes when a column is resized.	**http://support.microsoft.com/ support/kb/articles/Q168/1/55.asp**
DBGrid bound to a Remote Data control displays only a single record after a MoveLast method is executed.	**http://support.microsoft.com/ support/kb/articles/Q168/1/53.asp**
Applications built with the VB4 version of an unbound DBGrid control display invalid data under VB5 SP1.	**http://premium.microsoft.com/ support/kb/articles/Q171/5/46.asp**
Untrappable error generated when editing data on machines that previously had the VB4 DBGrid control installed.	**http://premium.microsoft.com/ support/kb/articles/Q171/5/47.asp**

Note: As of this writing, the latest service pack was Service Pack 3. This service pack contains the fixes included in Service Packs 1 and 2. You can obtain Visual Studio Service Pack for free by downloading it from **http://www.microsoft.com/vstudio/sp/download.htm**.

GETTING STARTED WITH THE DBGRID CONTROL

This section walks you through the basics of the DBGrid control, the version of True DBGrid control that comes with Visual Basic. If you've already upgraded to the commercial True DBGrid product, this section applies to you as well, because the basic techniques for both versions of the control are the same.

The DBGrid control contains a number of other objects used to manipulate the grid. The DBGrid control's object model is illustrated in Figure 11.1.

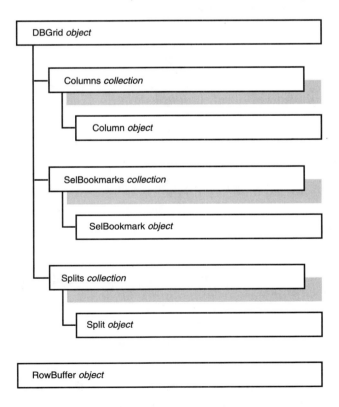

Figure 11.1: Object model of the Apex DBGrid control.

The DBGrid control is installed on your computer when you install either the Professional or Enterprise editions of Visual Basic. Its filename is DBGRID32.OCX.

To use the DBGrid in a Visual Basic project, do the following:

1 In Visual Basic, select Project Components.

2 The Components dialog box appears. In the list of components, scroll down until you see Microsoft Data Bound Grid Control.

Note: The Data Bound Grid control does not change in Visual Basic Service Pack 2, but it is updated in Service Pack 3. Apex Software periodically makes updates of the control available for download on its Web site. Check out http://www.apexsc.com for more details.

3 Check the control in the list, then click on OK. The DBGrid control is added to your Visual Basic toolbox, as shown in Figure 11.2.

Figure 11.2: The DBGrid control in the Visual Basic toolbox.

To display the contents of a recordset in the database grid, bind it to a Data control just as with other data-aware controls. To do this:

1 Add a Data control and a DBGrid control to a VB form.

2 Set the Data control's DatabaseName and RecordSource properties as you normally would.

3 Set the DBGrid control's DataSource property to the name of the Data control. (Because it displays many fields, the DBGrid control has no DataField property.)

4 Run the application. The data should be displayed in the grid, as shown in Figure 11.3.

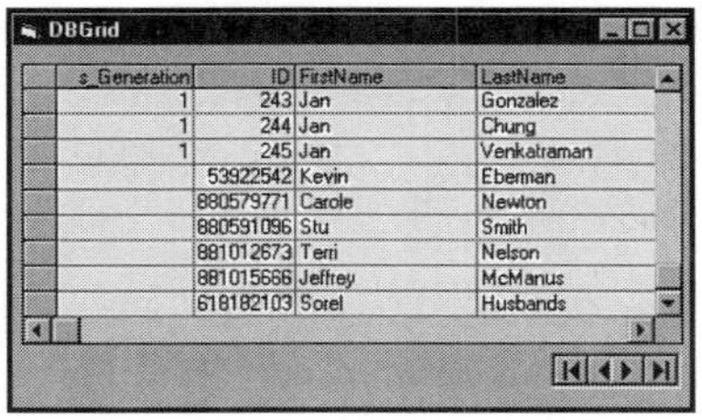

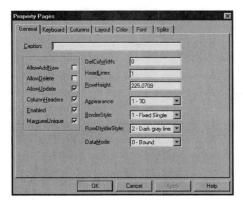

Figure 11.3: Information from a Data control displayed in the DBGrid control.

This application is easy to build because it requires very little code, but it has a few problems. First, the columns from the recordset are displayed randomly. Second, the data is read-only. Those problems are resolved in the next few sections.

Selecting Columns to Display at Design Time

The DBGrid control has a powerful property sheet that permits you to determine several aspects of the grid's behavior and appearance. In this example, you use the property sheet to denote which columns to display and in which order.

1 In the Visual Basic design-time environment, right-click on the DBGrid control.

2 Select Properties from the pop-up menu.

3 The Properties dialog box appears, as shown in Figure 11.4.

Figure 11.4: DBGrid Properties dialog box, enabling you to make design-time changes to the control.

4 In the Properties dialog box, click on the Columns tab. By clicking on the Column combo, you can see that at design time, there are two columns by default: Column0 and Column1.

5 Assign the DataField property of Column0 to FirstName.

6 In the Column combo box, select Column1. Assign the DataField property of Column1 to LastName.

7 Click on OK, then run the application again. You should be able to see that only the first and last names of customers appear in the grid.

The appearance of a set of columns in a DBGrid control is referred to as a *layout*. In the commercial True DBGrid component, the control stores a collection of Layout objects. This permits you to easily manipulate and switch between multiple layouts.

In both versions of the grid control, you have the ability to manipulate grid columns at runtime, using code. This topic is covered in the section "Manipulating Grid Columns in Code" later in this chapter.

Manipulating Columns at Design Time

You can add columns to the DBGrid control at design time by using the control's context menu. After you've added columns, you can bind each new column to another field in the database using its Properties dialog box.

1 In the Visual Basic design-time environment, right-click on the DBGrid control.

2 Select Edit from the pop-up menu. The grid is now in edit mode (even though its appearance remains the same).

3 Right-click on the DBGrid control again. This time the pop-up menu is different, reflecting the fact that the grid is in edit mode. This is shown in Figure 11.5.

4 Select Append from the pop-up menu. A new column appears to the right of the two existing columns.

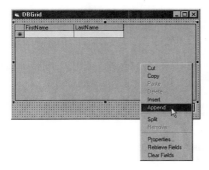

Figure 11.5: The DBGrid's pop-up menu when it's in edit mode.

To delete a column:

1 While the grid is in edit mode, click on a column to select it.

2 Right-click on the grid. Select Delete from the pop-up menu.

To resize a column:

1 While the grid is in edit mode, position your mouse pointer in the grey header area, directly on the boundary between two columns. The mouse pointer turns into a double-headed arrow, as shown in Figure 11.6.

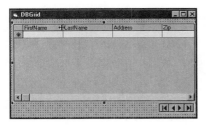

Figure 11.6: Resizing a column at design time using the mouse pointer.

2 Click-drag to resize the column.

Using a combination of mouse actions and the Properties dialog box, you should be able to set up the grid so it displays four fields: FirstName, LastName, Address, and Zip. This interface is shown in Figure 11.7.

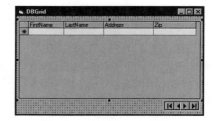

Figure 11.7: DBGrid interface displaying four fields from the recordset.

Making the Data Editable

By default, the DBGrid control permits users to alter the data it displays, but it doesn't let users delete or add records. You can manipulate properties of the grid control to control whether users can change data and insert or delete records.

The properties that the DBGrid control uses to manage editability of records are:

▶ AllowAddNew   Determines whether the user can add new records. False by default.

▶ AllowDelete   Determines whether the user can delete records. False by default.

▶ AllowUpdate   Determines whether the user can edit existing data. True by default.

To make the data displayed in the grid fully editable, appendable, and deleteable, simply set all three of these properties to True at design time. When the AllowAddNew property is set to True, you must scroll to the bottom of the grid to add a new record, as shown in Figure 11.8.

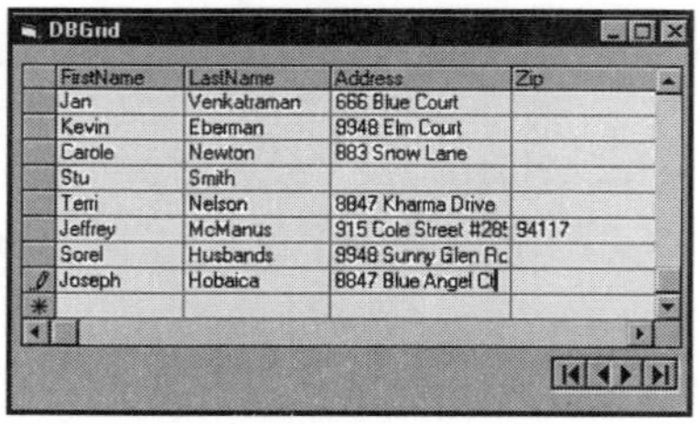

Figure 11.8: Adding a new record in a DBGrid whose AllowAddNew property is set to True.

This is the same technique you use to add records in a Microsoft Access datasheet.

Note: It's better to manage the editability of records at the database-engine level rather than at the user-interface level. For example, don't create a read-write Recordset object, then make it read-only by setting the DBGrid's AllowUpdate property to False. Opening database objects for write access is generally more computationally expensive than opening them read-only. For more information on how to open a Recordset object in read-only mode, see Chapter 8, "Multiuser Issues."

Inserting Splits at Design Time

You can split a grid into multiple sections. This makes it easy for users to view a large amount of data in the grid without having to scroll back and forth in the grid.

Splits can be either horizontal or vertical. When a split exists in a grid, two sets of scrollbars become available, one to control each split. Splits don't affect the data in the grid, only the way it's displayed; you can think of them as separate viewports onto the set of data displayed by the grid.

To create and configure a split at runtime:

1 Put the grid in edit mode.

2 Right-click on the control. Select Split from the pop-up menu.

3 A vertical split appears, as shown in Figure 11.9.

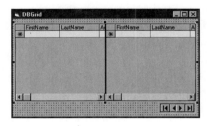

Figure 11.9: A vertical split created at design time.

4 With the control still in edit mode, right-click and select Properties from the pop-up menu.

5 Select the Splits tab. You should be able to see two splits in the Splits combo box: Split0 and Split1. You alter the properties of Split0 to make the first two columns visible at all times.

6 Change the SizeMode property of Split0 to 2 - Number of Columns. Then change its Size property to 2. This will cause the split to be two columns wide.

7 Finally, set the split's ScrollBars property to 0 - None, then click on OK.

8 Run the application. It should look like Figure 11.10.

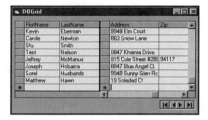

Figure 11.10: DBGrid control with a non-resizable vertical split.

As with the other elements of the DBGrid control, you have the ability to create and manipulate splits at runtime, using code, as well as at design time. The next section gives an example of how to do this.

Manipulating Split Objects in Code

There's one problem with the interface you've built in the previous examples. The right split, Split1, initially displays the same information as the left split. It would be better if Split0 showed columns 0 and 1 by default, while Split1 showed columns 2 and 3.

Unfortunately, you can't designate the initial column for a particular split at design time. Here's where you get to delve into the DBGrid control's object model—specifically, the Split object. You declare a Split object in code the same way you declare any other object:

```
Dim sp As Split
```

Your sample grid control has two splits: Split0 and Split1. Because these objects are members of the Splits collection, you can also refer to them ordinally, as Splits(0) and Splits(1). To assign the Split object variable to one of your control's two splits, use the following code:

```
Set sp = DBGrid1.Splits(1)
```

This sets the object variable sp to the rightmost split. You can now manipulate the properties and methods of the rightmost split through the object variable sp. Listing 11.1 uses this technique to set the rightmost split's default column.

Listing 11.1: Assigning the Default Column of a Split Using the Split Object's LeftCol Property

```
Option Explicit

' References DAO 3.5

Private Sub Form_Load()
Dim sp As Split

    Data1.DatabaseName = App.Path & "\novelty.mdb"

    Set sp = DBGrid1.Splits(1)
    sp.LeftCol = 2

End Sub
```

In addition to manipulating existing splits, you also have the ability to create and delete splits in code at runtime (using the Add and Remove methods of the grid's Splits collection).

Manipulating Grid Columns in Code

You have the ability to manipulate the columns of a grid in code. This technique is similar to the technique you used to access the properties of a split in the previous section: Create an object variable to represent the element of the grid you want to manipulate, then access the properties and execute the methods of the object variable.

For example, say you're interested in permitting the user to easily hide a particular column of the grid, then make the column visible again later. You can do this by setting the Visible property of a Column object. Listing 11.2 shows you how to do this.

Listing 11.2: Manipulating the Properties of a DBGrid Control's Column Object

```
Private Sub cmdHide_Click()
Dim c As Column
```

continues

Listing 11.2: Manipulating the Properties of a DBGrid Control's Column Object (Continued)

```
    Set c = DBGrid1.Columns(1)  ' LastName column
    c.Visible = Not c.Visible

End Sub
```

Applying the Not operator to the Column object's Visible property means that the Hide button will display the column if it's hidden already.

In addition to manipulating existing columns, you also have the ability to create and delete columns in code at runtime (using the Add and Remove methods of the grid's Columns collection).

Navigating with the Bookmark Property

You can refer to the currently selected row in the grid by the grid's Bookmark property. This property, which is analogous to the Bookmark property in Data Access Objects, permits you to save the location of a particular record so you can return to it later.

Listing 11.3 gives an example of two command buttons—one to set a bookmark, the other to return to the bookmarked record.

Listing 11.3: Setting Bookmarks and Returning to Bookmarked Records

```
Private mstrBookmark As String

Private Sub cmdBookmark_Click()
    mstrBookmark = DBGrid1.Bookmark
End Sub

Private Sub cmdGo_Click()
    DBGrid1.Bookmark = mstrBookmark
End Sub
```

When the user clicks on the Bookmark button, the value of the current record's bookmark is stored in the module-level variable mstrBookmark. When the user clicks on the Go button, the value of mstrBookmark is assigned to the grid's Bookmark property, causing the grid to move to the row with that bookmark.

Selecting Records Using the SelBookmarks Collection

In addition to bookmarking a record, you can use the Bookmark property in conjunction with the SelBookmarks collection to visibly select one or more rows in the grid. You select a row in order to highlight it to the user, or to pre-pare it for a later operation, such as deletion.

The SelBookmarks collection is a collection of bookmarks of selected rows of the grid. To select a row in the grid, you add its bookmark to the grid's SelBookmarks collection, using code like this:

```
DBGrid1.SelBookmarks.Add DBGrid.Bookmark
```

This code adds the current row to the SelBookmarks collection—with the side-effect of selecting the current row.

As a practical example of this technique, say your application needs to have a search feature. This feature uses the FindFirst method of the Data control's Recordset object to locate a record. After it does that, it would be helpful if the application selected the record to make it easy for the user to see what took place. Listing 11.4 gives an example of code that does this.

Listing 11.4: Searching a Recordset and Highlighting a Found Record in the Grid Using the SelBookmarks Collection

```
Private Sub cmdSearch_Click()
Dim strFind As String
    strFind = InputBox("Enter the last name to find.", "Find")
    Data1.Recordset.FindFirst "LastName='" & strFind & "'"

    If Data1.Recordset.NoMatch Then
        MsgBox "The name was not found.", vbExclamation
    Else
        DBGrid1.SelBookmarks.Add DBGrid1.Bookmark
    End If

End Sub
```

Figure 11.11 shows the DBGrid application after it's found and selected a customer in response to a user query.

Figure 11.11: DBGrid application containing a selected record.

The fact that SelBookmarks is a collection implies that a number of rows in the grid can be selected at the same time. This is, in fact, the case. You might do this in a situation in which the user performed a search on the records in the grid and the search retrieved a number of rows.

Using the DBGrid Control in Unbound Mode

Until now, all the examples in this chapter have been predicated on the concept of a DBGrid control connected to a database through the Data control. You have the ability, however, to display and manipulate data in a DBGrid control without a Data control. This is referred to as *unbound mode*.

You use unbound mode when you need greater control over how information is retrieved and displayed in the grid control, or when you want to overcome the performance or flexibility shortcomings of the Data control. The DBGrid control provides a number of properties and events that support unbound mode.

To use a DBGrid control in unbound mode, start by setting the control's DataMode property to 1 - dbgUnbound. When you do this, you're telling the control that your code takes complete responsibility for manipulating and displaying data in the control.

In an unbound control, you write code that handles data manipulation in response to four events. These events include:

▶ UnboundAddData   Triggered when the grid needs to add a row to the data source.

▶ UnboundDeleteRow   Triggered when the grid needs to delete a row from the data source.

▶ UnboundReadData   Triggered when the grid needs to retrieve a row of data from the data source.

▶ UnboundWriteData   Triggered when the grid needs to write data back to the data source.

Note: The commercial True DBGrid control adds a new type of unbound mode, *unbound extended mode,* that is simpler to code against (because it requires fewer events) and is a bit more efficient. The technique described in this section, however, has the advantage of working in DBGrid as well as the commercial True DBGrid control.

The big disadvantage of using unbound mode is the fact that it's fairly complicated to code. To make it work, you need to write code to all the events, interacting with the RowBuffer object passed to your application from the grid through the events as an argument.

Developing Database-Aware Applications Using True DBGrid Pro 5.0

The commercial version of the DBGrid control is called True DBGrid Pro 5.0. This control contains all the features of the DBGrid control, is nearly 100 percent backward-compatible with earlier versions of the control, and provides some significant additional features that permit you to customize the control's appearance and behavior.

Some of the features available in the commercial True DBGrid 5.0 that aren't available in the version that ships with Visual Basic 5.0 include:

▶ Support for extended unbound mode and storage mode, two unbound modes that permit the grid to display information without a Data control

▶ The capability to include unbound columns in a grid that's bound to a Data control

▶ The capability to embed user-interface controls and bitmap images in grid cells

▶ The capability to apply formatting to individual cells in the grid

▶ Support for *celltips*, a feature similar to the ToolTips you find in a toolbar control, but assignable to each cell in the grid

▶ The ability to load and save predefined sets of formats called *layouts*, and to program layouts at runtime through the Layout object

Some of these features are demonstrated in the remainder of this chapter.

The object model of the commercial TrueDBGrid control is a superset of the object model of the DBGrid control that ships with Visual Basic. Figure 11.12 shows the object model of True DBGrid 5.0.

The True DBGrid control does not ship with Visual Basic; it's a separate product. A trial version of the commercial control is available on the CD-ROM that accompanies this book; you can purchase the control online at the Web site for this book, **http://www.redblazer.com/vbdb/**.

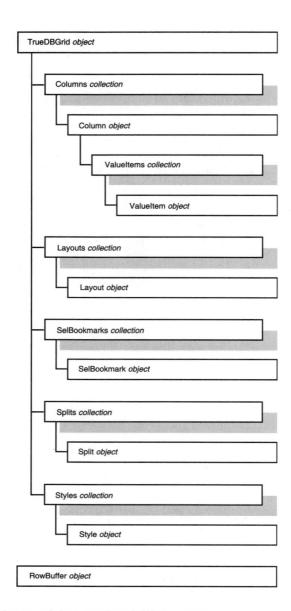

Figure 11.12: Object model of the True DBGrid control.

The True DBGrid control's filename is TDBG5.OCX. To use True DBGrid in your Visual Basic project, do the following:

1 In Visual Basic, select Project Components.

2 The Components dialog box appears. In the list of components, scroll down until you see Apex True DBGrid Pro 5.0.

3 Check the control in the list, then click on OK. The True DBGrid and TDBDropDown controls are added to your Visual Basic toolbox, as shown in Figure 11.13.

Figure 11.13: The True DBGrid control in the Visual Basic toolbox.

Note: Apex Software periodically makes updates of their controls available for download on the company's Web site. Check out **http://www.apexsc.com** for more details.

Bear in mind that this chapter is designed to give you a brief introduction to True DBGrid 5.0's features—it's not even close to being a complete reference to the control. The current edition of the (very helpful and well-done) manual for the commercial version of the control runs about 400 pages and covers the features of the control in much more depth than this chapter has room for.

Migrating from Previous Versions of True DBGrid

Because there have been changes in the programmable interface of the True DBGrid control over the years, the True DBGrid Pro 5.0 package comes with a migration tool. This tool inspects your code, picking out incompatibilities and updating calls to the elements of the control's interface that have changed. This migration tool is installed when you install True DBGrid.

1 Because the tool makes changes to your code, start by backing up your source code files.

2 Open a Visual Basic project based on a previous version of the True DBGrid control.

3 Activate the migration add-in by selecting Add-Ins, Add-In Manager.

4 The Add-In Manager dialog box appears. Check True DBGrid Pro 5.0 Migration Utility in the list, then click on OK.

5 The Migration utility is loaded; it appears as a button in the Visual Basic toolbar (it does not appear as an item in the Add-Ins menu, as many add-ins do). This toolbar button is illustrated in Figure 11.14.

Figure 11.14: The True DBGrid Pro 5.0 Migration utility in the Visual Basic toolbar.

6 Run the migration utility by clicking on the button in the toolbar. The Migration Utility dialog box appears, as shown in Figure 11.15.

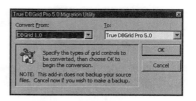

Figure 11.15: True DBGrid Pro 5.0's Migration Utility dialog box.

7 Using the combo box in the Migration Utility dialog box, select the version of the DBGrid control your current application uses, then click on OK.

8 The Migration utility analyzes your code, commenting out any that doesn't conform to the new version of the control and replacing that code with the True DBGrid 5.0 version of the code.

Storing and Applying Formatting with the Style Object

In True DBGrid Pro, you have the ability to manipulate sets of formating attributes composed of such things as font, color, and alignment. These sets of attributes are called *styles*. Styles in True DBGrid Pro are conceptually similar to styles in the Microsoft Office applications—they can be named, applied to sections of the grid, and altered to suit your needs. When you change the definition of a style, all the grid elements that have that style change to reflect the new style definition.

You can create and manipulate grid styles using True DBGrid Pro's property dialog box. You can also manipulate styles in code. You use the Style object when you're working with styles in code.

You can create styles yourself; True DBGrid Pro comes with a number of predefined styles. These are listed in Table 11.1.

Table 11.1: Predefined Styles Available in True DBGrid Pro 5.0

Name	Description
Normal	The basic style upon which other styles are based.
	Font: MS Sans Serif 8.25
	BackColor: Window Background
	ForeColor: Window Text
	Text Align: Left
Heading	Parent: Normal
	BackColor: System Button Face
	ForeColor: System Button Text
Selected	Parent: Normal
	BackColor: System Highlight
	ForeColor: System Highlight Text
Caption	Parent: Heading
	Alignment: Center

continues

Table 11.1: Predefined Styles Available in True DBGrid Pro 5.0 (Continued)

Name	Description
HighlightRow	Parent: Normal
	BackColor: System Window Text
	ForeColor: System Window Background
EvenRow	Same as Normal style
OddRow	Equivalent to the Normal style

Note: System colors (such as System Button Face) are defined by the user through the Windows Control Panel. Accordingly, you can't predict with certainty to what those colors will be set.

Applying Styles in Code You can apply style formatting to the entire grid by setting the Style property of the grid control. This property is a string that corresponds to an existing style in the grid's Styles collection.

For example, use the following code to set the grid's formatting to the preset EvenRow style:

```
Private Sub cmdStyle_Click()
    TDBGrid1.Style = "EvenRow"
End Sub
```

This sets the entire grid's formatting to the EvenRow style, but you can also apply styles to individual rows and columns in the grid. For example, use the following code to apply the EvenRow style to the first and third columns in the grid:

```
Private Sub cmdStyle_Click()
    TDBGrid1.Columns(0).Style = "EvenRow"
    TDBGrid1.Columns(2).Style = "EvenRow"
End Sub
```

Using the Style property, you can apply a style to the entire grid control, a single column within the control, or a split within the control.

Creating Your Own Styles in Code You can create your own styles in code at runtime. You might do this in situations where you want to enable the user to apply style-based formatting to the grid, or if you simply prefer to describe your styles in code as opposed to using the control's property sheet.

To create a style, create a new Style object, add it to the grid's Styles collection, and assign its properties. For example, assume you need a style to highlight a particular type of customer. Listing 11.5 shows how to do this.

Listing 11.5: Creating the Preferred Style at Runtime

```
Option Explicit

' References DAO 3.5

Private Sub Form_Load()

Dim st As Style
    Set st = TDBGrid1.Styles.Add("Preferred")

    With st
        .Parent = "Normal"
        .Font.Bold = True
        .BackColor = vbYellow
        .ForeColor = vbRed
    End With

End Sub
```

As soon as your custom style is created, you can apply it to grid elements (as demonstrated in the previous section).

Note: This just scratches the surface of what you can do with styles. True DBGrid Pro's style features are much more involved than this chapter has space to cover. The grid comes with additional documentation and sample applications that give you more information on how to use its extensive style features.

Applying Custom Styles Using the FetchRowStyle Event   The True DBGrid control provides a number of features that make it easy for you to apply custom style formatting based on the contents of cells. One way to do this is with the FetchRowStyle event.

The FetchRowStyle event is triggered whenever the grid control needs to display a row of data. In the event procedure, you can write code specifying how each row of data should be formatted, based on data contained in cells or any other criterion you specify.

Enable the FetchRowStyle event by setting the grid's FetchRowStyle property to True. You can then write an event procedure in the FetchRowStyle event that formats cells based on the criteria you specify. Listing 11.6 gives an example.

Listing 11.6: Using the FetchRowStyle Event Procedure to Apply Styles to Cells

```
Option Explicit

' References DAO 3.5


Private Sub Form_Load()

Dim st As Style
    Set st = TDBGrid1.Styles.Add("Preferred")

    With st
        .Parent = "Normal"
        .Font.Bold = True
        .BackColor = vbYellow
        .ForeColor = vbRed
    End With

    Data1.DatabaseName = App.Path & "\novelty.mdb"

    ' Enables row-by-row style formatting
    ' via FetchRowStyle event
    TDBGrid1.FetchRowStyle = True

End Sub

Private Sub TDBGrid1_FetchRowStyle(ByVal Split As Integer, Bookmark As _
            Variant, ByVal RowStyle As TrueDBGrid50.StyleDisp)
    If TDBGrid1.Columns(2).CellText(Bookmark) = -1 Then
        RowStyle = "Preferred"
    End If
End Sub
```

This code highlights all of Jones Novelties' preferred customers with the Preferred style (created in the previous example). The result of this code is illustrated in Figure 11.16.

Figure 11.16: Formatting data in the True DBGrid control with styles according to data in each record.

Changing the Display of a Column with the ValueItem Object
Occasionally, you need to alter the display of information in a column in order to clarify or highlight the data. TrueDBGrid Pro 5.0 provides this functionality through the ValueItem object.

The ValueItem object has the Value and DisplayValue properties. The Value property is the actual value of the cell, while DisplayValue is the information you want to display in the grid.

For example, the Preferred column in the example application displays 0 for False and -1 for True. It might be easier to make out this information if the column displayed the textual values Yes and No. Listing 11.7. gives an example of how to use the ValueItem object to change the display of data in a column.

Listing 11.7: Using the ValueItem Object to Alter the Display of Information in a Column

```
Private Sub cmdValue_Click()
Dim Item As New ValueItem

    With TDBGrid1.Columns(2).ValueItems
        Item.Value = -1
        Item.DisplayValue = "Yes"
        .Add Item
        -
        Item.Value = 0
        Item.DisplayValue = "No"
        .Add Item
```
continues

Listing 11.7: Using the ValueItem Object to Alter the Display of Information in a Column (Continued)

```
        .Translate = True
    End With

End Sub
```

This causes the grid to display data as shown in Figure 11.17.

Figure 11.17: Grid displaying data translated with the ValueItems object.

Because it's no longer displaying the numeric values 0 and -1, but instead the textual values Yes and No, applying this change to your application breaks your FetchRowStyle event procedure. To fix that, change the grid's FetchRowStyle event procedure as shown in Listing 11.8.

Listing 11.8: Change to the FetchRowStyle Event Procedure to Accommodate the Translated Value

```
Private Sub TDBGrid1_FetchRowStyle(ByVal Split As Integer, Bookmark As _
          Variant, ByVal RowStyle As TrueDBGrid50.StyleDisp)
    If TDBGrid1.Columns(2).CellText(Bookmark) = "Yes" Then
        RowStyle = "Preferred"
    End If
End Sub
```

An interesting variation on the ValueItem object available in True DBGrid 5.0 is the capability to display graphics in cells. To do this, simply set the ValueItem object's DisplayValue property to a picture retrieved with the Visual Basic LoadPicture function. Listing 11.9 gives an example.

Listing 11.9: Displaying Graphics in the Grid Using the ValueItem Object

```
Private Sub cmdValue_Click()
Dim Item As New ValueItem

    With TDBGrid1.Columns(2).ValueItems
        Item.Value = -1
        Item.DisplayValue = LoadPicture(App.Path & "\pref.bmp")
        .Add Item

        Item.Value = 0
        Item.DisplayValue = LoadPicture(App.Path & "\norm.bmp")
        .Add Item

        .Translate = True
    End With

End Sub
```

Figure 11.18 shows what the grid looks like when this code is run.

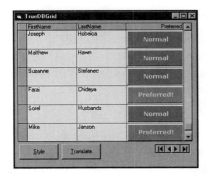

Figure 11.18: Grid displaying a graphic instead of a text value in a column.

Providing Help for Users with CellTips

A new feature of True DBGrid 5.0 is the capability to provide CellTips to users. CellTips are visual cues similar to the ToolTips in Microsoft Office applications, except CellTips can be different for each row, column, or cell in your application.

You set up CellTips in your True DBGrid application by setting the grid's CellTips property to something other than 0 (which is the default). When you've set this property, write code in the FetchCellTips event to supply text to the cell tip. Listing 11.10 gives an example.

Listing 11.10: Populating the Grid's CellTips

```
Private Sub TDBGrid1_FetchCellTips(ByVal SplitIndex As Integer, ByVal _
        ColIndex As Integer, ByVal RowIndex As Long, CellTip As String, _
        ByVal FullyDisplayed As Boolean, ByVal TipStyle _
        As TrueDBGrid50.StyleDisp)

' Set CellTips property to make this work

    Select Case ColIndex
        Case 0   ' First Name
        CellTip = "The customer's first name"


        Case 1   ' Last Name
        CellTip = "The customer's last name"


        Case 2   ' Preferred
        CellTip = "Preferred customers have this field set to -1."


    End Select

End Sub
```

The FetchCellTips event takes a large number of arguments, permitting you to supply CellTips in a variety of contexts. In this case, the code simply supplies a description of the various columns displayed in the grid by setting the CellTip argument to a text string.

Setting the grid's CellTips property to 2 - Floating produces the effect shown in Figure 11.19.

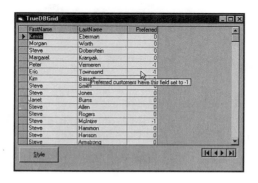

Figure 11.19: Floating CellTips over a True DBGrid control.

SUMMARY

This chapter gave a brief summary of the DBGrid and True DBGrid Pro controls' features. In addition to providing examples of using the control with a data control, you learned how to use the grid in unbound mode, as well as take advantage of techniques that permit you to display data differently based on the contents of a particular field.

The next chapter introduces another grid control, the MSFlexGrid control, and its commercial counterpart, the VideoSoft VSFLEX control. You can use this grid to work with data in a manner similar to the DBGrid control, but with a number of user-definable customization features.

QUESTIONS AND ANSWERS

Q. Is there an easy way to permit the user to select from a list of choices when entering information in a grid cell?

A. Yes. The True DBGrid control provides support for controls—such as a drop-down list box—to appear in a cell when a user is editing data. True DBGrid 5.0 provides a drop-down list called TDBDropDown. The benefit of using this control is the fact that it supports many of the properties and methods of the full grid control, including the display of data in multiple columns. You can even bind the TDBDropDown control to a different Data control than the True DBGrid control is bound to.

Q. Can I apply an input mask to a grid cell the same way I can with a masked edit control?

A. Yes. To do this, use the EditMask property of the grid's Column object. The same formatting characters supported in the Visual Basic Masked Edit control are supported in True DBGrid. (The Masked Edit control is introduced in Chapter 10, "User-Interface Controls.")

The MSFlexGrid and VideoSoft VSFLEX Controls

How can I analyze data using a direct connection to the database instead of a printed report?

How can I build a user interface that permits users to easily customize their views of data?

How can I sort and retrieve information displayed in a grid after it's already been displayed in the user interface?

Chapter 122

The MSFlexGrid control is the newest grid control to ship with Microsoft Visual Basic. Although you'd think that VB is "gridded out" (as of now, the Professional and Enterprise editions come with a total of three separate grid controls), you find that the FlexGrid control provides some significant features the others don't.

These features include the capability to display and analyze data by clicking and dragging with the mouse. When you do this, the FlexGrid control regroups data and combines it in ways that let you see trends across a large amount of data without forcing you to analyze every bit of information in your database.

Using Online Decision Support

Database tools are generally divided into two categories: transaction-processing tools and decision-support tools. *Transaction processing* involves entering and altering data in the database, while *decision support* involves evaluating data that's already in the database.

A database report is an example of a decision-support tool. In most cases, report data is non-interactive; a user can't generally edit the numbers (often because the report is presented to him or her in the form of printed numbers on a piece of paper). Most importantly for the developer, if the report's consumer needs to see the data in a different way (sorted by date and grouped by region, for example), the developer must go back to the grindstone and create a whole new report.

An alternative to this is a process known as *online analytical processing* (OLAP). OLAP tools have the following characteristics:

▶ **Displaying data in multiple dimensions.** This generally involves a minimum of two dimensions (which makes a database grid ideal for use as an OLAP tool), but sometimes involves views of data that exceed three dimensions.

▶ **Drill-down.** This process permits you to expose detail about a specific statistic. For example, if your application displays a list of sales figures for each division of your company, you might want to see details on how each salesperson in each region fared. A drill-down feature makes this process a no-brainer. In a GUI, drilling down is typically accomplished by clicking on the piece of data about which you want more detail.

▶ **Grouping.** This is the opposite of drill-down; it's also known as roll-up. This process involves hiding or summarizing information in situations where you don't need to know the detail. For example, if you're a company's CEO, it's unlikely that you'd need to know how many rubber chickens were sold in retail store #485 yesterday. Instead, you'd roll that data up into a storewide or a regional statistic. OLAP applications permit you to do that.

The MSFlexGrid control permits you to create highly effective decision-support applications; the commercial vsFlexArray control lets you do even more, particularly in the area of roll-up and drill-down. This chapter introduces both controls, showing how you can use them in applications both with and without the Visual Basic Data control.

USING THE MSFLEX CONTROL

Microsoft Visual Basic comes with an ActiveX component that lets you incorporate OLAP capabilities into your VB applications. This component, the MSFlexGrid control, displays data in a grid that makes it easy for users to group information in order to view and summarize data more easily.

Note: The MSFlex control is a "light" version of the VSFLEX component developed by VideoSoft Corporation. For more information on the full version of VSFLEX—including a working version of the control you can download and evaluate—check out the VideoSoft Web site at **http://www.videosoft.com**. There is also more information on the commercial version of VSFLEX (including differences between it and the MSFlex control that comes with VB5) in the section "Using VideoSoft VSFLEX 3.0," later in this chapter.

The MSFlexGrid control ships with the Professional and Enterprise editions of Visual Basic 5.0. The MSFlexGrid control's filename is MSFLXGRD.OCX. To use the MSFlexGrid in your Visual Basic project, do the following:

1 In Visual Basic, select Project Components.

2 The Components dialog box appears. In the list of components, scroll down until you see Microsoft FlexGrid Control 5.0.

Note: If you're running a service pack edition of Visual Basic, the name of the control in the Components dialog box might reflect the name of the service pack; for example, if you're running VB 5.0 Service Pack 2, the control is listed as Microsoft FlexGrid Control 5.0 (SP2).

VideoSoft periodically updates its controls available for download on the company's Web site. Check out **http://www.videosoft.com** for more details.

3 Check the control in the list, then click OK. The MSFlexGrid control is added to your Visual Basic toolbox, as shown in Figure 12.1.

Figure 12.1: The MSFlexGrid control in the Visual Basic toolbox.

To start using the MSFlexGrid control, add an instance of the control to a Visual Basic form. You can then optionally bind the MSFlexGrid control to a Data control. This chapter takes you through the process of creating an application based on the MSFlexGrid control, first in unbound mode, then bound to a Data control.

Adding Data to the MSFlexGrid Control

When the MSFlexGrid isn't bound to a Data control, you can add data to the control using its properties and methods. You start populating an unbound FlexGrid by setting the grid's Rows and Columns properties. This provides cells into which you can insert data.

```
FlexGrid1.Rows = 12
FlexGrid1.Columns = 4
```

This code creates a grid with 48 cells—12 rows by 4 columns. After you've created a number of rows and columns in the FlexGrid, you can navigate from one cell to the next in code, adding data to each cell. Navigate to the cell to which you want to add data by setting the Row and Col properties of the grid; this sets the position of the current cell. You can then assign data to the current cell by using the Text property. The Text property returns or assigns data to the current cell (as set by the Row and Col properties).

Listing 12.1 gives an example of code that populates a single-row grid with data.

Listing 12.1: Populating a FlexGrid Control with Hard-Coded Data

```
Option Explicit

Private Sub Form_Load()
    FlexGrid1.Cols = 4
    FlexGrid1.Rows = 1

    ' Place text in header
    FlexGrid1.Row = 0
    FlexGrid1.Col = 1
    FlexGrid1.Text = "Jan"

    FlexGrid1.Col = 2
    FlexGrid1.Text = "Feb"

    FlexGrid1.Col = 3
    FlexGrid1.Text = "Mar"

End Sub
```

This code produces a header for the grid, but doesn't add any data to it. The grid produced by this code is illustrated in Figure 12.2.

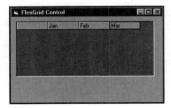

Figure 12.2 Using the Row, Col, and Text properties to populate the grid header.

Adding Data to the FlexGrid Using the AddItem Method   As an alternative to determining the number of rows and columns in advance, you can use the AddItem method to populate the grid with as much data as you prefer, without having to know in advance how much data you have.

Listing 12.2 modifies the code example in the previous section, populating a FlexGrid control with three rows of hard-coded data using the AddItem method.

Listing 12.2: Populating the Grid Using the AddItem Method

```
Option Explicit

Private Sub Form_Load()
    FlexGrid1.Cols = 4
    FlexGrid1.Rows = 1

    ' Place text in header
    FlexGrid1.Row = 0
    FlexGrid1.Col = 1
    FlexGrid1.Text = "Jan"
    FlexGrid1.Col = 2
    FlexGrid1.Text = "Feb"
    FlexGrid1.Col = 3
    FlexGrid1.Text = "Mar"

    ' Place data in grid
    FlexGrid1.AddItem "Rubber chickens" & vbTab & "100" & vbTab & "200" & _
```

continues

Listing 12.2: Populating the Grid Using the AddItem Method (Continued)

```
                        vbTab & "250"
    FlexGrid1.AddItem "Hand buzzers" & vbTab & "75" & vbTab & "125" & _
                        vbTab & "65"
    FlexGrid1.AddItem "Squirt flowers" & vbTab & "15" & vbTab & "35" & _
                        vbTab & "115"


End Sub
```

Note: The FlexGrid control is designed to be compatible with the (non-database-aware) Grid control, which has shipped with Visual Basic since time immemorial. Consequently, many techniques in this section of the chapter (pertaining to the Cols and Rows properties, for example, as well as the AddItem method) are applicable to the plain-vanilla Grid control as well.

The grid produced by this code is shown in Figure 12.3.

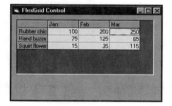

Figure 12.3: Grid populated with hard-coded data using the AddItem method.

The tab character, expressed in code as the constant vbTab, is used to delimit data when using the AddItem method. When you use AddItem, each piece of data separated by a tab character goes into a separate column.

In addition to using the AddItem method, you can also add information to cells in the grid using the TextMatrix property, described in the section "Adding Data Using the TextMatrix Property," later in this chapter.

Creating a Grid Header Using the FormatString Property   The FlexGrid control provides one additional method of creating a header row—the FormatString property. This is probably the simplest method of assigning text to the header row, and it has the advantage of being usable at design time. It has the additional advantage of permitting you to align the cells in the grid at the same time you supply header text.

To format a grid's header, assign a string that contains special formatting characters to the grid's FormatString property. You can do this at design time or at runtime, using code. For example, to enter data in the grid's header, you enter text separated by a pipe character (|). Using the semicolon character, you can assign values for the row header as well as the column header. You can also use formatting characters to specify the alignment of information in columns.

The formatting characters available in the FlexGrid's FormatString property are shown in Table 12.1.

Table 12.1: Formatting Strings Available in the FlexGrid's FormatString Property

Character	Meaning
|	Delimiter; separates text that should be placed in different columns of the grid's header row
<	Left-align the column
>	Right-align the column
^	Center the column
;	Begin row information

For example, to create a grid with three columns labeled with the first three months of the year, use the following format string:

```
"January¦February¦March"
```

Use the following format string to create a grid to illustrate the sales of various products over a period of months:

```
"¦>January¦>February¦>March;¦Rubber Chickens¦Hand Buzzers¦Squirt Flowers"
```

This formatting string contains an extra pipe character (to the left of the month of January); this causes the upper-left cell of the grid to be blank. This format string produces the grid shown in Figure 12.4.

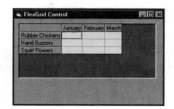

Figure 12.4: Grid formatting produced by applying the FormatString property.

Adding Data Using the TextMatrix Property In addition to adding information to the grid the old-fashioned way using the AddItem method, the FlexGrid control also provides a technique that the classic VB grid control doesn't support—the TextMatrix property. This property is an array that represents all the cells in the Grid control.

To assign a value to a cell in the grid using the TextMatrix control, you must first create the cell you're attempting to address. You've seen a number of techniques for creating grid cells in this chapter—the AddItem method, the FormatString technique (which creates cells as a side-effect of creating row and column headers), and the simplest method, which involves assigning the Rows and Cols properties of the grid.

After you've created cells, populate them by addressing their x-y coordinates using the grid's TextMatrix property. For example, use the following code to place a piece of information in Column 3, Row 2 of the grid:

```
FlexGrid1.TextMatrix(3, 2) = "Rubber Chicken"
```

Remember when you're assigning values to cells in the grid that rows and columns in a FlexGrid control begin numbering at zero.

Sorting Data in the FlexGrid Control

You sort data in the FlexGrid control by selecting the column you want to sort by, then setting the grid's Sort property to a sort constant.

The sort constants available with the FlexGrid control are listed in Table 12.2.

Table 12.2: Sort Constants Used with the FlexGrid's Sort Property

Constant	Value	Description
flexSortNone	0	No sorting
flexSortGenericAscending	1	Sort in ascending (A to Z, 0 to 9) order; in a generic sort, the control guesses whether a piece of data is textual or numeric
flexSortGenericDescending	2	Sort generically, in descending order
flexSortNumericAscending	3	Sort in ascending order, treating stings as numbers
flexSortNumericDescending	4	Sort in descending order, treating strings as numbers
flexSortStringNoCaseAscending	5	Sort in case insensitive, ascending order
flexSortNoCaseDescending	6	Sort in case insensitive, descending order
flexSortStringAscending	7	Sort in case sensitive ascending order
flexSortStringDescending	8	Sort in case sensitive descending order
	9	Use a custom sort order determined by the grid's Compare event

Listing 12.3 gives an example of a Command button that sorts a list of products by product name.

Listing 12.3: Sorting a List of Items in the FlexGrid Control

```
Private Sub cmdSort_Click()
    ' Select the column you
    ' want to sort by
    FlexGrid1.Col = 0

    ' Apply the sort constant
    FlexGrid1.Sort = flexSortStringAscending
End Sub
```

The sorting capability becomes important in an application based on the FlexGrid control, because values that are adjacent to each other in the grid can be merged if they share the same value. However, the items in the grid tend to appear next to each other in the grid only if they're sorted. This is different than grouping, as you find in database reports. When data is merged, duplicate values in adjacent cells are displayed in one merged cell; in grouping, a number of records' values are added together, averaged, or combined in some other arithmetical way.

Merging the contents of cells makes for a more concise expression of data; it's introduced in the next section.

Note: Bear in mind that in a database access application, it's almost always faster to let the database engine sort data rather than sorting it in the user-interface level.

Merging Data in Cells Using the FlexGrid Control

In order to take advantage of the FlexGrid control's full capabilities, you must set it up to merge cells.

To set up your grid to merge cells, you follow these general steps:

▶ Set the grid's MergeCells property to a value that permits merging. By default, MergeCells is set to zero, which prohibits merging cells.

▶ Use the MergeRow and MergeCol properties to designate which rows and columns are eligible to be merged.

▶ Write code that responds to an action in the user interface—such as clicking on a column—that indicates that the user wants to merge data based on a particular field.

To begin creating an application with data cells that can be merged, you set the grid's MergeCells property. The MergeCells property dictates how cells are going to be merged. With the least restrictive setting, flexMergeFree, any cell that is adjacent to (that is, to the left or on top of) a cell with the same value is merged with that cell. The MergeCells property has five settings in all, shown in Table 12.3.

Table 12.3: Settings of the MSFlexGrid Control's MergeCells property

Setting	Description
flexMergeNever	Don't permit merging. This is the default setting.
flexMergeFree	A cell can be merged with the value in the row or column adjacent to it.
flexMergeRestrictRows	Data can only be merged by rows.
flexMergeRestrictColumns	Data can only be merged by columns.
flexMergeRestrictAll	Data can be merged by both rows and columns.

Note: Visual Basic 5.0's online help topic for the MergeCells property lists the constant flexMergeRestrictBoth. This is an error; the constant is actually named flexMergeRestrictAll.

For example, suppose you start with the following basic data set:

Product	Region	Units Sold
Rubber chickens	North	100
Rubber chickens	South	125
Joy buzzers	North	75
Joy buzzers	South	85
Squirt flowers	North	25
Squirt flowers	South	65

With a data set like this, the first two columns are mergable (because it wouldn't make sense to group matching values in the Units Sold column). Use the following code to enable this:

```
FlexGrid1.MergeCol(0) = True
FlexGrid1.MergeCol(1) = True
```

Now you have the ability to set the MergeCells property to see the data in different ways. If you set MergeCells to flexMergeFree, the grid looks like this:

Product	Region	Units Sold
Rubber chickens	North	100
	South	125
Joy buzzers	North	75
	South	85
Squirt flowers	North	25
	South	65

Notice how much more compact this data is than the previous data set. This information display is clearer, as well. Now watch what happens when the Region column is moved to the leftmost side of the grid (remember that in this grid, MergeCells is set to flexMergeFree).

Region	Product	Units Sold
North	Rubber chickens	100
	Squirt flowers	125
North and South	Joy buzzers	75
South		85
	Rubber chickens	125
	Squirt flowers	65

Because the grid is set to flexMergeFree and the Joy buzzers product appears twice in the Product column, Joy buzzers are merged across the North and South regions. It's still clear how many buzzers were sold by each region, but only because you suppressed merging in the Units Sold column. To prevent Joy buzzers from merging across regions like this, set the grid's MergeCells property to flexMergeRestrictRows. This prevents cells from merging vertically. The grid now looks like this:

Region	Product	Units Sold
North	Rubber chickens	100
	Squirt flowers	125
	Joy buzzers	75

continues

continued

Region	Product	Units Sold
South	Joy buzzers	85
	Rubber chickens	125
	Squirt flowers	65

This organization makes things a bit clearer.

Listing 12.4 gives a complete example of a grid application that populates itself with this data and permits you to rearrange its columns by double-clicking to see data differently.

Listing 12.4: Sales-Tracking Application that Permits You to Rearrange Data

```
Option Explicit

Private Sub Form_Load()

    Dim x As Integer

    FlexGrid1.FormatString = "Inventory Item Name¦Region¦Amount"

    FlexGrid1.FixedCols = 0
    FlexGrid1.Cols = 3
    FlexGrid1.Rows = 1

    With FlexGrid1
        ' Product sales data by region
        .AddItem "Rubber chickens" & vbTab & "North" & vbTab & "100"
        .AddItem "Rubber chickens" & vbTab & "South" & vbTab & "125"

        .AddItem "Joy buzzers" & vbTab & "North" & vbTab & "75"
        .AddItem "Joy buzzers" & vbTab & "South" & vbTab & "85"

        .AddItem "Squirt flowers" & vbTab & "North" & vbTab & "25"
        .AddItem "Squirt flowers" & vbTab & "South" & vbTab & "65"
    End With

    FlexGrid1.MergeCells = flexMergeRestrictRows

    ' Make the product and
    ' region columns mergable
```

continues

Listing 12.4: Sales-Tracking Application that Permits You to Rearrange Data (Continued)

```
    For x = 0 To 1
        FlexGrid1.MergeCol(x) = True
    Next x

End Sub


Private Sub FlexGrid1_DblClick()
    FlexGrid1.ColPosition(FlexGrid1.MouseCol) = 0

    ' Without the sort, the merge
    ' doesn't work
    FlexGrid1.Col = 0
    FlexGrid1.Sort = flexSortStringAscending
End Sub
```

The important thing about this application is the fact that it is interactive—the user gets to determine which column is merged by double-clicking on it. When the grid's DblClick event is triggered, the column the user double-clicked on (as determined by the grid's MouseCol property) becomes the leftmost column (as a result of the ColPosition property). The grid is then resorted, which causes adjacent cells with the same value to merge.

Figure 12.5 shows what this application looks like when it is running. In the figure, the user has moved the Region column to the leftmost side in order to aggregate sales by regions.

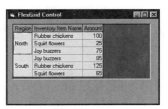

Figure 12.5: FlexGrid application whose data has been sorted and merged.

The one remaining unsatisfying aspect of this application is that it populates itself with hard-wired data embedded in the code. That problem is fixed in the next section.

Using the FlexGrid with a Database

You can bypass the various programmatic techniques for populating the FlexGrid control with data by simply connecting it to a Data control. When you do this, the data displayed by the grid is determined by the Data control; you don't need to use the AddItem or any other property or method to populate the grid with data.

Bear in mind that the version of the MSFlexGrid control that comes with Visual Basic can't alter the data it displays when it's connected to a Data control (this might be a good thing). However, if you need the grid to be able to write information back to the database, use the commercial version of the control— vsFlexArray, which is introduced later in this chapter.

The version of the novelty.mdb database in this book's accompanying CD-ROM's Chapter 12 folder contains data that demonstrates how the FlexGrid control interacts with information provided by a Data control. To see how this works:

1 Create a new VB project.

2 Create a Data control and a MSFlexGrid control on the project's main form.

3 Set the Data control's DatabaseName property to the version of the novelty.mdb database in this book's Chapter 12 folder on the CD-ROM.

4 Set the Data control's RecordSource property to qryOrdersByCustomerType. This is a query stored in the database that returns three columns: CustomerType, Month (a calculated field that expresses the month the order took place expressed as a two-digit number), and Amount. The query returns this information by joining three tables in the database: tblCustomer, tblCustomerType, and tblOrder.

5 Set the Grid's DataSource property to the name of the Data control, Data1.

6 Because the user won't interact with the Data control, set its Visible property to False.

7 Set the grid's FixedCols property to 0, then run the application. It should display the data, as shown in Figure 12.6.

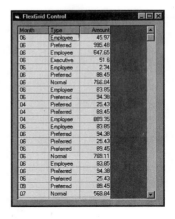

Figure 12.6: Application displaying query results in a MSFlexGrid control.

8 Make the cells in the grid mergable. To do this, set the grid's MergeCells property to 2 - flexMergeRestrictRows.

9 Enable merging for the first two columns by adding the following code to the form's Load event:

```
FlexGrid1.MergeCol(0) = True
FlexGrid1.MergeCol(1) = True
```

10 Now permit the user to determine which column is merged by adding the following code to the grid's Click event:

```
Private Sub FlexGrid1_Click()

    FlexGrid1.ColPosition(FlexGrid1.MouseCol) = 0

    FlexGrid1.Col = 1
    FlexGrid1.ColSel = 0
    FlexGrid1.Sort = flexSortStringAscending

End Sub
```

11 Run the application. The grid initially sorts by customer type, showing you the purchases by each type of customer from one month to the next, as shown in Figure 12.7.

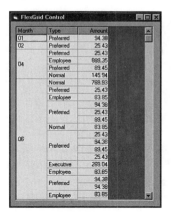

Figure 12.7: A database-enabled grid application that groups orders by month.

12 Finally, click on the Type field's header. The grid rearranges itself to show which types of customers made purchases in which months. This reveals new information about your data source you may not have been able to infer before. For example, as Figure 12.8. shows, employees only made purchases in months 4, 6, and 11 (April, June, and November).

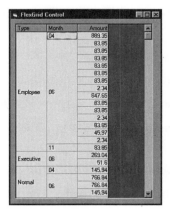

Figure 12.8: FlexGrid control merging information based on customer type.

USING VIDEOSOFT VSFLEX 3.0

The commercial version of the MSFlexGrid control is called VideoSoft VSFLEX.

The VSFLEX product actually consists of two controls—vsFlexArray, the commercial version of the FlexGrid control, and vsFlexString, used to find patterns and expressions in data.

 Note: A trial version of the commercial VSFLEX package is on the CD-ROM that accompanies this book. For more information on the commercial VSFLEX package, visit the VideoSoft Web site at **http://www.videosoft.com.** You can also buy the package online through the VBXTras catalog; there's a link to their online software store at **http://www.redblazer.com/software.**

The full version of VSFLEX offers a number of new features and performance enhancements over the MSFlexGrid control included with VB5. These features include:

▶ The capability to bind to a Data control in read-write mode (the MSFlexGrid control can bind to a Data control, but the data is read-only)

▶ The capability to edit text inside a cell

▶ The capability to present subtotals and display data in outline format, similar to the way Windows Explorer displays folders and files

▶ Columns that resize themselves automatically to fit their contents

▶ The capability to select rows that are not adjacent to each other

▶ Enhanced sort capabilities, including support for international sort orders

▶ Display of flood values in cells, giving you the ability to graphically display data similar to a progress meter

▶ Additional options for controlling the appearance of the control

▶ The capability to embed controls such as check boxes and combo boxes in grid cells

▶ The capability to save the entire contents of the grid to a file, then reload the file into the grid later

▶ Increased performance

The VSFLEX controls do not ship with Visual Basic 5.0; VSFLEX is a separate product. The filename of the VSFLEX controls is VSFLEX3.OCX. Do the following to use the VSFLEX controls in your Visual Basic project:

1 In Visual Basic, select Project Components.

2 The Components dialog box appears. In the list of components, scroll down until you see :-) VideoSoft vsFlex3 Controls. This should conveniently appear toward the top of the list of components, because of VideoSoft's crafty practice of placing an emoticon at the beginning of the names of each of their software packages.

3 Check the control in the list, then click on OK. The vsFlexGrid and vsFlexString controls are added to your Visual Basic toolbox, as shown in Figure 12.9.

Figure 12.9: The vsFlexArray and vsFlexString controls in the Visual Basic toolbox.

Many of the MSFlexGrid control enhancements provided by the vsFlexArray control are discussed in the remainder of this chapter. In addition, the commercial VSFLEX package contains the vsFlexString control, which lets you perform lookups on data based on expressions.

Editing Data in Cells

When your application uses the MSFlexGrid control, the only way you can change the contents of a cell at runtime is in code, by selecting the cell and altering its Text property. An important improvement in the vsFlexArray control over the MSFlexGrid control is the fact that users can edit data in cells directly; you needn't write any code to support this feature. In-cell editing works whether the grid is bound to a data control or not.

In-cell editing is deactivated by default in vsFlexArray. To permit users to edit values directly in cells, you set the control's Editable property to True. You can do this at design-time or runtime.

To permit users to perform in-cell edits on data when your grid is bound to a data control, you must also set the grid's DataMode property to 1 - flexDMBound. This tells the grid to commit edited data in cells back to the data source through the Data control.

It's important to bear in mind that if the DataMode property isn't set correctly, the user can edit the contents of a grid cell, but the update won't be sent back to the database, and no error is triggered.

Displaying a Combo Box in a Cell

You have the ability to display a list of choices in the form of a combo box control in a vsFlexArray cell. You do this in situations where you want the user to pick from a list of choices.

You create the combo box control by using the grid's ComboList property. This property takes a string variable that permits you to designate the list of choices, delimited by pipe characters (|).

You write the code that assigns the ComboList property to the Grid control in the control's BeforeEdit event. This event is triggered at the time the user attempts to initiate an in-cell edit. This event receives the grid's current row and column as arguments, so you can display a different list of choices for each column.

> **Note:** Providing combo boxes only makes sense if the grid is editable. For information on how to make a grid editable, see "Editing Data in Cells," earlier in this chapter.

For example, consider a vsFlexArray control that contains a list of customers. You want to enter each customer's name, address, and state of residence. Because there are a finite number of states, it might be nice to provide a list of states. Listing 12.5 shows an example of this.

Listing 12.5: Displaying a List of Choices Using the vsFlexArray's BeforeEdit Event and ComboList Property

```
Option Explicit

Private Sub Form_Load()
    Data1.DatabaseName = App.Path & "\novelty.mdb"
```

Listing 12.5: Displaying a List of Choices Using the vsFlexArray's BeforeEdit Event and ComboList Property (Continued)

```
    FlexGrid1.Editable = True
    FlexGrid1.DataMode = flexDMBound

End Sub

Private Sub FlexGrid1_BeforeEdit(ByVal Row As Long, ByVal Col As Long,
Cancel As Boolean)
    If Col = 3 Then
        FlexGrid1.ComboList = "AZ¦CA¦ID¦MT¦NM¦NV¦OR¦WA"
    Else
        ' Shut off list for other columns
        FlexGrid1.ComboList = ""
    End If
End Sub
```

This code assumes you've set the RecordSource property of the Data control to return data from the tblCustomer table. The code also includes only eight of the 50 U.S. states for brevity.

In the BeforeEdit event, the list is displayed when the user edits Column 3 (the column that contains states) but it's set to an empty string when the user attempts to edit another column. This is important—if you don't do this, the list appears in every column after the user edits a value in the State column.

Figure 12.10 shows what the drop-down list looks like when it's being edited.

Figure 12.10: Editing a vsFlexArray cell based on a list of choices provided by the ComboList property.

Saving the Grid Contents to a Disk File

The VSFLEX 3.0 vsFlexArray control enables you to save the control's entire contents to a disk file, then reload the data from disk later. This is an exceptionally handy feature, particularly if you must minimize impact on a server in a client-server configuration. In this scenario, your application connects to the server, downloads the data it needs, adds it to the grid, and disconnects from the server. The user then saves the data locally and begins to slice and dice the data. If he must use the data again at a later date, he reloads the data from his disk file as opposed to reconnecting to the server.

Save the contents of a vsFlexArray grid by using its SaveGrid method. Load the contents of a previously saved file using the grid's LoadGrid method.

Note: When using the SaveGrid and LoadGrid methods, you have the option of saving and loading just the data, just the formatting, or both.

Listing 12.6 gives an example of an application that loads data (through its link with the Data control), saves the data to a file, disconnects from the Data control, then reloads the data from the file. This application assumes that the Data control called Data1 has been connected to a database at design time.

Listing 12.6: A vsFlexArray Application that Saves and loads Data Using the SaveGrid and LoadGrid Methods

```
Option Explicit

Private Sub Form_Load()
    Data1.DatabaseName = App.Path & "\novelty.mdb"
End Sub

Private Sub cmdLoadDB_Click()
    ' Data is displayed in faBound
    faBound.Visible = True
    faUnbound.Visible = False
End Sub

Private Sub cmdSaveFile_Click()
    faBound.SaveGrid App.Path & "\savegrid.dat", flexFileAll
End Sub

Private Sub cmdLoadFile_Click()
    faBound.Visible = False
    faUnbound.Visible = True
```

Listing 12.6: A vsFlexArray Application that Saves and loads Data Using the SaveGrid and LoadGrid Methods (Continued)

```
    faUnbound.LoadGrid App.Path & "\savegrid.dat", flexFileAll
    MsgBox "Local data loaded.", vbInformation
End Sub
```

The tricky thing about this application is the fact that when a control is bound to a Data control, it's bound to the control forever—you can't disconnect it. This is because the Data control's DataSource property isn't read-write at runtime. In addition, if you attempt to use the LoadGrid method with a bound control, you get a runtime error.

A possible solution to this problem is to include two identical vsFlexArray controls in the application, one bound and one unbound. When the user asks to save the data, the application takes the contents of the bound grid and writes it to a disk file called savegrid.dat. When the user reloads savegrid.dat to the grid, the application loads the data into the unbound grid. It's a kludge, but it demonstrates how to save and load data in the grid.

Automatically Resizing Rows

One of the enhancements to the commercial version of the FlexArray control is the fact that it automatically resizes columns to accommodate information in cells—no more resizing columns in order to see what's there.

The grid does this through its AutoResize property, which by default is set to True. This means that you don't have to do anything to take advantage of this feature.

SUMMARY

This chapter showed you how to analyze data using the MSFlexGrid control. It showed you examples of the control in bound and unbound mode, as well as the enhanced capabilities of the commercial vsFlexArray control, part of the VideoSoft VSFLEX control suite.

In the next chapter, you'll see how to construct a data-aware user interface with the ActiveX controls in the Sheridan DataWidgets suite. In addition to providing a grid that has slightly different capabilities than the MSFlexGrid and DBGrid controls, the package contains several additional user-interface controls, such as data-aware list boxes and command buttons.

QUESTIONS AND ANSWERS

Q. **I want to look up data in the grid control, but the search facilities provided by SQL aren't sufficient. Do I have any other options?**

A. The commercial vsFlexArray version of the Grid control comes with a second control, vsFlexString, that permits you to search on regular expressions. The control's search facility could find, for example, the fifth occurrence of a word that contains a vowel in a FlexArray control. In addition to this kind of search, the control permits you to search on substrings that come at the beginning, end, or within a string, strings that contain upper- or lowercase letters, or any type of number. The control also has the capability to evaluate expressions and provides search-and-replace functionality.

Q. **Is it possible to use this control as a reporting tool?**

A. There's not enough space in this chapter to go into many of these features, but yes, the grid control provides a number of formatting features, including the capability to apply font formatting on a cell-by-cell basis and the ability to integrate with the Visual Basic Printer object. VideoSoft also sells another product, VSVIEW, introduced in Chapter 4, which provides print preview capabilities and serves as a replacement for the VB Printer object. VSFLEX integrates with VSVIEW, permitting you to use the controls together to print data after you've sliced and diced it.

Creating User Interfaces with DataWidgets

How can I build a user interface that permits me to display information from a database?

How can I extend the functionality of the Visual Basic Data control and other data-aware controls by replacing them with enhanced controls?

Chapter 123

The Sheridan DataWidgets suite contains a variety of user-interface controls that permit you to create database-aware applications.

This chapter provides an introduction to each control, demonstrating how to get started using the controls and giving an example of how they are used in applications.

OVERVIEW OF THE SHERIDAN DATAWIDGETS SUITE

The Sheridan DataWidgets suite comprises six ActiveX controls. They are packaged as both 16- and 32-bit controls, so if you need to support Windows 3.1 development using the 16-bit version Visual Basic 4.0, you can use the same controls (or a reasonable facsimile thereof).

The controls in the DataWidgets suite include:

▶ **DataGrid.** A control to display a recordset in rows and columns.

▶ **DataCombo.** A combo box that binds to a database field and displays values from another recordset.

▶ **DataDropDown.** A combo box designed for use with the DataGrid control to provide the user with a list of choices when editing.

▶ **DataOptionSet.** A set of option buttons that can be bound to a database field.

▶ **EnhancedData.** A control designed to work with, as well as replace, the Visual Basic Data control.

▶ **DataCommand.** A data-aware Command button that can trigger certain data access actions (such as navigating through a recordset, creating and deleting records) without code.

Each of these controls is demonstrated with a code example in this chapter.

Note: For more information about DataWidgets and Sheridan's other ActiveX packages, check out Sheridan's Web site at http://www.shersoft.com.

A trial version of Sheridan DataWidgets package is on the CD-ROM that accompanies this book. You can also download the latest version of Sheridan DataWidgets directly from the Sheridan Web site. The package comes in three files; you must download all three files to install the package. The files can be found at:

http://www.shersoft.com/download/trials/dat20c_1.zip

http://www.shersoft.com/download/trials/dat20c_2.zip

http://www.shersoft.com/download/trials/dat20c_3.zip

Note: Sheridan recommends that users of Windows NT 4.0 install Windows NT Service Pack 2 on systems that use the DataWidgets controls. You can download the latest Windows NT 4.0 Service Pack from the Microsoft BackOffice Download and Trial Center at http://backoffice.microsoft.com/downtrial/default.asp.

The Sheridan DataWidgets controls are packaged in two OCX files. The file SSDATA32.OCX contains the Enhanced Data, OptionSet, and DataCommand controls. The file SSDATB32.OCX contains the DataGrid, DataCombo, and DataDropDown controls.

Do the following to use the DataWidgets controls in a Visual Basic project:

1 In Visual Basic, select Project Components.

2 The Components dialog box appears. In the list of components, scroll down until you see Sheridan DataGrid/Combo/DropDown and Sheridan dbData/dbOptSet/dbCmd Controls.

3 Check the set of controls you want to use, then click on OK. The controls you chose are added to your Visual Basic toolbox, as shown in Figure 13.1.

Figure 13.1: The DataWidgets controls in the Visual Basic toolbox.

Using the Sheridan DataGrid Control

The Sheridan DataGrid control provides many of the features offered by the True DBGrid control (covered in Chapter 11, "Using the DBGrid and Apex True DBGrid Controls"). The Sheridan DataGrid provides much of the same functionality as the DBGrid control; in fact, some of its properties and contained objects are identical to that of the DBGrid control.

Figure 13.2 shows an example of the Sheridan DataGrid control displaying data from the Jones Novelties database.

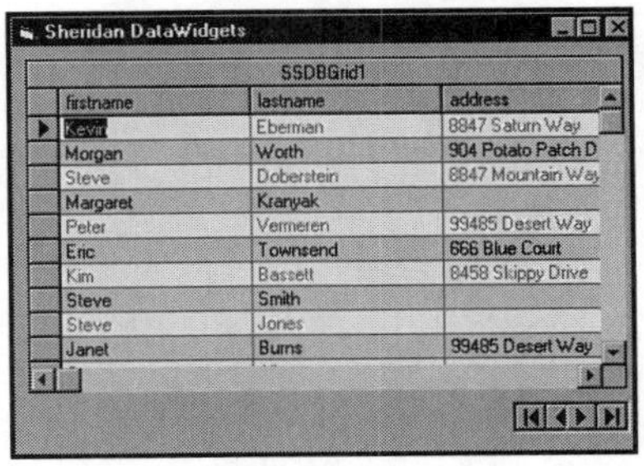

Figure 13.2: A bound Sheridan DataGrid control displaying information from a database.

You use the same technique to bind the DataGrid to a Data control as you use with the DBGrid control—simply create a Data control, assign its DatabaseName and RecordSource properties, and assign the control's DataSource property to the name of the Data control. Like the DBGrid control, the DataGrid requires no DataField property, because it is designed to display multiple fields. You can create a basic data browser application based on the DataGrid with no code, as you'd expect from any self-respecting bound control.

You can see that by default, the DataGrid control shows rows of data in alternating colors. This is designed to help you read data in a row; it's particularly helpful if your application contains very long rows of data. If you'd prefer to view data in a single color, or a color of your choice, you can set the grid's ForeColorEven, BackColorEven, ForeColorOdd, and BackColorOdd properties.

Like the DBGrid control, the DataGrid control permits you to determine whether the user can add, update, or delete data in the grid with a series of design-time properties. These properties even have the same name as their DBGrid counterparts—AllowAddNew, AllowDelete, and AllowUpdate. Setting the AllowAddNew property to True at design time adds a new record row to the bottom of the grid; you can use this row to insert new records, as shown in Figure 13.3.

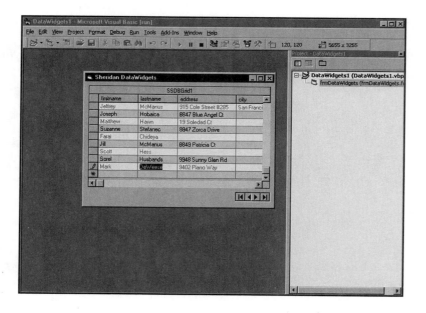

Figure 13.3: Inserting a new record in the DataGrid control after its AllowAddNew property is set to True.

Altering the DataGrid's Design-Time Properties   Like the DBGrid control, the DataGrid provides a design-time property dialog box that permits you to visually assign a large number of the grid's properties. Because this dialog box contains a very effective interface and gives you access to so many more properties than the Visual Basic property sheet, use the grid's own property dialog box to set its design-time properties.

To see how this works, do the following:

1 Create a VB project with a DataGrid control bound to a Data control. Set the Data control's properties to a database, and set the grid's DataSource property to the name of the Data control.

2 Right-click on the DataGrid control. The control's property dialog box appears, as shown in Figure 13.4.

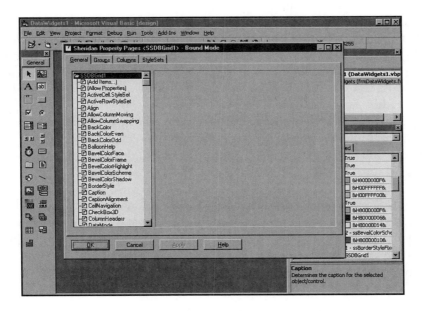

Figure 13.4: The Sheridan DataGrid Custom Properties dialog box.

3 As an example of how to change a property with this property sheet, select the Caption property in the list under the General tab. When you do so, the Caption property should appear. Change the Caption property to Jones Novelties, then click on OK.

4 You should be able to see that the Grid control's caption has changed to the value you assigned.

Considering how involved a grid control's set of properties can be, it's nice to have an enhanced properties dialog box to minimize the complexity of working with the control at design time. In the next few sections of this chapter, you manipulate the design-time properties of the grid control using this property dialog in order to take advantage of some of its unique features.

Working with the DataGrid's Object Model   Like the DBGrid, the DataGrid contains an object model that permits you to manipulate its properties and behaviors in code. Figure 13.5 shows this object model.

Notice that elements in the DataGrid's object model are suspiciously similar to the DBGrid's object model—there's a Columns collection, but there's also a SelBookmarks collection that permits you to select rows, and a variation of the RowBuffer object that permits you to receive rows as arguments to event procedures. It's clear that the DataGrid and DBGrid controls were designed to be at least conceptually similar to each other.

The Group object provided by the DataGrid control permits you to refer to and display a number of related columns as a group. For example, when displaying customers, you might place properties pertaining to the customers' addresses, cities, states, and zip codes in one group, while putting their customer status, credit rating, and order history in another group.

The StyleSet object is similar to the DBGrid Style object. It permits you to create formatting objects (composed of background color, font, and foreground color) that can be assigned to cells, columns, groups, the active row, or the entire grid control.

Dividing Columns into Groups at Design Time   You can divide your grid into groups of columns at design time. You do this in situations where you want to visually denote that a number of data fields fall into the same category. This is particularly useful when you want to indicate that a number of different columns are in the same recordset.

To assign groups to a DataGrid at design time:

1 Connect the grid to the tblCustomer table in the database novelty.mdb using a Data control (you don't have to use a bound grid to take advantage of groups, but it makes this demonstration easier to follow).

2 Right-click on the grid and select Properties from the pop-up menu.

3 Click on the Groups tab. The Group Properties tab is displayed, as shown in Figure 13.6.

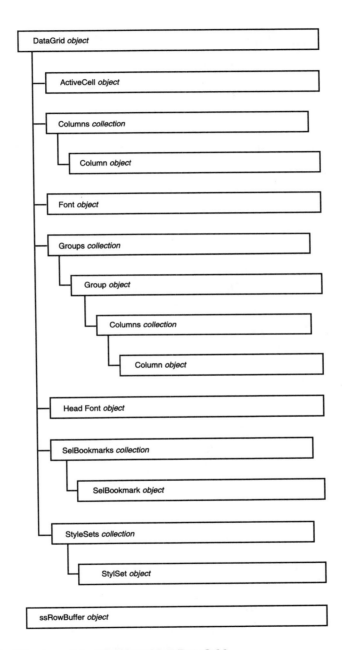

Figure 13.5: Object model of the Sheridan DataGrid.

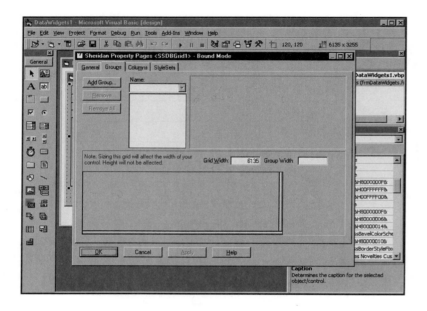

Figure 13.6: Groups Property tab in the DataGrid Custom Property dialog box.

4 Click on the Add Group button. The Add Group dialog box appears. Type Person, then click on OK.

5 The Person group appears in the property dialog box. Add another group, Address, using the same technique.

6 You should see two groups in the Custom Property dialog box. You have the ability to resize the width of these groups by click-dragging with the mouse. Resize the Person group so it's approximately 2000 twips wide, then resize the Address group so it's approximately 4000 twips wide. (A twip is the standard measurement unit in Visual Basic programming, equal to a twentieth of a point; there are 1440 twips to the inch.) You can resize the overall grid control by click-dragging on the right edge of the sizing control, as shown in Figure 13.7.

7 Now you can add columns to each group. To do this, start by clicking on the Columns tab in the Custom Properties dialog box.

8 Because your grid is bound to a database, you can select columns from a list of data columns in the database. To do this, click on the Fields button.

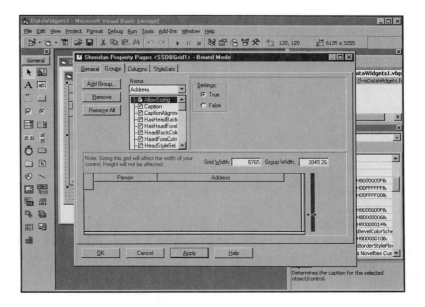

Figure 13.7: Resizing groups and the grid in the Groups tab of the DataGrid's Custom Property sheet.

9 The Field Selection dialog box appears. Click on the FirstName field, then hold down the Shift key and click on the LastName field. The dialog box should look like Figure 13.8.

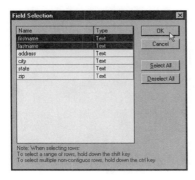

Figure 13.8: Selecting fields from a database to add to the columns in a DataGrid group.

10 Click on OK. The fields are added to the Person group, as shown in Figure 13.9.

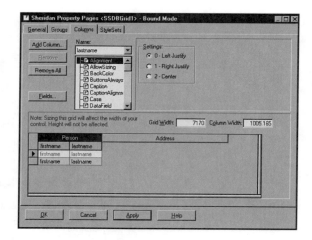

Figure 13.9: Fields in a group in the Columns tab of the DataGrid's Custom Property dialog box.

11 Click on the Address group, then use the Field Selection dialog box to add the Address, City, State and Zip fields to the Address group. Use your mouse to appropriately resize the columns. When you're finished, the grid looks like Figure 13.10.

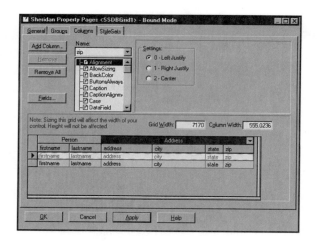

Figure 13.10: Resizing the columns of the grid in groups at design time.

12 Run the application. Your data is displayed and organized in groups, as shown in Figure 13.11.

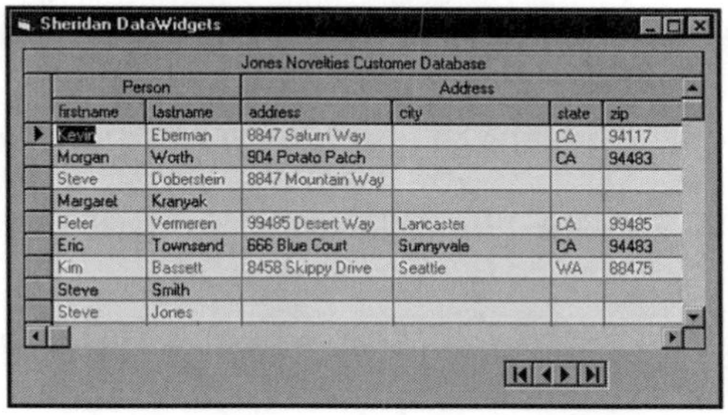

Figure 13.11: Viewing data in a grid comprised of groups.

> **Note:** In addition to assigning groups to the grid at design time, you can also add them in code at runtime by manipulating the DataGrid's Groups collection. Additionally, when you have a grid that contains groups, you can access columns at runtime in code using either the grid's Columns collection or each Group object's Columns collection. This can make it easier for you to navigate through a grid in code when your grid contains a large number of columns.

Using the DataCombo Control

The Sheridan DataCombo control is a combo box that binds to a database field and displays a list of choices from another recordset. The control gives you the ability to create data-access interfaces without writing code.

Figure 13.12 shows an example of the Sheridan DataCombo control.

Figure 13.12: Using the DataCombo control to create a data-entry interface.

Do the following to create this application:

1 Create a database access application using the Data control. Name the Data control datCustomer and bind it to the tblCustomer table.

2 Create three text boxes bound to the FirstName, LastName, and Address fields.

3 Add a reference to the Sheridan DataWidgets controls in your project, if necessary.

4 Create a DataCombo control on your form. Because this control binds to the TypeID field in the tblCustomer table, name the control cboCustomerType.

5 Bind cboCustomerType to the TypeID field the way you would for any other bound control—by setting its DataSource property to the Data control datCustomer, and setting its DataField property to TypeID.

6 Populate the list of choices provided by this control. To do this, create a second Data control. Give this control the name datCustomerType and connect it to the tblCustomerType table in the database.

7 Because the user won't be using the Data control to navigate, set datCustomerType's Visible property to False.

8 Set cboCustomerType's DataSourceList property to datCustomerType. This property governs which Data control is used to display choices in the combo box's list.

9 Set the cboCustomerType's DataFieldList property to ID. This field represents the value copied into the main record when the user makes a selection—that is, the primary key of tblCustomerType to be inserted into the foreign key of tblCustomer.

10 Set cboCustomerType's DataFieldToDisplay property to Type. This ensures that the control displays the textual description of the customer type, as opposed to the numeric ID of the customer type.

11 Run the application and choose from the list. You should see the full list of choices displayed. Best of all, this application requires no code.

Using the DataDropDown Control

The Sheridan DataDropDown control is a combo box specifically designed for use with the DataGrid control. It provides the user with a list of choices when editing data in a grid cell.

Figure 13.13 shows an example of the DataDropDown control in action, displaying a list of choices from the Jones Novelties customer database.

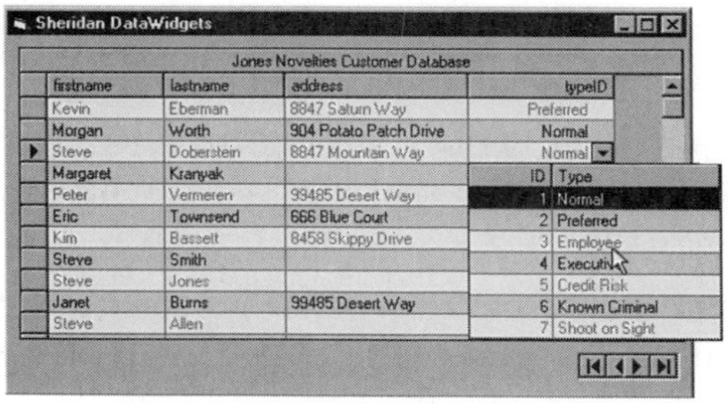

Figure 13.13: Accessing a list of choices in a DataGrid control using the DataDropDown control.

The technique for assigning a DataDropDown control to a column in the grid is similar for building a DataCombo control. To do this, follow these steps:

1 Create a project based on a Data control and a DataGrid. Connect the Data control to the tblCustomer table. Name the Data control datCustomer.

2 Name the grid dbgCustomer and connect it to the Data control by setting its DataSource property to datCustomer. When you run this application, it displays the contents of the TypeID field as a number, as shown in Figure 13.14.

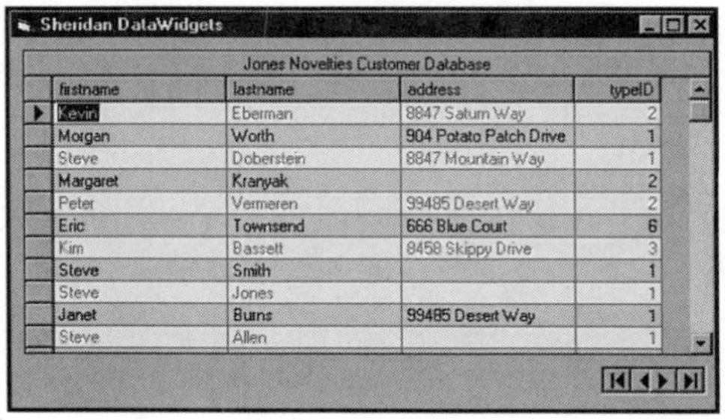

Figure 13.14: DataGrid control displaying a numeric field before adding a DataDropDown control.

3 Instead of displaying the TypeID, display the contents of the tblCustomerType table in order to let the user know what the type IDs mean. To do this, create a second Data control. Name that control datCustomerType and connect it to the tblCustomerType table.

4 Create a DataDropDown control on the form. Name this control ddCustomerType. You can place this control anywhere on the form; its exact position on the form at runtime is determined by which cell the user edits.

5 Assign the DataDropDown's DataSource property to datCustomerType, assign its DataFieldList property to ID, and set its DataFieldToDisplay property to Type. This causes the control to display the textual customer type, but store the numeric customer type ID in the database. (These settings are identical to the settings you used for the DataCombo control in the previous section's example.)

6 You must write a line of code in order to assign the DataDropDown control to a column in the DataGrid. Do this in the grid's InitColProps event. The code assigns the DataDropDown control's window handle to the DropDownHwnd property of one of the DataGrid's column objects:

```
Private Sub dbgCustomer_InitColumnProps()
    dbgCustomer.Columns(3).DropDownHwnd = ddCustomerType.hWnd
End Sub
```

Note: The *window handle*, or hWnd, of a control is a unique value the operating system uses to identify a control or other window. It isn't used much in Visual Basic programming, but you run across it every so often. It's used more often when you place calls to the Windows Application Programming Interface (API).

7 Run the application. You should be able to see that now, instead of the TypeID, the textual customer type is displayed. When you click on a Customer Type cell, the DataDropDown displays the list of customer types in tblCustomer.

Note: Remember to make the recordsets that provide non-editable lists to read-only. This alteration improves performance greatly.

Using the DataOptionSet Control

The DataOptionSet control provides a database-aware set of option buttons. You can bind as many option buttons as you want to the same database field; when the user chooses a particular button, the value associated with that button is stored in the field.

Figure 13.15 shows an example of the DataOptionSet control displaying data from the Jones Novelties database.

Figure 13.15: The DataOption control at runtime, displaying the contents of the TypeID field.

Do the following to create this application:

1 Create a database access application based on a Data control connected to the tblCustomer table in the Jones Novelties database. Create text boxes bound to the FirstName, LastName, and Address fields.

2 Create two DataOption controls on the form. Give the first control the caption Normal, and give the second control the caption Preferred.

3 Assign the OptionValue property of the first control to 1. Assign the second control's OptionValue property to 2. This will cause the option buttons to store the numeric values 1 and 2 in the database.

4 Assign both controls' DataSource properties to datCustomer, and assign both controls' DataField properties to TypeID.

5 Run the application. You should be able to see that for the first record that appears, either the Normal or Preferred fields are selected. To change this customer's status, simply click on the appropriate option button.

The obvious disadvantage of the DataOptionSet control is the fact that you have to hard-code the controls' values through the OptionValue property; you can't bind the list of option buttons to a Data control like you can with the DataCombo. However, the DataOptionSet control contains a collection of

Button objects that you can use to add buttons to the control at runtime. You can use this to make the DataOptionSet control more useful in situations where you need to make a set of buttons appear based on the value stored in a related database table.

Using the Sheridan Enhanced Data Control

The Sheridan Enhanced Data Control isn't a replacement for the standard Visual Basic Data control; rather, it's designed to work alongside VB's Data control to provide features not provided by the standard Data control.

These enhanced features include

▶ The capability to display the control horizontally, like the conventional Data control, or vertically

▶ The capability to navigate through the recordset with bookmarks

▶ The capability to browse through records quickly by clicking and holding on a button (a feature called Speed Buttons)

▶ A Find dialog box that tailors itself to your record source

Figure 13.16 shows an example of the Sheridan Enhanced Data control in an application that displays data from the Jones Novelties database.

Figure 13.16: The Sheridan Enhanced Data control in an application at runtime.

Do the following to create this application:

1 Create a database access application using the standard Visual Basic Data control. Because you use the Enhanced Data control to navigate the recordset, set the Data control's Visible property to False.

2 Add an instance of the Sheridan Enhanced Data control to your form.

3 Set the Enhanced Data control's Caption property to nothing, then set its Align property to 2 - vbAlignBottom. This causes the control to align to the bottom of your form and to resize along with the form.

4 Run the application. You can now use the Enhanced Data control to navigate through your recordset. Your application can now use the control's buttons to provide a number of features not offered by the standard Data control.

Table 13.1 lists each of the Enhanced Data Control's buttons with descriptions of what each button does. The buttons are listed in the table as they appear on a default Enhanced Data control—from left to right.

Table 13.1: Description of the Buttons on a Sheridan Enhanced Data Control

Button	Description
MoveFirst	Equivalent to the conventional Data control's MoveFirst button
Previous Page	Moves back to the previous page of data
MovePrevious	Equivalent to the conventional Data control's MovePrevious button, except you can hold down the button to move through records in a rapid-fire fashion
Add	Adds a new record to the interface; the Cancel and Update buttons become available when you click on this button
Cancel	Aborts the creation of a new record
Update	Commits the creation of a new record
Delete	Deletes the current record
Add Bookmark	Adds a bookmark to the current record, permitting you to return to it later using the Go To Bookmark button. The number of bookmarks that can be stored by the control is governed by its BookmarksToKeep property; the default is 10
Clear All Bookmarks	Clears any bookmarks you may have previously created

continues

Table 13.1: Description of the Buttons on a Sheridan Enhanced Data Control (Continued)

Button	Description
Go To Bookmark	Moves the current record to the next bookmark you've created
Find	Displays the Enhanced Data control's Find dialog box, permitting you to locate records based on criteria you specify
FindPrevious	Finds the previous record; available only if you've specified a Find criterion using the Find button
FindNext	Finds the next record; available only if you've specified a Find criterion using the Find button
MoveNext	Equivalent to the conventional Data control's MoveNext button, except you can hold down the button to move through records in a rapid-fire fashion
Next Page	Moves ahead to the next page of data
MoveLast	Equivalent to the Data control's MoveLast button

You can disable the additional buttons on an Enhanced Data control. Do so by assigning the Boolean values of the control's Show properties at design time; for example, to suppress display of the control's Delete button, set the control's ShowDeleteButton to False. (All the control's Show properties are set to True by default.)

Using the Data Command Button

The Sheridan Data Command button provides several common database access functions (such as navigation and the creation and deletion of new records) with a minimum of code. You can use it as an alternative to, or in conjunction with, the Enhanced Data control described in the previous section.

You use the DataCommand button by binding it to a Data control, then assigning an action to it. The action taken by the DataCommand control is governed by its DatabaseAction property, as shown in Table 13.2.

Table 13.2: Values for the DatabaseAction Property of the Sheridan DataCommand Control

Value	Description
0	MoveFirst
1	Previous Page
2	MovePrevious
3	MoveNext
4	Next Page
5	MoveLast
6	Save Bookmark
7	Go To Bookmark
8	Refresh

Figure 13.17 shows an example of an application that uses Data Command Button controls to navigate through a recordset. This isn't the most visually impressive control in the suite, but it does cut down on the number of lines of code you write in your application, which is usually a good thing.

Figure 13.17: An application that uses the DataCommand buttons for navigation.

Do the following to create this application:

1 Build a database access interface based on the Data control.

2 Create four DataCommand buttons on your form.

3 Set the buttons' Caption properties to MoveFirst, MovePrev, MoveNext, and MoveLast.

4 Set the buttons' DatabaseAction properties: 0 - ssFirst, 2 - ssPrevious, 3 - ssNext, and 5 - ssLast, respectively.

5 Set the button's CaptionAlignment property to 7 - ssAlignmentCaptionCenterMiddle. (Buttons' captions are aligned to the bottom by default because the button supports a Picture property, which lets you assign a custom graphic to the button.)

6 Run the application. You should be able to navigate through the recordset using the DataCommand controls.

In addition to supporting database actions without code, the DataCommand buttons support automatic text wrapping (through the WordWrap property) as well as rapid-fire navigation through the recordset. To see how this works, run the example application, then click and hold the mouse on the MoveNext button. You should be able to see that the button moves you through one record at a time very quickly.

SUMMARY

This chapter provides a quick introduction to the Sheridan DataWidgets suite's six controls.

Bear in mind that the third-party controls discussed in this book aren't necessarily the be-all, end-all of database-aware controls—but hopefully they give you an idea of how easy it is to build a database-aware user interface with a minimum of code.

QUESTIONS AND ANSWERS

Q. I'm interested in displaying data in a heirarchical format—not in rows in columns, but in more of an outline format, like the Visual Basic TreeView control. Is there a data-aware control that does this?

A. I don't know of a TreeView-style control that connects directly to a database through a Data control. However, Sheridan Software provides a control called ActiveTreeView, which is compatible with the VB TreeView control and supports a number of additional features (such as an event-driven virtual mode that lets you populate the control with only the data needed for display—as opposed to having to dump thousands of records in the control at once).

Index